Body Talk **Philosophical Reflections on Sex and Gender**

Jacquelyn N. Zita

COLUMBIA UNIVERSITY PRESS

NEW YORK

Columbia University Press
Publishers since 1893
New York   Chichester, West Sussex

The "Kinsey Scores" graph on page 123 is reprinted by kind
permission of Simon & Schuster from *The Science of Desire* by
Dean Hamer and Peter Copeland. Copyright © 1994 by Dean
Hamer and Peter Copeland.

Library of Congress Cataloging-in-Publication Data

Zita, Jacqueline N.
     Body talk : philosphical reflections on sex and gender /
Jacqueline N. Zita.
          p.   cm. — (Between men~between women)
     Includes bibliographical references and index.
     ISBN 0–231–10542–8 (hbk. : alk. paper). —
ISBN 0–231–10543–6 (pbk. : alk. paper)
        1. Body, Human—Social aspects.   2. Feminist theory.
     3. Sex role.
     I. Title.   II. Series.
HM110.Z58   1998
305.3—dc21   97-48958
                                                            CIP

For Karen, my FemFire

Contents

Acknowledgments

It has been difficult to imagine that I would have a tomorrow when this book would be finished, but it has now crossed that magical line of completion. There are many individuals and organizations to thank for this. First of all I would like to thank the by now several thousand students I have taught over the years as waves of new feminist theory and other shocking ideas filtered into the classroom and into our discussions and readings. Second I want to thank my nearest colleagues and coworkers involved in our Women's Studies Department at the University of Minnesota, Susan Geiger, Helen Longino, Guadalupe Luna, Amy Kaminsky, Mary Jo Kane, Myrna Klitzke, Toni McNaron, Jessica Morgan, Richa Nagar, Naomi Scheman, and Eden Torres, who have *been there* for discussions on some of these ideas and for comments on some of these chapters. I would also like to thank Pam Olano, Eva Hill, Catherine Orr, Kerry Brooks, and Marilyn Walker, whose help in various stages of production made this book possible. I am grateful to the Midwestern Society for Women in Philosophy and the National Women's Studies Association for providing an intellectual space that grounded me in a more philosophically complex professional world and enabled me to create a more innovative style of inquiry. I especially want to thank my friend Hilary Sandall and my partner, Karen Clark, for their intellectual support, patience, and family, and the time they allowed for the necessary isolation this book demanded on my weekends, late nights, and summers. Love and appreciation I give to my parents for their generous hearts and hugs. Ann Miller and Susan Heath with Columbia University Press deserve my appreciation for their efforts to keep me focused on the final production and editing of this book as the administrative demands of our small department seemed to prolong its completion. Finally the readers of this book should be thanked for completing a circle of bodies, theories, and revolt. I have deeply enjoyed writing *Body Talk* and hope you will find in these words a labyrinth of contemporary struggles. Have it!

Body Talk

Introduction

 Over the last few decades there has been increased interest in corporeal philosophy and cultural studies of the body. Much of this intellectual interest has been sparked by political liberation movements based on sex, race, gender, disability, or class struggle that have exposed the centrality and social construction of the body in ideologies that discriminate against groups marked by corporeal differences. This book explores new ways of understanding bodies as normative and cultural formations involving articulation, domination, resistance, and violence. I have entitled the book *Body Talk: Philosophical Reflections on Sex and Gender* because I focus primarily on the ways we think about sex, gender, and the body in theory and other cultural rhetorics. Theory, as I understand it, is an ongoing conversation, a not-so-lonely way to talk across texts, bodies, and revolution.

 This book is an attempt to cross generations of contemporary body theory I have experienced in my own life. The transition from the 1970s to the 1990s is marked by the emergence of multicultural and ethnic studies, postmodern theory, queer theory, and attacks on disciplinary formations—all of which challenge the way in which feminist philosophers and theorists were thinking and writing about the body in work that started in the 1970s. For feminist philosophers influenced by 1970s radical feminism, writing about the body was at first a way to bring the body to theory and politics. The female body was uncovered as a site of personal narrative and memory that disclosed how women were implicated in social relations, sexual domination, and oppression. A decade later the questions posed to radical feminist philosophy by multicultural and ethnic studies, postmodern theory, queer theory, and the critique of disciplinarity have in some ways deeply challenged the assumptions of radical feminist philosophical thinking about the body. A complete erasure of radical feminist thought from contemporary theorizing about the body is wrong, however. Such a move would constitute an intellectual form of genocide, an academic annihilation once again calling for the disappearance of women or, at least, certain kinds of women.

In spite of the recent Foucauldian seduction of the academy, there are realities that we should not eclipse in our contemporary ways of thinking about the body. I have noticed in recent years that there seems to be less and less talk in academia about the persistence and violence of male domination and oppressions based on sex, race, gender, class, disability, age, and other social hierarchies of power. However, misogyny did not disappear into performativity. Sexual violence did not disappear into S/M stop words. Race did not disappear into style. Date rape did not disappear into consent. Identity politics need not disappear into liberalism. This book is an attempt to stay committed to certain tenets of a progressive and inclusive radical feminist philosophy while embracing the challenges that threaten its disassembly and encourage a stronger re/vision.

Two images inspired me as I wrote this book. The first is an image of an incident that happened at a gay, lesbian, bisexual, and transgender political meeting in Alexandria, Minnesota, where activists and organizers came together to discuss statewide issues related to our political work. We were greeted at the hotel restaurant, where the conference was being held, by food handlers wearing latex gloves, purportedly to protect the waitresses and waiters from possible transmission of the HIV virus. The hotel manager spoke strongly of his right to protect his employees, who, by contract and because of the recently passed state civil rights protections, were forced to interact with a group of dangerous outsiders. From his perspective, there seemed nothing perverse about the gloves; they were justified as a second skin to protect employees from possible viral transmission. The political uproar caused by this incident was considerable. In writing this book, there still remains for me a fantasy of the gloved hand serving food, paused in tentative disassociation, marking a border between self and the stealth of otherness. This seems a tangible border between bodies and identity.

The second image that stays with me is an incident that happened to a middle-aged Mexican woman, who had recently immigrated to the United States with her husband and children. She found work at a local meat-production plant, where she suffered a severe back injury while working on the floor of the plant. During this same period the United

States government entered into the NAFTA agreement with the Mexican government, a trade agreement that sent United States capital investments to Mexico to develop factories and strengthen trade across the Mexican-American border. As this woman became my friend, she continued her efforts to learn English in hopes of keeping her family in North America. Her back injury incapacitated her from work, but she continued to study for her citizenship exam in hopes of gaining her life ticket to North America. Because her papers were delayed by a government shutdown, she was finally deported to Mexico against her will, leaving her husband and children behind. She feared the bodily agony of the journey home to her father's house, half-way by plane and half-way over rocky roads that would exacerbate the pain in her back.

The deportation came as a violent disruption across the white skins of immigration officers and lawyers and the massive anti-immigration rhetoric that was filling the airwaves. My friend's was one of many deportations that passed silently over the border; there was no political uproar. I imagine the meat-production plant responding with indifference or relief, hunting down its next labor reserves while spitting out limbs and lives from its hidden interiors. Still today, I observe many workers of color drawn through its doors. I am left wondering about the border we call nation and the flow of transnational capital across that line, greedily feeding on bodies of cheap labor in poor countries and sucking the life out of blighted neighborhoods in the inner city. I wonder how that border called nation, imprinted on the back of my friend, is related to the smaller gloved border of Alexandria, and the borders of writing that make up this book. Each seems related to body, identity, and political struggle.

These images guided me through the writing of this book, bringing together two discursive planes: the micropolitics of borders, barriers, skins, and identities that operate in our everyday interactions to define self and not self, and the boundaries and demarcations of macropolitics defined by ownership of land, language, weapons, governments, and technologies: the materialisms of history. These global materialisms cut out from the land a new entity called "nation," an entity used to conscript bodies into surrendered loyalties, devoted fertility, and massive sacrifice in the name of war. Disciplining human bodies is necessary for the effective functioning on both the micro- and macrolevels of body economies, from the intimacies of sex and bodily practices to the institutional and cultural organization of a nation state and transnational corporations. While this book focuses primarily on the microlevels of the disciplined body and in particular on the construction of identities in sexuality, race, and gender, I am drawn toward what such analysis excludes—its absences—a different kind of study of the larger forces constructing sexuality, race, class, gender, geography, and historical location in the mega-narratives of nature's sheer force or history's brutal terror. What is the relationship between the microborders of self and other—a worker's glove as a protection, a surface up against personal annihilation—and the heaving forces of capital and high-tech weaponry organized to preserve a border marking land and resources for national possession or corporate annihilation? There is a movement of matter across many borders that I want to understand as interconnected. This book is only the first step.

The bodies studied in these essays are caught not only between the space of these two images but also in the contemporary tensions between modernism and postmodernism, feminist theory and queer theory, and philosophical and more experimental ways of writing about the body. I understand these tensions as coming from overlapping and distinct lineages of intellectual, political, and creative work and from different places within myself. Collected together they generate an ongoing dialogue on the body's biological matter and its social and historical formations. What is very real about bodies is a matter written on and through the body, a matter of discursive production developed and disciplined in the physicalities of the body. As others have argued, the body is a *materialization*, a socially mediated formation, lived individually and in communities as *real effects*. The *physicality* of the body establishes some of the potentials and limits for what we can do with our bodies, but these limits are not always absolutely fixed. The social world enters the physical body as we develop skills and capacities, altering even the body's molecular structures, its anatomy, physiology, and metabolism. The body is thus a sturdy but fragile thing, an historical matter of political struggle.

I have divided the essays of this book into three sections, each with an introduction, as a way to organize three movements in my own reflections on sex, gender, and the body. In the first section, "Articulations," I explore how normative bodies are constructed and articulated through deployments of power across sexuality, gender, race, disability, and class. In the second section, "Disarticulations," I pursue various ways in which postmodern theory relaxes the seeming sturdiness of our sex and gender assumptions. I analyze a variety of unruly bodies that do not fit the norms of a modernist body order: the male lesbian, lesbian femfire, and the omnisexual nomad. In thinking about these bodies, the categories of linear "straightness" and modernist assumptions about the body are challenged by the loss of prior material origin and ontological foundation.

In the third section, "Rearticulations," I explore various ways in which contemporary theorists have attempted to return *the matter of bodies* to cultural and philosophical theory. I think about this by considering the location of the writing body in writing about the body. The writing body is unlike the body of modernist thought—a body that presents itself as a prediscursive object with an organic structure and hierarchy of function, best comprehended by a reductive sciencism such as genetics or neurobiology. This Cartesianized body of modernist thought is often premised both metaphysically and epistemologically on the separation of the disciplined mind from that which it studies—the body. In the four essays in this section I explore other ways of returning the body to theory that abandon and challenge our modernist assumptions about the body of the knower and the known.

The place of my personal body in writing this book remained throughout the writing process, and even today, a puzzle. Introducing too much of one's personal life seems an unnecessary narcissism and perhaps an unwanted burden for the reader, but the absence of any personal voice seems ultimately antifeminist and overly Cartesian. In three kinds of writing I experiment with different ways to bring a more personal edge to body theory ("FemFire: A Theory in Drag," "Venus: The Looks of Body Theory," and "A Suite for the Body"). While engaged in this experimental writing, I have found the movement from personal to theoretical, mediated by nonphilosophical writing, an intriguing way to create new ideas.

I was astonished to find in finishing this book that the body became all the more a mystery to me. Certainly knowing the body is a task of many different methods, discourses, and practices, and I pursue here a modest interdisciplinary approach to various kinds of body talk as they *articulate, disarticulate,* and *rearticulate matters of the body.* In the end the seeming sturdiness of our bodies is rendered more fragile, and the fragility of our bodies is rendered more physically durable—a paradox I can live with. And in the end I have found only a few things I can know for sure about the body, elicited by desire, touch, feeling, and meaning. The panic attack produced by knowing so little of the body's ultimate mystery—why bodies?—inspires us to more body talk of theory, politics, and love.

One Articulations

The heterosexual body is often considered natural and normative.

Biological and medical discourses on the body suggest that parts fit functions, that millennia of sex drive and natural selection explain how these parts and functions evolved, and that sex and race differences can be given biologically grounded explanations. This way of writing about the matter of bodies has been challenged by new social construction and performativity theories in which notions of *the natural* and *the normative* are analyzed as functions of discursive practices, power relations, and performative effect. In such theories the body is often depicted as either culturally produced through disciplines and practices[1] or as semiotically produced through categories of meaning and identity mapped onto the body.[2] In this regard the athlete's body epitomizes discipline, meaning, and identity in perfecting the body's physicality.

I open this section of the book with "The Magic of the Pan(eroto)con," an exploration of black male athleticism in the body of Magic Johnson. This body, like all cultural bodies, is produced and extended institutionally beyond its actual physicality into a "third corpus." This "third corpus" situates the body as an object of cultural and cash value in an electronically and technologically mediated postmodern and imperialist world. Although Magic's body is lived uniquely by Earvin Magic Johnson, it is also produced beyond itself by the machinations of power and capital interests. The body of Magic Johnson provides a remarkable convergence of personal, historical, cultural, and political forces that produce the magic of Magic.

While the fetishized appropriation of Magic relies on the image of natural black sports excellence, my analysis of a cultural apparatus I have named "the pan(eroto)con" reveals the multiple labors and social tensions that hold Magic in place and produce his social meaning and cash value. In 1991, when he publicly announced his positive HIV status, Magic created a stress fracture in this system, one that makes more tangible the realities behind the appearance of his megastar image. In this chapter I seek another reading behind the appearance of what seems to be Magic's restorative hyperreality. From this perspective the body is articulated beyond itself. It is more than *the natural* and more fragile than it appears to be.

In a similar manner, the white heterosexual body is constituted through the institutional practices and social categories that define the meanings and status of sex, race, and gender. In the chapter "Heterosexual Anti-Biotics" I develop this idea further by exploring *the stretch* of this body into a semantic and institutional "third corpus" that gives privilege and protection to bodies of like kind, while regulating other bodies to lower status and more endangered life conditions.[3] By "first corpus" I refer to the body as an apparently unified biological organism, its living physicality; by "second corpus" I refer to the body as an incorporation of skills and disciplines and a conscription to culturally specific body vocabularies, practices, and identities; and by "third corpus" I refer to the extended institutional, semantic, and technological structures that produce the body in culturally significant relations of power and meaning. The heterosexual body appears as *the natural* and *the normative* through this layered recursive production of power.

Finally, in "Prozac Feminism" I explore how the heterosexual body also functions as a *yielded norm*, a norm often desired and a desire that yields itself to commodified completion. Proof of heterosexual desire and desirability requires an ongoing preoccupation with the private body, one that often generates an enormous need for help that inspires a desire for commodities promising bodily pleasure and perfection. In the last essay in this section, "Prozac Feminism," I explore how Prozac has been marketed to more socially privileged females (mostly white, heterosexual, employed, and middle-class) as a way to increase women's labor marketablity and improve their sex appeal and self-presentation. While radical feminism of the 1970s positioned itself as a mark of resistance against the dominant male culture, Prozac feminism, as marketed in the 1990s by Peter Kramer, becomes a sign of compliance with the norms of efficiency, buoyancy, and sexual jocularity. Prozac feminism, emerging within a new postmodern technologically and pharmaceutically mediated life, reveals a production of the heterosexual body in the feeding frenzy of capitalism. Resistance to Prozac feminism may require more than a return to antiquated notions of *the natural* as an organic or bodily origin. The body is always already a discursive, desiring production of its physicality. Resistance in the name of a more radical and treacherous feminism may require a postmodern disruption of Prozac's marketed promise.

The Magic of the Pan(eroto)Con

*From Othello to Mandingo, the predominant stereotype
of black masculinity is of an unrestrained, predatory, and
rapacious heterosexuality. The image of the black "stud"
is a classic (white) sexual fantasy.*

—PETER JACKSON, "Black Males"

*The figure of black masculinity consistently appears in
the popular imagination as the logical and legitimate
object of surveillance and policing, containment and
punishment. Discursively this black male body brings
together the dominant institutions of (white) masculine
power and authority—the criminal justice system, the
police, and the news media—to protect (white) Americans from harm.*   —HERMAN GRAY, "Black Masculinity"

On November 7, 1991, Earvin "Magic" Johnson[1]
held a press conference to announce his immediate retirement from the
L.A. Lakers and the National Basketball League. The reason stated by
Magic: "I do not have the AIDS disease. I know a lot of you want to know
that. I have the HIV virus. . . . Sometimes we think only gay people can
get it, or it's not going to happen to me. Here I am, saying it can happen
to everybody. Even me, Magic Johnson."[2] This statement set off a world-
wide panic of grief and shock, a public reaction much stronger than that
triggered by Rock Hudson's unexpected disclosure of his HIV-positive
status in 1985.[3] The heterosexual world realized that AIDS was not just a
closet issue for Hollywood celebrities like Hudson but a plague that could
penetrate as far as the idealized body of Magic Johnson. The over six-foot
seven-inch, thirty-two-year-old superstar of the L.A. Lakers, a giant

among sports giants, the NBA's Most Valuable Player for three years, had become a black male body infected by the AIDS-endangering virus. Its vector of sexual transmission—the alleged body of some woman some-where—seared the heart of heteromasculine invulnerability, as this hero of sports heroes surrendered his professional career to the microjourney of the virus.

President Bush commended Magic with the following public state-ment: "He's a hero to me. . . . I think he's a gentleman who has handled *his problem* in a wonderful way."[4] What is this problem, its content and magnitude; how much of this is Magic's *personal* problem; and how much of this is a problem related to the construction of Magic's mythi-cal body in the fantasy matrix of heteromasculine panoptic desire that holds at bay the vicious forces of sexual racism, AIDS phobia, and homo-phobia? Magic's revelation should have unleashed these emotional vul-tures, but instead restorative operations were almost immediately set in motion. Magic did not fall to pieces. He remained heroic, a fate not com-monly shared by thousands of other African-American, HIV-positive males. As Steven Feedback from the San Francisco-based National Task Force on AIDS Prevention has suggested, "The most despised people with AIDS in this society are black males. Black men are feared as crim-inals, as drug addicts. You add the stigma of AIDS—a black man with AIDS is treated like garbage."[5] This demise has not happened to Magic, because power resurrects bodies selectively just as it ignores bodies selectively.

In this chapter I will explore why Magic does not fall to pieces, by analyzing the machinations of what I call "the pan(eroto)con," a multiple media production of images and meanings that restore Magic's body to the American public. The pan(eroto)con *enters* our everyday life through thousands of screens, images, printed matter, recorded sounds—interwo-ven with color, texture, and design, to *enter*tain us, in this case with the body of Magic Johnson, a body celebrated for saving the L.A. Lakers from bored fans and low profits. These many bits of matter, literally dots and waves collected against a grainy, opaque threshold, have fleshed out a body—on television and elsewhere—that matters, a discursive represen-tation that is the magic of Magic and that promises the real thing. This "realness" is a tangible reality in both the flesh and blood of Magic and in the physical sublimity of his athleticism. Magic's body is produced by his talent and his personal devotion to sport disciplines, as well as through a larger apparatus of power—the pan(eroto)con that magnifies, manipulates, and multiplies images of Magic's body into a mythic apex of black, hyperabled, masculine physicality.

Magic stands as an edifice of this power: his announcement generating the need for discursive restoration.[6] As a transcendental icon of "the naturalized" black male athlete, this investment has not been without risk. Magic Johnson was symbolically invited into the American living room, where his disciplined black physicality could be spectated upon and experienced in pleasure, but this was cast against a black masculinity otherwise perceived by white racist America as amorphous, dangerous, violent, and degenerate. Magic's public announcement of his positive HIV status threatened to re-race Magic into this amorphous denigration. It was as if millions of flickering television screens and commercial images had also been invaded by the virus and the impending threat of Magic's dissolution. Magic's body, threatening to fall to pieces, was situated in a precarious intersection, where the construction of deviant bodies crosses over into the white man's "terror of race and desire."[7] The restoration of Magic required a massive sweep of the pan(eroto)con.

Magic's Body and the Pan(eroto)con

The notion of the "pan(eroto)con" is a hybrid theoretical term. It relies on Foucault's "panopticon"[8] as a central metaphor for the modern production of bodies subjected to multiple spectral and omnipresent surveillance techniques that foster disciplined bodily practices and self-management regimes to produce docile, high-functioning, and "normalized" bodies. My idea of the pan(eroto)con is also derived from Elizabeth Meese's notion of "(sem)erotics,"[9] which suggests that meanings of the body are at least partially "produced" in a semiotically infused physical exchange of erotic energy between beloved and lover, writer and reader, object-looked-upon and the adoring gaze. In the pan(eroto)con Magic's physical body is produced in the value and meanings of a unifying series of historical, plural, and culturally mediated presentations.[10] The pan(eroto)con makes Magic *magic* through a multifocal kaleidoscope of re-presentational points and interpretive schemas, pleasuring the viewer's gaze with a viscerally felt connection and a fanciful identificatory release into the male transcendental physicality of Magic's mythical body.

I consider this pleasure erotic and kinesthetic, though not necessarily genital in the location of bodily pleasure. Although women can join court erotics on varied terms, this is mostly man-to-man stuff, with the machinery of pleasure and connection flowing from Magic's body to the adoring male spectator, remuscling boyhood memories, real or imaginary, in a vital, agile, and hyperabled male body ideal. Power produces this M(m)agic and visual pleasure in the materiality of a sports hero—Magic's trained and disciplined body—and has dispersed his embodied transcendence into multiple screens, sounds, and images in the millions of tributaries of the pan(eroto)con's theaters. In truth most everybody loves this magic. When Magic announced his HIV status to the public, a shock reverberated in Magic's multiple theaters, on screens and images across the world, where his heroic stature was threatened by AIDS slippage and racial disintegration. As this ugly gash in the semiotic screens of social reality began to appear, the body panics that ensued were largely money and manly matters. The pan(eroto)con—as the corporate body machinery of America—labored to put the pieces back together again.

Observed looking through the pan(eroto)con, Magic's body is a composite of many different "bodies." His *physical body* threatens to collapse from the siege of the virus. His *practical body* displays the cultural imprint of discipline and training—the habit, skill, movement, timing, coordination, language, and grace of this paragon of male physical being. His *semiotic body* carries the meaning of his power, read against the grids of race, gender, sexuality, health status, and sports heroics. His *corporate body* exists for the exchange of capital in images of specular masculinity—a body owned by white capital and "owned" for twelve years by millions of Laker fans who adored "their" Magic. Magic also has a *home body* and is in some ways a familiar guest in the American family. Jim Reeves of the *Fort Worth (Texas) Star-Telegram* personalized Magic's impact at home: "AIDS came home to our neighborhood Thursday. Mine and yours. It pulled up a chair, sat down in our midst, and began shaking hands, as if it belonged there, as if it wasn't wearing the dark hood of death mask of the Grim Reaper. As if—and this is the scary part—it was an old friend, come to pay its respects."[11] Magic's smile has always been welcomed into American homes. As Cheryl Cole and Harry Denny have suggested:

> Johnson's marketability was established through promotional strategies that articulated Magic as the embodiment of an accept-

able, non-threatening face of masculinity, of having a personality and character consistent with the values of what Cindy Patton has called the "Africanized Horatio Alger trope of athletics"—family, modest beginnings, skill, hard work, discipline, courage, determination, and social mobility.[12]

There is also Magic's *mythic body*—the magic of Magic—which makes his body *more real than the real*, the supranormal ideal of masculinity that unifies and solidifies Magic's other bodies into one referent. In this consolidation the excess of Magic is not that of deviance but that of magnificence, magnifying what makes a man superior and godlike in his disciplined physicality. As Margaret Whitford suggests, "In the male imaginary, the transcendental, the *ec-stacy* (*ek-stase, hor-de-soi*) or *ek-sistance*, corresponds to the projection of erection, male narcissism extrapolated to the transcendental."[13] In this construction what the subject cannot dominate threatens the subject with castration—"the cavern, the womb, the inside of the mother's body is a dangerous place (whose dangers are represented by the phantasy of the *vagina dentata*)."[14] In the case of Magic's mythic body and his positive positioning within male transcendental excess, phallic trouble is displaced onto the female body, transforming it into an infecting and evil hole, markedly not male, a further displacement of anal deviance, "monstering" the female body, re-racing the black sexual body, and feminizing the queer body. In the discursivities of AIDS, Magic's physical body caught in the grip of HIV is a fact—the meanings of his body, produced through the changing social and political theaters of the pan(eroto)con, teeter unsteadily between the excess of deviance and the excess of mythic transcendence.

Strategies of Restoration

Inside Magic's body the virus threatened physical depletion and semantic damage, in effect re-racing Magic's sexuality and emasculating his almost transcendental status. This would have created a rift between the referent (his body) and the cultural representations of his superheroic and fabulous physicality (an ensemble of signs and meanings). A disaster seemed imminent. Magic's HIV-positive body might become an AIDS body, a hypersexual black and deviant body, and as the rumors began to fly, possibly a closeted queer body.[15] However, his body did not fall to pieces, because *strategies of discursive restoration* were quickly deployed to resuture a tear and to rescue the slip in the pan(eroto)con's representational system. I want to understand this reaction, not only in terms of Magic's warrior will, positive attitude, and good health—all very admirable in themselves—but also in terms of the cultural anti-gravity that restabilizes his mythic heteromasculine status. I will exam-ine four "strategies of restoration" that restore Magic's stability, nor-malcy, innocence, vitality, and power as an infallible sports hero. These strategies include: (1) the normalization of his heteromasculine promis-cuity, (2) the vilification of the vagina, (3) the disavowal of his queer-ness, and (4) the rebuilding of Magic's body. These four strategies work to resolidify and restabilize the cultural meanings of Magic's body, a body that began to slip from the screens of popular imagination and careen toward a capital disenchantment. America still wanted the plea-sure of looking at Magic, the stellar body of blackness in motion. It was a matter of how *to overlook* the dis/pleasure and dis/integration occa-sioned by the real and symbolic meanings of the virus in the hero's body.

Strategy 1: Normalization of Heteromasculine Promiscuity

> *If it happened to a heterosexual woman who had been with 100 or 200 men, they'd call her a whore and a slut and the corporations would drop her like a lead balloon.*
> —Martina Navratilova, USA Today

> *A publicly gay athlete like Martina, she'd be gone (if she tested positive). No way can I imagine endorsers would stick with her, that she would be asked to speak in schools. And that's criminal.*   —Mary Carillo, USA Today

How Magic got the virus is a matter of speculation, but its publicly announced route was casual and unprotected heterosexual intercourse. This promiscuity is constructed as an extension of Magic's magnetic power over women and his willingness to accommodate the women who flocked to him. Similar to Wilt Chamberlain's claim that he has had sex with close to twenty thousand women,[16] Magic comes off as a hero—perhaps less reckless than Wilt,[17] but more unlucky. The *National Enquirer*[18] did, however, sensationalize Magic's number at more than one thousand women. Magic now stands before the press and the public as remiss about his sexual irresponsibilities, a narrative that oscillates between the wrongness of having had too many women or having had too little protection. The strategy of restoration that operates here does not vilify Magic for his exuberant male prowess. Instead Magic was "wronged" by a bad encounter—the wrong woman, the wrong vagina, the wrong way. He appears repentant, soft-hearted, likable, and unlucky. As Will Perdue of the Bulls said, "it's difficult to say no to a beautiful woman."[19] Magic's error seems forgivable. The restorative strategy creates a picture of Magic as heterosexually errant but not deviant.

Such is not the case with gay or female heterosexual promiscuity, indicating how this strategy of restoration relies on the double standards of gender and heterosexual privilege. Magic's heterosexual promiscuity is seen as excessive behavior, less damning than gay or female promiscuities that are often considered fatal flaws in personal character or a sexual nature pathological in content. As female tennis players Martina Navratilova, Pam Shriver, and Mary Carillo have pointed out,[20] Magic was able to keep his endorsers because he did not get the virus through drugs or gay sex—he got it "the natural way" through sex with women.

Magic's heterosexual promiscuity also fulfills a heteromasculine fantasy for fast, easy, and satisfying sex with an interminable number of female bodies—a scoring that measures heteromasculine power rather than pathology. It was not Magic alone who did this but Magic as the personification of power. As he describes this:

During the 1980s, the Lakers were seen as the sexiest and most glamorous team of them all. Los Angeles was glamorous. Winning was glamorous. Our fast break was sexy. And being the best team in the league made us *very* sexy. Just about every time the bus brought us back to our hotel after the game, there would be forty or fifty women waiting in the lobby to meet us. Most of them were beautiful, and a few were just unbelievable.[21]

When I got up to my room, there would always be a stack of phone messages. Dolores called, she's waiting in the lobby. Arlene called, she's wearing a red dress. Marian called, she's by the elevator. Often, before I even checked into the hotel there would a dozen or more calls from women I had never met.[22]

Some of the mail got pretty explicit, and it wasn't just letters, either. Sometimes women would send along photographs of themselves— usually out of uniform. And even videotapes, just to make sure you got the idea. Others sent their underwear. There was nothing subtle about it.[23]

In some hotels you could open your door at just about any time of day or night and find a beautiful woman standing there in the hall, hoping to be invited in.[24]

Although Magic claimed he enjoyed "making women's fantasies come true,"[25] the invasion of the virus has caused him to call his unprotected sexual practices into question. He does this without a vindictive or mean spirit toward the women who wanted him; that work is already done by a cultural misogyny that despises female promiscuity. In this strategy of restoration, Magic's mythical body is recouped with a double reading of his HIV status as the yet invisible mark on his Titan body and as a high mark of heteromasculine sexual power.

Strategy 2: Vaginal Vilification

> *Coupled with the self-assurance that I project, I become*
> *like a majestic mountain many feel they'd like to scale*
> *and conquer. Wilt as Mount Everest.*
>
> —WILT CHAMBERLAIN, *Minneapolis Star Tribune*

The arena of sports, especially basketball and football in America, provides a specular display for hyperabled male physicality, demonstrating male physical superiority over the female sex and ranking males over males on the basis of skill, violence, and power. This often spills over into physical and sexual acts of aggression against women. Recent studies on college campuses suggest that a disproportionate number of gang rapes and assaults are perpetrated by male athletes.[26] Melnick has suggested that the increasing number of recent sexual assaults by male athletes is not a set of random occurrences but "part of a larger pattern of behavior with roots firmly planted in the very structure and culture of (men's) sports." [27] Where aggression, violence, and "power over" relationships mark excellence in sport for the male body, it is not surprising these same behaviors are sexualized, normalized, and even idealized in sexual relationships with women as the other proving ground of male physical and sexual hubris. The male athlete as *the male body in the real* is exonerated for his excesses in sport with men and in sex with women. Even in the case of Mike Tyson, where his sexual violence was well-documented and horrific, desperate attempts were made to rescue the athlete from his imprisonment for rape.[28]

I am not suggesting here that Magic Johnson is a rapist or that all male athletes assault women. What is interesting in Magic's case is the semantic inversion (in this second strategy of restoration) that overdetermines Magic as a victim. His excess is a seduced excess. The women who swarm his body are caricatured as vampire gold-diggers, narcissistic sex addicts, and beautiful and glamorous spoilers. These women are known as "groupies," sex drifters who follow the teams, gluing their bodies to the vulnerable and sex-driven heroes of sport. Whatever their motivations, they blend into a whoring mass of "no names," attacking their prey with a sex-exalted lure. Magic comes off as a victim of some woman somewhere, indecipherable from the others. Perhaps only one woman infected Magic, but this woman is to blame. Her "fault/fall" is found in her promiscuity and her infecting fluidity. In this narrative of Magic's sex life, *woman X* and her body secretions are vectors of danger.

This vectoral property appears to be unilateral. A year after Magic made his announcement to the world, he was faced with a lawsuit by a woman in Michigan who claimed that Magic infected her with HIV.[29] She claims to have sent a letter to Magic with this information eight weeks before his fateful life-insurance test and two weeks before his marriage to Cookie. On the basis of an eight-month period of celibacy prior to her sexual intercourse with Magic and previous HIV blood tests that were negative, she claims that Magic infected her in June 1991. Johnson himself does not deny the night of sex passed with this woman, but his lawyer, Howard Weitzman, claims that the woman was promiscuous and could have contacted the virus "from any number of men."[30] In the tabloids other women have come forward exposing affairs with Magic. One of them, a porn model, claims that Magic had unsafe sex with her after he knew he had the virus. These women are, however, already sexually sensationalized and culturally marginalized as the real or imagined predators of the sex-beleaguered star. Their promiscuity damns them against the greatness of Magic's body.[31]

Other athletes confirm Magic's story:

> We come into town, and the women come out in force. They call the hotel, they follow the bus. They hover and wait to get you.
>
> KEVIN JOHNSON [32] *(Phoenix Sun)*

They want the thrill of being with an athlete. And they don't want
safe sex. They want to have your baby, man, because they think that
if they have your baby, they're set for life.

DOMINIQUE WILKINS [33] *(Atlanta Hawks)*

If you're in this league long enough, you know women all over the
country willing to yield to your request. Were the same women
yielding to the request of, say, the Philadelphia Eagles the week
before? Maybe.   DEXTER MANLEY.[34] *(Tampa Bay Buccaneers)*

This sexual frenzy mixes with sexual racism, a subtext that conjures
black men as oversexed animality and black women as uncontrolled, rapacious, and reckless sex. As Evelynn Hammonds has pointed out,[35] African-
American women constitute not only the majority among women with
AIDS but also the most invisible category of persons living with AIDS.
According to Hammonds, this is to a large extent fostered by sexual
racism: "For a Black woman to expose that she had a sexually transmitted
disease was for much of this century to render herself multiply stigma-
tized, bringing up older images of immorality and uncontrolled sexuality
that neither class nor educational privilege could protect her from."[36]
While these stereotypes work to silence the experiences and circumstances
of an African-American woman's experience with HIV/AIDS, they also
magnify her danger to the black man, falsely inverting the truth that
women are at much higher risk for HIV transmission through intercourse
with an infected male than men with an infected female.[37] Over-inflated
male fears that associate AIDS with "the polluting fluids of woman," primarily the prostitute of color, were fanned by the splurge of publicity in
the black press about C.J., an African American HIV-positive prostitute in
Dallas, who was having unprotected sex with men as an act of revenge.[38]
This story, like that of the Lolitas, the Amy Fishers, the Lorena Bobbits,
and other fatal attractions of the white press around the same time, further overdetermines the meaning of woman as a sign of sexual danger and
death; in this, the African-American woman comes off even more stigma-
tized and silenced because her sex is already "raced" as dangerously polluting, inferior, and reckless. In Magic's case, she—not surprisingly—has
no name. Magic's tragedy, caught through the vector of this no-name
woman, situates *that woman* in the unknown territory of race and desire.
However, the blame for all of this, filtered through the sexual racism of

contemporary culture, is not colorless and not innocent. She disappears into a dangerous black amorphous mass.[39]

In contrast to these women, Cookie Johnson, Magic's wife, whom he married six weeks before he learned about his condition, appears as a *phallic angel*, miraculously untouched by the virus and capable of delivering an uninfected son, Earvin Johnson III. Cookie represents purity, understanding, forgiveness, fidelity, patience, the balancing symbolism of "motherhood/wifery" that redeems Magic's manhood as a family man.[40] Against the dirty tide of furies, Cookie's presence restabilizes the repentant hero in a second performative of masculinity: a phallus that does not infect but "fathers" in the sanctity of a clean woman's womb. The fear that Magic was an "infector" is erased by Cookie and by Magic's relief that all the women he called "came up clean," with the exception of Michigan, who called him. Cookie by his side, Magic regains his heteromasculine status as a family man with a newborn son, a portfolio worth millions, and the luck of Gabriel: the virus has not harmed his seed.[41] "Nasty rumors and ridiculous gossip"[42] fall by the wayside.

Strategy 3: Disavowal of Queerness

> *I've already said it, but I'll say it again: I have never had a homosexual experience. I'm not gay or bisexual. If I were, I would say so. It's not my style to hide or deny something like that.*   —Magic Johnson, *My Life*

> *First of all, I am far from being homosexual.*
>   —Magic Johnson, *The Arsenio Hall Show*

> *I sympathize with anyone who has to battle AIDS, regardless of his or her sexual preference, but I have never had a homosexual encounter. Never.*
>   —Magic Johnson, *Sports Illustrated*

> *I was upset about hearing about a thing I didn't do. There are no skeletons in my closet.*
>   —Magic Johnson, *Larry King Live*

> *But I'm not. And it didn't happen that way. And it didn't happen by sharing a needle, because I have never done drugs.*   —Magic Johnson, *My Life*

These disavowals of homosexual interest and desire read loud and clear to the American public. The specular and mythic body of Magic Johnson does not lie. Unlike Rock Hudson, Magic's late marriage should not be read as a sign of homosexual hesitance or deception[43] but as an effect of Los Angeles hetero high life, an intoxication of women seducing a steady man into the euphoria of interminable pleasure. This is explained by his wife, Cookie:

> No wonder Earvin took so long to get married. He didn't want to let go of that world. What man would? Look at Hugh Hefner, with the big mansion and the parties where who knows what goes on. Could a man like that exist in any other city? Only in L.A. . . . During these years I knew about Earvin's personal life in general terms. But I didn't know the details, and I didn't want to know.[44]

However, the narrative travelogue of the HIV virus in the United States threatens to tell another story—a story that leads to the "queering" of this heroic body, a painful metaphysic threatening to reveal a dislocation between the body's truth and its public appearance. Even if Magic's encounter with the virus did not happen through homosexual acts, this suspicious discourse surrounds his body like prairie fire, and his sex, like the sex of gay men, has become a matter of public fascination.

In this restorative strategy, the pan(eroto)con, desperately reproduces the hetero/homo divide, while smearing the edges with homophobic panic. Cindy Patton has argued that AIDS in the contemporary psyche is always in some way related to deviant sex. According to Patton, heterosexuals fit into this paradigm as victims of temptation: "the underlying message is that heterosexuals don't normally do these things unless they are exposed to these exotic sexual elements."[45] Heterosexuals get the virus when they venture into danger zones associated with Haitians, Africans, prostitutes, IV drug users, gay and bisexual men, and bad blood. In the heterosexual AIDS panic there is a link between AIDS and sex outside the norm of man-on-top-penis-in-vagina-between-married-(to-each-other)adult sex. Patton argues that even when the route of transmission does not involve sex, these "others" are marked as "sexually feminized" or unmasculine "honorary queers."[46] What results is a feminized immune system made vulnerable and weakened by the virus. As Patton suggests: "the paradigmatic representation /embodiment of the "AIDS virus" is the gay man. . . . The world of AIDS knowledge mobilizes a dispersed panopticism which directs everyone's eyes to the sex lives of gay men."[47] "The AIDS body," condensed to queerness, an object of cultural hatred, signifies a gay male body.

This "queering" of "the AIDS body" allows heterosexuals to return to the security of their heterosexual practices and to a virulent form of AIDS-inspired homophobia that polices the borders of heterosexual communities. However, when Magic Johnson announced to the world that he was HIV-positive, the fluid boundaries of "high risk" groups merged into the threatening category of "heterosexually acquired HIV."[48] Magic's body became a kind of "border body"[49] ambiguously crossing the terrains of Africa/race/sex/risk and the norms of white American everyday life. If it could happen to Magic, it could happen to less physically heroic straight men. It was difficult "to other" Magic with categories of degradation without psychic hazard to heteromasculine body fantasy. Instead, Magic's body oscillated between an "HIV anomaly" and an "HIV messenger" as the fans adjusted to the news.

However, the heteromasculine gaze requires Magic's heterosexual purity. This third strategy of restoration works overtime to separate Magic from the stain of queerness, to make him straight and honest. We understand this by what Magic is *not*: (1) there are either innocent or deserving victims of the HIV virus; Magic is an innocent victim, an HIV anomaly; he did *not* really deserve this; he is *not* gay;[50] (2) the AIDS body as the homosexual body is usually represented showing obvious signs of the virus; Magic's body shows no obvious signs of the virus; he is heterosexual and *not* categorically unhealthy; (3) HIV/AIDS is a consequence of abnormal gay promiscuity; Magic's male promiscuity was *not* abnormal but supernormal; his mistake was in not taking safe-sex precautions rather than in being gay; (4) homosexuals are liars and "closeted"; Magic does *not* lie; he is honest and trustworthy; (5) the gay AIDS body is not worth saving; this is *not* the case for Magic as the world will never be the same without Magic; (6) how homosexuals get *it* is a matter of moral panic; Magic has *not* done this—his only crime was being too much a woman's man; (7) homosexual spokesmen on HIV/AIDS are not credible authorities to the public; Magic as "a spokesman for the virus" is "God's gift to the virus"; [51] if he came out as a bisexual he would lose this credibility and power; Magic is *not* one of them; (8) homosexuals are soft, effeminate men; Magic is a hardened gladiator; he has a soft heart but an amoured body; his softness signifies innocence *not* gayness.[52] In fact, his hard body is a sign of post-Nam Reagan-era masculinity. Magic Johnson is *not* a pervert. As is typical of heterosexual identity, Magic's straightness is constructed by a series of oppositional negations.

Strategy 4: Rebuilding Magic's Body

> "Magic Urges Bush to Get in AIDS Game"
>
> —USA Today

> "Magic to Bush: Get into the Game, Spend More Money on AIDS Crisis"
>
> —Atlanta Constitution

> "Magic Johnson Urges Bush to Lead AIDS Battle"
>
> —New York Times

It is not uncommon when Magic appears on talk shows after his November 7th announcement that he mentions his good health or that he has just finished a long workout. While it might be expected that the public sincerely wants to know how he has been feeling and whether the virus has caused any trouble, the meaning of these disclosures is double-edged. Just as a male-to-female transsexual must "talk out" her feminine condition to overdetermine its positivity,[53] so Magic must "talk out" his body as evidence of his Titanic health and as proof that the virus remains defeated. It is no longer taken for granted that Magic's body will be in top condition. Magic's work to maintain his health, bulk, and conditioning provides him some hope of returning to the court and a demonstration of his will to power over the virus. What is most feared is the virus altering the flesh of Magic. As Larry Kramer has articulated this: "I think he'll turn into the same pariah that all the rest of us turn into when we become sick. When his body becomes skin and bones and pus and runny sores, there won't be so many people running to embrace him."[54] This fourth strategy of restoration targets Magic's physical appearance.

Investment in the appearance of Magic's body is no small matter.[55] His body is a site of capital investment—millions in contracts, endorsements, and franchises—and a site of psychic investment for a heteromasculine admiration of Magic's sheer physicality. Capital interests in the appearance of Magic rely on an intensive medical management of Magic's HIV-positive body, as well as aggressive cosmetic "makeovers" if opportunistic infections should set their mark on Magic's body. What the public doesn't see when Magic appears before them is a likely entourage of medical and technical expertise, perhaps the best AIDS experts in the country, who stand behind him. For as long as possible, Magic's appearance must remain unmarked by the virus.[56]

This "behind-the-scene" management separates Magic from other HIV-positive African Americans, many of whom have very little access to the medical attention given to Magic or to the capital required for the best possible medical care and restorative production.[57] These unlucky victims of HIV remain invisible, not at all magical, and at least doubly jeopardized by the effects of racism and AIDS-phobia that result in small, ignominious, and publicly unattended deaths. Magic appears to be magic in his resilience, but this is a collective and capital-intensive effort invested in Magic, not because he is black and HIV-positive but because he is a sports hero who dares not perish too quickly in front of America. His is a body not only "worked out," "bulked up," and "talked out" but labored upon by the many interests who manage his public presentations and commercial impressions.

Similar to the positioning of the body in other masculinist representations of pathology, Magic positions his infected body in an adversary, calling for a "struggle against" and "victory over" its encumbrance. He often does this through the discourse of sports metaphors. In a letter Magic sent to President George Bush on January 14, 1992, Magic, who had been recently appointed to serve on the Bush AIDS Commission, uses such metaphors to implore the President to provide more funding for research on and treatment of AIDS and Medicaid care for HIV-positive people. Magic's choice of metaphors fits consistently with the fleet of masculinized metaphors of war, battle, and intercommunications already mapped onto the AIDS body.[58] Using sports metaphors, Magic calls on the Commander and Chief in this man-to-man style to be more responsive to the AIDS crisis.

Magic writes in his letter to President Bush:[59]

In the last two months I have switched games, from basketball to, I guess, the biggest game of all—life and death. . . . In asking me to join the Commission, in fact you were asking me to join your team. You are the owner. . . . I have given this much thought and realize that the fight against AIDS demands a full court press. We can win this game, but not without a total commitment from everyone.

In President Bush's letter of response, there is an appended handwritten note that reads: "I like your 'team' analogy. Good luck, Come back."[60] Magic subsequently resigned from the Commission in public disapproval of President Bush's inadequate efforts to deal with the AIDS crisis. In his resignation letter to the President, Magic wrote, "I am disap-

pointed that you dropped the ball."[61] Between one of the greatest contemporary male athletes in the country and the highest ranking white
male official in the United States, the game was over. These sports
metaphors in the Magic/Bush correspondence remind us that Magic's
body is special, that his special status is a result of sports heroism, and that
he is probably one of very few African-American males in the country
who could write to a president of the United States and receive a personal
response, an invitation to serve as a high-level appointee in a government
commission, and a handwritten note sporting their comradery. The
racism inhabiting these masculine repartees is both screaming at Magic
and silenced by presidential honor.

In this communication between President Bush and Magic, some saw
both seeking photo opportunities and political gain.[62] As Magic's body
entered the press-driven deployments of the 1992 presidential campaign,
he was positioned as a new hero on Bush's AIDS team. The deployment
of sports metaphors was marshaled into overtly political and conservative aims. With Magic's resignation from the commission, the sport
metaphors were redeployed in a personal domain where he teams up with
his own body to continue his workouts and health management. The
scope of sports metaphor application was reduced to Magic's physical
body rather than the social and political structure of the AIDS crisis. The
battle becomes a matter of one man's struggle. Perhaps Magic realized he
had gone too high up in his brush with the President, that his mythical
power failed to have effect in the body politics of the AIDS crisis. Magic
retreated, his image still intact.

All four of the strategies of restoration within the pan(eroto)con aim to
restabilize and revive Magic's heroic status. They stave off the negative
images of AIDS, homosexuality (bisexuality), heterosexual wrongdoing,
disability, and death. Magic is kept from slipping over the edge, but the
tension remains delicately balanced by the need constantly to restore the
image of Magic against the frayed edges of these discursive dangers. I
would like to explore two of these areas of recalcitrant discursive danger,
where Magic's body is threatened by semantic failure. In these areas
Magic's excess cannot be easily contained by the operations of the
pan(eroto)con. They mark out the shadows of race hatred and white paranoia in sexual racism, held in check as long as Magic stays magic, a body
buoyed up by the forces of the pan(eroto)con and its constant restoration
of Magic's power and purity. However, these are also areas of cultural

anxiety that can invade the pan(eroto)con and multiply—like a virus—excessively.

Re-Racing Sex and Basketball

> *Johnson will perceive that he is as marginal as we are. The difference between him and the gay community will dramatically lessen as time goes on. That is a good linkage. Let our enemies be his enemies. He's a strong ally.*
> —PAUL BONEBURG, *Advocate*

> *Black is the color of the "dirty" secrets of sex—relentlessly represented in the image of Black "boy" as stud, and Black woman as whore.* —LYNNE SEGAL, *Slow Motion*

Magic's mythic power relies on his adamant disavowal of homosexual desire and his deification as a sports hero. While Magic's body is situated at the intersection of number of significant determinants—race, class, gender, sexuality, AIDS, impending disability, and athletic genius—the magic of Magic is also his fabulous life story hailing the American dream. Magic grew up the son of a General Motors factory worker in Lansing, Michigan, one of many young black men in the pick-up games on the asphalt city courts who rose through talent, discipline, and will power to the very top of the NBA. This is the story of hope for many young black males who sit on the benches of poverty, racism, environmental hazard, and the institutional decimation of African-American males. Magic's is the story of race victory and devotion to a disciplined black masculinity.

As Richard Majors has pointed out, "the influx of Black men into sports has happened since World War II, when sport became one of few respectable avenues for black masculinity.[63] While a disproportionate number of young black males are drawn to sport, the selection of only a few for the top ranks leaves its toll on those left behind.[64] As Majors tabulates this: 6 percent of all athletic scholarships given in the United States go to African-American athletes; 25 to 35 percent of high school black athletes do not qualify for scholarships because of academic deficiencies; of those who do acquire scholarships, 65 to 75 percent may not graduate from college; of those who do graduate, 75 percent graduate with "jock degrees" especially designed for athletes and not especially useful for later career work.[65] In this context Magic's story of ascent to the top of the NBA becomes an even more fabulous American dream. He stands as an idol for many African-American youth, perhaps more especially so than he does for every other American child. However, this personal story of "making it" serves to foster an implicit racism blaming those left behind for their lack of success.

Race and sex differences collide and reassemble themselves in the body of the black male athlete, where black athleticism signifies the exalted physicality of the male sex. As others have pointed out,[66] sport as mass spectacle began to take on its modern form with the declining relevance of the physical body in work and war. Socially and economically privileged masculinity was absorbed into capital and wealth production, which prioritized mental over manual labor and valued the disembodied practices of instrumental reason, abstraction, and surplus accumulation over the labor of muscle, local barter, and man-to-man combat. With these changes in privileged forms of heteromasculinity, sport especially tailored to the extreme potentialities of the male body became a way to reify the differences between the sexes *as natural* and to reclaim a form of male superiority through public displays of exalted male physicality. The representation of hegemonic physical masculinity in the force and skill of the sports hero's body is literally "played out" for the "sitting spectator" in the most capital-intensive sports—baseball, basketball, and football. As Clarke and Clarke have argued, because sport "appears as a sphere of activity outside society, and particularly as it appears to involve natural, physical skills and capacities [it] presents these ideological images as if they were natural."[67] Superior male performance over females in most sports and especially in heavy contact sports reaffirms a certain kind of physical ontology of valued difference between the sexes.

The historically recent influx of black male bodies into the arena of specular sport reinforces the mind/body split in a racialized male supremist system as it reinforces the physicalities of sex difference. In white racist America, black male athletes enter these equations seemingly even closer to nature, closer to the physical, and as proof of male physical superiority over women; blackness still performs as the buck for the master.[68] This is the cultural location in white America where Magic's body enters as a magnificent machine. In turn, white America appropriates his body, invests in its promise, and uses its meanings to reinforce the sex and race differences in the majesty of Magic's performance.

However, the entry of black male bodies into the sport of basketball did more than provide a socially acceptable form of disciplined black masculinity for sports fans. It also changed the nature of the game, introducing black style and an aesthetic that fused African-American norms and practices with the competitive skills of the game. The disciplining of blackness redefined the sport of basketball, privileging black agility, style, and performativity. Michael Eric Dyson describes this as cashing in on the symbolic danger of black sports excellence, in which black athletes "captured and catalyzed the black cultural fetishization of sports as a means of expressing black cultural style, as a means of valorizing craft as a marker of racial and self-expression, and as a means of pursuing social and economic mobility."[69] Nelson George adds, "there's no question that certain African-Americans execute their court magic with a funky attitude akin to that of the race's greatest musicians."[70] Black basketball created new shots and plays—the behind-the-back pass, the alley-oop, the jammin'-dunk—that changed the vocabulary ("trash talking")[71] and physical motion of the game. In this context Magic's talent expressed by a flamboyant intensity and a stylized way of intimidating through improvisation, helped rank the Lakers on top as Johnson pushed through the middle. The beauty of this physical aesthetic is what many spectators adore in Magic: his ability to see the whole court from on high and orchestrate from there. With Magic on the court, the game again produced an African-American stylization of the performing body in motion that condensed physical grace and sheer power. Magic's mythic transcendence is about excess, an excess of style and athleticism and an excess of sex and race. An anxious white cultural pleasure fell in love with Magic, and this love was pure.

The Queerity of AIDs and Sexual Racism

Sexual racism imagines the black phallus as excess—too much sex and too much power.[72] Magic's affliction indicates a masculinity gone over the edge, an unruly physicality, a body of black danger that hides behind his splendid Magic. While Magic denies any association with gay sex and happily produces his smile, his confessional moment evokes a call for surveillance of Magic's sexual truth: who, when, how, how many, why? This is a narrative of shadow speculations that perversely haunt the pan(eroto)con's operations. It is a response that typically hovers around the AIDS body, interrogating the body's sex as the spectral economy looks for blame and innocence. However, the stain of race,[73] like the stigma of homosexuality, makes that innocence more difficult to achieve in the pan(eroto)con's rescue of Magic's image. Likewise, the queerity of

the AIDS sign—plagued by its continuous slippage and lack of containment—though literally denied by Magic, continues to refigure the hero.
Along with a fascination about Magic's past sexual excess, there are three
additional tropes that reinscribe the queerity of the AIDS in the margins
of Magic's story: the anxiety of other players toward his bodily fluids,
Magic's stylized "return home" as the sexually reformed son (a common
trope of gay return), and the lingering terror *in a story of AIDS origin*
that links the virus to race and sexual excess.

In the first trope, fluidophobia[74] was commonly expressed by players
fearful of contact with Magic's body. In 1992 Karl Malone of the Utah Jazz
team demanded Magic resign from the Lakers because he feared getting
infected from Magic's sweat and blood during court play. Despite the inaccuracy of this transmission lore, Magic resigned from the L.A. Lakers for
a second time in 1992. Malone stated that he said what many other players were thinking but were afraid to say.[75] When Magic returned to the
Los Angeles Lakers in 1996 after four years of retirement, there were still
concerns. Dallas Mavericks guard Lucious Harris supported Magic's
return, stating that he would not have a problem playing against Mr.
Johnson, "but there's always the question in the back of the mind, What
if? It's a one-in-a-million chance of becoming infected, but who wants to
be that one in a million?"[76] Vernon Maxwell of the Philadelphia 76ers
reportedly told the *Los Angeles Times*: "I don't want to be there with that.
I have a wife and kids."[77] Surrounded by these fears, Magic's images are
now redispersed at various nodal points within the pan(eroto)con. He is
stabilized at these points, however tenuously, through the positive discursivities that make him shine, while the negative tropes work like a
malevolent virus in the skein of the pan(eroto)con itself.

In a second trope, Magic returns home to the American family the
prodigal son, asking us to accept him as the same person he was before, a
script now commonly assumed for the repentant gay and infected son
who returns home for family forgiveness and a place to die. Columnist
Jim Klobuchar sentimentalizes Magic's return: now "he will live in the
shadow of a disease that is lethal and *was once regarded as repugnant.*"[78]
The shift in evaluation of AIDS is significant here. Similar to syphilis in
the nineteenth century, the moralism surrounding that disease, long associated with prostitutes and low life, began to dissipate when the disease
began to affect the respectable classes. Magic returns home with a body
marked by its vulnerability to opportunistic infections and cancers, a victim of a natural disaster, a disaster allegedly caused by dirty female secre-

tions. He asks not to be burdened with moralism or blame and dedicates himself to educating African-American youth about the dangers of unprotected sex. He returns home an all-American heterosexual son. He returns home a black son to help the youth of his community. The absolution mirrors the equally difficult return of many gay sons to heterocentric households. Magic returns repentant but not gay. As Douglas Crimp suggests, Magic's innocence and adoration depends on this disavowal:

> Accommodating Magic—for queers—means accommodating this contradiction: safe sex will be accepted, taught to teenagers, adopted by heterosexuals at risk, save lives—because of Magic, because it is necessary to protect the sanctity and prerogatives of his heterosexual union. Accommodating Magic—for queers— means accommodating the continued homophobic construction of AIDS discourse. . . . The spectacle of someone who's HIV-positive being revered and physically embraced is deeply gratifying. But *our* gratification is diminished, because we know the boast to Arsenio makes it possible.[79]

Finally, a third negative trope further subverts the restoration of Magic's image: the anguish of white capital and heteromasculine psychic investment, subtly redirecting its hatred toward the gay phallus—the alleged "patient zero" and the underclass of color—the story of origin that explains the fate of America's Magic through the channels connecting female vaginas with gay anality[80] and third-world bodies of color.[81] The other side of the world is hidden in the anxious shadows of a heterosexist and imperialist race-driven discourse that seeks to restore its token first-world Hero. However, Magic's buoyancy has put a strain of compassion and panic in a semantic field ordering itself and us around the mythic dimensions of "male natures" and "phallic invulnerability." Capital investment may become more risky as endorsers shun Magic's indelible association with AIDS. Similarly, heteromasculine psychic and cultural investment may become more tenuous if signs of virus mark the surface or the solidity of the hero's physical body. The spectator may become more queasy with the thought of this stealth virus sleeking through Magic's body, a viscerally felt disruption in the flow of the spectator's kinesthetic and aesthetic pleasures in watching Magic move. The thrill of his body in motion may be lost in the somatically felt fluidophobia slipping between men—in sweat, cuts, and scratches "infecting" players. As Magic's body is cashed out through the racist operations of the pan(eroto)con, he may become a dangerous hero—too costly, too black, too honest, and too demanding on spectator compassion.

The strategies of the pan(eroto)con keep Magic stabilized and his mythic value tentatively restored. Yet as a production of the pan(eroto)con, Magic's body is located at the intersection of homophobia and misogyny, promiscuity and anality, race and capital, disease and drugs. After his announcement Magic emerges repentant, rich, and respectable, but his symbolic and mythic value remains fragile and tethered by the queerity of AIDS and the violence of sexual racism. To his credit, Magic has taken some remarkably progressive actions: he has called for and made possible controversial safe sex education, he has especially reached out to African-American youth with his sex-education programs,[82] he has challenged the homophobia in Arsenio Hall's audience,[83] he has made a public plea of compassion for *all* people living with the virus,[84] he has started an AIDS foundation, he has "joined the trenches" with his new HIV-positive/AIDS teammates, he has called into question the invulnerabilities of heterosexual promiscuity and carelessness, he has stood up to school board censorship of his sex education materials, and he has affronted a president of the United States[85] for his laxity in AIDS-prevention measures. He does this with intelligent cunning, pushing the edges of sex and gender conservativism while attempting to hold his place in the eroto-heroics of exonerated black heteromasculinity.

Magic's body produced by the pan(eroto)con as a phallic transcendental pinion of heteromasculine physicality explains why Magic has not careened into rapid free fall. However, the pan(eroto)con is a white power machine, situating the technologies of race, gender, sexuality, ableism, and class in the new world order of electronic and surface reproductions. At the moment Magic's body seeks a balancing point between the positive excess of heroism and the negative excess of panic and phobia flowing through the psychic ledger of the pan(eroto)con. Time will unveil this story, but the story needs a body much more powerful than Magic's. It is a story that will require a magic/Magic strong enough to reveal the psychic infrastructure of heteromasculinity and the homo/erotic and race panic in the pan(eroto)con, where white capital rides the backside of black athleticism in its need for specular aesthetic. This is more than Magic's personal problem, and though he may have handled *his* personal problem "like a gentleman," the real problems of racism, homophobia, ableism,

AIDS-phobia, misogyny, and the metaphysics of male physicality reified in the black sports celebrity—the very "matters" making the magic of Magic—are not entirely Magic's. Sex and race in the pan(eroto)con relocate the problem in the black male body, but like the virus, the total cure for this requires a more radically caring politic that is collective, social, economic, personal, and global.

While the power of the pan(eroto)con works on all of us in our more ordinary lives, we are its consumer/spectators not its raw material. We enter its stream of production through the screens and surfaces that have created America's Magic as a phantasm of cultural heroism. We hold him together by looking and overlooking, the twin gazes, directed toward Magic's briefly restored performances on the court where the virus has joined our consciousness. The pan(eroto)con has produced the majesty Magic's hyper-ableism, a state of exalted being seemingly immune to the devastating physical assaults of racism, homophobia, and AIDS-phobia. Ordinarily, a black male body with HIV infection transmitted by sexual contact would have already disappeared into the amorphous mass of danger and incivility that marks a body as black in the white racist psyche. This disaster does not affect Magic, because power resurrects bodies selectively just as it ignores bodies selectively. However, this is a power that resurrects for men, for whites, for the able-bodied, for heterosexuals, and for capital.[86] Magic stands at risk.

For me it came as no surprise that over a year after Magic officially announced his HIV status to the world, I encountered a seven-foot, stand-up poster of Magic highlighting an enlarged tape measure to mark and emphasize his physical stature. This poster was located outside the entrance to a lingerie store in a Minneapolis mall. Magic's image was being used to sell a T-shirt for Safe-Sex Clothing, Inc., which reads on the front, "Protect Your Johnson. No Matter How Magic You Think It Is"; the second line is a simple list: "Abstinence. Monogamy. Condoms. AIDS Hotline." This T-shirt, admirable in many ways, also signified a condensation and reversal of phallic troubles in Magic's didactic commodification. Its metonymy with Michael Jordan's signature sneaker seems uncanny: Johnson's name was indirectly selling condoms for safe sex. As Michael Dyson has commented on the Jordan sneaker, "at the juncture of the sneaker, a host of cultural, political, and economic forces and meanings meet, collide, shatter, and are reassembled to symbolize the situation of contemporary black culture."[87] I found in Johnson's newly signatured commodity a similar but more ominous set of collisions. The T-shirt, advertising Magic was available in large and extra large; black only. The whites were already sold out. I stood there next to Magic's image, wondering if we really could become allies in all of this clean and shiny whiteness. His steady smile, high above the crowded North American mall, was haunting.

Looking at them can provoke a number of emotional and behavioral responses:

Fear . . .

Disgust. Disregard. Abhorrence.

Scorn. Anger. Rage.

Anxiety. Nausea.

Panic. Derision. Flight.

Pain. Loss. Grief.

Shame. Silence.

Hate . . .

Given the complexity of these emotional responses, it seems rather simplistic to define "homophobia" as "an irrational fear and intolerance of lesbians and gays."[1] The psychological content of "homophobia" seems more diverse and complex than the reduction to a singular emotional substratum such as irrational fear. Others share my concerns with this reduction. Celia Kitzinger has pointed out that "homophobia," defined as "an irrational fear," is misleading since the "irrationality" exhibited by homophobes is a *rationally* consistent and prudent component of their worldview.[2] I also find that an exclusive focus on "fear" condenses a large repertoire of emotional and behavioral responses to a common denominator easily rejected by homophobes, who never tire of saying, "I'm not homophobic; I'm not afraid of them, but I disagree with their lifestyle." A focus primarily on the fear component in "homophobia" tends to homogenize class, race, gender, regional, generational, as well as idiosyncratic antigay sentiments.

Theorists as diverse as Gregory Herek and Suzanne Pharr have also argued that the term "homophobia" misnames the problem as a function of a personal frailty, like an irrational fear of snakes, better cured in therapy than by social transformation. Accordingly, they suggest that the term "heterosexism" more accurately depicts social and institutional practices that exclude and devalue lesbians and gays.[3] This is further reflected in Audre Lorde's approach to systems of oppression, where "heterosexism" is a defined as a belief in the superiority of one sexuality over other sexualities and thereby the right of those considered "the superior" to dominate over and discriminate against "the lesser."[4] This shifts our concerns to the warrants for heterosexuality's alleged superiority and to the way its power is constructed through institutional privileges, exclusionary practices, and entitlements to disfavor and even violate "the lesser" sexualities. A similar perspective shift is accomplished by Joe Neisen, who argues that "internalized homophobia" in gays and lesbians is better described as "shame due to heterosexism," shifting the locus of problem to the effects of heterosexual institutions and practices on gays and lesbians.[5]

These two considerations—that homophobia is not accurately defined as an irrational fear and that it is more useful to analyze homophobia as a function of heterosexism—seem basically right to me. Starting with heterosexism allows one to analyze its similarities and differences with other intersecting social oppressions such as sexism, racism, classism, ageism, ableism, etc. A theoretically rich understanding of heterosexism would always include an attempt to understand how it is formed through and within other social oppressions, as well as its diverse institutional, social, economic, cultural, political, and personal expressions.[6] To focus on homophobia as an internal feeling does not immediately give us the larger structural analysis offered by an approach that starts with heterosexism as an institutional and social set of practices. By claiming that the subjective state of homophobia is an effect of these practices, this starting point exposes the homophobe as the problem.[7]

While this strategic approach is valuable, it still seems to leave blank the emotive space where homophobia dwells. I recall a relative who once shared his personal view with me that the thought of two men kissing was beyond vomit. This statement stuck with me, mainly because of its forthright honesty and visceral discontent, and because of what it implies: a body at risk, unable to find a mechanism strong enough to eject the intrusions of this particular "otherness." The subject reacts with an unbearable bodily feeling ("beyond vomit") that seeks a border between "self" and "not-self," between inner and outer. Because the simple reflex of vomiting is not enough to eject this vileness, it seems closely allied with what Julia Kristeva has referred to as "abjection," where the fear associated with abjection is related to a border crisis of ambiguity. According to Kristeva, abjection never quite releases the subject, "because, while releasing a hold, it does not radically cut off the subject from what threatens it—on the contrary, abjection acknowledges it to be in perpetual danger."[8]

These thoughts have led me to reconsider the meaning of "homophobia" as a threatened and troubled subjectivity necessary for understanding heterosexism. Just as the cultural practices of sexism are fueled by the psychodynamics of misogyny, so I think the term "homophobia" names the psychological dimensions of heterosexism. In this chapter I will attempt a new analysis of homophobia that begins with the body and ends with social structure and that links homophobia to class, race, gender, sexuality, and other social oppressions. Although it is beyond the scope of this chapter to do full justice to the kind of analysis explored here, I will attempt to sketch out why the racialized state might have an interest in queer kisses. I will replace the term "homophobia" with "straight repulsion," both to suggest the performative drama involved in such feelings and to indicate a continuum of more vaguely defined emotional responses that terminate in the desire to push away and annihilate queerness, both in the self and in others. I surmise that straight repulsion is not an irrational fear but a viscerally cogent response inhering within hegemonically constructed heterocentric genders that foster social relations of oppression.[9]

Straight repulsion is an emotive response directed toward certain kinds of "border bodies,"[10] bodies defined by their transgression of normative sex and gender boundaries. Border bodies are "queer" when they do not clearly align with the linear prescriptions of sex, gender, and sexual orientation: they do not fit the linear entailments of *if-biologically-male, then-masculine-and-heterosexual* or *if-biologically-female, then-feminine-and-heterosexual*.[11] Queer border bodies are perceived as deviant: a man who is *too* feminine, a woman who is *too* masculine, a man who desires men, a woman who desires women or a bisexual who desires both men and women, a man who becomes a woman, and vice versa.

These bodies are out-of-bounds, defying conservative cultural norms and habitual expectations about how bodies are supposed to be sexed and gendered. Straight repulsion is a conserving heterosexual anti-biotic.[12]

I surmise that what the homophobe finds vile about border bodies is not "them" but "himself"[13]—his own border anxiety and dread of crossing over into another kind of sexual or gendered body. A panic may emerge from wayward desires—a deluge threatening to refigure how bodies are supposed to be gendered, sexed, socially ordered, and reproduced. Straight repulsion is protection against this "queerness," which includes lesbian, gay, bisexual, transgender, intersexed, and other gender-mixed border bodies. This repulsion can solidify into hate expressing a potential will to perpetrate violence against *the other*, preconditioned by a dehumanization of border bodies along a continuum of increasing levels of acceptable violations of queer life.[14] For the homophobe, this repulsion toward *the other* can also merge into a fear of self-sameness with *the other* or the terror of becoming "the opposite sex." Straight repulsion engenders a need to create an image of horrific difference and monstrous queerness, to attack what is queer (*not self*), where this *other* appears in a discursive space becoming more visibly filled with a multiplication of pleasures in sex and gender.[15]

As a way to begin I will theorize "institutions from the body up" while recognizing that bodies are "already oriented to institutional contexts."[16] This approach is unlike arguments based on sociobiology that attempt to explain social institutions and relations from the biological body. I will analyze social institutions and social relations of power from the body up, while recognizing that the body, as a basic building block, is always already in the process of its social formation. How bodies become inscribed and conscripted into embodied subjectivities is the cultural achievement of heterosexuality. I understand this in two ways. First, heterosexuality is an ensemble of cultural and institutional practices that requires desiring bodies to shape its mechanisms, meanings, and terrains. Second, central to this social and psychological production is a cultural panic located in heteromasculinity and "recursively saturating" institutional and interpersonal transactions of power in sex, race, class, gender, and other social relations. Straight repulsion is a viscerally cogent heterocentric response to the threat of corporeal recompositions in sex and gender.

Closer to home, straight repulsion is a palpable border crisis: a fear and loathing of the body's possible arousal to forbidden touch or erotic glance. It is a response to pleasure and loss of control and to the personal and social consequences haunting these quivers of the private body. The primary labor of straight repulsion is to insure that *my* body does not do or want *that*. Its secondary labor is to suppress and destroy border bodies—defined by the mark of deviant desire and gender transgressions. Theorizing from the body up, I will explore how heterosexism and male domination over women seem to hold the hetero-body of both sexes in place so as to produce *the cultural phallus*, a racialized heteromasculine fetish of part-to-(w)hole.[17] Theorizing from the body up, I also find the body an insurrectionary location of contradictory desires and recalcitrant indocility. Thankfully, the body can make a mess of theory.

In what follows I surmise that hegemonic white heteromasculine embodiment is a primary site in the cultural production of straight repulsion.[18] This may fly in the face of presumptions that homophobia is more virulent and violent in communities of color or in working-class or rural areas. I do not presume to know this. The measure for that sort of a claim seems puzzling to me. I believe, however, that there is a deep connection between the social formation of white hegemonic heterocentric masculinities and the origins of contemporary straight repulsion, regardless of how "others" may carry out the work of straight hegemony. I will explore how this masculinity relates to the "otherness" of queers, heterowomen, transgendered bodies, and racially marked (nonwhite) others. This is mirrored in the introjected fears of pollution/contagion/invasion—potential harms threatening the dissolution of the white male heterocentric body—and the macropolitics of sexual oppression and border policing aimed at ejecting these harms from nations, neighborhoods, families, and the children. A consequence of this is a new version of "the homosexual enemy," expressing a crisis in a heteromasculinity now confronted with the civil rights rhetorics of lesbian, gay, bisexual, and transgender people.

In my reflections on straight repulsion, I have come to see heteromasculine embodiment as a more fragile and more tenuous cultural formation.[19] The labor required for its mythic power seems repeatedly jeopardized by body sprees of "spilling over," of *"devenir femme,"* "turning queer"—of crossing over—an "undoing" of heteromasculine embodiment that is an object of both great visceral fear and disgust as well as fascination and errant desire. The analysis I pursue in this chapter attempts to locate a significant origin of straight repulsion in the intrasubjective and institutional "recursive structuration" of an historically modern and racialized heteromasculinity. This is a relational identity and social formation in which male domination, racism, heterosexism, and other social relations of power are continuously reproduced through emotive-bodies-in-motion and in-relation. At the vortex of this cultural production is white heteromasculinity, and it is the very instability and fragility of this center that makes its straight repulsion both excessive and perversely common. My hope is to elucidate its stealth and make visible its systemic deployment.

Heteromasculinity and Straight Repulsion

> *The sexual pervert's body haunts society and reminds it*
> *of its fragility.*   —THOMAS LAQUEUR,
> "The Solitary Evil, the Solitary Vice, and Pouring Tea"

Gregory Herek has developed a definition of "heterosexual masculinity" that seems to fit the privileged hegemonic white gender norms of contemporary America.[20] He elaborates on three components of "heterosexual masculinity":

1. The embodiment of personal characteristics such as success and status, toughness and independence, aggressiveness and dominance
2. The manifestation of these characteristics by adult males through exclusively social relationships with men and primarily sexual relationships with women
3. A definition of self defined by what it is *not*: not feminine, not homosexual, not being compliant, dependent, or submissive, not being effeminate (a "sissy") in physical appearance or mannerisms, not having relationships with men that are sexual or overly intimate, and not failing in sexual relationships with women.

While there may be variations on the constructions of heteromasculinities across races, ethnicities, and classes, Herek's analysis captures the norms of modern white hegemonic masculinity that often serve as an ideal against which other nonwhite masculinities in racist contexts are read as compensatory hyper-reflections using other available resources and expressions.[21] According to Herek contemporary Euro-American heteromasculinity seems to rely on a sexual entitlement to female bodies and a claim of superiority over queer bodies. Herek's notion of heteromasculinity is conceived as relational—enacted in relations of success, status, aggression, and dominance over others; in social relations with men and sexual relations with women; and in relations of negation of those behaviors and characteristics considered not masculine—the feminine and the queer. Thus modern hegemonic heteromasculinity rests on an eroticism of power asymmetry, compulsory heterosexuality, and coital sovereignty.

Jonathan Dollimore[22] suggests two ways of conceiving the dynamics of heterosexual homophobia in the construction of heteromasculinity: the psychoanalytic model of repression (the "othering" from within), which represses the content of homosexual desire, and the materialist cultural model (the "othering" from without), which comprises all the personal and social practices to keep gay and lesbian people out of the family, the school, the military, the nation, and other institutions:

> On the Freudian model it is the repression and sublimation of homosexual desire that helps secure identity and social organization. Conversely, on the materialist model it is much more homophobia itself, as an aspect of the construction of heterosexuality and independently of the question of the actual subjective repression of desire, which helps secure a coerced identity and social organization; homophobia enforces the heterosexual norm by policing its boundaries.[23]

According to Dollimore this formation requires its abhorrent "otherness," albeit in a repressed or socially excluded form, against which it must be continuously reconstituted and protected from the flooding and "queering" of the body. I find this analysis helpful in understanding how *the labor of "othering" that holds all of this at bay is at the heart of straight repulsion.* This is not an easy labor, since heterosubjectivity dwells close to the knowledge, however suppressed this may be, of its possible annihilation, a point that Dollimore makes in his comparison of psychic and material homophobias:

> Both theories suggest an eventual return of homosexuality: in the one (psychoanalytic) it is a psychic return of the repressed from within, in the other (materialist) a social or cultural return from without; either in inner resurgence of desire through the breakdown of psychic repression, or the oppositional approach via the proximate of the demonized other from beyond, from the social margins where he or she has been discovered, constructed, displaced.[24]

Both Herek and Dollimore suggest an understanding of homophobia as an aspect of heteromasculinity, involving an "othering from within" (the disowning and repression of a potential self) and an "othering from without" (the political suppression or psychological projection of this homoerotic self onto border bodies). The relationship between sexism and homophobia appears in what is feared: the loss of manhood—emasculinization, effeminization, castration, and a passive and tender surrender to the erotics of men.

A point missed by Herek and Dollimore is that heteromasculinities also belong to a larger matrix of race struggle, where the aim of sexual reproduction is sometimes politicized as a duty-bound regeneration of "raced" bodies, hence necessitating a sexual allegiance to a people, a race, or a nation. As long as this reproductive project is seen as the sacred domain of heterosexuals and not an option for homosexual or bisexual couples or other alternative families, queerness in such contexts can be used to signify antinatalism or antireproductivism. Straight repulsion becomes complicit in race survival, especially when race purity or survival is threatened by genocide or the siege of miscegenation. Queerness and interracial sex may be rhetorically read as signs of race betrayal.

For the white heteromasculinized subject, the mixing of genes and different lineages—the birth of *mestizaje, mesla,* mulatto, and mixed bloods—may be deeply experienced as a threat to his own race purity, though not his pleasure. More likely, he will be threatened when "his" white women carry out these deeds. This fear is not absent, however, from the nonwhite race-centered nationalist rhetoric designed to keep women of color in their place—racially committed to the reproduction of a people and straight to the bone.[25] Thus compulsory heterosexuality and its straight repulsion converge in heterosexually controlled, pronatalist, race-centered mandates, especially those controlling women's sexuality. This results in a racialized heterocentric will to wield power over and even to violate the bodies and life circumstances of those marked by the danger of difference in sex, skin, and blood.

While straight repulsion is deeply interpolated in race regenerative politics, it is also shaped by how differently males and females are stationed in heterosexual practices. Straight repulsion depicts a fear of crossing over the boundaries that render one queer, an experience that may have differently valenced meanings for females and males. Pursuing this will elicit some additional insights into the relationship between racialized straight repulsion and what I believe to be its modern origin in recursive heteromasculine embodiment. In this next section I draw on empirical studies of homophobia. Because these studies undertheorize categories of race and generally consider race as neutral, I will name the object of these studies as white Euro-American homophobia.[26] With this assumption, I will pursue my hunch that a primary locus of modern straight repulsion originates in this more privileged heteromasculinity.

Gendering and Racing Straight Repulsion

What available empirical studies suggest is that white heterosexual men are more homophobic than white heterosexual women.[27] While both male and female heterosexuals seem to have similar views on moral and civil issues in national opinion poles, the difference between the two sexes is revealed in small-scale experimental studies where heteromales are more homophobic in their emotional reactions. These homophobic attitudes have been correlated with authoritarian personality structure, racist attitudes, intolerance based on religious beliefs, cognitive rigidity, conservative sex attitudes, and stronger sex-stereotype beliefs. Where homophobic attitudes are strong, these correlations are high, presenting a composite of male straight repulsion as rigid in categorical thinking, dependent on authority, invested in sexual conservativism and traditional gender roles, as well as attitudinally racist, xenophobic, and nationalistic.[28] Herek's study of these heterosexual men finds them notably high in defensive homophobic attitudes, which he defines as an attitude projecting an unacceptable part of the self onto gay and lesbian people. By rejecting (or even attacking) gay and lesbian people, these heteromen are able to attack an unacceptable aspect of the self and distance themselves from the object of their aggression, thereby solidifying heteromasculine group boundaries and identities.[29]

Why these heteromales are prone to homophobic behavior and emotions has been a matter of some speculation. Herek has argued that a strong linkage in American culture between masculinity and heterosexuality creates considerable pressure on males to affirm their masculinity by distancing themselves from what is culturally defined as not masculine (male homosexuality and male effeminacy) and from what is perceived as undermining the importance of males (lesbianism).[30] According to Herek, heterosexual women may be less prone to perceive the rejection of homosexuals as integral to their identity; in addition, because they may have more personal contact with male homosexuals, this may decrease their homophobia toward gay men in particular.[31] Heterosexual women are also given more permission to engage in emotional and some physical expressions of same-sex affection[32] and have been socialized to associate penile penetration with pleasure and love.[33] The threat of too much physical intimacy or sexual penetration by another man would seem to threaten male heterosexual identity.

Herek and Pleck have argued that greater conformity to the male role results in increased homophobic "defensiveness" among heterosexual men.[34] Dollimore has pointed out that this conformity, often expressed through homophobia, increases the secondary gains in heteromasculine male bonding, but on the negative side the rigidity of heteromasculine role conformity increases anger and frustration.[35] Lehne suggests that the policing of "fag-baiting" is often deployed by heterosexual men against other heterosexual men, chasing after behaviors which might appear to be "gay."[36] In this "gay-baiting" real male homosexuals may be incidental or occasionally bashed to set an example of what can happen to you if you cross over the line.

As many theorists have noted, homosexuality is stereotypically associated with transgendering: lesbians are no longer perceived as *real* women but are stereotypically perceived as mannish or butch; gay men are longer perceived as *real* men but are stereotypically perceived as emasculated or effeminate. Regardless of the inaccuracy of these totalizing stereotypes, the values and relative weights placed on the alleged gender transgressions have a bearing on the gender valences of these border crossings. From the dominant culture's point of view, normative masculine qualities and character traits are considered more valuable and more "adult" than feminine qualities and values. Hegemonic white masculine characteristics train one for primary instrumental and dominant social roles, handsomely rewarded in our culture, while normative white feminine qualities lend themselves to secondary expressive and cooperative social roles, not highly rewarded in the stratification of bodies in the public and corporate domain. Accordingly, when this is further reinforced by generalized cultural misogyny, there is more to give up when a male body crosses the border into feminine territories. He will be called "queer" *and* "sissy"—signifying a double loss of power.

In contrast, when a white middle-class female traverses gender terrains, she is perceived as "strong," "assertive," "independent," and "*uppity*" —at least if she does not go too far. She is leaving behind what has less value—femininity, passivity, weakness, and dependence—a residue of incapacities accompanying whatever other privileges she might have. In contemporary advertising, female border-crossing becomes a titillation for the privileged female consumer, moderately fostered in the image of the "the fashionable and playful female androgyne." As long as these "softly butched" women stay within the domain of heteroeroticism, the semimasculinized attire, demeanor, and body language are seen as sexy garb. A male in a skirt, however, unless he is a bagpiper, pope, prince, or priest, risks direct violent assault against his ambiguously signifying "border body." The lines are more thickly drawn around the male body, although violence against transgendered butch women (the border "he/shes" and the visible butches) gives testimony to a straight repulsion that targets these more seriously intended female crossings.[37] Violence against women is in the mix of emotion and violence expressed and delivered against the bodies of transgendered and transsexual people.

Following the logic of sex/gender alignment in the dominant culture, one would have to have more compelling reasons (or an overwhelming cause) to shed one's white *masculinity* than to cast away the disempowering aspects of white *femininity*. The meaning of border-crossings for the two sexes is different: more homophobic force circulates around the male body to keep him in place, since his queer desires threaten noncompliance and disloyalty to other straight men. He apparently gives up the double privileges of his heterosexuality and his masculinity. I speculate that this power deployment is what I have encountered in gay men's preference for explanations of sexual orientation that rely on biological determinism—the overwhelming and inevitable cause that makes a man do this—while lesbians and especially lesbian feminist analyses have generally suggested a wider latitude of choice in the creativity/discovery of sexual orientation.[38] In a quite controversial and provocative essay, Eriadni has argued that the whole construction of sexual preference may largely be a male item.[39]

A closer analysis of the systemic oppression of women within the institution of heterosexuality reveals that women, when compared to the men of their class, are likely to be "held in place" by a number of nonsexual forces, such as economic deprivation and discrimination; a greater threat and incident of sexual violence; more unequal access to education, wealth, land, food, literacy, health care, reproductive rights, and other resources; and less access to the police and military powers, world and national governments, global capitalism, and the world's judiciary, medical, educational, artistic, religious, and scientific power elite.[40] This has the effect of forcing many—but not all—women to be more materially dependent on men of their class or community or dependent on the male-commanded state for their survival. Women who are not directly dependent on men or the state do, however, suffer related material consequences, such as depressed wages, fewer high-level job opportunities, higher risk of sexual harassment, absent child care options, and so on.

Heteromales are also "held in place" by nonsexual forces, but for heteromales who have privileged access to the resources mentioned above, as well as race privilege, the policing of homophobia and adherence to class and race specific norms of masculine gender conformity become significant factors in "keeping heteromen in place." For heteromales who have less status and less access to wealth or class-privileging capitals,[41] the interpersonal aspects of heterosexuality, such as *being explicitly heterosexual* (e.g., clearly not queer) and *being a real man* about it (e.g., various styles of macho/machismo) may dominate the formations of heteromasculinity.[42] Despite these class, race, and ethnic differences, the heteromasculine male in our contemporary United States cultures seems a curiously armored being, who will likely find great treachery in the tenderness, touch, and taste of other male bodies.

For heteromasculine men displays of passivity toward other men may be coded as border-crossings. When this display is explicitly sexual, one risks the demise of manhood: one can be raped like a woman. Anal postures of sexual openness "vaginate" the male body, coding "womanliness" onto the body's cheeky surface. As Pleck has commented,[43] male passivity toward other men is emasculating because it indicates a refusal to compete. Homosexual sex, coded as one man sexually and emotionally surrendering to another man, can also be seen as a refusal to be a man in traditional competitive terms.[44] Of course, as others have pointed out, homosocial expression thrives in a heteromasculine world where male bonding is clear and in the open, crossing carefully through the shadows of border bodies. In that world, "the closet" variously choreographs public and private space, a sexual architecture reminding heteromasculinity of its perpetual danger. Indeed, "closets" are a part of every heterosexual domain, where homoeroticism must remain out of sight, or, what is the same, disembodied between men.[45]

In the gendered reality of heterosexual hegemony, there are two different border crossings: when a man submits to the phallus, he refuses (fails) to be a man, and when a woman will not submit to the phallus, she refuses (fails) to be a woman. In general, men are punished for what gets done to them and women are punished for what they do or what doesn't get done to them.[46] Heteromen and heterowomen are constructed in and through the phallic signifier and by the violence of border policing that keeps heterobodies in place. As Luce Irigaray has suggested, "once the penis itself becomes merely a means of pleasure, pleasure among men, the phallus loses its power."[47] The phallus is an imploded cultural signifier creating the meanings of biological sex difference central to the construction of heteromasculinity, which further necessitates the absorption and symbolic castration of women. Misdirected into the bodies of men, the phallus no longer exists in the heteromasculine world, and by this means, it no longer *is* a signifier of real manhood.[48] In allowing oneself to be penetrated by another man, the phallus is at least temporarily "off frame" and the body recoded as "feminine." The synonymy of "faggots" with women is secured by this somatic/semantic logic of heterodomination: both are castrated and in need of a good fuck. Both can be raped without necessarily naming the rapist a faggot.

To prevent the possibility of this border-crossing into queerness, male straight repulsion requires "the closet" (the abjected queer body) as it requires "woman" (the objectified and open body).[49] The phallus grounds a semiotics of sexual suppression and women's oppression. In this scheme, the only body to possess the real phallus is the heteromasculine body, and for the sake of this heteromasculine identity, heterowomen and queers must be kept in their place: women in the home and in the brothel, readily available; faggots in the closet and in the latrines, bars, and parks, (invisible and omnipresent); and both, when they fight back, incarcerated or beyond the guarantee of civil dignities. Straight repulsion is a viscerally cogent response, *making sense* in the heteromasculinized body: protecting its orifices, armoring its skin, disciplining its behavior, and policing its aggrandized body boundaries of family, religion, culture, and nation state against the threat of queer desire and passive surrender to the erotics of men. Receptivity and the fluidly open male body are the problems; a semantically and physically closed body and a hyperaggressive, armored, and possessive heteromasculinity are the solutions.[50]

From this perspective a female straight repulsion can be read as derivative.[51] Heterowomen are paradigmatically situated in relation to men. They are *to be there* for men: sexually available, institutionally loyal, and emotionally present. "Lesbian" signifies an absence—one who does not usually or willfully place her body in the spermatic economy of male desire as she is drawn in her lustful ways to the bodies of other women. Her access into the spermatic economy for the purposes of reproduction, when that occurs, is usually self-chosen, deliberate, often overtly contractual (and hand-delivered), and seldom, except in the case of rape, unwanted. Like the gay male, her existence threatens the borders of heteromasculinity, but in a different way. She is not perceived as a potential rapist of men, but she "emasculates" by *not being there* as a sexually available woman, as instead she offers a possibility of exit for other women.[52] She represents a desiring sexual subject of lesser sexual value to men. Her sexuality is her own domain and her reproductive interests potentially threaten culturally sanctioned male entitlements to fatherhood and female wombs. Straight repulsion in women may be a fear of "doing these things to men" (or of the consequences "of not being there" for them), the fear of losing an identity confirmed by a male-commanded racialized spermatic economy. Her lesbian desires are frequently interpreted as female disobedience to men (be that directly to one man or to the manly manifestations of family, race, nation, and meaning), and acting on them makes her a potential target of cultural hatred and violence. Condensed to the body, female straight repulsion is a fear of the meanness of these social consequences and a fear of the pleasures and arousals that compel a woman to love another woman. This does not mean that female straight repulsion is less intense or less violent than that of heteromales, but the sources of her expression are both in her visceral response and derived from the discursive involution of the hetero-phallus.

As I am suggesting, straight repulsion has a significant origination in a rigidly closed heteromasculine male body, threatened by the possibility of spilling over or becoming engulfed in his own abjected "otherness." This would mean losing control of what stabilizes a man's heterosexual identity, namely, his penis, "his" women, "his" off/spring (and/or fetuses), "his" sons and daughters, "his" race and "his" brotherhood, "his" cosmos, and "his" god. For the male sex, straight repulsion haunts the danger zones of male tenderness, the pleasurable softness and hardness of male bodies and spirits, and the fear of rape that can terrorize this intimacy.[53] For the female sex, straight repulsion haunts a woman's *willful* abandoning of heterosex and her sexual lust for other women.[54] Lesbians, gays, and bisexuals are shamed and punished by the dominant culture for these sexual desires and acts. Though different in kind, dykes are scorned for not behaving like women; faggots are hated for behaving like women; and bisexuals are ridiculed for not standing firm, a seeming feminine ambivalence that haunts the monosexual binary. Trangendered and transsexual bodies literalize the uncanny. All abandon the mandates of heteromasculinity in different ways. Thus the social menaces of gay, lesbian, bisexual, and transgendered bodies have different cultural and social meanings ascribed to them and represent different kinds of challenges to the heterosexualized body/politic. For both sexes, however, straight repulsion seems intimately related to male violence against women, heterosexually controlled race politics, and culturally encouraged violence against border bodies.

Purity and Danger in the Emergence of Modern Homophobia

In her book *Natural Symbols: Explorations of Cosmology*, Mary Douglas argues that human social relations are structured by two models: *grid* and *group*.[55] A "group" refers to an association of people, who experience a strong allegiance to the social whole to which they belong. "Grid" refers to rules and an interlacing formal structure that relate one person to another as an aggregate of people held together by compliance to the rules. In grid-based social relations, the individual is less constrained by group loyalties and follows a set of rules that enable individuals to enter reciprocal transactions and engage in interpersonal exchange. The rules, rather than a sense of group belonging, hold this aggregate of individuals in relation to one another.

In most cultures grid- and group-based associations are both present. When the body is primarily constructed as isolate and monadic in grid-based social relations, group loyalties are experienced as making counterdemands on this body-ego. When the body is primarily bound by an allegiance to a larger social whole, the relationship between members of the group is usually less well articulated and "individuation" is experienced as making counterdemands on the socially bounded self. In *group associations*, the body is part of something larger than itself; in *grid-based associations*, the body is singular among other isolated units of self-interest.

Douglas's distinction between group and grid social relations is useful in understanding the social construction of *the individual* in modern Euro-Amercan cultures and the crisis in heteromasculinity that now generates an historically modern form of straight repulsion. The formation of the European state, the ascendance of rights discourse, the impact of industrialization and its new divisions of labor, the increasing privatization of self, and new technologies and sciences aimed at disciplining the body and normalizing behavior have led to the historical emergence of the individual. This formation of the individual emerges within the *grid*-based liberalization of the nation state, which sought to replace *groups* bonded to sovereignty and local community. While democratization of Eurocentric cultures accompanied a rhetoric of new respect for individual uniqueness—for inwardness, the integrity of personhood, and the dignity of human rights—the body was transformed into an ownership of oneself, protected by law and the boundaries of "privacy."[56]

As others have argued, this eighteenth-century construction of the Eurocentric individual had as its primary site *the male body*. In discussing the Eurocentric story of social contract, Carole Pateman comments:

> The standard commentaries on the classic stories of the original contract do not usually mention that women are excluded from the original pact. Men make the original contract. . . . Only masculine beings are endowed with the attributes and capacities necessary to enter into contracts, the most important of which is ownership of property in the person; only men, that is to say, are "individuals." . . . Sexual difference is political difference; sexual difference is the difference between freedom and subjection. Women are not party to the original contract through which men transform their "natural" freedom into security of civil freedom. Women are the subject of the contract. The (sexual) contract is the vehicle through which men transform their "natural" right over women into the security of civil patriarchal right.[57]

Using Douglas's distinction between group and grid, one can interpret the transition from premodern social relations to civil society as a transition from a heteromasculinity based on the group lineage of patriarchs (Father-Right) and the kinship paradigm—a group-based alliance of male loyalties extending from the Patriarch to the Sovereign to the Deity—to a new form of *fraternal male domination* based on a social contract (in grid-based civil society) and a sexual contract (in a residual group-based domestic sphere). The sexual contract, according to Pateman, marginalized women from full participation in the public domain as individuals. The subjugation of women to men served as a precondition for constructing a new hegemonic heteromasculine individual and provided a mechanism for holding privileged women out of the public domain while also assuring male access to female bodies.[58]

While grid-based social relations in modern civil society were represented as politically neutral and open to all, they were in fact strategems of power hiding an implicit sexual contract that subordinated women to men, protected race and class interests of the new male elite and created a hidden and sometimes heartless domestic haven where male violence against women and children was left mostly unattended by state interests. By domiciling the "properly civilized woman" to the private world of the home and rendering women of other classes and races less visible and valuable, grid-based liberalism maintained the supremacy of a racialized sex-class of men. Thus the white heteromasculinity of modernity was stabilized through a mythic fraternal pact within civil society that implicitly assured privileged male access to the labor, hearts, and wombs of female bodies and to the labor powers of the less advantaged.

By the late nineteenth century, anxiety about male-to-male intimacy was pervasive in the construction of this new heteromasculinity.[59] Concentrations of men in the male workforce could not tolerate erotic "misinterest" in the bodies of coworkers; the emergence of male sports created an exclusive enclave for displays of masculine physical power and sex difference;[60] new medical interest in the schoolboy's body made a symptom of his masturbation;[61] and medical science busied itself "pathologizing" same-sex intimacy in the new medical categories of "invert" for women and "pervert" for men.[62] As the predominant norms of modern heteromasculinity shifted their group-based alliance with Father-Right to the emerging market economies, a new homophobic anxiety came to inhabit the male body.[63] In response to this, a new group-based ideology of manhood appeared in the promotion of "muscular Christianity,"[64] measured by productivity, family providership, heterosexual prowess, and loyalty to a closely scrutinized homosocial brotherhood. At this historical juncture, homosex in the brotherhood was best contained by the sexual colonization of women, the racialization of bodies, and the pathologizing of queers.

Modern white heteromasculinity is thus supported by at least four primary structures: a group loyalty to a male-sex class, the white male grid pact within civil society, a racialization of bodies into a race hierarchy, and the historical emergence of the sexual closet.[65] Using Douglas's framework, what has been called a recent homophobic backlash in contemporary North America is perhaps best understood as a phenomenon located in a conflict between grid- and group-based masculinity constructions, a conflict incited by a collective movement of minority groups to create a more inclusive civil society. This threatens to undo the categories of heteromasculine sex/gender ontology.[66] Hence the vehement and violent force behind contemporary straight repulsion draws its energy from a heteromale retreat into group formation, re-marking the borders of manhood as *not* female, *not* feminine, *not* homosexual, and *"not* any in my family."

Recursive Body Panic

> *We cannot possibly interpret rituals concerning excreta,*
> *breast milk, saliva, and the rest unless we are prepared to*
> *see in the body a symbol of society, and to see the powers*
> *and dangers credited to social structure reproduced in*
> *small on the human body.*
>
> —Mary Douglas, *Purity and Danger*

In her analysis of group- and grid-based social relations Mary Douglas notes that in group-based associations body symbolism is often used to define the boundaries of the group. This is reflected in the heteromale retreat into group formation in contemporary North America, where body imagery emerges repeatedly on a number of different levels of representation, solidifying heteromasculine group boundaries. According to Douglas, group-based associations foster a more ambiguous zone between individuals:

> A man recognizes a very strong allegiance to a social group, and at the same time does not know how he relates to other members or what his expectations should be. He tends to use the image of the human body to express both the exclusive nature of the allegiance and the confused social experience. The group is likened to the human body; the orifices are to be carefully guarded to prevent unlawful intrusions, dangers from poisoning and loss of physical strength express the lack of articulated roles within it.[67]

The emergence of body-panic symbolism in a predominantly grid-based civil society suggests that heteromasculinity has gone into a reactive formation in response to the political organizing of women, people of color, immigrants, and queers. In my reflections on this I have found three different kinds of body-panic imagery associated with this recent threat:

1. *The Private Body*. Panic is expressed as a fear of fluids entering the body through vulnerable membranes, open sores, or ruptures in the body wall. Perhaps first formulated as fear of sex and germs,[68] this fear has been amplified by the AIDS crisis and by the mundane fact that sex is often wet and messy. The most recent imagery that emerges at this site is a militarized immune system representing the "unpolluted" interests of the body, an inner barrier reinforcing the outer skins of latex barriers and the abjection of sexual fluidity.

2. *The Normative Body*. Panic is expressed as a fear of bodies' crossing over the boundaries of sex and gender categories; of women's refusal to be women and men's refusal to be men; of bodies that appear to be liminal, standing on the threshold or reappearing on the other side. Most recently the imagery that emerges here is that of a freak body, documented in gay pride marches and used by the religious right wing to evoke horror, disgust, and fear of bodies without limits.

3. *The Social Body*. Panic is expressed as a fear of queer bodies' crossing the boundaries of the family, schools, the military, religious institutions, and nations and getting too close to home. Recently the imagery that emerges here is a defense system for the boundaries of the social body, legislated through laws and policies designed to block the admittance of foreign bodies, to zap them at the border and send them back—out of sight and beyond mattering.[69]

Each of these domains depicts a border crisis on three different levels of unification—the private body, the normative body, and the social body—all vulnerable points of weakness in the construction of heteromasculinity. I would like to examine more closely how these three high-risk areas relate more directly to heteromasculine identity formation. As I have argued, male straight repulsion is a viscerally cogent response to the unruliness of border bodies and the chaotic dangers of sexual desire. In my definition of straight repulsion I have used the term "visceral" to suggest that this is more than an intellectual response and more than a mere attitude, that this may involve a physical, emotional, behavioral, and internal response in the whole body. I have used the term "cogent" to suggest that this response in the heteromasculinized body is not irrational but consistent with the boundary and categorical distinctions required for heteromasculine identity formation and male domination. I have referred the phenomenon of straight repulsion back to the body to emphasize how the semantic meanings of sex and gender embodied in male flesh require this visceral emotive response to prevent a "queering out" of the body. I have tried to bring heterosexism back to the body and to theorize institutional practices *from the body up*, to reveal heteromasculinity in its social formations of power and its multiple levels. Returning to these three cultural bodies—the private, the normative, and the social—I will examine more carefully the effects of these different border crises and their mutual and recursive saturation in and through the embodiment of contemporary white heteromasculinity and the new fragilities of the nation state.

The Private Body

Straight repulsion as a viscerally cogent heteromasculine response often relies on a symbolic representation of a straight body struggling for survival in a hostile environment. The boundaries of skin and orifice are threatened by foreign body fluids, such as sperm, ejaculate, saliva, blood, and female discharge encountered in sexual or fluid-mixing contacts. This is a literal and metaphorical fear of holes in the body wall, especially brought to cultural awareness with the AIDS crisis. The virus (HIV) carried by sex and body fluids is given a nonwhite story of origin, coming from male homosexuals, bisexuals, people of color, the underclass, prostitutes, IV-drug users, and Africans—a conglomerate of "subpopulations" thick and "dark" with viral flow.[70] These racialized and disqualified bodies are personified as a threat to the privileged white heteromasculine body of the "first world." Under siege and engulfed by body fluids from the other side, this privileged body threatens to fall apart, to dis/integrate under the crisis of a weakened immune system, a feminizing frailty that fragments the body as cells lose their defining boundaries and body portals are left open to opportunistic pathogens of death. Under the threat of disintegration, "real men" must remain put together, clearly defined, on alert, and in present danger.

The cultural representation of this imperiled male body is overtly militaristic, with the immune system represented as an internal defense system. [71] This is reflected in representations of the AIDS threat as covertly emasculating, inspiring on one level heteromen to fight off queers, and inciting the microlevel immune system to act as an internal battalion, armed with killer cells and a legion of white nurses.[72] The body is circumscribed by death and danger in its commingling with queerness.

The Normative Body

Male straight repulsion relies on the belief that for men *to be* men, they must be masculine and heterosexual, and for women *to be* women, they must be feminine and heterosexual. This is grounded on an ontology allegedly derived from nature or structured by natural law. Given this perspective, the dance of queerness on the fringes of the heterosexual world is threatening. This is where lesbians, gays, bisexuals, transsexuals, transvestites, gender benders, gender blenders, male lesbians, female faggots, pregnant lesbians, leather daddies, female impersonators, drag queens, gay and lesbian coparents, fag hags, gender-fuckers, fems and butches of all sexes, *and their friends and family* outrageously appear as bodies out-of-control. These "deviants" of the sex-gender system, unified by the word "queer,"[73] scramble the categories of a heterosexual sex/gender ontology and open the possibility of playing against the edge of meaning with the body. In the world of these border bodies, the body appears as a location where meaning is created and reversed, however tenuously; where body identities and parts are movable and removable; and where the pleasures of the body can erupt in socially unspoken spaces. This "dance of queerness" reverses the ontology of heteromasculine belief, turning "nature" into partial performance and potential subversion.[74]

To keep "nature" in order it is best to re/present these bodies as freaks, as contagious, and as sick. "Freakishness" replaces their play and pleasure, "contagion" replaces their liminality, and "sickness" replaces their invitation to new panoplies of wholeness. The body metaphors used here are relational, suggesting the danger of a malady that threatens the body's normative definitions and limits. Such "freaks" strung together in parades provide a visible streak of outrage running through the body politic. Norm-preserving straight repulsion acts as an antibiotic against the alien matter and pleasures of these border bodies.

The Social Body

The sex/gender ontology of heteromasculinity is further threatened by another border crisis located within the grid-based matrix of civil society where lesbian, gay, bisexual, and transgender activists have taken up the liberal rhetorics of civil rights and minority discourse. These strategies threaten to diminish the mark of difference and inferiority as they attempt to "normalize" queerness: progay research minimizes the dif-

ferences between heterosexual and homosexuals;[75] civil rights legisla-
tion humanizes gay, lesbian, bisexual, and transgender persons;[76] new
cultural images eroticize and sexually objectify white male bodies,
opening up legitimate erotic subject positions for both heterowomen
and male homosexuals;[77] bisexuals organize for sexual choice, transgender consciousness begins to tell its story, and feminism and race liberation politics continue to fight against subordination and discrimination.

For privileged heteromasculinity much is becoming "uncontained"
as this scene comes close to home and work: heterowomen are breaking
out, queers are coming out of the closet and showing up in the living
room, and the HIV virus—apparently escaping the strong arm of science—is everywhere on the loose. Even the maintenance of exclusive heterosexual male orientation has become more difficult[78] as many more
men than imagined slip their fantasies into anonymous encounters with
other men. The "everywhereness" of this "contamination" and the ontological shock of "deviants" going public with pride challenge the scientific, ideological, and civil supports of a beleaguered heteromasculine
hegemony.

The response in the conservative social body parallels that in the private body: a macro-immune system sends law and order to the borders of
the nation and its institutions to prevent entry of these foreign bodies or
to force them into hiding. As Naomi Goldenberg has suggested: "Male
identity often seems to be built around a concept of the tribe and its territory as anxiously guarded parts of the masculine body . . . Thus male
tribal hierarchy with its insistence on unity of allegiance and the separation of groups largely defines the terms of human association on this
planet."[79]

In all three domains—from the private body to the normative body to the
social body—the threat that appears recursively to saturate each level, is
represented in the body-centered metaphors of infection, contagion, pollution, and in the threat of catastrophic displacement—a border-crossing
that turns one queer. Straight repulsion, theorized from the body up,
moves from the drama of membranes and fluids and a border anxiety
physically demarcated by a militarized immune system and queer bashing (the private body) to the body dysphorias of "freaks" devoid of "natural" body boundaries (the normative body) to the policing of national
and community borders (the social body). The social body responds by

deporting queers, denying basic civil and marital rights protections to lesbian, gay, bisexual, and transgender people, criminalizing queer sex acts, promoting straight repulsion, censoring school and library books, "homosexualizing" the enemy, and fostering heterocentric fantasies of queer genocide and genetic annihilation.

As Foucault has suggested, "the phenomenon of the social body is the effect not of a consensus but of the materiality of power operating in the very bodies of individuals."[80] From the level of the private body to the social body, border bodies are perceived as a threat to national security and to military/immune system defenses. The panic loop between the private body and the social body is completed by images of hate and violence—originating significantly in the visceral logic of a phallic-centered construction of heteromasculinity. The heterophallus reverberates on all levels of this crisis—the private, the normative, and the social—as heterosexual males retreat into group formation, using body-panic reactions to stop the flow of border bodies. On each level the body symbolism indicates a cultural inquietude inhabiting the heteromasculine body, which fears its dis/appearance, both figuratively and literally, into sex and gender chaos. Douglas summarizes this isomorphism: "The body is a complex structure. The functions of its different parts and their relations afford a source of symbols for other complex structures."[81]

The Movable Queerness of Being

"Heterosexualizing" is a constant activity, reenacted in many everyday moments of life and in all the technologies and institutions that further produce and protect its effects. As Connell has pointed out in his analysis of masculinity: "the dominion of men over women, the supremacy of particular groups of men over others, is sought by constantly reconstituting gender relations as a system within which the dominance is generated."[82] To "heteromasculinize" is a verb that doesn't exist in the dictionary, hiding the process and activities of bodies that create a pseudosubstantive "heteromasculinity." Likewise "heteromasculinity," is also absent from the dictionary but *thought to be found in nature* and grounded metaphysically on a belief in the stable ontologies of sex and gender differences. This binary ontology is used to delineate heteromasculinity from the "otherness" of sexual deviants and heterowomen. Same-sex lust on all accounts threatens to undo this, blending the heteromasculine body

into what it is not—its abjected queerness and the polymorphically heterogeneous possibilities of flesh and pleasure. *Kissing the right kind of
body is important here.*

Robert Mapplethorpe's "Untitled 1972"[83] is a black and white photo
of two male bodies lying side by side, naked and engaged in a languid
and open mouth-to-mouth kiss. A stark border and contrasting color, a
box outlining the kiss in lifelike color highlighting reddened lips,
demarcates it from the background of the two bodies, which seem to disappear into the greys and shades of a soft and fluid male body. What is
important in this image is the kiss against the background of the same
sex in a loving embrace. The tenderness and mutuality of the two bodies in this kiss suggests openness, willfulness, equality, consent, the possibility of love, qualities that Foucault has labeled perhaps more disturbing than the heteroculture's predominant stereotype of the rough
anti-intimacy in gay sex.[84] A mutual kiss opens into the interior of each
body, allowing the exchange of fluids and the play of tongues, inciting
the flesh with desire and will. Kissing like that transforms the body
from its dailiness of clear physical boundaries into an indefinite merging across the touch of skin. What does one call oneself after doing or
wanting this?

A "queering out" of the heteromasculine flesh takes one to the other
shore, to the other side, a palpably different order of reality physically
symbolized between men by turning backside to another man. In two languages, the male homosexual body is referred to this *elsewhere*: in German, *am andern Ufer* (on the other shore) and in Spanish, *del otro lado*
(on the other side). As I have suggested in my reflection, this turning of
the male body to the other shore or to the other side can be symbolically
read as becoming woman, as castration, as falling before an external
enemy, who steals desire away from its proper phallic register. *The labor
of straight repulsion is to keep bodies from crossing over and to hide the
monstrous woman on the backside of male flesh.*

This monstrous woman is a misogynist transmutation. In the premodern world the seduction of the purest of men was carried out by what
was most evil—a lustful and insatiable female body. In the modern world
the queer male body competes with her as a new sign of sexually saturated danger. Woman's flesh may still be considered vile, but women, so
dearly needed to reinforce the proof of heteromasculinity, are not as
overtly imploded with the staggering evil of lascivious female bodies in
the middle ages. In modern heterosexual practices a nuanced dehuman-

ization of women can happen within an acceptable range of normalcy. The misogyny behind these scenes is not often acknowledged, as women's secondary status is accepted as *a matter of nature* or untroubled consent. Female bodies reaffirm and consolidate the meanings of heteromasculine identity[85] and provide a buffer zone for needy male libidos that could fall prey to homosexual impulse in the absence of women. Turning queer is another matter: straight repulsion is often overtly acknowledged and openly promoted. It is frankly permissible to transfer an excess odium of woman-hatred onto gay male bodies, reinforcing the efficient cruelty and the righteousness of those who are "Proud to be a Homophobe."[86]

In all of this the queer male body occupies a precarious and endangered place in a political system of heterosexual male dominance. The male body is the terrain where violence and tenderness between men can cross over: a kiss is sometimes enough to do this. The thought of this for some may be surprising; for others, repulsive; and for some, exquisitely common. However, the simple pleasures of this must not be told. Queers must disappear for bodies to remain visible, regular, heterosexual, and in place. Yet queer male bodies also reappear for heterocentric masculinity as the outer limit, on the other shore, on the backside of male flesh, the woman-side of man, where difference begins and ends, and where kissing can make men disappear: *am andern Ufer, del otro lado,* over there, voiceless, unsightly, vanishing into the not.

Warning Danger

Looking at them can provoke a number of emotional and behavioral responses:

Curiosity

Fascination.

Desire. Longing. Fantasy. Revery. Secrecy.

Touching. Tasting. Rubbing. Penetrating. Rolling.

Engulfing. Biting. Grinding. Licking. Sucking. Receiving.

Reveling. Transgressing. Surrendering. Controlling. Releasing.

Jouissance. Fluidity. Liminality. Ecstasy.

Wanting. Adoring. Loving. Deciding. Going over.

Becoming that. Coming on. Coming out.

A lascivious slip into a deterritorialized space where the obdurate fact of the body's physicality is transformed into bewildering pleasures and wild ontologies.

Prozac Feminism

There is a sense in which antidepressants are feminist drugs, liberating and empowering. In this scenario, it is the failure to prescribe medication that keeps the wife trapped, apparently by her own proclivities.

Prozac does not just brighten mood; it allows a woman with the traits we now consider "overly feminine," in the sense of passivity and a tendency to histrionics, to opt, if she is a good responder, for a spunkier persona.

Thymoleptics are feminist drugs, in that they free women from the inhibiting consequences of trauma.

She will attend to them [her anxiety, guilt, shame, timidity, depression, and low self-worth] in a new way, reading them not exclusively as signs of and stimuli to transcendence, but in part as scars of old injuries, in part as her family's physical heritage, burdens it would not be shameful to modify chemically.

—PETER KRAMER, *Listening to Prozac*[1]

In the late twentieth century, probably no other licit drug has received such a standing cultural ovation as Prozac.[2] Known as Lilly 11014 or fluoxetine hydrochloride, a drug released by the Food and Drug Administration (FDA) in 1987 for its moderate effectiveness in altering severe depressive moods, Prozac was hotly marketed in the mass media.[3] Prozac has made the cover of *Newsweek* magazine. It has weathered cross-examinations on Phil Donahue, Geraldo, Larry King, and Oprah, held up to the attacks from the Church of Scientology, and enjoyed its zigzag career in almost all United States media outlets.[4] Five years after it was released for prescription consumption, over eight million people were users, and an estimated 80 percent of these were women.[5] "Prozac" has become a household word, referring to a little green and white capsule that millions have added to their daily regime along with vitamins and morning coffee. In its brief life history, Prozac has become a respectable middle-class and professional antidepressant, a way for depression to come out of the closet.

But Prozac is more than this. Peter Kramer, in his book *Listening to Prozac*, which appeared in 1993, argues that Prozac ushers in a new age of psychopharmaceutical cosmetics and personality sculpting in which we may alter our moods and temperaments to suit the demands and stresses of our everyday lives. For women, Kramer proclaims, the news is particularly good. Prozac acts as a feminist drug able to turn women who are mildly depressed, sluggish, rejection-sensitive, and anhedonic into quick, vivacious, and resilient hyperthymic personalities,[6] the kind of woman who is in demand in the contemporary world of work and sex. This transformation of personality can be acquired within weeks of the drug's ingestion, short-circuiting months and even years of psychotherapy that may or may not bring women to the same level of high-functioning and sexual vivacity. According to Kramer, the news from Prozac puts women in both the driver's and the passenger's seat, since the driver is given the right to control her life (or her biochemistry), and the passenger has but to listen to Prozac to discover a self that is active, energetic, and whole. In this picture of the mind and body, human personality becomes largely a function of neurons and neurotransmitters, a mix that can be altered and rearranged like a recipe for white cake. For the Prozac-activated female, this portends not only the possibility of sculpting our corporeal bodies by discipline, surgery, and dieting but also designing our personalities by altering our brain chemistries. Pharmaceuticals may have entered the world of fashion, fitness, and feminism.[7]

In this chapter I will explore the construction of this new Prozac discursivity. Although I am less interested in the medical and popular debate on the pros and cons of Prozac use, what interests me is Kramer's representation of Prozac as a feminist drug. This raises some interesting questions on how feminism is rescripted by Kramer's Prozac industry to help produce middle-class "hyperthymic babes" in a rhetorical stroke that not only redefines Prozac as the drug for feminist hypernormalization but also calms the cultural panic surrounding the newly emerging postmodern body.[8] The experience of living a postmodern body becomes more commonplace as the body loses its prior symbolic unities and is instead experienced as a confluence of intersecting codes and chemicals. It becomes a less distinct nexus, merging boundaries of nature/culture, body/mind, self/not-self.[9] Prozac is more than a medical remedy for a mental dysfunction. It appears on the contemporary scene with a promise to reconstitute out of the chaos of unlimited postmodern disintegration the individual-based, white middle-class norms for gender, sex, and work. Prozac feminism proclaims its difference from past reactionary attempts to medicate women's social problems by tranquilizing them, but its "feminist" strategy of energizing individual women is also distinctly different from earlier forms of radical feminism that were based on collective acts of resistance to middle-class norms and disciplines of the female body.

I explore how Prozac feminism and the promotion of personality sculpting (in tandem with contemporary body-sculpting disciplines for women) can be read resistantly—against Kramer's discursive production of Prozac's promise. Medicating the "liberation" of privileged women in the name of Prozac feminism reveals a potential market-driven nightmare: a hypernormalized conformity, a solipsism of power, and a foreclosure on a more radical collective feminist consciousness. In this scenario the postmodern body—hybridized by pharmaceuticals as well as cybernetics—poses as a matter of self (ob)literation. Barring a return to an essentialist organic notion of the body, the place of more radical feminisms in this moment of the potently new "first world" informatics of domination[10] is yet to be disclosed.

Listening to and Talking Back to Prozac

By the middle of the 1990s the dominant Prozac discourse established by the press and media hype is referenced by two texts, Peter Kramer's *Listening to Prozac* (1993) and Peter and Ginger Breggin's *Talking Back To Prozac* (1994). Peter Kramer's work is specifically well-crafted in its appeal to women, known by far to be the primary consumers of pharmaceuticals and hence a primary marketing target for Prozac.[11] Unlike the psychotropic drugs marketed to women in the 1970s, Prozac is not promoted as a tranquilizer that will help mollify women's unhappiness with housework.[12] Prozac is marketed to women as a way to keep up with the multiple demands and rapid pace of family, career, sex, and relationships. Kramer's feminist drug normalizes feminism as superwomanism.

In the meantime Kramer appropriates as his own the rhetorical tropes of feminism, such as professional *receptivity* (enlisted through the metaphor of *listening*) and *concern for the victim* (a woman assaulted by biochemical imbalance).[13] The *personal voices* of his clients convince Kramer that Prozac is liberating them from the *tyranny of their biology*: the enemy within. *Listening*—that is, allowing the patient to *tell her story* (before and after Prozac); treating the before-and-after story as a *salvation narrative*; and not allowing one's professional voice to dominate over the voice of Prozac—these rhetorical maneuvers feminize Kramer and make Prozac (in the transgendered voice of Kramer) the feminist pill of the middle class. The Breggins' book, *Talking Back to Prozac*, continues the appropriation of feminist rhetorical tropes, as in *talking back* strategies that are widely used in feminist and anti-oppression discourse as ways of speaking from "the margin" to the dominant center.[14] However, the Breggin text merely takes up the personal and medical side effects of Prozac rather than the positioning of women in Kramer's discursive production of Prozac's promise.

Consider for example Kramer's famous case of Tess. Tess came to Kramer mildly depressed. She was the eldest child of ten children from a poor housing project, a victim of sexual and physical abuse, and from a family with a passive mother and an alcoholic father. Her father died when Tess was twelve, at which time her mother became clinically depressed, never to recover. Tess subsequently helped raise her siblings, had an adult history of degrading relationships with men, and was involved with a married man, Jim, who had recently returned to his wife, leaving Tess in shambles. At the same time she was having unusual difficulty at work in her administrative position where she negotiated with the union leaders for her company. After several weeks on Prozac, Tess left Jim for good, initiated a vivacious dating life, dropped her old friends who enabled her depression, experienced a burst of confidence, settled stalled union negotiations, and received a substantial raise from the company. According to Dr. Kramer, "the masochism just withered away and she seemed to have every social skill needed" (p. 8). Kramer writes, "Prozac redefined Tess's understanding of what was essential to her and what was intrusive and pathological"(p. 19). In this response Kramer continues to argue that self, personality, and temperament are perhaps no longer best thought of as mere accretions of personal history and memory. The day-to-day functional aspects of self are better conceived as the direct consequence of biochemical casualties.

Eight months after first stopping Prozac, Tess telephoned Dr. Kramer to ask whether he might resume her medication. She was not presenting symptoms, but she was losing her edge, and new union negotiations were underway. She said, "I am not myself." Kramer listens to Tess and resumes her medication as a way to enhance her work performance. Given again Tess's extraordinary improvement, Kramer asks us to consider how medication may "reshape a person's identity"(p. 18). With Prozac, Tess seems to have "located a self that feels true, normal and whole"(p. 20). With Tess's interpretation of her experience, Kramer (listening to Tess) raises further philosophical and practical concern: are we willing to allow medications to tell us how we are constituted or define who we are? This question is carried further in Kramer's ruminations on the practices of psychiatry. In the case of Tess, she was not just restored to her premorbid self, she had been transformed and had become "better than well." While he considers this effect possibly unnatural, unsafe, and uncanny (p. 13), Kramer later lauds it as a possible breakthrough for pharmacologic self-actualization and cosmetic psychopharmacology.

What is the role of the old-fashioned psychotherapist in the Prozac story? Kramer's reinterprets the role of the psychotherapist, who still continues to work through the medium of words and analysis, as best delivered in the mode of drug transference. This is suggested in Kramer's work with Susan, a rejection-sensitive client, who came to see him because she had decided her marriage was bad for her and she found herself unable to leave her husband. Susan was also unwilling to take Prozac. As Kramer writes, the role of the psychotherapist, in such cases, may be most effective if he mimics the role of Prozac. Kramer writes about his own experience:

> I saw this woman differently than I would have before my exposure to Prozac. I did not perceive her as ambivalent, or at least I did not imagine that mixed feelings toward her husband were the main contributor to her current paralysis. I saw someone who wanted a divorce but could not make the move because of the overwhelming feelings of pain and disorganization she anticipated from separation. . . . In the course of psychotherapy, Susan and I discussed her personality structure—her difficulty letting go, her demands for admiration—and the reasons, based on her family history, that she had formed strong ties to the particular man she had married. But for the most part, in my role as

psychotherapist, I acted like a medication—like Prozac—helping to mitigate my patient's sensitivity to loss. Soon we may be able to go further and say that the therapy mimicked medication more closely—that it altered Susan's serotonin levels—but that speculation is as yet a barely tested notion. (p. 286)

The leading popular press critics of Kramer's work, Peter and Ginger Breggin, authors of *Talking Back to Prozac,* have taken Kramer to task for his selective attention to the "good news" of Prozac based on a handful of stories told by his patients.[15] The Breggins, in "talking back," speak for the victims of Prozac who are the invisible fatalities ignored by Kramer's Lilly-financed work. They are victims who are organizing Prozac survivor groups (another feminist motif). The Breggin analysis highlights the minimal testing Prozac received before it was put on the market,[16] the various side effects caused by the drug, Kramer's misleading classification of the drug, and the stories of Prozac users who barely survived the effects of Prozac on their personalities. In the early 1990s the media and the press responded in kind, bringing into view alleged dramatic side effects of Prozac: impulsive relationship break-ups, attempted suicides, homicidal fantasies, and other irrational impulse-driven behaviors.[17]

In this public contestation, the biological and psychological effects of Prozac became the primary issue between Kramer and the Breggins. Prozac is a synthetic drug, engineered by Eli Lilly Pharmaceuticals to have the molecular structure capable of blocking serotonin reuptake from the synapses in the brain.[18] Its mode of action maintains a higher level of available serotonin in the brain, which is correlated with relief from depressive symptoms. This explanation is supported by the lower than normal levels of serotonin found in autopsies of those who die by suicide with clinically depressed brains.[19] Since the molecular structure of Prozac is technically designed to be a serotonin reuptake inhibitor, it has a more or less specific singular effect on brain chemistries; because of this, it has fewer side effects than other antidepressants. According to Kramer, Prozac is *a clean drug,* which eliminates acetycholine-related side effects and is selective only for serotonin and not for norepinephrine. However, though it may be a clean drug, it has a *dirty field of action.* According to Kramer, this means that Prozac brings about a diverse number of changes in human temperament, affective states, and felt capacities. In some senses what the drug does is so diverse that it may be unpredictable.[20] While Kramer focuses on Prozac as a clean drug that eliminates messy internal targetry, the Breggins focus on the multiple effects of Prozac as dangerously unconsidered in Kramer's selective listening.

The debate between Kramer and the Breggins sets the focus on cause-and-effect circuities, with evidence largely gathered from the experiences of biochemical "victims" on both sides.[21] The popular press loves this kind of pro-and-con debate (the shallow liberalism of "equal time"), but such debate also obfuscates how the trope of listening actually functions in Kramer's rhetorical strategies. The premium he places on listening helps to manufacture demand for a new hegemonic figuration of the body; a new articulation of traditional psychiatric categories, practices, and boundaries; and a recuperation of the meaning of feminism as female hypernormalization. These effects emerge outside the terms of the public debate between Kramer and the Breggins, indicating the emergence of a new cultural formation of body, agency, and feminism.

Postmodern Bodies and Diagnostic Bracket Creep

The instant popularity of Prozac is best understood as part of a postmodern cultural formation. In a world where all that is solid melts, where the boundaries between self and other seem less clear, where the body's immune system frequently turns on itself, and where the traditional forms of family, work, and other community institutions are becoming unstable guarantees of survival and success, a panicked self emerges, set afloat by a scheme of recombinant historical circumstance in the fast-moving economies of global capital. This is a self parsed by a remote control of multiple channels and bombarded by momentary images and contingent relationships, a self at risk for psychic dis/assembly.[22] Much of what seems organically whole and solid becomes unsteady, fragile, and less distinct. Through the application of technologies and disciplines to the body, the body becomes one location where the self can find an anchor and a place from which to narrate a foundation for itself.[23] Prozac provides such an anchor, assuring the user that at least the boundaries of personality and temperament can be controlled, however much they may become discontinuous with a previously unmedicated self. To gain acceptance, Kramer's *Listening to Prozac* rejoins the self to the stability of middle-class norms fending against the flood of apparent class dissolution and psychic disintegration. The relocation of women at this moment is critical, as Prozac's medicated women become the blissful and energized managers of home, family, relationships, career, and sex. Prozac is marketed as a drug that gives women enough energy to be equal to men in a restoration of middle-class stability.

If we listen to Prozac attentively, according to Kramer, we discover a new language for the body and personality, a new lexicon of personality dysfunctions, and a new portrait of the self as a composite of neural chemistries. The body in this new Prozac discursivity is no longer clearly divided by mind and matter, by culture and nature, or by self and not self, but is rebuilt, reshaped, and manipulated by new biotechnologies. Similar to Donna Haraway's notion of the "cyborg" (a hybridization of cybernetics and organism) as a new paradigm for the postmodern body,[24] I will explore a subspecies of this, "the pharmorg," a hybridization of pharmaceuticals and organism. For the pharmorg, the boundary between mind and body becomes both literally and figuratively leaky as medical and pharmaceutical expertise enables us to construct any number of possible personalities.

The infrastructure of this postmodern body is mirrored in how Kramer understands the professional consequences of listening to Prozac. According to Kramer categories of psychiatric diagnosis and personality should rest upon our ability to listen to drugs and catalogue their effects. In the field of descriptive psychiatry, the descriptive categories of diagnosis or cosmetic pharmacology should be revised to match the effects of various drugs on personality. Kramer labels this "diagnostic bracket creep": the boundaries between diagnostic categories are either "creeping out" as the penumbra of the category becomes a drug-treatable conditions or the category distinctions become less clear and distinct as different conditions respond positively to the same drug. In the case of Tess, Kramer's original diagnosis of mild depression was later expanded to include obsessive compulsive disorder (OCD) because she responded so positively to Prozac, a response that he would have expected from an OCD patient (p. 36). In this new vision of psychiatry, the expert is to listen to drugs, and, in a style mirroring the old empirics of medicine,[25] to catalogue a drug's effects as a way to establish better categories for medical diagnosis. As a sign of postmodern transition, "diagnostic bracket creep" shifts the ontology of disease and wellness to a pragmatics of treatment based on a reduction of human personality to biochemical determinants and the effects of psychotropic drugs. Kramer suggests how this merges psychiatry more directly with market demand:

> Some people might prefer pharmacologic to psychologic self-actualization. Psychic steroids for mental gymnastics, medicinal attacks on

the humors, anti-wallflower compound—these might be hard to resist. Since you only live once, why not do it as a blonde? Why not as a peppy blond? Now that questions of personality and social stance have entered the area of medication, we as a society will have to decide how comfortable we are with using chemicals to modify personality in useful, attractive ways. We may mask the issue by defining less and less severe mood states as pathology, in effect saying, "If it responds to an antidepressant, it's depression." Already, it seems to me, psychiatric diagnosis has been subject to a sort of "diagnostic bracket creep"—the expansion of categories to match the scope of relevant medications."(p. 15)

"Diagnostic bracket creep" captures the shifting surfaces and chemical reassemblies that constitute the pharmorg as a distinctive kind of postmodern body. Normalizing the pharmorg is referenced by culturally specific norms of efficient social functioning and work ethic success, which discursively define a "natural" or "healthy" body. Psychiatric professionals as the ideologues of this new class-based notion of the body are not held accountable for its fabrication. As Kramer views the work of psychiatrists, "It is easy to imagine that our role will be passive, that as a society we will in effect permit material technology, medications, to define what is health and what is illness" (p. 16). If professionals would only listen to Prozac, its predictable consequences can be reified into diagnostic or cosmetic categories of mental science and personality sculpting. The pharmorg body emerges in a Prozac delivery.

According to Kramer listening to Prozac occurs on four distinct prescriptive levels: psychiatrists should listen to their patients who say that Prozac helped them find their true selves; psychiatrists should listen to Prozac and revise ways of thinking about diagnostic categories; psychiatrists should listen to Prozac's potency for transforming and creating "better than normal" personalities; and consumers should listen to their Prozac-medicated selves and increase the popular demand for Prozac so that professionals will better listen to their clients and patients. In all of this listening, the boundaries between consuming and medicating bodies may be shifting. Imagine a *Diagnostic and Statistical Manual* and *Consumer Reports* in coordinate intertextuality for consumers and patients interested in reshaping their personalities. Medicine and insurance companies have already begun the struggle to establish new limits for medical coverage of treatments for the "worried well," blending psychiatry and fashion into biochemical normalization. Licit psychopharmaceuticals and street drugs may venture an odd tryst in their class warfare as the need for a medicated self reveals the hypocrisy of the war against unmarketable drugs. What is ironic in this picture is that professionals have become receptive. They listen to Prozac only to become the voice of a chemical whose agency and effect are changing what we mean by body, self, and personality. Through the fractionating of a cultural hegemony[26] established by pharmaceutical companies, medicine, media, and advertising, Prozac nation[27] appears in this mirror of irony as a grassroots movement, where the experts have been forced to listen. Demand becomes voice, and women all-star consumers.

Kramer is concerned that this new power of Prozac may usher a dreadful scene of coercive pressure to embody our cultural biases concerning temperament and character traits: "Prozac highlights our culture's preference for certain personality types. Vivacious women's attractiveness to men, the contemporary scorn of fastidiousness, men's discomfort with anhedonia in women, the business advantage conferred by mental quickness—all these examples point to a consistent social prejudice" (p. 270). While Kramer raises such concerns in *Listening to Prozac*, he fails to follow their implications once the smiling and happy faces of his chemically "born again" clients line up against the hesitations of his second thoughts. For feminists, listening to Prozac, I believe, involves a double echo of wonder and terror, a tension that I would like to pursue in my critique of Kramer's Prozac feminism.

The nightmare is real. One can foresee a world where women are expected to discipline their bodies and modify their personalities into high-premium hyperthymic "first world babes," energetically self-injected into the capital-intensive corporate and increasingly hypersexualized capital markets of an expanding transnational and male supremist economy. This is a form of disciplinary expectation that goes beyond Michel Foucault's now rather quaint notions of body disciplines emerging in the schools, the military, and asylums[28] and beyond Sandra Lee Bartky's and Susan Bordo's application of Foucauldian networks of power to the daily micro-labors of disciplined feminine flesh.[29] Pharmaceutical discipline is an expectation that calls for a physical rearrangement of body's most intimate matter—that of a self that matters. In the physical and cultural displacement of postmodernism, the traditional unities and determinacies of self and body may in the end support a world of privileged and freely sculpted pharmorgs: the new hyperthymia of first-world chemical happiness.

Talking Back to Prozac: Tess Revisited

> *The way neurochemicals tell the story is not the way*
> *psychotherapy tells it.*
>
> —PETER KRAMER, *Listening to Prozac*

As a resistant reader to Kramer's *Listening to Prozac*, my concerns are not those of an unconverted and unmedicated outsider unwilling to listen to Prozac. Nor am I an antipharmaceutical protester unwilling to fathom any chemical manipulation of the brain. I do, however, want to raise some questions about gender, women's oppression under capitalism, and the role of Prozac as Kramer's new feminist drug. My concerns are social and political, since I question Kramer's representation of the pleasures and promises of Prozac against the backdrop of other dispersions of power that hold women in place and incarcerate them more deeply in their bodies. I also want to explore what constitutes a continuous autobiography of the self and the lexicons of reductionism that retell this story of the self on the short side of a present tense.

Kramer's female "makeovers" are indeed impressive. A sampler reveals the following:

Julia, a registered nurse, was married, had a short day job so that she could manage her children and household. She came to Dr. Kramer because she had read about Tess and Prozac. She explained to Dr. Kramer she had a problem with her controlling need for perfectionism, which alienated her husband and children. She was employed at a job that was not challenging. On Prozac Julia became more relaxed and less controlling. Her husband was much happier with her, and she managed to move up the career ladder in pay and status to become a pediatric nurse. Apparently Julia said to Dr. Kramer, "I am enjoying the unpredictability of pediatric nursing"—a change that would have been unavailable to her in her pre-Prozac morbidity. (pp. 22–36)

Gail, a medical doctor, came to Dr. Kramer because she suffered "rejection sensitivity," which expressed itself in her inability to weather social slights and in her inordinate spending on clothes. On Prozac Gail experienced a new confidence. She was able to make public presentations without notes and capable of withstanding confrontation without breaking down. She applied for a higher post as the hospital assistant to the medical chair and was able not to fall apart when she was turned down. Her husband found her more affectionate. As for her spending, "I don't feel guilty about spending. My husband can say what he wants." (pp. 92–95)

Hillary arrived at Dr. Kramer's office after having tried psychotherapy, Rolfing, and hang-gliding to retrieve a sense of enjoyment in life. Her anhedonic state dissipated with Prozac. She was able to enjoy the ordinary pleasures of life, no longer felt intimidated by men, and developed a felicity in moving in and out of relationships with considerable ease. Although she had ambled her way through college and professional school in her pre-Prozac life and had failed to show up for job interviews, when she was on Prozac she found a new lease on work—she called her work "the perfect job." (pp. 224–227)

Sonia, a talented graphic artist, presented the symptoms of a mild depression—a "forme frustre of dysthymia"—when diagnosed by Dr. Kramer. She was an ethereal young woman, who was having problems showing up for scheduled events. She was murky in her thoughts according to her husband, unable or uninterested in managing her finances, and slow in her speech and focus. With Prozac she became an energetic, more socially assertive, more clearly focused, and fast-talking and nuerologically aroused woman. Prozac has given her a more fluent voice, overcoming the tongue-tied effects of depression's psychomotor retardation. (pp. 237–239)

No one would deny that these are remarkable stories of transformation and that Prozac brings this "substantial minority"[30] a precious gift of renewed energy and apparent self-actualization. According to Kramer, Prozac can offer to many women relief for minor depressions, loss of self esteem, rejection-sensitivity, perfectionism, dependency on abusive relationships, sexual abuse trauma, inability to enjoy ordinary pleasures, intimidation by men, dysfunctional sluggishness, timidity, tongue-tiedness, speech retardation, and applause-seeking behaviors. These personality flaws seem worthy of a fix given a corporate world rewarding the quick and productive and a sexual market putting a premium on the fast and the fit. As Kramer points out, men now prefer sexually hyperthymic women to the hypothymic personalities of subservience, passivity, and male-dependency: the anhedonic Victorian is both out of style and no longer in male demand. Marketed in this way to women, Prozac is an individual solution responding to the demands of a work and heterosexual ethic most pronounced in the lives of middle-class women. This new norm requires a steadied and pricey femininity.

What is the story of the self told by neurochemicals? Kramer writes the story of Prozac to provide us with a framework for writing a story of the self. Prozac was created for that story—literally designed in the lab as a serotonin reuptake inhibitor, interpreted as a personality shaper, and promoted as a gateway to effective and high-achieving normality. Where commonly many people experience the self as an accretion of experience, memory, self-reflection, imagination, and social interaction—a mix of fact and sense-making that seems continuous, historically located, and connected to communities of meaning—Prozac can be seen as a plot device for a newly constructed postmodern self whose story includes a host of characters and molecules not previously found in oedipalized, social-historical, or politicized metanarratives of the self's biography.[31] The way neurochemicals tell the story of the self makes the self an affective-behavioral complex in which the flaws of personality can be added or subtracted from its intimate matter. The question becomes one of whether or not we want to inhabit the story of the self as told in this new pharmaceutical discursivity, where Prozac seems to provide the missing pieces.

Kramer's story of the self assumes that emotional states are the effects of neurochemical substrata and that by getting all the pieces in place, the self has but to listen to know itself and even to enjoy itself. In examining the ontology of this story, the body's intimately recombinable neurochemistries become the matter of a self that knows itself by listening to these chemicals. How then can we do this? Is it really possible to listen to Prozac as a way of authoring a story of the self? For whom and for what purpose is this story?

Naomi Scheman's work on the emotions helps elucidate some of the problems in Kramer's analysis.[32] In her early reflections of women's anger, Scheman critiques the traditional Freudian view of human emotions in which emotions are characterized as definable psychological entities buried deep in the silt of human consciousness and discoverable through the labor of psychoanalysis. In arguing that "psychical acts" such as parapraxes, dreams, and neuroses "have a sense" and are not just an effect in somatic, biochemical, or materialist causalities, Freud extended the domain of psychological phenomena useful in constructing a story of the self. However, rather than posit the emotions—such as anger and depression—as particular states in the individual that exist independent of social context, Scheman argues that the social context and its political dimensions are critical to the construction of meaning and cognitive direction in naming and understanding one's emotions. She uses the hypothetical but typical case of Alice to make her point:

> Alice belongs to a consciousness-raising group. When she first joined she was generally satisfied with her life. But she became gradually more aware of those times when she felt depressed, or pressured and harried, as though her time were not her own. However, she didn't believe her time ought to be her own, so in addition, she felt guilt. She would sometimes snap at her husband or children, or cry without quite knowing why, and then put her "moodiness" down to various causes, such as her neuroses or her husband or children, or cry without quite knowing why, and then put her "moodiness" down to various causes, such as her neuroses or her menstrual cycle. She didn't think she had any reason to feel this way; she never took the bad feelings as justified or reasonable; she didn't identify with them; they came over her and needed to be overcome." (p. 24)

In the process of sharing her experiences and feelings with the group, Alice comes to understand her guilt and depression as a response to and cover for feelings of anger. This anger she comes to see as legitimate—sincere, not self-deceptive—and justifiable given her growing political understanding of women's life situations. According to Scheman, Alice's discovery of her anger and her willingness to name it as such rest upon a political redescription of her life situation.

> The crystallization of her feelings will be impeded in part by her unwillingness to face the sort of person she thinks she would be were she really angry. But in the group women she has grown to know and to like confess to similar feelings. As the other women realize that they are angry, Alice's certainty that they are not monsters will make it easier for her to accept that she is angry too. . . . The bestowing or the withholding of a name can be personally and politically explosive. To see that some state of affairs counts as oppression or exploitation, or that one's own feelings count as dis-

satisfactions or anger is already to change the nature of that situation and those feelings.(29)

Our assessment and categorization of feelings depend for Scheman on the entire context of a person's life story. This includes our social interactions, where feelings get named, legitimated, and justified, and a political framework that at least partially articulates female discontent. In Scheman's account, emotions are not ghostly entities there to be discovered but are more likely to be an inchoate and confusing turmoil, which takes on shape and meaning in the contexts of social interaction and in a continuous narrative construction of the self. Accordingly, when we are confused about our emotions, it is because the emotions are confused: "there is no reason to think that under the muddle is a clear fact, a leaf beneath the silt (p. 28)." The story of the self as told by Scheman is told through this collective articulation that locates the self in a world structured by power and oppression and in a context of women's political resistance. *Finding personal voice* in this location and context is to settle meanings in a new way of understanding personal experience, identity, and the self. It is this cognitive grasp of that larger world that gives a woman like Alice a means for naming her emotions differently. Rather than consider these troubling emotions a flaw to be eradicated with psychotropic drugs, as in Kramer's approach to Tess, Scheman's framework allows for an alternative personal and political articulation of a radical fault line that splits our lives into the open.

As most studies confirm, we live in a world where women are more depressed than men by an average ratio of two to one,[33] a matter that can be given different social interpretations. From a social/psychological framework, women's depression and dysthymia can be understood as deeper distress occasioned by disconnection and isolation. The higher prevalence rates of depression among women can be read as a gendered function of women's oversocialization into relational and interpersonal orientations. Women's experience of disconnection is perhaps more terrifying and devastating than men's experience, because male socialization into autonomy and individualism raises the threshold for isolation's discontent. Additionally, some have argued that women are given fewer outlets for legitimate anger, which turns inward to work its way through depression and somatic response.[34]

In Scheman's constructionist view of the emotions, women's contextual and collective articulation of emotions can become an indication of women's political discontent with a larger system of social oppressions, perhaps a deserving target of female rage and resistance. It would seem that Prozac feminism, transacted in Kramer's office, displaces the language of this feminism—women's need for autonomy, self-determination, resilience, and defiance—as qualities of personality made available through Prozac. In Prozac feminism the problem is in the body; the solution is individual; and the emotions, named in the context of therapy and diagnosis, are reduced to the effects of neurochemicals. Prozac enters the self under the sign of postmodern informatics, devoid of its own authorship while authoring the self. Given Susan Faludi's analysis of therapeutic trends of the 1980s that have come to blame feminism for women's discontents and in turn to blame the individual woman for her unhappiness,[35] Kramer's promotion of Prozac as a new feminist drug of the 1990s fits very neatly into the backlash against a more radical and collectively spirited feminisms.

Talking Back to Prozac Feminism: The Pharmorg Revisited

> *Our culture is caught in a frenzy of biological materialism.*
> —Peter Kramer, *Listening to Prozac*

> *Liberation rests on the construction of consciousness,*
> *the imaginative apprehension, of oppression, and so of*
> *possibility.*   —Donna Haraway, *Simians, Cyborgs, and Women*

There are several challenging ways for feminists to talk back to Kramer's Prozac feminism. Some feminists may oppose the use of any psychotropic drugs to ameliorate women's discontent. Though not necessarily calling for the complete immiseration of the female sex, these feminists may fall back on the notion of a "natural body" or a body purified of contaminations from the dominant culture. This is not the approach taken by Scheman in her Wittgenstinian analysis of emotions and their context-dependent articulation. Nor is "the natural body" an approach that I think successfully talks back to Kramer's discursive construction of Prozac, since a drug-free female body is only one of many physicalities of the body that could be called "natural." Such an option may not be the best for a particular woman suffering from dysthymia or other emotional complications. The appeal to a natural body does, however, provide an anchor for discursive resistance to Prozac, as does an appeal to some original and fictive unity of the body unpolluted by the "dirty work" of pharmaceuticals.[36] Such a cumbersome ontology is, however, not really necessary.

In contrast, Scheman's analysis operates at the level of experience and meaning where emotions are named in a politicized context of oppression. Emotions are experienced as somewhat dependent upon how words are used to make sense of "what's going on inside," regardless of whether the body's physicality is considered natural or unnatural. The articulation of an emotional self in Scheman's work is not diced by a vocabulary of neurochemicals or constructed by neurochemical building blocks; rather, it becomes what it is in a narration of self told in the living context of a collective conversation and a politics of feminist dissent. To the extent emotions are context-dependent, the emotional body is socially constructed by such practices and destabilized as it moves through various contexts.[37] The agency of self is moved to a different level in deciding which narrations of self to inhabit and how. Given this reading, Scheman's analysis provides a more direct way to move beyond the evocation of "the natural body" or "the plot of original unity" and to talk back to Prozac feminism at the level of politics rather than side-effects.

Scheman's analysis does not preclude an incorporation of the post-modern pharmorg body, a fabricated hybrid of animal/human/pharmaceuticals structured as a series and multi-tiered "coded texts through which we engage in the play of writing and reading the world."[38] Similar to Haraway's construction of the cyborg body, the pharmorg body does not rely on an imagined organic unity or an appeal to nature to integrate or sponsor collective social resistance or cultures of opposition. Like the cyborg, the origin of its physical ontogeny is at least partially constructed by what Haraway calls an informatics of domination that seeks to control and profit from its induced compliance and unconscious utilities while also creating small but dangerous spaces for imagination and oppositional agency. If I may take the liberty to substitute "pharmorg" for "cyborg" in Haraway's text, another way to talk back to Kramer's Prozac feminism emerges:

> *Pharmorgs* are not reverent; they do not re-member the cosmos. They are wary of holism, but needy for connection—they seem to have a natural feel for united front politics, but without the vanguard party. The main trouble with *pharmorgs*, of course, is that they are the illegitimate offspring of militarism and patriarchal capitalism, not to mention state socialism. But illegitimate offspring are

often exceedingly unfaithful to their origins. Their fathers, after all, are inessential.[39]

Kramer's new Prozac discursivity can be understood as a form of biotechnology that recrafts our bodies under the paradigm of communications sciences. The emotions are presented as a problem of neurochemical coding. In crafting the body as an ensemble of codes, where "all heterogeneity can be submitted to disassembly, reassembly, investment and exchange"[40] an enforcement of prescribed meaning can bear down on the pharmorg's sense of unity. Kramer's promotion of Prozac feminism attempts this as he reassembles a unity of self ("the true self") holding together the values of middle-class work ethic, efficient wifery, hyperthymic heterosexuality, and perhaps a special kind of whiteness.[41] This story of the self steps only cautiously into the instabilities, fluidities, and loss of alleged purity enjoined and enjoyed by the postmodern body. However, the pharmorg need not become a reverent docile body. She need not re-member the old cosmos. In taking on the responsibility to tell the story of her self and body, to draw her own boundaries of domain and potency, and to reside in collectivities of political resistance, the pharmorg can become, if need be, a Prozac-tipped but not Prozac-promised feminist. This may not be a story of the self as told by neurochemicals; rather, it might be the story told by pharmorgs and cyborgs acting with *and* against the new epistemologies of the self emerging in the informatics of domination.

Like the cyborg body, a pharmorg body "is not innocent; it was not born in a garden; it does not seek unitary identity and so generate antagonistic dualisms without end (or until the world ends); it takes irony for granted."[42] Kramer's attempt to recuperate white middle-class values in the production of female pharmorgs in effect works to discourage the liberating potentials of women's multiple identities and of our "dysfunctional selves," our affinities with gossip and heteroglossia, and our monstrous joy in re/fusing the (ob)literation of radically and collectively spoken selves. Both Scheman and Haraway give us ways to embrace the body's postmodern physicality without surrendering to the way neurochemicals tell a flat story of the self and without the need for "the natural body" or "the plot of essential unity or origin." The postmodern emotive body is thus crafted at the level of microrecodings in neurochemical matter and in variable frameworks of the self continuously recorded and recoded by shifting location, boundary, identity, relation, and alliance.

This can become a radical crafting of the self with or without Prozac, but a crafting rather than a compliant listening to Prozac's media-promoted promise.[43] I urge this craft as a woman's pleasure as well as her responsibility to constitute a radical literation of her self as an antimodernist body and, if necessary, as a noisomely resisting reader to Kramer's Prozac promise.

Two	Disarticulations

The metaphor of production allows us to think of bodies as somewhat culturally and personally assembled and thus capable of disassembly and rearrangement. This approach challenges the modernist concept of the body as an autonomously integrated organic unity that is *as it is* by nature. Consistent with this assumption, sexuality, race, and gender are often considered attributes of the body and effects of genetic or hormonal causes that create deep and entrenched differences in the morphological and physiological features of different body kinds. The view I am developing in this book opposes this modernist concept by exploring the cultural and social materialization of matter. The three essays in this section engage a process of "disarticulation" in which the articulated bodies of modernism's normativity, in this case the gendered heterosexual normative body, is disassembled and refigured.

"Male Lesbians and the Postmodern Body" was originally written as a didactic piece to introduce students to contemporary discussions on the performativity and historical weight of sexual identities. Many readers have asked me questions about the male lesbians I mention in this essay. However, how they actually experienced their dysphoric embodiments is incidental to my philosophical reflections on how such a claim—to be a male lesbian—can make intelligible sense. On the surface, it appears an impossible state of being. However, by lifting gender and sexual identities from their modernist nexus with nature, the disarticulation of modernist body paradigms allows for new sexes, sexualities, and genders that can dislodge the signs of gender and sexuality from the trump of genital signification. Gender and sexuality categories become corporeal terrains open to all kinds of bodies and various communities of meaning. Still these postmodern articulations of the self must face off against the larger and more oppressive sturdiness of cultural forces that continue to produce sex and gender norms. The crushing weight of this social and discursive structuring bears down on bodies, selecting the best-fitting for easier survival and rejecting the disarticulated body as "a freak of nature." The male lesbian as an intellectual interlocutor asks us to disarticulate our modernist notions of corporeal intelligibility. I explore this as an intellectual and practical challenge.

"FemFire: A Theory in Drag" furthers these postmodern ruminations on gender and sexuality in an experimental writing that merges personal and philosophical reflection. I fashion a fem lesbian persona who confounds the 1970s lesbian feminist critique of femininity by turning her fem seductive power on the lesbian philosopher. The seduction becomes critique as poetic analytics disarticulate the meanings of power, harm, loyalty, and resistance in an erotics of hetero/lesbianism. Winning the argument is replaced by butch surrender to a fem's pleasure in intellectual play. Such gender migration and refiguring disengages both modernist and early radical feminist paradigms of sex and gender. FemFire would rather mix and match in the ethos of postmodern bodies.

The final essay in this section, "Fiddling with Preference," explores new biological research on gay genes. I examine Dean Hamer's construction of the sexual body in *The Science of Desire* and his rhetorical construction of sexual desire as a phenotypic trait. What eventually emerges from my analysis is an understanding of how empirical work such as Hamer's relies on modernist assumptions about sexual desire and a suppression of bisexual and omnisexual forms of desire. I contrast Hamer's research methods with two other approaches: postmodern sexual theory and multidimensional sexual orientation research, which provide other ways of understanding the personal, cultural, and historical aspects of sexual identity formation.

The essay concludes with a new metaphor for thinking of sexual identities as *shelters* identified by the signs of sexual kinds. The image of a shelter suggests a respite or haven from harsh forces that might destroy the life it protects. Generally, shelters are wide-open structures though sometimes a port of access may be controlled in various ways. Shelters are generally made by humans for the purposes of protection or survival, and when we find them in nature, it is because we give them such uses and meanings. In thinking of sexual identities as shelters, signs harboring the integrity of a life form, sexual desire can be more clearly understood as extended and articulated beyond the body itself and implicated in a history of human struggle.

4   Male Lesbians and the
       Postmodernist Body

The owner's manual, interior, and T-shirt all say Porsche.
But it still runs like a Volkswagen. And no matter how
much you scream at it, beat it, love it, or hate it, it is still,
deep down a Volkswagen. . . . I felt somewhat awkward
about a car analogy, but I love cars and my Volkswagen
is very much a part of my life and my identity. No, it
does not have a Porsche engine in it, but I have often felt
that I'm a lesbian trapped inside a man's body.
                           —Commentary written by a male student

My Future Memories: Being the Recently Discovered
Ideas of a Twentieth-Century Penis-Wielding Androgy-
nite; or, The Possible Accounting of a Lesbian Trapped In
a Man's Body   —Essay title written by a male student

You're not welcome in this bar/ You're not welcome at
this party/ You're not welcome in my home. And I say I
don't know why separatists won't let me in—I'm proba-
bly the only lesbian to have successfully castrated a man
and gone on to laugh about it on stage, in print and on
national television.   —Transsexual KATE BORNSTEIN, 1991

The "male lesbian" seems to be an oxymoron. Yet I
have met more than a few. Other lesbians report similar encounters. Is
there a problem here? Our commonsense definition of "lesbian" as a
woman who has emotional and sexual relationships with or erotic desires
for other women renders the "male lesbian" a foolish fantasy since "sex
with a woman" in his case would clearly make him heterosexual. My personal response to "male lesbians" has often been a mixture of suspicion,

befuddlement, and sometimes anger toward the arrogance of this appropriation. These are men who claim not merely to act like lesbians or to be
lesbian-identified or to feel like lesbians, but to be lesbians, to take on the
identity of lesbian as I have in my own existence as a genetic female. They
are sometimes men who claim to be more lesbian than I am in our conflicting interpretations of lesbian writings. They are usually men who
want access to lesbian-only space in all its varieties.

Feminists have struggled for years with the concept of a male feminist. While some are willing to acknowledge that there are men who are
trustworthy and who can join feminist circles by virtue of sharing an ideological perspective and by giving up some power and privilege, others
fall back onto body ontologies: "No, they can't really be feminists; they're
not women." From this perspective the difference of sex is perceived as an
insurmountable obstacle to becoming a real feminist in some deeply
authentic sense. Regarding the "male lesbian," these same sentiments
bring the body even more into focus "No, you can't be a lesbian; you're
not a woman." Being a lesbian seems to require more obviously and at
least minimally a certain kind of body. It is questionable whether men can
be authentic feminists; it seems unquestionable that men cannot be lesbians. Only the second possibility interests me.

Why take this seriously? I am intrigued by the chimera of the "male
lesbian" and the questions posed by this construction of identity within
recent postmodernist theorizing on the body. If, according to some postmodernists, the body is itself a product of discursive construction and a field
of interpretative possibilities that can occupy different locations or positionalities, what prevents a male body from occupying the positionality of
"woman" or "lesbian"? How does any body, even one with XX sex chromosomes and primary sex characteristics identified as female, become a
woman? Is it possible to become a woman trapped in a male body? Would-
n't a preference for women in this case imply a lesbian trapped in a male
body? How do lesbians know when we are with other lesbians? Are genetic
males who claim to be lesbians exhibiting great pretense or denial toward
the real meaning of their genitals or their sexual desires? How do genitals
or desires come to mean anything? What makes any sex or gender identity
real when it is possible that humans make up these meanings through the
disciplinary practices of "doing gender" or "having sex"? Why should we
privilege genital anatomies in defining the truth of our sex? In light of these
questions, the "male lesbian" strikes me as a proverbial Trickster whose
self-proclaimed identification presents an interesting philosophical puzzle.

In this essay I will explore this special case of lesbian identity through an analysis of how sex, gender, and sexual identities are established by heterosexual codes of the dominant sex culture and by similar rules informing various lesbian communities. I examine "lesbian identity" as a construction defined by normative positioning, empirical inspection, and sex-specific acts. In each of these frameworks the "male lesbian" creates a stress on established social categories, which are further challenged by postmodernist theorizing about the body. Using the theoretical tactics of postmodernism, a male can argue his way into "lesbian-only" community as a "lesbian." "He" becomes a "she" who desires "her." Surprisingly for me, my exploration of this special case has lead to a critique of postmodernism as well as a new way of conceptualizing the cultural construction of the sexed body.

The Historicity of the Body

Human bodies as a species form have remained relatively constant throughout Western history. What has changed more dramatically are the ways in which subjectivity has been embodied and made sense of its embodiment. Premodernist, modernist, and postmodernist modes of embodiment provide a topography for thinking about the history of these changes. In the Western premodernist world, bodies were tightly integrated into the collectives of kinship and social wholes. In deeply internal connections, bodies belonged to larger social aggregates—the family, the manor, the church, the village, the clan, or the tribe and were in a sense owned and controlled by higher social powers that determined the body's place, meaning, and use. Only with great difficulty can words such as "homosexual" be applied to isolate bodies in a premodernist world, since "individuals" who "owned their body and its sexual rights" did not exist as a possible self-construction. Bodies were woven into the tapestry of larger social aggregates. David Halperin makes this point when he argues against using the modernist concept of "homosexual" to categorize male-to-male sexual activity in Greek society. Such sex, Halperin contends, was used to reconstitute the hierarchical structure of male social relations, to solidify and honor social status roles between older and younger Greek males. Sex was not being used to constitute homosexual identities in the modernist sense.[1]

The modernist construction of "the homosexual" awaited three important historical developments: the Cartesian separation of the body from the contexts of folk and social nexus (the construction of the intelligible body); the "invention" of sexuality as a truth about the body and as such a truth about the individual (the construction of the clinical body); and, consequently, the historical emergence of communities of sexual minorities (the construction of sexual identification). An example of an early foreshadowing of a modernist homosexual politic can be seen in 1726 when William Brown responded to his arrest at one of London's Molly Houses with the claim that "there is no crime in making what use I please of my own body," a claim that reflects a new sentiment of private ownership of one's own body and a public flaunting of kinship moralism.[2] In the modernist world individuals would increasingly flock to networks and communities where sex attraction drew strangers together and where the organization of sexuality relied increasingly on the individuation of the subject's agency in sex.

By the end of the nineteenth century socioerotic identities were constructed by reference to preferred "object choice." This aspect of personhood was seen as a deep truth about the individual and as a resource for creating medical categories and communities of affinity. In the transition into this secular world, the status of homosexuality moved from sin to pathology, as bodies were assigned a place on either side of the great homo/hetero divide. Linking sexual deviance to pathologies, whether mental or physical, required a new authority—the modern medical expert—who saw the body as a thing controlling and defining the stricken homosexual. Through a confluence of institutional changes, these discursive practices both created and discovered "the pervert" and "the invert," signified by "abnormal" object choice or gender dysphoria. Many lesbian and gay liberation movements have been built on a reversal of this modernist sex discourse.[3]

A critique of the modernist body has been recently articulated in postmodernist thinking about the body. Although postmodernism is primarily thought of as an epistemic critique of Enlightenment philosophy, its belief in the power of reason and in the autonomy of the "knowing" self, this critique of traditional epistemology also spawns a new way of conceptualizing the cultural constructedness of the body. By challenging the Archimedean ideal of disembodied knowledge, postmodernism brings into focus first of all the "locatedness" of one's body as a place from which particular viewpoints on reality can be generated. Thus any universal reading of reality from one perspective can be challenged by a multiplicity of different selves in different locations. For some postmodernists, subjectivities can ambulate into these multiple locations, each generating a particular discursive view of the world, which in turn "constructs" the subjectivity of that location. The subject becomes a product of discourse or intersecting textualities, as the world becomes a ceaseless play of interlocking and conflicting texts, spoken from different locations and negotiated across different perspectives.

The body under postmodernist imagery can be extracted from its historically concrete daily context and "shifted" into an ever-increasing multiplicity of positionalities, a creative movement, according to Suleiman,[4] which "invents" the body itself. The simple unities and stabilities of self in the modernist world are shattered in this choreography of multiple selves, as the body loses its surety of boundary and its fixity of truth and meaning. As Susan Bordo has suggested, "here is where deconstruction may slip into its own fantasy of escape from human locatedness—by supposing that the critic can become wholly protean, by adopting endlessly shifting, seemingly inexhaustible vantage points, none of which are 'owned' by either the critic or the author of the text under examination."[5] Similarly, the body becomes a portable site for reinventing the meanings of flesh.

I would like to explore this idea further in my reflections on "male lesbians." The theoretical assumptions of postmodernism seem to make possible the transmutation of male to female as a matter of shifting contextual locations that "reinvent" the body. Whereas modernism considers the body to be fixed, by nature, in its sexedness, the tactics of postmodernism suggest that there are indeed more things possible on heaven and earth than we may be willing to grant a rightful status of being.

Lesbian Identity as Normative Positioning

A lesbian is the rage of all women condensed to the point of explosion. —RADICALESBIANS, 1971

In the primacy of women, of women creating a new consciousness of and with each other, which is at the heart of women's liberation, and the basis of cultural revolution. —RADICALESBIANS, 1971

Feminism is the theory; lesbianism is the practice. —TI-GRACE ATKINSON, 1974

In the early 1970s an effort was made by some lesbians to remove lesbianism from its sex bed. Definitions of "lesbian" were desexualized and presented as a political choice. Lesbian feminists were represented as woman-identified, in contrast to heterosexual feminists, who were considered male-identified with their energies continuing to flow "backward toward our oppressors."[6] This downplay of sexual stigma purified the "female deviant," whose identity was less essentially defined by how and with whom she had sex (in all its graphically, clinically, and culturally hegemonic representations) and more essentially defined as a political position in opposition to heteropatriarchy. This approach, which disembodies "lesbianism" of saturated sex and separates it from explicit genital reference to the bodies and pleasures pursued by many lesbians, allows a possible port of entry—strained though it may be—for the "male lesbian." "Lesbian" becomes a role, a positionality open to insertion.

This is especially true if "lesbian" is defined as an ideological, ethical, or political posture: a way of being in the world or relating to others, a way of seeing the world that is "woman-identified" or "woman-seeing," a special way of loving, preferring, or "sexing" women—any number of political oppositional practices engaging or disengaging the domination of heteropatriarchy. I take it that many males who claim to be lesbians identify with these ideological positions as preferable to masculinist options or as more "true to their selves." Males who claim to be inside these "lesbian" positions may embody in their actions or character a number of principles that comply with these ways of being, relating, or acting in the world. In lesbian reader theory, for example, a male might read a particular text like a lesbian or with a lesbian sensibility and come to conclusions similar to those of a number of other lesbian readers.[7] He could be said to share a normative worldview, occupy a position, or participate in a role that constitutes a significant component of lesbian identity.

The question remains—does he read like a lesbian or does he read as a lesbian? Our "male lesbian" is likely to claim the latter. This shift from a similarity claim to an identity claim assumes that we know what it means to do anything "as a lesbian," and thus to know when we are in the presence of lesbians. The claim that there is such a way of being, seeing, and doing is minimally epistemologically separatist: there must be some way in which lesbians are different from other human beings and that way is what it means to be a lesbian. Some lesbians do make such claims, but others don't. Given any normative definition of "lesbian," there will always be some self-identified lesbians who do not fit the norm and who are categorized as "male-identified," "gay," "educable or not," or "not real lesbians." The "misfits" are frequently able to contest the norms used to exclude them. Can our "male lesbian" similarly decry this totalitarianism of the norm?

Lesbian identity as normative positioning implies an identity construction that is prescriptive and often exclusionary. For a male to claim a lesbian identity in this normative sense is to claim to be a particular kind of lesbian, usually a highly politicized lesbian who sees lesbianism as anti-establishment separation from men or as a radical directive for social change. To be "lesbian" in this sense is to be ethically or politically postured toward the world in a particular way. Oddly, our "male lesbian" could claim to be a "male lesbian separatist," separating himself from other men and from his own body in order to be ideologically consistent. A postmodernist perspective, which construes the subject as protean and the body as a neutral field open to interpretation or as constructed by its contingently discursive positionality, makes plausible this creation of identity.

From a modernist perspective, however, a genetic male who claims to be lesbian by virtue of occupying the normative positionality of "lesbian," while clearly having the wrong body, is mistaken. The identity of lesbian, unlike other positionalities, is defined by explicit reference to a particular kind of body—namely female. His body is different, in fact "the opposite sex" of female bodies, and certainly because of that, his bodily and embodied experiences will in some ways be different from those of women. You have "to body" lesbian in order to be one. However, what does it mean "to body" lesbian? Am I assuming that there is something deeply incommensurable between a male's acting like a lesbian and my being a lesbian? Is it a male's XY chromosomes, his testosterone profile, testicles, sperm, penis, or ejaculate—in general the distribution of substances in his body—that makes it impossible for him to be a lesbian? From a modernist perspective, the answer relies on the physical criteria that we commonly use to demarcate one sex from the other; from a postmodernist perspective, we are thrown back onto the question of why the body is given this criteria-bound interpretation from among others.

Perhaps the issue here is not one of identifying some Lesbian X-Factor in the body or of justifying sex-differentiation criteria, but simply a question of preference or desire. A male body is not what most lesbians hope to find under the sheets or under "her" clothes. If physical sexual preference is our reference, then lesbians are customarily defined by a preference for sexual encounters generally involving four breasts, two vaginas, and two clitorises, among other things. The male body is lacking. However, we may ask, what counts as having any of this? Women who have had mastectomies, vulvectomies, hysterectomies, and other surgical operations removing body parts can still claim to be female and self-declared lesbians. Likewise, persons who for whatever reason were born without any number of these parts may claim identities as women and sometimes as lesbians. Consider, for example, an individual born with testicular feminization, with an XY chromosomal constitution, undescended testicles, a short-ended vagina, a clitoris, labia minora and labia majora, who has been raised as a female only to discover at puberty, with the absence of menses, that "she" is a genetic male. "She" may continue to think of herself as female, feel comfortable with this, and if "she" experiences deep erotic desires for other females rather than males, "she" may choose to call herself "lesbian."

The defining mark of "female" in most instances is not the presence or absence of certain female body parts but the absence of phallic genitalia or their genetic correlates, a fixation confirmed by our culture's concern about the "overly enlarged clitoris," surgically corrected at birth to its proper life dimensions, and by chromosomal tests for female athletes. But how much is too much? If a body exists with a "penoclitoris" but is incapable of producing sperm, what have we here? If a body has a smaller clitoris and the capacity of producing sperm, what have we here? If a lesbian friend is given a sex reassignment after a chromosome test, what have we here? My fear is that we may too quickly subscribe to a very rigid cultural binarism by insisting that bodies fit consistently and permanently into two exclusive and exhaustive sex types, using the same genetic-gonadal-anatomical master norms of the dominant culture. Is it always the case that having nothing short of a female body is what is required before one can feel like a woman? become a woman? know that one is woman-to-woman? before one can "body lesbian"?

To further complicate the issue, lesbians who fall for men sometimes claim that they do not feel as though they are any different from their former selves. In spite of community responses to their purported "backsliding," they insist on claiming a lesbian identity, just as Jan Clausen has identified herself as "the dyke sleeping with a man."[8] In this case the experienced continuity of self-identity survives, while the naming of difference is lost. Others may be inclined to describe these phenomena as bi-phobia, acute denial, unusual sex fantasy, or just plain confusion, guilt, and cowardice. The pregnant man-loving lesbian, who claims to be a lesbian, who happens to be in love with a man, who, as luck would have it happens to be a "male lesbian" (a "sperm-bearing lesbian," in this case), has created a miracle for some lesbian couples: a positive pregnancy! Not all lesbians desire this. Is there not something amiss in this picture?

Lesbian Identity as Bodily Inspection: A Question of Evidence

> *What exactly does "membership" in the queer community entail? Who makes up the rules and decides who belongs and who doesn't?* —ROBYN OCHES, 1990

> *A National Lesbian Purity Board is called for in this time of wavering allegiance to the cunt. Laminated identity cards with small, colorful photographs could easily fit into one's wallet. And random vaginal smears would be helpful in culling impostors from the ranks.*
> —MARY WINGS, 1990

> *At first women simply undressed for "visual inspection," or what the press called "nude parades," in front of a panel of gynecologists. In 1968, the International Olympic Committee (IOC) adopted a chromosome measure. . . . It's called the buccal smear, and it has nothing to do with the way a woman looks, feels or was raised. Instead, it's based upon the sex chromosome pattern found in cells scraped from inside her cheek.*
> —ALISON CARLSON, 1991

It would seem that the dilemma posed by the "male lesbian" could be resolved in most cases by bodily inspection. Sex identity is understood to have clear biological criteria, measurable and countable in kind and number. Sex chromosomes, hormonal profiles, genitals, gonads, and secondary sex characteristics are traits often used, in various combinations and with different weights, to determine the male or female sex status of a given body. Since lesbians are females, the special case of the "male lesbian" can be quickly closed. However, I will explore an incident that confounds the simplicity of this procedure.

I have heard a story about a lesbian who was an active member in a metropolitan lesbian community. She defined herself as a lesbian separatist and in the late 1970s was active in a community coffeehouse that was a social gathering place for lesbians. She lived in a lesbian collective, where one day the awful truth was discovered. She had male genitalia and had over the years been "passing" as a lesbian. The community response was swift and definitive: reject, abject, exclude. Friends who had known "her" as a lesbian turned against "him." The coffeehouse was no longer a welcome space for "him."

Why did this discovery make such a difference? In oppressed communities there is obviously a fear of intruders, spies, and government agents, but in a lesbian community these will most likely be women passing as lesbians rather than "male lesbians." From all that was known, this individual was not a spy (unless considered so by definition). Understandably, male entry into lesbian or woman-only spaces was at the time experienced as intrusive. However, this individual felt like a woman, was attracted to women, was at home in lesbian separatist spaces and politics, was reliable and trustworthy in those relationships, and had for years self-identified as a lesbian though outwardly celibate and body-shy. The community test had little to do with how "she" felt, how "she" was raised, or how "she" appeared in public. Was anatomy a justifiable reason for the community's response? Would surgical reconstruction of the body to the anatomically correct requirements of membership have resolved this problem? Or would the knife always fail to go deep enough to cut out the traces of difference disqualifying "him" from community membership? How does anyone successfully "pass" as a lesbian?

In both the frameworks explored so far—lesbian identity based on normative positioning and lesbian identity based on bodily inspection—the "male lesbian" emerges as a figure oddly out of place. This person claims to be "lesbian" but seems to be male in somatic appearance and heterosexual in his preference for women. The challenge of the "male lesbian" reflects back onto the practices we commonly use to attribute sex and gender categories to the body, raising some new possibilities for undoing how we have done such things.

Lesbian Identity as Doing Sex and Gender

In attribution theories about gender and sexual identity there are two starting points of reference: self-to-other and other-to-self. In the first the attribution of gender or sex identity is ascribed to the self by the self and presented to others; in the second it is ascribed by others to the self and presented to the self by these others. I will label the first "self-intending attribution" and the second "other-extending attribution." It is usually the case that self-intending and other-extending attributions are the same, as when the self sees itself as female (sex identity) as do others or sees itself as a woman (social sex identity) as do others. For the individual the consolidation of gender and sex identity as a meaningful aspect of self is an achievement that requires this mutually reinforcing and consistent interaction between self and others. However, when self-intending attributions and other-extending attributions contradict one another, the criteria for making such attributions come into question as does their application to a specific individual. The case of a "male lesbian" claiming to be "a woman trapped in a male body" presents an intriguing example of this. Here the inner sense of self may be regarded as a deeper "figuration of the body" that rests uneasily in its externalized somatic form. In this case self-intending and other-extending attributions of the same body may contradict one another. The table below presents a grid that is helpful in understanding the different kinds of sex and gender attributions and their relationships to one another.

Identity Category	Oppositional Categories	
Sex[a]	Female	Male
Gender[b]	Feminine	Masculine
Socioerotic[c] (heterosexual)	Male	Female

[a]Sex Identity is considered a physical category where bodies are sorted into clearly identifiable kinds, female and male, on the basis of biological criteria.

[b]Gender Identity is a behavioral and psychological category in which individuals are considered to fit or misfit expected behaviors, functions, and personal attributes associated with one sex or the other, as in femininity and masculinity.

[c]Socioerotic Identity is a behavioral and psychological category in which individuals are differentiated from one another on the basis of erotic desire for and/or sexual acts with the same or "opposite" sex. This is also referred to as sexual preference or sexual orientation identity.

Several comments need to made about this sex/gender grid.[9] It maps the relationships and assumptions most commonly operative in the everyday world: that there are two kinds of people (male and female), that males are masculine and females feminine, and that everyone is heterosexual. Commonly held ontological beliefs about the body assume that these identities represent naturally determined facts about the body and the self. According to this "naturalist perspective," this order of things is nature. Where there are misfits, these are considered "mistakes of nature" or "sicknesses of soul."

There is another interpretation of the grid. Some social construction-ists argue that all three of these binary categories are imposed on the con-tinuum of human natures, forcefully dividing bodies into mutually exclu-sive and exhaustive types, ignoring the significance of "misfits" and press-ing a relationship of entailment between these categorical levels. From a naturalist perspective, "maleness" grounds "masculinity" which grounds "female" as object choice, which implies a "heterosexual orientation"—reflecting a seeming logical and maturational order in the body's nature. In contrast, some social constructionists argue that establishing such "lin-ear" identities is an achievement of many discursive practices and policing mechanisms that invest in the body and inspire a desire in the subject to belong unambiguously to one social sex category or the other. The grid does not reflect nature; it reflects personal and social formations of sex, gender, and sexuality as meanings and identities made out of nature.

There is one additional composite category that combines all three of these identities into an individual's "social sex." The "social sex category" is what it means "to be a man" or "to be a woman" in the fullest cultur-ally specific and culturally appropriate meaning of these categories—a gendered ideal. Popular belief assumes that membership in a social sex category is not completely confirmed by simple genital inspection: it requires and is further confirmed by evidence of appropriate gender and sexual orientation presentations. To be a real man in the fullest sense requires biological, psychological, social, and sexual evidence. Accord-ingly, gay men are stereotypically not seen as real men and lesbians are not seen as real women. While both are seen as less than human (i.e., less than a real man), not being a real man demotes one to "womanly status"; not being a real woman demotes one to nonexistence. The personages of the "heterosexual stud," "the reproductive breadwinner," "the pregnable wife," "the feminine faggot," and the nonexistence of lesbians are deriv-atives of these representational strategies.

John Stoltenberg defines "male sexual identity" as "the conviction, held by most people born with penises, that they are male and not female, that they belong to the male sex." He also notes

> In a society predicated on the notion that there are two "opposite" and "complementary" sexes, this idea not only makes sense, it becomes sense; the very idea of a male sexual identity produces sen-sation, produces the meaning of sensation, becomes the meaning of how one's body feels. . . . Most people born with a penis between

their legs grow up aspiring to feel and act unambiguously male, longing to belong to the sex that is male and daring not to belong to the sex that is not, and feeling this urgency for a visceral and constant verification of their male sexual identity—for a fleshy connection to manhood—as the driving force of their life. The drive does not originate in the anatomy. The sensations derive from the idea. The idea gives the feelings social meaning; the idea determines which sensations shall be sought.[10]

According to Stoltenberg, in sexual activity itself there is a correlation between doing a specific act in a specific way (what, with whom, and how) and one's self-ascribed socioerotic attribution: "for many people, for instance, the act of fucking makes their sexual identity feel more real than it does at other times, and they can predict from experience that this feeling of greater certainty will last for at least a while after each time they fuck."[11] The repetition of sex acts is used as a partial confirmation procedure—as significant evidence for assignment to appropriate sex, gender, socioerotic, and social sex categories. Sex acts in a sense "sex" the body. The intensification of sex in Western cultures has a lot to do with maintaining the stability of these categories in a modernist world.

Using the sex/gender grid and Stoltenberg's insights into the cultural construction of the "sexed body," we can understand how the commonplace construction of lesbian identity relies on the assumptions behind this grid: a "lesbian" is someone with a female body and someone who is consistently and erotically drawn to—or more regularly than other females engaged in—genital sex acts with other females. When such a person claims a lesbian identity, there is consistency between her self-intended attribution and other-extending identity attributions ascribed to her. By claiming or being claimed by such an identity, she becomes a special category of person, defined by her sex and her sex acts, whether potential or actualized. As Stoltenberg points out, confirmation of socioerotic identities rests on sex-specific sex acts or, I might add, on probable or desired sex-specific sex acts in the case of asexual lesbians. In this commonplace construction of lesbian identity, bodies come to occupy an historically preestablished category of existence. The "male lesbian" is not saying that occupants of this category should include nonlesbians, but that the category needs to be stretched—not by adding men, but by adding men who happen to be lesbians.

Male Lesbians: The Undoing of Sex and Gender

"Do we truly need a true sex?" This question, asked by Michel Foucault in his preface to the English edition of *Herculine Barbin: Being the Recently Discovered Memoirs of the Nineteenth-Century French Hermaphrodite*,[12] brings into focus two considerations: how do we construct a "true biological sex" for any body, and, once we understand how we do this, do we truly need to continue doing this to ourselves and others? In modernist Eurocentric cultures, baseline criteria for such attribution appear to be genitocentric. Kessler and McKenna describe the criteria as follows:

> There are two, and only two, genders (male and female); one's gender is invariant; genitals are the essential sign of gender; any exceptions to two genders are not taken seriously; there are no transfers from one gender to another except ceremonial ones; everyone must be classified as a member of one gender or another; the male/female dichotomy is a "natural" one; membership in one gender or another is "natural"[13]

This "natural attitude" toward the sex identity is for Kessler, McKenna, and Foucault a matter of cultural construction, achieved either through the transactions of symbolic interaction[14] or through the discursive practices of power that make "true sex" an important truth about the body.[15] In both approaches, sex and gender attribution are activities, something that we do to ourselves (self-intending attribution) or to others (other-extending attribution) within layer upon layer of institutional controls and accepted confirmation procedures. The challenge presented by the "male lesbian" is whether or not we can undo how this is done. To have a sex, gender, or sexual identity requires self-presentation and displays of behavior that are interpreted, read, and finally judged as evidence for belonging to one social sex category or the other, using the grid of identities and linear entailment I have already discussed. Do we truly need to go on doing sex and gender as we have done it in the past?

The "male lesbian" usually lives in a body originally assigned at birth to the male sex category. He was expected to take on a masculine gender identity and to maintain an active heterosexual practice, all evidence of his membership in and allegiance to the social sex category of manhood. Undoing this involves two generic and any number of specific transsexing strategies. The two generic strategies ask us first, to reconsider the criteria we use to assign "sex identity" (to prioritize criteria in a different manner, to overlook certain characteristics and valorize others, or to replace our fixation on a select set of "essentialized" biological criteria) and second, to become active "readers of the body," implementing the new criteria into our everyday life transactions. For the male lesbian, specific strategies designed to realign self-intending sex attribution with other-extending attributions can be marshaled in the following ways:

1. Change the physical structure of the body to fit the genital or morphological criteria for "female"; ask that others overlook the man-made reconstructions of these genitalia and the chromosomal traces and internal organization left unaltered in your body (a postoperative transsexual strategy).
2. Valorize the feeling of inner certainty of being a woman trapped in a male body; ask that others look beyond the somatic form of your body and look for signs of this "inner figuration" of your body's sex or its reconstitution in deep gender identity (a transgendering strategy).
3. Request a reading of your body that decenters genital and gonadal anatomy as the essential criterion for sex identity; ask that others "overlook" these indicators in attributing sex identity to you (a genital de-essentializing strategy).
4. Engage in "genderfuck," taking seriously the centrality of meaning-in-sex-acts as sufficient criterion for sex category membership and construct sex scenes in which your sex acts take on the meaning of acts performed by the "opposite sex"; ask that others agree to these readings and to this criterion for sex category membership (a special "genderfuck" strategy).

All of these strategies allow the body to enter a conversation with others, with a request for a particular reading of the body, an acceptance into a particular group, and a respect for the subject's desire to name "her" own sex identity. Rejection of this would simply mean that the wayward "male lesbian" must search until "she" finds a community of "lesbians" ready to embrace her membership and life energies as a lesbian. Note that I have not questioned the authenticity of "her" sexual desire for other females. "She" claims to be "monosexual" (rather than bisexual) and a "lesbian." What is at stake here is whether, through negotiation of behav-

iors, interpretations, expectations, meanings, and agreed-upon readings of
the body, a genetic male, usually penis-bearing and sperm-producing, can
find a community of lesbians who would welcome "her" as a "lesbian"
into their community. Is anything more required? As Sarah Hoagland has
suggested, the "essentialism" that we may wish to give to "lesbianism" is
a product of community will, not a metaphysic threatening to pound the
daylights out of our mistakes."I think of lesbian community as a ground
of lesbian being, a ground of possibility, a context in which we perceive
each other essentially as lesbians, a context in which we create lesbian
meaning. This context exists, not because it has walls, but because we
focus on each other as lesbians."[16]

If "essentializing" what it is to be "lesbian" is enacted by the way we
focus on each other as lesbians in any particular community—by a consensus of community will and vision—then the "male lesbian" can be
seen as requesting a certain kind of selective focus from a particular community. Strategy 1 asks that we "essentialize" external genital and primary sex characteristics (regardless of origin) as criteria of membership
and acceptance. Strategies 2 and 3 ask that we overlook the body as we
habitually read it and attend to other evidence of sex identity. In these two
readings the penis is not disposed of, but its significance is deposed: it is no
longer the phallus. It remains an appendage, useful perhaps, interesting
perhaps, a location of pleasure like the clitoris, but a perforate clitoris with
some optional functions. As Kessler and McKenna have suggested: "Some
people, at some points in their lives, might wish to be identified as sperm
or egg-cell carriers. Except for those times, here need be no differentiation
among people on any of the dichotomies which gender implies."[17]

Strategy 4, which challenges our "natural attitudes" toward sex identity even more, suggests the possibility of temporary or permanent travel
or transformation into the body of the "opposite sex" without surgery or
cosmetic reconstruction. I realize that I am using the word "genderfuck"
in a special way, since most practitioners of genderfuck are not so much
interested in "passing" or "becoming" the opposite sex as much as tam-
pering with the codes of sex identity by mixing male and female, masculine and feminine, man and woman signifiers on a specific body. I am
using the term "genderfuck" to indicate a means of passage from one sex
to the other through the meanings given to sex-specific sex acts. Within
this special framework of "genderfuck," a male can have sex "as a female"
with another female (perhaps genetic), where "having sex as a female"
might be defined as a style of erotic encounter that decenters attention

from the penis and its essentially definitive acts of intercourse. Sex acts, mutually interpreted as "female" sex acts, would establish membership for both bodies in the same sex category. In and through such sex performances, both subjects come to enjoy the sexually expressed "femaleness" of both bodies. "Genderfuck" for females can involve a female fucking another body "as a man" and in those acts claiming identity in the male sex category. When appropriated in lesbian contexts, "genderfuck" would allow two genetic females in a relationship to be different sexes. It would also allow heterosexual women to enjoy "heterosexing" with another woman or heterosexuals to have "queer sex." Sex identity becomes transitive, liminal, and momentary—a veritable riot against *un sexe véritable.*

Joan Nestle explores this unspeakable border-crossing: "I feel I am being kind to myself as I caress the false cock. No need to hide the word any more. No need to hide my desires. Let me be butch for you; I have been a femme for so long. l know what your body is calling for."[18] Nestle's declaration of desire can be variously interpreted—as a transgendering moment in lesbian sex, as a pangendering exploration of lesbian eroticism, as role occupation in one of many erotic scripts for lesbian sex, as just another way to be a lesbian in the thrill of unspeakable passion, or as a way to do something else with your hands. However, many lesbians are loath to interpret this as "wanting to be or to be with a man." However, this forecloses transsexuality. Where in lesbian erotics is there a space for female transsexual desire, however temporary or continuous, however "metaphysicalized" by roles and role-playing or by the chimerical masking of "butch" and "femme"? Why is there such hesitation to open up the possibility of a "lesbian male" trapped in a genetic female body? I am not arguing that all lesbians are this or want this or that Nestle's statement implies this, but I am suggesting that lesbian communities may house a small minority of transsexuals just as one finds transsexuals in gay, bisexual, and heterosexual communities.

The existence of this transsexual minority in lesbian communities has been highly undertheorized, a situation that is complicated by transsexual males and females "passing" as lesbians. At the 1991 Michigan Womyn's Music Festival, the following commentary was made:

> There have been transsexuals on the land for many years, mostly undetected. Many are uncomfortable about revealing too much about themselves, fearful of encountering hostile reactions from participants. . . . Some women would exclude transsexuals on the

basis that they have not been socialized as women. Should we then exclude women who were raised as boys? How about men raised as girls? If we accept a person's sex at birth is immutable, should we allow female-to-male transsexuals at the festival on the basis that they are still "really" females, penises and all?[19]

Transsexuals as a sex minority in lesbian communities may desire a nonsurgical means of transsexing, in which their sex identity can be liberated from soma and respecified by sex-specific sex acts. Such an interpretation meets a great deal of opposition in some lesbian communities. I suspect that the reluctance on the part of some lesbians to embrace preoperative female-to-male lesbian-identified transsexuals is not so much a function of sex-negative attitudes as a desire to defraud the stereotype of the mannish lesbian that has been so abusively used against lesbians and to define lesbianism as a political and sexual positionality in opposition to men or male dominance. Perhaps this politics of opposition could be separated from the desire to engage in the erotics of "opposite sexing," a code of erotic scripts that is itself a cultural construction and arbitrary division of possible erotic terrains.

The challenge of the four transsexing strategies suggests the possibility of reversing the assumptions of our "natural attitude" toward sex and gender categories. I propose the following fanciful reversal on the ethnographic observations of Kessler and McKenna:

> There are two, and only two, sexes (male and female); one's sex can be variant; genitals are not necessarily the essential sign of sex; any exceptions to two sexes are to be taken seriously; there are transfers from one sex to another; not everyone must be classified as a member of one sex or another; the male/female dichotomy is a constructed one; membership in one sex or another is a matter of "passing" and consensus in "reading" the body one way or the other.

All that remains in place in this new schema of body travel is the binarism of the original grid. When that is abandoned, we bring into view many genders and many sexes—a thickness of contiguous diversity and individual uniqueness that escapes easy categorical theorization and provides the play of multiple transfers. The assumption of binarism and belief in the unalterable ontology of one's sex and gender identities become suspect. However, the hold of this binarism and its fix on identity persists. Perhaps the desire to keep this binarism intensifies a desire to transgress constructed barriers, an erotic risk of transcategorical pleasure, rather than the risk of nonidentity in an in/different world of many genders and many sexes. Perhaps some bodies and not others really are set by this binarism at a very early age. Regardless of individual variation, the politics of this culturally specific binarism are best captured by Kate Bornstein, a self-identified lesbian transsexual:

> Why is there gender? Why do we insist that there's this? The only thing it comes down to is that it gives roughly half the people the chance to be oppressive to roughly the other half. That's the only reason that I can see that we keep it in place. There's always an "other" for half the people to oppress. And if it were all fluid, if it were kind of rainbowy kinds of genders, who could oppress whom? Everybody would be an "other."[20]

The Return of the Body

Women only.

Lesbians only.

Women-born women only.

Genetic female dykes only.

No boys over the age of twelve.

These signs that hang around the edges of what precious little lesbian space there is in the world suggest that lesbians not only would like some time to be alone together in social public spaces but that some lesbians are also suspicious of males trying to invade community-defined lesbian-only space. However, the "male lesbian" presents an interesting dilemma for community standards, especially where the rights of a subject to name "her" sex seem parallel to the rights of a subject to name "her" sexuality. The "male lesbian" who feels like a woman stuck in a male body may attempt to align "her" external male body by altering the body's somatic form, by altering its cosmetic appearance, or by requesting a different read of the body's sex. All of these strategies described earlier attempt to do away with the contradiction between a self-ascribed sex identity and other-extending sex attribution by maintaining the original entailments of the sex/gender grid. To this extent these strategies oddly conserve and reinforce linear constructions of sex and gender identities, but they are also strategies that can be used to argue male admittance into lesbian community.

Perhaps this is seen as the path of least resistance for the "male lesbian." One might ask why "woman" and "lesbian" are the chosen arenas of contestation, rather than the culturally constructed world of "hetero-masculinized maleness." For some men feelings of identity kinship with lesbians don't require a sex reassignment as much as a space for different ways of being a man. It follows that such men need not hastily reverse the sex binarism "if not man, then woman" because of deeply felt disloyalty to masculine codes of social sex category membership. However, it may be easier to contest the meaning of "lesbian" and "woman" than to contest the normative rules for heterosexual males. In other circumstances alleged "male lesbians" may suffer from body hatred and self-loathing that is better treated by release from sex binarism and the narrow confines of heteromasculinity than by the surgeon's knife. If there were not two sexes but many and in turn many genders and sexualities, a number of different ways to inhabit the body could be engendered. A "male lesbian" could then see himself as multiply gendered and erotic. No longer needing to infuse the category "lesbian" with his maleness, he could become a "lesbian-identified-non-lesbian-hating male," who loves his own body and acknowledges his heterosexual privilege. However, challenging the norms of the heteromasculine world is perhaps more hazardous than gutting out a space where a man can become a lesbian. Similarly, attempts to challenge the categorical binarism of sex/gender identities seem to meet an unmovable material resistance to change. The "male lesbian" is endangered in both straight and lesbian worlds: "she" doesn't want to be a man, "she" finds it difficult to be a lesbian, and "she" desires women lovers, preferably lesbians, who may not want "her." It's difficult to find a support group with others of "her" own kind.

The paradox of the "male lesbian" reveals some insights into how sex identity attributions are customarily established for all of us in our culture. Membership in social sex categories is determined through gender performance and sex acts, through meanings imposed on the body and its anatomical functions, through the uptake of community readings of the body's sex, and through the essentializing of genital anatomy as the overdetermined master text for "sexing" the body. The range of lived interpretations for the body is less determined by anatomy and more determined by the interpretations and prescriptions given to that anatomy. The perspectives of postoperative "lesbian transsexuals," transgendered "male lesbians," genitally deessentialized "male lesbians," and the transsexing practitioners of "genderfuck" suggest that:

1. sex categories themselves are less unified and stable than everyday thinking admits,
2. criteria for membership in sex categories can be contested,
3. sex identity may be experienced by some as transitive and liminal, or as genuinely dysphoric and discontinuous, and
4. "stability" in sex identity is an ongoing achievement dependent on particular social contexts and practices.

Postmodernism supplies a set of ontological commitments needed for a world in which the body appears to be malleable, protean, and constructed through and within discourse. Postmodernism makes the "male lesbian" a real possibility.

However, I remain stuck in a modernist closet. My mind is anxious with the question, how can a male really be a lesbian? Is there any way to reconcile my resistance with postmodernism and its marvelous insights into the constructedness of the body and the playful potentials of the flesh? Has the body all but disappeared in the wash of multivalences and multivocalities? One of the consequences of this traveling flesh as it bends in and out of categories is that there may be no such thing as lesbians. If men can become lesbians, if women who sleep with men can still be lesbians, if anybody can visit lesbian positionality or transsex it with anybody else, then what would such a category really name? Postmodernism not only makes the "male lesbian" possible; it may in addition make lesbianism, at least as we have known it, impossible. The theory seems a bit pitiful.

Perhaps we should pursue the male lesbian as "she" leaves the charmed circle of her lesbian community. It is clear that a "male lesbian" best thrives in "her" charmed circle of postmodernist lesbian friends. However, entry into the charmed circle also implies the possibility of exit into an external world that overshadows the dear delights of the circle's warmth. When our "male lesbian" leaves this circle, outsiders will most likely not read his body in the same way or take kindly to his identity claim. In that world, he will be seen as male by assumptions regarding his genitalia if nothing else and will be granted the full registers of meaning, privilege, history, and expectation that go with that.

What about the "male lesbian" who successfully passes in the straight world as a "female"? Isn't it the case that successful passing in that world would "make up" the sex of "her" body ? The difference between the response of the charmed circle in the lesbian community and the straight world is that the request made in the postmodernist lesbian circle is to change the criteria by which the body's sex is determined, to rename the sex of the body so that the body is seen, read, experienced, and respected as the "sex" desired by the authorizing subject. This is an ontological shift into the "opposite" sex category, not a masquerade of belonging to it. The conventional world may be fooled by the artifice of a passing "female" but also violent in its discovery of the "truth"—"you can get killed for this sort of thing." This is because the straight world is overly invested in a naturalist ontology supporting sex binarism and the strict linear entailments of the sex/gender grid: a man with a vagina and a woman with a penis do not (and shall not) exist. "Passing" implies pretense and lying, not a new ontological reading of the body's sex. Postmodernism with its notion of the body as an invention of discursivity makes plausible the "transsexualizing" of the body, a possibility dependent on the adoption of new criteria and alternative readings of the body's sex. In this context the subject's desire "to sex" a body of one's own becomes a defensible right. However, when our "male lesbian" fails to maintain a consistent female identity at all times, this is not a failure in postmodernist imagination but an indication of the individual's inability to control overdetermined hegemonic readings from the outside world forced on the body. When these readings numerically outnumber the less frequent "lesbian" attributions in the charmed circle, this external world definitively "sexes" his body. From this perspective conferring a "sex" on the body is not only about meaning but also about access to gendered asymmetries of power. These privileges and points of access granted to male bodies and not to female bodies may be rejected or "disowned" later in life or variously distributed among males early in life, but they cannot be denied or discounted in the life experiences that generally mark male somatic existence. Flesh so named makes difference.

I refer to this "maleness" or "femaleness" as *the historical gravity* of the sexed body. It is not clear to me that the historical gravity of the male body can be completely negated in the charmed circle where the male lesbian is embraced as a legitimate member of a lesbian group qua lesbian. It is clear, however, that the hegemonically more numerous and controlling contexts that "sex" our bodies by genitocentric criteria serve the interests of heterosexual and male domination. The "male lesbian" is a strikingly odd figure in this scene, challenging the naturalness of "maleness" and "heterosexuality" by the bizarreness of his self-ascribed sex and gender attributions. From this perspective, the "male lesbian" is perhaps more of an impostor to the heterosexual world than she seems to in some lesbian communities.

What I am suggesting is that the stubborn return of the body's sex, its "maleness" in this case, is nothing more than a hegemonically overdetermined set of readings made apparently "continuous" and "natural" by their seriality, redundancy, and consistency that confer "a sex" on the body without regard to the will or authorship of the subject. These meanings are perhaps metaphysically and historically contingent, utterly constructed and arbitrary, but encumbering. What agency the subject has to move in, around, and against these readings in this culture is a question for exploration and struggle. What agency we have in this culture to move beyond these assigned categories, to become "unstuck" from our constructed bodies, to travel transgendering and transsexing journeys of relocation, or to deconstruct sex binarism altogether are questions left uncomfortably unanswered in my thoughts. Perhaps all is "drag" made up of cells, soma, and style marked redundantly in memory and public repetition.

In/Conclusion

My conclusions are tentative. Postmodernism is right in bringing into focus the contingency of sex identity imposed on and incorporated into the body's soma but wrong in supposing these to be lightweight and detachable. This body is not only a thing in the world, subject to physical gravity, but a thing that carries its own historical gravity, and this collected weight bears down on the "sexedness" of the body and the possibilities of experience. Postmodernism is right in revealing the "inventedness" of this body but wrong in supposing that this implies a protean self ambulating between "positionalities." The "male lesbian" is perhaps right in challenging the commonplace criteria of sex but unable to transcend straight realities. Failure to become a lesbian in all her fullness—dare I say "a real lesbian"—is not a failure of postmodernist tools but a lacuna in postmodernist ontology and a failure to recognize the "male lesbian's" real powerlessness against the imposition of other-extending attributions that "sex" the flesh. In this failure is a discovery of the historically located body—a discovery of the historical gravity of a culturally constructed "sexed" body. Against the intellectual anorexia of postmodernism, this body with its biology and history stubbornly returns with a weight that defies the transcendental promises of postmodernist fantasy and its idealist mechanism. We are more firmly called on to "own" what is ours, where we sit, breathe, and theorize in the Cartesianized circles of postmodernist academia as we attempt to think and travel beyond the binary divisions of humankind.

5   **FemFire: A Theory in Drag**

In much of 1970s radical feminist analysis, there was nothing more politically abhorrent than the patriarchal construction of femininity. According to Mary Daly, femininity is a mutant fembird, the evil simulacrum of patriarchal embodiment. Encased in paint, clipped at her wings, and lost in her own self-absorption, she cannot fly away.[1] My own body owes much to radical feminism: as a teenager I slept on my forehead with brush-rollers covering my scalp; I bouffed, ratted, and sprayed my hair into wind-resistant porcelain; I endured electrolysis, shaved, and plucked; I waited for the school bus bare-legged under heavy jackets, shifting my weight from side to side in January, Missouri, high school; I toned over my sock-line and quite willingly starved, high-lighted, and softened. I fixated on body flaws and melted my self-worth into male approval. I suffered in a political vacuum without words.

As a young woman I guarded my pubescent crotch and reputation, understanding vaguely their connection. I married rather early and learned to wear a dirndl, cook sauerbraten, and love Bartok, European coffee, and intercourse. I soundly lost my virginity and eventually came into my body. He and I fell in love with the same woman. It was the late 1970s. The Vietnam war was over. At that time I took my distance from men, closed the door, forgot their games and cues, their need for my femininity. Edna said, "no men beyond the first floor"—our collective Big Birtha's Heartbreak House became a Powderhorn refuge for separatists looking for home. We fought hard for ourselves and our communities. As Ti-Grace said, sisterhood was powerful: it killed us!

This is an essay about femininity and two waves of feminism. It is in part historical, biographical, and imaginary, just as the sign of femininity ghosts its way in and out of my life. It is in part personal and in part political. It is about body pleasure and power, danger and ecstasy, butch and

fem, excess and desire: about the spirit of containment that always hates
and loves the excess clipped from the picture to make the scene neat and
regular. This is an essay about the reclamation of fem power in lesbian
erotics. It is about my body and hers.

Radical Feminists Attack Femininity

In the 1970s with the emergence of radical feminism, the slogan "the personal is political" charged an enormous wave of political consciousness,
and for good reason, since many Movement Women, wives, and girl-
friends were at last rebelling against male management. In this second
wave of feminism, the arena of personal experience, largely articulated by
white and middle-class women, was more closely scrutinized for imbal-
ances and abuses of power between the sexes. Gender and its masculine
and feminine embodiments became a focus of attention: what was horri-
ble and objectionable about male behavior and attitudes became a function of masculine power and privilege, and what was harmful and debili-
tating about women's complicity was relocated in our socialized femininity. While we as feminists gave ourselves a chance to unlearn this, men
were sometimes thrown back into a biological end zone. Under the sign
of the times, we set about rebuilding the social categories and institutions
of gender. For some women this resulted in a very real construction of
androgynized bodies, and for others it inspired a quest for mutuality,
equality, and balance in separatist communities or liberated coupledom.
In this new ungendering of free space, fems were seldom welcome, and
butches from the fifties were considered male-identified and out of order.

Four Anti-Fem Premises

A period of fem-bashing emerged from several prescriptive premises as
the sex/gender distinction operated everywhere.

1. *Femininity is a gender category of negative excess, but the female
sex can be separated from this and redeemed from the disturbance of a
socially fabricated femininity.* Many voices made this claim:

> In our culture, not one part of a woman's body is left untouched,
> unaltered. No feature or extremity is spared the art, or pain, of
> improvement. Hair is dyed, lacquered, straightened, permanented;
> eyebrows are plucked, penciled, dyed; eyes are lined, mascaraed,

shadowed; lashes are curled, or false—from head to toe, every feature of a woman's face, every section of her body, is subject to modification, alteration. This alteration is an ongoing, repetitive process. It is vital to the economy, the major substance of male-female role differentiation, the most immediate physical and psychological reality of being a woman. From the age of 11 to 12 until she dies, a woman will spend a large part of her time, money, and energy on binding, plucking, painting, and deodorizing herself (Dworkin).[2]

In exchange for our psychic servicing and for performing society's non-profitmaking functions, the man confers on us just one thing: the slave status which makes us legitimate in the eyes of the society in which we live. This is called "femininity" or "being a real woman" in our cultural lingo. We are authentic, legitimate, real to the extent that we are the property of some man whose name we bear (Radicalesbians)."[3]

Pain is an essential part of the grooming process, and that is not accidental. . . . *The tolerance of pain and the romanticization of that tolerance begins here,* in preadolescence, in socialization, and serves to prepare women for lives of childbearing, self-abnegation, and husband-pleasing (Dworkin).[4]

The "painted bird" functions in the anti-process of double-crossing her sisters, polluting them with poisonous paint (Daley).[5]

2. *The fem in femininity is a sign, a mark, a labor done to the body, a stylization of the flesh disciplining women into oppression.*

Female subjectivity is constituted in any significant measure in and through the disciplinary practices that construct the feminine body. The socialization and training that constitute the feminine as a style of flesh also inscribe female subjectivity, rendering this subject frequently powerless against an onslaught of psychological, physical, and sexual harm.[6] The perfect feminine body has a smooth and hairless texture, in which the inner is the outer, a mask holding hidden labors from the consumer's eye and producing a woman's power of seduction. To be wanted for your body is the fem's prize. This femininity is often infantilized and forever under construction, producing the illusion of an ageless Platonic wonder, preserved in antiwrinkle treatments, acid face peels, silicone injections, cosmetic liposuctions, hair dyes, surgical face lifts, and chin tucks. In the earlier phase parasitic eating disorders, endangered self-esteem, and stairmaster reveries dissolve in the deep psychic distress of feminine subjectivity. Hers is a paranoid subjectivity eminently fearing her replacement by a younger woman. She is sworn to discipline her body into an orderly arrangement of parts, pieces, and smiles. Losing this form is the inner terror of femininity. "The fact is, from this moment on beautiful skin is simply a matter of Discipline . . . rewarding you with skin that is sleek. . . . Skin that has to be disciplined. There are no miracles. There is only Discipline."[7]

3. *The fem is a pawn in male spermatic race wars.*

Traditional representations of femininity are "normed" by the white, Caucasian body. The cult of true womanhood emerged in America when African-American women were kept as breeders, slaves, and properties for sexual violence and rape, spawning from gentle white men the "beautiful young quadroons and octaroons, who became increasingly (and were deliberately bred to become) indistinguishable from white women."[8] Mixing white with black, they became the highly prized slave mistress— a border body between wife and livestock, culture and nature. Border children emerged from the North, South, East, and West, born in the descent of mixed blood and sometimes in the violence of a white rape against a brown mother's body. White femininity required the racist otherness of color, the "de-formities" of the Hottentot Venus, whose dead genitals were encased in a Parisian museum as proof of significant female differences. White femininity is a social skin. Because only white women are truly allowed to wear this social skin, whiteness hides from view the stain of female lust and animality projected onto female bodies of color. "The race/gender nexus fostered a situation whereby white men could then differentiate between the sexualized woman-as-body who is dominated and 'screwed' and the asexual woman-as-pure-spirit."[9]

4. *The fem is a commodified fetishism.*

To become the perfect fem requires considerable expense, time, and luck. Though femininity is a production, a matter of discipline, and a labor of love and terror, it is re/presented without this memory or fear. It appears as simply there, as if from nature, *the nature of woman*, alienated from the social relations and discursive practices that produced her cultural form. She is a phallicized commodity fetish, a specular body, that makes men hard and powerful, making them men. To maintain the simulacrum of "the real" and "the natural," she must absorb the flow of commodities promising improvement, maintenance, repair, and eternal reformation. Her entire soma is marketed piece by piece by hawkers hunting her desire. She is indeed "the painted bird" in the "anti-process of double-crossing her sisters, polluting them with poisonous paint."[10]

Given this analysis from the 1970s, what radical feminist would dare to become a fem—an artificial creature of dubious origin? What kind of feminist lesbian could possibly presume this impostor's pose? What radical woman could face herself in such a get up? in such a masquerade? in such a victimhood? I hear a voice inside of me. In this unconscious mass of ideological skin that holds me in place, in a dangerous place, "she" comes to me, without invitation, to take advantage of my body for her existence and her sex. She begs me to drag this into theory. I find her wanting the opposite in me. How can I con[this]text?

FemFire

I sat there. My legs crossed at the knee, slightly rocking the back cusp of one knee against the other. My blouse is low-cut, inviting and drawing the gaze across my painted face into the line that runs down, hardening my nipples and curling its way further down into the wetness that pulses lightly with my leg swinging against my thigh. This "passive" body grants me inward retreat, through my porous flesh and skin, open and waiting, wanting to be touched, wanting to be taken down by your strong and direct command. This body is naked and waiting, open to the contingencies of dangerous surrender, in a compliance that is soft and sweet, in contrast to your hard moves, taking control of me, taking me, taking off the feminine surface to find my Fem complying and receptive, a generous, gentle giving that melts your butch fire as you come over me/under me wet with pumping heart as I control your pleasure. My passivity is my power.

Dangerous Fems. In itself there is nothing wrong with this form of physical being, filled with the longing to receive a touch, a glance, in fully pleasured skin. This is my body proudly open to public spaces—exposing legs, buttocks, upper breasts, and the long languid energies of my soft body flow—swish, turn, pivot, following your lead—filling up the territories of my body where butch bodies dare not go in their own flesh.

You appear in your turtleneck, covered, unadorned, ready to move, strong and in control, in your "practical" clothes, your "neutral" cut, and your hard edge. My space is smaller compared to yours. But, come here! Look at me! I appear with lips painted red, engorged ruby lips. I strut with color, creams, and scents swirling my body and pulling you into my orbit, cutting the talk with the lure of my sex, hot, baby, hot for you. You know what to do, but I control you with my want, my sex, my body thrilling you and me. My hot steamy butch, come here, come home, come over, come to me. You know my "girl glow" is hard for your butch love.

We Fems have been ridiculed for putting on too much makeup, for removing, fixing, and coloring hair, for curling lashes and lining our lids, for painting our skin and nails, for creaming, cleansing, softening, and reworking our faces, stomachs, and buttocks. We eat too little. Exercise too much. We have been ridiculed for showing too much and for the sexy sound of our hose swishing and our heels cutting the floor with sharp staccato steps. The sounds we make a r o u s e.

We have been ridiculed for allowing you to see the cleavage of our breasts; for wearing our clothes, both scant and tight, to draw you closer, so we can lean against you and close in on your intimacy and control. Why are you suspicious of our bodies, with surfaces shaved smooth and "lotioned" for the pleasure of your touch, my pleasure and yours? We are shape-shifters and body-artists of a craft not made for museums but for lookers. We are mortal skins, painted for pleasure, for now. Chameleons of pleasure.

We have been called unnatural pawns in a male game of power-rape, narcissists shaping our bodies for the ignominious events of back alleys, back seats, one night stands or long journeys into monotonous monogamy and slavish wifery. We have been blamed for other women not feeling good about their bodies, and we have been told we hate our bodies as well. Our preoccupation with the body is seen as a sign of captivity and incarceration, a symptom of immanence and compliance, an undesirable way to flesh "out" the body. A hollow waste of a double-crossing fembird.

That is one way to harm a Fem. The system does it. Men have done it. Feminists also. It has been thought that we cannot stand up against this, but there is a resilience in this-my-flesh as it pushes into the light of day, defiant in a world of danger, because this body is a work of art and pleasure wanting your gaze and turning your head. I want this to arouse your desire through glancing fantasies and harmless plays of sensuality on the loose.

A Fem is an endangered being, abused by the system of gender oppression, misogyny, and fem-bashing, but in her stride she is a body that takes a chance, puts it out there, unashamedly exposing, weaving in and out of the impulses of strangerdesire and strangerlooking. She is a body not afraid to trust, even you. My FemFire will let you touch, make it safe, even run the risk of enduring your sudden panic and uncertain disdain. Why do you insist on seeing me as a dupe, a pathetic victim of cultural manipulation? Woman, let me fix your tie!

Foolish Fems, they say: cover up and stay out of sight—use fear or shame or common sense to stop this non/sense—whatever works, stay out of the line of vision and fire. Yet this defiant Fem is a body playful and proud of itself—dancing and revealing. Passivity is a tease, an active reception, a receiving activity. Passivity is a plenitude not a lack. Come here, again. Let me fix it. Look at me! Please me!

Fem is the street poet of sensual grace and beauty, not a mask or masquerade, but a "face put on" the body for the sake of flesh, luring us to take joy in multiple pleasures, dense intensities, and small places of feminine excess. The horror/whore of the Fem is that she trusts in the open in a world that might kill her soul and rape her body. A Fem lives on the edge.

In itself, my Fem immanence requires no transcendence, but like any art form, Fem is a constant labor, of making artful and apparent what I put there. Art-official, I am there to be seen and enjoyed as I take pleasure in the erotic connection of you watching and wanting. The gaze is not unidirectional, seeing how it is to-be-looked-at. Yes, I am asking!

"Fem passivity" is my way to inhabit all the inner and outer spaces of my body, to make beauty where the flesh stands lonely, to snare your heart as I wrap my legs around your torso, coaxing you to surrender to my feminine exuberance. I want to hold you down to this euphoric con-tradiction—to the Fem you can really love in a sexual and emotional sur-render of all your power. I'll ride you if you let me. My passivity is what is most feared . . .

FemFire, girl glow, butch baby.

A Philosopher Confesses

How can I not (be) like FemFire? The question seems ambiguous and filled with pleasure and danger. The radical wave that rescued my body in the 1970s called for the destruction of all gender categories. Transcenden-tal figures emerged then and still persist—the Lesbian Body of Wittig's utopias,[11] the Elemental women of Daly's spirited journeys,[12] the Willful Virgin of Frye's imagination,[13] the original women of Raymond's pas-sion,[14] and the Amazons of Atkinson's odysseys.[15] These figures of les-bian imagination, transcendental escape artists, one by one ran away from femininity's patriarchal skins. But FemFire is also a figure in my lesbian imagination, able to place the conventional signifiers of femininity on her skin without harm, mean consequence, or violent abuse. Is FemFire my double-crosser? Is her style an arbitrary device? Why does she haunt me? What tracking of lesbian desire calls out for a new confession to sex.

FemFire, I left you.

I stopped all of it. I let my body "return to nature." I took off all the paint and scents. I unadorned my body of feminine signs. I took off my hose, garters, brassieres. I liberated my body from the pain of all artificial encumbrance. I learned a new language of the body. I threw out my dresses, skirts, heels, chokers, and T-straps. I found painter pants, hiking boots and Birkenstocks, second-hand flannels, and black watches. I stopped the process of my prior socialization.

I let go. I was free to walk with stride and take up space. I was released from years of discipline. I named this my freedom.

She /you left . . . My imagination changed. My desires changed. My identity changed. My body changed.

I became a willful, wild, and undomesticated woman seeking a world outside of the institution of female heterosexuality and compulsory femininity. A refusal "actively, perversely, and obstinately" created in my body and its daily disciplines.[16] Frye's willful virgin, a woman unto her own.

According to Frye, such "virgins do not attire and decorate themselves in the gear which in their cultures signal female compliance with male-defined femininity and which would form their bodies to such compliance. They do not make themselves 'attractive' in the conventional feminine modes of their cultures."[17]

Living according to this, these were years of sweet transgression in a text of resistance.

Then you returned. My lips and skin remembered a deep and rushing hunger. The motions came easily. I unbuttoned her, unzipped her, undid her, lifted her, released her, unsnapped her, setting her free . . . she demanded this much of me and I asked back—loving the lace and leather skins and scents she brought thick and wanting into my own flesh and desire. I was on the other side of the great hetero divide. She was real. I was liquid frenzy.

Or is this the same house of fictitious anatomies?

I am confused and oh-so pleasured in the mirrors of lesbian transgression—desiring and identifying in the dizzy worlds of secret ceremony and in the tender /hard spaces of lesbian sex.

How do I take up the struggle of political and sexual resistance in my body's enigma? This is not a problem of capitalist anomaly.

A Philosopher Professes

It can be a hazard for a philosopher to have changed one's mind in print, in order to get to a truth. It can be a hazard for a lesbian to have changed her identity in public, in order to get to an ecstasy. Where is the body's desire in philosophy?

The problem is that no one really owns the signs of femininity—heterosexual productions of femininity do not constitute *the* original, *the* real or *the* more authentic ontology. Heterosexuals are not the sole possessors of gender rituals and their erotic division. The territory is large enough for different inhabitants.

The problem is that femininity is abused in heteropatriarchal realities, read as a sign of *O*, the open, *lack*, the castrated, *hot*, the ready, *mamma*, the nurturer, the giver. *O, lack, hot mamma*—a mother-fucking that has killed many women.

The problem is that femininity is a social and sexual skin of vulnerability and diffuse eroticism—a social skin worn like a nylon's second nature—questioning a fetishized need for penile performativities, but still sometimes wanting something somewhere. Spreading and condensing pleasured surfaces, every cell becomes a cunt, a clit, a ruby lip. Commanding and wanting, femininity is an erotic aesthetic of sex—a possibility of pleasure, not the property of heterosexuals, not the property of rich whites, not even the property of females.

The problem is that there is both pleasure *and* danger in whatever gendered skins we assume—the fem is not always in pleasure; the fem is not always in danger. She negotiates her terrain whether in a female or male body, just as butches of either sex and transcendental lesbians balance the pleasures and dangers of their *different* journeys. There is no salvation from the body. Its enigma persists beyond and in the performance and within the games of personal truth and pleasure.

The problem is that radical feminism did not understand all the pleasures of the conventional fem. *The problem* is that FemFire is said to provoke her rapes and murders. *The problem* is that no one wants to be a *really bad motherfucking hot mamma* . . . except on *her own terms*.

The problem has long been posed as sex against spirit, as pleasure against danger, in the vernacular of white against color, stacking power against a woman's body and displacing her pleasures with the fear of falling into dis/appearance.

Private Solutions

We have to stop this language and its harm, full of inference; understanding that our skins wanted and worn are choreographies of pleasure
and danger, desire *and* taboo, movement *and* flight. A dance of power and
desire begins from inside with fragments of the familiar. Some stolen
pieces for escape artists and some for our hearts, "homing" our desires
into the flesh.

     Gendering is a metaphorical talk, my way to move you, your way to
move with me, one of many asymmetrical languages for releasing sensu-
alities into the grainy bareness of being. Playful perpetual asymmetries
of power's pleasure.

FemFire, haunt my lesbian imagination, sliding as you do in and out of
uncustomary grace,
I do not hate you or me as a category of being.
. . . what really matters is who creates our scene.
. . . what really matters is where you and I will stand when the enemy is
present.
. . . what really matters is that no harm be done to you or to me.
FemFire, glow girl, your lesbian angel is home, your butch baby wants,
your fem sister aches. Melt these our bodies with your soft soft skin,
knowing well, want, power, and pleasure . . .
. . . knowing well that danger is everywhere and that pleasure's persis-
tence is a secret agent in the Regime and of the Resistance.
FEMFIRE, YES!

> *Bisexuality—a state that has no existence beyond the word itself—is an out-and-out fraud. . . . The theory claims that a man can be—alternatively or concomitantly—homo and heterosexual. . . . Nobody can dance at two different weddings at the same time. These so-called bisexuals are really homosexuals with an occasional heterosexual excuse.*   —Bergler

The existence of bisexuality presents a conceptual challenge that has not been seriously recognized. Instead, bisexuality is often ridiculed as a transitional stage, a trendy posturing or a denial of one's real sexual orientation. When it is acknowledged, it often remains a puzzle. It comes with a prescription to wait. Because a bisexual identity formation seems less linear, more open-ended, and in some ways less fixed than heterosexual or homosexual identity, bisexuality is often perceived as an inauthentic and untrustworthy state of being. Likewise, traditional models of the coming out process[1] seem less universally applicable to bisexuality, where neither one sex nor the other is exclusively desired and where *coming out* does not end in a monosexual definition of the sexual self. However, our cultural reluctance to acknowledge bisexualities may hide the reality and possible ubiquity of a bisexual responsiveness that contradicts the strict closures of the hetero/homo divide. In this essay I explore some of the theoretical aspects of bisexuality, namely its challenge to a modernist *science of desire*.

A Modernist Science of Desire

While homosexuality has been explained by some sociobiologists as a possible genetic benefit, the status of gay genes in sociobiological theory has remained somewhat speculative. At most, the function of gay genes is rendered consistent with a story of genetic utility that refers to kinship selection.[2] According to this concept, lesbian and gay relatives in a family will nurture and care for their extended family offspring, thus increasing the viability of family genes and their chances of replication and continued survival. This conjecture accounts rather awkwardly for homosexuality's contemporary experience function, since not all gay uncles and lesbian aunts are interested in performing a quasiparental role and many families feel deeply threatened by the chill of sexual deviance in the family line and often react with hostility and distrust toward their gay relatives. None the less, the quest for gay genes continues.[3]

Dean Hamer and Peter Copeland's *The Science of Desire: The Search for a Gay Gene and the Biology of Behavior*[4] elaborates on a new empirical study that begins to give some matter to gay gene theory. In Hamer's research project, gay genes are purportedly located on a portion of the X sex chromosome known as the Xq28, where there seems to be a pattern of gene sequencing that is different in homosexual men. Reasoning that brothers are likely to have a 50 percent chance of inheriting one or the other of the mother's two X chromosomes, the significantly higher than 50 percent rate of inheritance of this specially marked Xq28 segment of the X chromosome in gay brothers suggests that this portion of the X chromosome may be associated with the queering of male desire.

Hamer seeks a genetic explanation for sexually orienting desires. Since these desires and fantasies may not always be acted upon, a modern science of desire must focus on desire itself, as an inner manifestation of a genetic molecular difference marking a variation among human kinds.[5] While I am not interested in pursuing various criticisms of Hamer's reductionist assumptions,[6] I would like to draw attention to the initial and perhaps most constructivist moment in Hamer's research project. This is his representation of sexual desire as a phenotypic trait, a constructivist moment in which the data to be explained—persistent orientation in human sexual desire—is rhetorically shaped into a phenotype.[7]

Phenotyping Sexual Desire

There are two ways to understand the relationship between genes and specific phenotypic traits. Commonly, a phenotype is construed as the effect or expression of a specific gene. In this case genes are distinguished by their effects on observable phenotypic differences. In a more weakly determinist approach, a phenotype can be defined as a discrete although variable characteristic of the body the manifestation of which is also dependent on nongenetic factors as well as genetic predispositions. In this more open-ended construction phenotypic traits and their manifest heritability are not the sole effects of a gene or subset of genes. On either interpretation the notion of phenotype requires a way of partitioning the totality of an organism's characteristics into "heritable traits" that seem to have a genetic cause, either strongly or weakly determining.

Many phenotypic traits are expressed along a continuum of phenotypic variation. Balding is an example of a phenotypic trait that has a measure of discreteness in its overt manifestations and a degree of variation across a mostly male population. In the case of baldness some men become bald and some men don't, and some are more bald than others. Even though these variations exist, there is still an identifiable trait called "baldness." If we take seriously the notion that a phenotype can be "extended," that the effects of a gene are not limited to the body's material structure and function but include behaviors or agential tendencies, then sexual orientation could be countenanced as a phenotype. It would seem, however, to be a trait like balding: some people have it, others don't, and some have it more than others.

In Hamer's approach to sexual desire, it must first be represented as an extended phenotype. This presupposes that sexual orientation can take on the qualities of a phenotype: that it is a measurably discrete though variable characteristic having a deeply engrained and heritable status in the body. Once sexual desire is couched in the language of "phenotypes," it is represented *as if* already referring to a genetic determinant. In what follows, I analyze the strategies used by Hamer "to phenotype" sexual desire or to represent sexual desire as a phenotypic trait. As I track this construction, one can see in its early moments of formation an active resistance to the evidence of bisexuality. To analyze Hamer's "phenotyping" of sexual orientation, I will explore four representational strategies that construct sexual orientation as a trait that is measurable, discrete, manifest, and heritable and further explore how these strategies rely on the assumptions of a modernist science of desire. Shifting to a postmodern framework, I pursue the implications postmodernism has for modernist sex research—namely, its dissolution—and suggest that we rethink the concept of sexual orientation as a category of political shelter rather than a genetically referential term. In contrast to Hamer, who advocates the phenotyping of sexual orientation, I call for the liberation of sex from modernity.

Making Desire Measurable

To conceive of sexual orientation as a specific phenotypic trait, one must first determine what aspects of sexuality seem observable and measurable and not so blended that they fail to mark a significant difference in variation. As Hamer argues:

> When we want to classify a trait such as sexuality, the definition of phenotypes becomes far trickier than with eye color. In part this is because sexuality encompasses so many different aspects of a person's physical, mental, and emotional makeup. A second complication is that these characteristics are not rigidly fixed during the life span. Most people do not have the same sexuality at age 50 as they had at age 20, and sometimes a person's desires can change within a period of a few days or even minutes. Because of the fluid nature of sexuality, it is important not only to isolate specific traits but also to know when they first appeared.[8]

To determine a measure for sexual orientation, participants in Hamer's study were given intensive interviews and asked about their sexual experiences in childhood, adolescence, and early adulthood; in their current sexual practices and feelings over the past year; and in various kinds of relationships. These interviews were used to determine initial sexual orientation attribution for his subjects, who were then asked a battery of questions related to sexual self-definition, attraction, fantasy, and behavior. Based on a Kinsey scale rating from zero to six,[9] the subject ranked himself in each of the four areas—sexual self-definition, attraction, fantasy, and behavior. Since all of Hamer's subjects were males, he describes the scale as follows:

> Zero stands for someone who identifies himself as exclusively heterosexual. One means a man is predominantly heterosexual but every once in a while is interested in other men. Two is a man who identifies as heterosexual but is attracted to or active with men more than just occasionally. Three is fully bisexual, meaning equally interested in men and women. Four is someone who is gay but is attracted to or active with women more than just occasionally.

Five is predominantly interested in or active with men. Six is exclusively gay.[10]

The deployment of this traditional Kinsey scale convinced the Hamer
research team that their subjects expressed sexual orientations in two
clearly distinguishable directions, with very few subjects located in a third
in-between category. According to Hamer, the data generated by the
application of the Kinsey scale resulted in the scores shown in the chart.

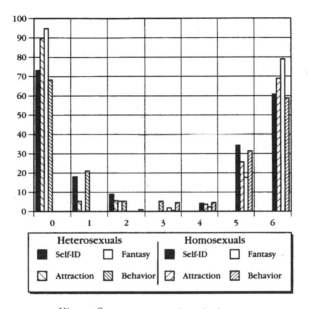

Kinsey Scores *(Hamer and Copeland 1994:67).*

The validity of typing people into discrete categories was based on
the belief that the Kinsey scale ratings do in fact measure sexual orientation. To guarantee the scale's reliability, Hamer refers to previous studies
using a penile plethysmograph,[11] which measures engorgement of the
penile tissues in response to visual stimulation. These earlier studies suggest that the Kinsey scale, while based on subject self-reports, correlates
with patterns of seemingly less voluntary penile tumescence in response
to heterosexual and homosexual erotic imagery.

The stability of the scale was also based on the stability of subject
invariance. Hamer points to the high degree of internal consistency
between the various facets of sexual orientation, indicating that generally
people's self-identification, fantasy, attractions, and behaviors correlate

consistently as homosexual or heterosexual identities. Heterosexual men in this study showed very little change over time in their sexual self-identification, attraction, and fantasy, although they did express some variance in behavior and occasional homosexual experiences. Gay men tended to be quite stable over time in their sexual attractions and fantasy but more variable in self-identification and behavior, an inconsistency that Hamer dismisses as a function of stigma management, peer pressure to conform to heterosexual norms, and the effects of homophobia. What Hamer fails to discuss is how these same aspects may have informed heterosexual identity formation, especially when some of Hamer's straight men had homosexual experiences and desires. However, given Hamer's collected data, he concludes that sexual orientation is "a reasonably consistent, reliable, and stable measure of one aspect of sexuality."[12] In this representation of desire, sexual orientation is beginning shape itself into a measurable phenotype.

Making Desire Discrete

Hamer addresses the question of whether sexual orientation is a discrete or bimodally, distributed phenotype or a quantitative, continuously distributed phenotype, usually represented by a bell curve. Clearly, Hamer's data presents "a striking feature" that almost all of his male subjects can be categorized as heterosexual or homosexual, with only 3 percent hovering in the Kinsey range of "two to four" and this only in some areas of sexual life. No one in Hamer's study self-identified as "a Kinsey three."

Two possible factors may have led to this result. First of all Hamer's research group sought subjects from the HIV Clinic of the National Institute of Allergy and Infectious Disease, which serves a large population of HIV-positive gay men; from the Whitman-Walker Clinic, which provides health services and programs for gay and lesbian alcoholics and substance abusers; from the Triangle Club, which offers 12-step programs for gays and lesbians; and from Emergence, an organization that serves gay and lesbian Christian Scientists. With the help of Parents and Friends of Lesbians and Gays (PFLAG) and an ad in the gay newspapers in Washington, D.C. and Baltimore that advertised for gay men who had biologically related gay brothers, Hamer's research group actively and almost exclusively sought out gay-identified males to contrast with a male heterosexual control group. A more aggressive outreach to bisexual populations might have yielded a different distribution of orientations, further complicating the question of what is it that makes a man gay? Second, using the Kinsey scale with his subjects, Hamer does not take into account how biphobia[13] may have skewed the data, since self-identification as a bisexual may not have been forthcoming—especially in the gay-identified organizations where Hamer sought his subjects. In any case, the absence of a sufficiently present bisexual population and Hamer's reduction of bisexuality to traditional Kinsey measures range results in the disappearance of the "in-between" and creates a representation of sexual orientation with a discrete bimodal distribution.

To enhance the dichotomous appearance of this trait, Hamer focuses on the variables of fantasy and desire, since the sexual behaviors of his subjects were more wide-ranging.[14] Applied to Hamer's subjects, Kinsey measures of sexual fantasy were consistently on the zero or six sides of the continuum, while their sexual behavior seemed more likely to stray. With 80 percent of his subjects scoring either a zero or a six in the category of sexual attractions, Hamer infers from this that sexual orientation is better defined by "attraction" than by "action," thus locating the original manifestation of sexual orientation in the inner erotic states of desire or arousing fantasy. Whereas a subject's overt behaviors may have been more suitable for objective measures, Hamer's *science of desire* circumscribes its object of interrogation as desire itself. As I have noted, the appearance of desire as fundamentally dichotomous rests upon the virtual absence of bisexuality and the avoidance of other measurement scales and subject recruiting methods that could better attend to bisexual responsiveness.

Making Desire a Manifest Trait

One of the problems in any genetic analysis is to determine the time of appearance and the content of a particular trait. As Hamer argues, this is true of a phenotypic trait such as baldness, since "if we studied only high school students, our analysis would be so distorted that we probably would end up 'proving' that baldness is linked to cancer. That's because among the few bald high school students we would find, many would have lost their hair during chemotherapy" (p. 70). One can easily see that this problem is compounded in considering sexual orientation as a phenotypic trait, since one needs to know when the trait is *really there*. Without examining his covert reliance on stage theories of sexual development, Hamer operationally defines the full expression of sexual orientation as that point in time when the subject acknowledges his or her sexual orientation to outsiders (p. 70). This astonishing move gives

Hamer a means to instant ontological accuracy, since the subject's sexual self-identification indicates the trait's full manifestation. In other words, the subject's "coming out' to outsiders, notably a recent historically based broad phenomenon encouraged by gay and lesbian political struggles, marks the full expression of sexual orientation as a phenotypic trait. This elision between a social-political discursive production of identity politics and the biology of the body seems conveniently overlooked by Hamer's positivism.

To reinforce the bipolarity of his assumptions, Hamer avoids the problem of phenotypes in the closet by complying with an epistemology of the closet: invisibility is a sign of absence. Accordingly, he argues that the average age the research subjects came out to outsiders was age twenty-one and since most of their subjects were age thirty-six, Hamer concludes "that most of our subjects who would be gay already showed signs of being gay" (p. 73). Further, since the timing of heterosexual and homosexual identity formations appeared to be similar to Hamer, he speculates that homosexual and heterosexual orientations may represent outcomes influenced by alternative forms of the same set of genes that in turn influence psychosexual development in all humans. With this unwarranted assumption, sexual orientation is seemingly represented as a phenotype—as a discrete, measurable, fixed, and manifest characteristic most likely determined in significant ways by genetic cause. Given the genotype/phenotype framework, those born with gay genes will usually experience the sign—"coming out to outsiders"—as the manifestation of a psychosexual developmental process. Like baldness, it is bound to happen. Unlike baldness, sexual orientation is a trait that must be spoken.

Making Desire a Deeply Somatic Heritable Trait

While Hamer defines public avowal of sexual identity as the discrete manifestation of an individual's sexual orientation phenotype, he notes that the trait expresses itself on a variety of levels and in a variety of ways over the lifetime of an individual. Early signs of the trait—such as childhood feelings of arousal and fantasy, sexual crushes on same-sex authority figures, early infatuations with peers, or cross-gender tendencies—are considered by Hamer as further evidence supporting a genetic hypothesis. As he notes, "early manifestation implies that sexual orientation is a deeply ingrained component of a person's psychological makeup, which again is consistent with a genetic predisposition" (p. 73). This *depth hypothesis* is used to explain away aberrant sexual behaviors, such as the heterosexual experiences of some of his gay subjects, dismissed by Hamer as attempts to conform to and comply with the norms of heterosexuality. Likewise, occasional homosexual experiences by some of their heterosexual subjects are not taken up as indicators of a derailed heterosexual orientation. Sexual orientation shaped by Hamer as a phenotypic trait is represented as deeply dichotomous and a seemingly stabilized aspect of psychosexual development, which presents some predictive, although not always consistent signs within the first six years of life. In the grid of phenotype/genotype, sexual orientation is represented as an heritable trait that establishes a fundamental indication in early life and later manifests itself in a matured sexual awareness. According to Hamer's *science of desire*, "coming out" as a sexual kind of person signifies the trait—a trait that requires this performativity for its ontology.

While I will not pursue the details of Hamer's research analysis, it is important to note that the genotype/phenotype model deployed by Hamer seems to ignore the role of environmental and agential factors in changing phenotypic expressions, especially those belonging to the inner life of human subjectivity. Although Hamer attempts to rule out the significant influence of environmental factors by focusing on genetic patterns of brother inheritance, his research strategies adopt a decidedly closed-model of genetic effect,[15] as they also blatantly ignore contemporary social and historical influences that inform sexual identity formation. In contrast, Barbara Ponse has pointed out that identity construction for various sexual minority groups often involves the construction of a consistent narrative of the self.[16] For gay people, this relies on a narrative device, "a gay trajectory," narrated by the subject as a series of remembered incidents or feelings that constitute evidence for a continuous monosexual orientation. To make sense of the past, behaviors that are inconsistent with current identity formations are read out of the past as mistakes or as hopeless attempts to conform to sexual norms or deny the truth of oneself. Sagarin has even more strongly argued that people who label themselves homosexual may become "entrapped in a false consciousness. They believe that they discover what they are (and by implication, since this is a discovery, they must have been this way all along). Learning their "identity" they become . . . boxed into their own biographies."[17] Obviously, the same could be said of heterosexuals.

This notion of identity work through identity narration is overlooked by Hamer, since for him sexual orientation is a discrete and isolable phenotypic trait. The work of the subject in identity formation is more that of a detective than an author. For Hamer consistencies in sexual self-identification, fantasy, attraction, and behavior are seen as evidence of a genetically determined core of invariance. In the individual, however, these same patterns are also produced by historical forces that pressure individuals to construct a narration of the self based on principles of consistency within a single monosexual trajectory. Without these cultural and historical factors, sexual orientation might be experienced as less discrete, less clearly measurable, less fixed, less isolable, and more fluid. Since a cultural experiment to test this idea is not readily forthcoming, it is not entirely clear then to what extent our contemporary constructions of sexual desire and identity formation belong to a particular historical and cultural regime of truth rather than to a fact about the body.[18]

Modernist Sex and the Phenotyping of Desire

While it is true that Hamer claims that he is doing real science, he misunderstands the historical and cultural conditions that make his project possible. The representation of sexual orientation as a phenotype rests on a suppressed understanding of its own genealogy or of the epistemic conditions of modernity that enable us to think sexual orientation as a phenotype at all. I would like to explore this genealogy to understand how we have come to think sex in modernist terms.[19] In other words, what are the presumptions of sex that make possible the representation of sexual orientation as a phenotype?

Hamer's project is clearly biased toward a reductionist explanation, referring sexual orientation to molecular cause. This is rhetorically reinforced by notions of sexual saturation, an idea that Foucault described as the modernist belief that sexual orientation saturates not only the soma of the body but also a deep psychic space within the individual, creating the possibility of sexual speciation of human kinds defined by sexual categories of desire. As Foucault argues, modernity rests upon the historical conditions that made possible the discursive construction of human sexual kinds as objects of scientific inquiry:

> The nineteenth-century homosexual became a personage, a past, a
> case history, and a childhood, in addition to being a type of life, a
> life form, and a morphology, with an indiscreet anatomy and pos-

sibly a mysterious physiology. Nothing that went into his total composition was unaffected by his sexuality. It was everywhere present in him: at the root of all his actions because it was their insidious and indefinitely active principle; written immodestly on his face and body because it was a secret that always gave itself away. It was consubstantial with him, less as a habitual sin than as a singular nature.[20]

This saturation of the sexual deviant with sex and sexual meanings, lodged in the smallest details of deviant soma and psyche, created the historical and theoretical presumptions for a modernist science of desire. After pirating the confessional from the Church, sex as an unruly composite of desires, fantasies, arousals, impulses, wishes, behaviors, and physiological events became an object of scientific inquiry, which was pursued in the intimate disclosures and observations between subject and expert. These private events catalogued by sexual science came to define who we are in sex. Sex became epistemic and saturating—"speciating" human beings into different sexual kinds. As Foucault suggests, "these polymorphous conducts were actually extracted from peoples bodies and from their pleasures; or rather, they were solidified in them; they were drawn out, revealed, isolated, intensified, incorporated by multifarious power devices."[21] Much of modernist sex research, which Hamer's work continues, is grounded on this commitment. Accordingly, sexuality becomes a hidden secret of the body, to be ciphered out by scientific methods that in turn redouble the representation of sexuality as a significant and saturating aspect of human bodies. Sexuality becomes a mode of speciation reflecting an ontology of difference, which in Hamer's work is largely limited to two discrete kinds, a bimodal phenotype based on the hetero/homo divide.

In this modernist turn, the presumptions of sex research and inquiry share some or all of the following features:

1. Sexuality is an object of knowledge and can be known pursuant to the right application of scientific and other methods of inquiry. *This results in the positing of sex as a secularized epistemic object.*
2. Sexual desire is a significant truth of the body that is often hidden from view, held as a secret either consciously or unconsciously, and as a core constitutive secret it holds a central key in understanding

a truth about the subject. *This results in the interiorization of sex as the body's inner secret and its representation as a significant if not essential truth of the individual.*

3. The hetero-homo divide marks a clinically and socially significant differentiation of human desire making the sex of one's partner one of the most salient categories of desire. This construction of categories of sexual desire, based on the sex of oneself and one's partner, creates a speciation of individuals into either homosexual or heterosexual. *This results in the hegemony of genito-sex dimorphism as a primary divide for establishing normative sexual kinds.*

4. These categories of sexual desire are often represented as discrete and nontransferrable and causally linked to inner structures or states in the body that significantly determine the direction and persistence of sexual desire. This inner structure or state may remain latent or muted until later expressed. *This results in a deep ontological foundation for the categories of sexual kinds.*

5. The emphasis on sexual object preference secures for heterosexuals a shield that places them initially beyond suspicion in their sexual object choice. This results in an increased scrutiny, surveillance, and study of marginal and deviant forms of sexual desire. Heterosexual desires and practices thus appear natural and transparent ("the way things are"), while nonheterosexual desires and practices seem to call for a special explanation. *As a result, categories of sexual deviance create a semantic, social, and medical space for an intensified saturation of sex and its effects on the body, mind, and behaviors of the sexual deviant.*

6. When the category speaks in the voice of a deviant, the category becomes *full of flesh.* The speaking deviant reproduces modernist sexual ontologies in the performativity of "coming out," especially when this is subjectively experienced as an act of becoming visible, disclosing a secret, or revealing a deep inner truth. *This results in the reification of sex in the body as a hidden ontological truth and the individual's conscription to that truth.*

Given this way of thinking sex, Hamer's "phenotyping" of sexual orientation can be seen as another modernist strategy for thinking sex as a deeply real ontology in the body. He does this by imposing a measure on desire, marking a dichotomous, fixed, and stabilizing inner state that reflects the hetero/homo divide as two alternative forms of a phenotypic trait. His ontological interiorization of sex puts sex into the genes and buries the secret of sex in micromatter rather than in the Freudian psyche. In this sense both psychoanalysis and Hamer's positivism incorporate an epistemology of modernism in thinking sex a significant truth of the individual and a secret to be dislodged by scientific mind and method. According to Hamer's approach, "coming out," as a psycho-sexual developmental process, is the final manifestation of a self-narration that, in fact, expresses a genetically determined trait. Since human beings may occasionally mistake or feign this truth, a professional expert is called upon to measure and determine the authentic manifestation of this trait.

In Hamer's study sexual orientation is represented as a phenotype by reliance on these modernist assumptions, as well as by discernible strategies of omission at the level of observation in his research. The methodological erasures of bisexualities or bisexual responsiveness in his data collection further erase the complexities of human desire—its volatility, instabilities, occasional slips, unconscious repressions, and less explicit thrills of the passing moment. The socially prestructured, and sometimes coerced, negotiations of the subject in establishing a consistent narration of the monosexual self are ignored. For Hamer these nuances are replaced by a construction of sexual phenotypes on either side of the hetero/homo divide. Desire is thus stabilized by conspiring with a modernist metanarrative of the sexual self and its ontology of sexual kinds.[22] The homosexual is thus rendered a genetic offspring and the geneticist the final expert on the matter of sexual desires.[23] In modernist frameworks the discursive construction of sex as an object of inquiry must never become so amorphous that it escapes modernist categories of explanatory containment. Under the influence of this will to know, we make of sex a tidy thing and ignore the deluge.

Postmodern Sex Ontologies

Modernist sex ontology has been recently challenged by the emergence of postmodern sexual theory and the development of multidimensional sexual orientation research. Quite differently, postmodern sexual theory and multidimensional sexual orientation research have put modernist sex ontology at risk by two complementary strategies: fluidity and mosaicism.[24] These new ways of thinking sex not only challenge the reductionist explanatory framework that researchers such as Hamer endorse; they also raise questions concerning the excluded middle—bisexuality—in the representation of sexual orientations. The metaphors of fluidity and mosaicism contrast with those of solidity, unity, and dichotomous purity and suggest, by that contrast, that sexual orientations may be multiple manifestations of unstable, shifting, and overlapping categories of desire. If sexual orientation bears this more amorphous complexity, a *science of desire* may lose its isolable and measurable trait, and the construction of sexual desire as a discrete phenotype may become a luxury of too few variables, oversimplified tools of measure, unrepresentative subject populations, and an ideological commitment to sex selection as an overly narrow divide of human sexual orientation.

Fluidity

While it is not my intention in this chapter to cover the full scope of postmodern sexual theory, one significant challenge postmodern queer theory brings to sex and gender studies is a critique of sexual identity as a monolithic unity based on dichotomous categories. Postmodern queer theory constitutes itself as the great discursive turn (on sex itself, so to speak) that challenges us to question the categories and genealogies of thought that enable us to codify and classify sexual desires and sexual kinds. Contrary to naive rejections of social constructionist theory, postmodern queer theory does not claim that sexual desire did not exist until it was named but, rather, that how it is named, depicted, represented, culturally organized, and socially regulated is considered relevant to its historical and epistemic appearance. Such an approach scrutinizes specific categories of normative and deviant sex, the social uses made of sex, as well as our lived experiences of sexuality and our ways of knowing about our own sexualities. These practices in turn have a gripping and metabolic effect in shaping the real.

Queer theorists often attempt to deconstruct the categories of sexual identity by softening the edges of the hetero/homo divide.[25] From this perspective, sexual desires, practices, fantasies, and acts are given more space to migrate and overlap across the boundaries of normative sexual categories. This challenges the fundamental assumptions of modernist sex ontology: that male and female sexualities are in some ways basically different, that male and female genders are grounded in biological difference, that heterosexual and homosexual sex acts and orientations are different, and that heterosexual orientation does not have its own queer secrets and queerness its straight closets. Postmodern sexual theory explores the possibilities of a new sexual pluralism, of a sexuality unleashed from the simple categories of the hetero/homo divide and a sexuality that becomes more nuanced: more lascivious, more tentative, more obstreperous, and less easily domesticated by the either/or obliqueness of sexual object choice. In this new approach the body is often metaphorically coded as fluidity or liminality, replacing the discrete and stabilizing ontologies of modernism with an inchoate drift of possibilities. As Eve Sedgwick has suggested in *Tendencies*, sexuality becomes "the open mesh of possibilities, gaps, overlaps, dissonances and resonances, lapses and excesses of meaning where the constituent elements of anyone's gender, of anyone's sexuality aren't made (or *can't be* made) to signify monolithically."[26]

Critics of postmodern queer theory have often pointed out that the possibilities opened up by the discursive play of desire on the loose create a vacuous transcendence of the real body, since queer life in the everyday world finds the hetero/homo divide very much intact and sometimes brutally violent. According to this criticism, queer theory's discursive turn (on sex itself) has at times gone too far, replacing flesh with the word. At the level of everyday experience, modernist categories of uncommon sexual kinds signify a place where sexual communities struggle to make sense and survive. *To be specifically sexual* on this earth is to live through an ongoing narration of self, community, and relationship within (or against) the categories of sexual kinds historically and culturally available during one's life. What is insufficient about these categories is their lived insufficiencies, not necessarily their intertextual cross-subsidies overly pondered in academic circles. While some postmodernism theory attempts to explore these everyday struggles, often these issues are way-sided by an intellectual fascination with fluidity as a critical and deconstructive device.

Mosaicism

In contrast to the discursive turn found in postmodern sexual theory, a new form of sex research is emerging that also challenges modernist sex ontology while supporting the need for empirically grounded inquiry. This new empiricism is postmodern insofar as it attempts to move beyond the dichotomous binaries of modernist sex ontology. It shares with modernism a will to know the secrets of sexual desire, but it postures itself as antimodernist in its unwillingness to endorse the oversimplified dichotomies of a modernist sex ontology. As a new postmodern empiricism, it relies on positivist methods to elicit subject disclosures on sexual matters, but its strategy is to create more complexity and more of a mess with sex.

This new research is based on multidimensional scales used to measure a variety of sexual orientations.[27] First developed because of the inadequacies of the Kinsey scale used in the 1950s, these new scales delineate a variety of sexual orientations based on sexual behavior, affectional attachments (close relationships), social preferences (friendships and social groups), erotic fantasies, arousal experiences, erotic preferences, life-style identifications, sexual identity ideals (or level of comfort with current identification), changes in sexual identity over time, and current self-identifications. Increasingly, multidimensional sexual orientation research has created new typologies for bisexualities, as in Klein's Sexual Orientation Grid, where bisexualities are measured across the scales of sexual attraction, fantasy, behavior, emotional preference, lifestyle indicators, and self-identification claims, and then further evaluated against four different temporal scales: transitional, historical, sequential, and concurrent.[28]

The term I have found useful in contrasting this new empirical research with postmodern fluidity is "empirico-mosaicism." In a mosaic framework, sexuality is composed of a collection of distinguishable impulses, pleasures, fantasies, memories, dreams, acts, and other experiential data. These pieces fit together to create an aesthetic whole. As a representation of an erotic life, this composite can be narrated into a coherent and unified identity as the subject struggles to *make sense*, literally and figuratively, of her or his erotic life. The significance of this new research is that it multiplies the number and kind of data that can be computed into this sexual narration, as it opens up differently nuanced categories of sexual identification. As a result, the negotiations of the subject *coming to terms* with her or his sexual desires becomes a more visible process, carried out in a panorama of multidimensional mono-, bi-, and omnisexualities that resist the easy closures the hetero/homo divide. "Empirico-mosaicism," unlike the abstract fluidity of postmodern sexual theory, is grounded on the experiences of an erotic life that an individual may or may not assemble into a coherent narrative of unified identity. These recollected pieces come from the differently felt ways erotic and sexual energies have connected for a particular individual. At the extreme, this new empiricism challenges sex selection (*either* male *or* female) as the fundamental divide of human sexual orientation. New questions emerge: *What if* sexual desire is not significantly based on the sex of one's partner(s)? *What if* sexual self narration has no particular ending or no particular identity formation? *What if* the field of pleasure and sexual identification could burst into the bloom of multiplicity rather than a duality of desire's division? Empirico-mosaicism provides an ontology of open departure that allows for the emergence of omnisexual nomadic desires.

This new multidimensional approach to sexual orientations challenges a number of common modernist assumptions: that heterosexuality and homosexuality are two mutually exclusive and autonomous orientations, that sex selection is necessarily a *primary* or *first order* criterion for sexual kinds of desire, that sexual orientation is immutable or nonfungible, that sexual orientation identity formation is a linear process with a fixed outcome, that monosexual identity constructions are based on a purity of content, and that bisexual identities have no monosexual dimensions. Monosexual beliefs in the linearity and purity of sexual orientation are replaced by an ontology of empirico-mosaicism and by what emerges from that, the remarkable agency involved in putting the pieces together to constitute an intelligible sexual self. To obscure the role of this human agency in sexual identity formation, it is first necessary to suppress the data of bisexualities from empirical research, a tactic that is clearly demonstrated in Hamer's attempt to phenotype human sexual orientation.

Compared to the theoretical solidity of modernity and the theoretical fluidity of postmodernity, empirico-mosaicism makes possible a science of desire that can merge the body's materiality with an historical understanding of contemporary sexual identity formations and provide a challenge to the sometimes violent closures of identity forced upon sex. With this new multidimentional approach, a *mosaic signature* emerges for each individual, a signature that is always in the process of identity formation, given the historically available categories for fashioning a sexual self and the erotic experiences or feelings an individual considers most salient or meaningful. Sexual identity formations are produced in culturally specific contexts as unsettled unities. This new way of thinking out loud through sex may involve less of a quest for a phenotypic representation of sexual orientation and less of a need for the grand theories of modernist sex ontology.[29] From this new perspective, sex can become many true stories rather than a truth of the body.

Hybridity, Persistence, and Resistance

Putting modernist sex ontology at risk may not seem a personally safe or politically wise consideration.[30] Most monosexual people have become accustomed to the feeling of a unified sexual identity, seemingly based on the persistence of desire, the consistency of sexual experiences, or the evidence of a familiar way of life. Causal hypotheses that our genes, hormones, prenatal environments, or hypothalamic nodes may strongly determine our monosexual orientations have provided for some the security of an immutable, hard trait as an ontic anchor for desire. In contrast, empirico-mosaicism allows for wider acceptance of inconsistencies in gay, lesbian, and heterosexual identity formations and opens up a wide discursive space for different kinds of sexualities. This does not mean that there are no real lesbians, no gay or heterosexual people, nor that one can necessarily change one's persistently felt orientation by willful strength or professional help. It does raise a question on what we mean by "real." I believe that the deep challenge of postmodern sexual theory and postmodern empiricism lies in the possibility, or, more rightly, in its gambit, that there may be a little of "the opposite" in many people. In anyone's sexual identity formation, there may be, though not necessarily, inconsistencies in expression and impulsivity that modernist inquisitions of sex, such as Hamer's, may easily dismiss. However, whether or not *these misfitting pieces* (the tell-tale traces of the opposite) will become a salient or deeply satisfying feature of one's erotic life, identity, and relationships is another matter. Agency in fashioning a sexual self operates on the level of self-narration through sex, on the level of pleasure's intensity and drive, and on the level of historical, political, and personal struggles for the survival of socially defined sexual kinds.

This agency and historical contingency are completely overlooked in the model of phenotype/genotype advocated by Hamer. In his framework biology is called to account for the formation and historical appearance of sexual identity claims. I have focussed on Hamer's ideological commitment to the hetero/homo divide and his selective construction of two discrete sexual orientations. As I have argued, this representation of sexual orientation relies on a methodological suppression of bisexual and multi-dimensional orientations and on the assumptions of a modernist sex ontology. As a result sexual agency in the construction of sexual identity formations is occluded by the closed biological circuitry. In contrast postmodernist sexual agency, reflected in the multiplication of sexualities and erotic vocabularies, places agency not in the defaults of biology but in a performative narration pieced together from memory, experience, and desire in the context of one's community, language, and history.

Shane Phelan argues a related point in her reflections on the traditional and individual-centered "coming out" model in lesbian communities:

> There is in this view a reality, a stable horizon of what it means to be lesbian or gay, but that stability is not given by discovery of a deep truth but by participating in particular historical communities and discourses. Coming out is partially a process of revealing something kept hidden, but it is more than that. It is a process of fashioning a self—a lesbian self—that did not exist before coming out began.[31]

Phelan's notion of coming out as a *(be)coming process* provides a way to bring postmodern sexual theory and multidimensional sexual orientation research into common alliance. Quite simply, the methods of empirico-mosaicism do not rule out a history and narration of the sexual self within communities, where sexual identity claims are established, debated, and negotiated. In this collective and discursive process each of us fashions a sexual self. We know this about ourselves by the performative acts that give flesh and meaning to our desires and experiences. These narrations of the self depend on the sexual vocabularies claiming us, as we work within, through, or against these ways of speaking sex. In this labor, we are making sense of our sexuality by making the kinds of people we think we are in sex.

We can thus understand sexual orientation as a community and intersubjectively mediated achievement. I recommend that we stop thinking of sexual orientation as a phenotype and start thinking of such categories as political shelters. A sexual orientation category is an *extended shelter* for those willing to bear and reveal the signs of its erotic kind. A sexual kind as a human construction and practice creates both the possibilities for a sexual self and a form of erotic life, positioned interrelationally with others both inside and outside the shelter. In a world hostile to a sexual kind, these shelters are critically necessary. In shifting the grounds of sex ontology to cultural and political struggle, we can ask whether it really matters how peope got themselves to the shelter: with or without the right biological markers or genetic evidence.[32] Regardless of how we come to these shelters, we take up a figurative and real residence in our surviving there.

In the name of these shelters, "lesbian," "gay," "bisexual," "queer," "ambi-sexual," "polysexual," "heterosexual," etc., we forge collective and per-sonal expressions of erotic life in a discursive public space where our sex-ual complexities enter historical and social relations of law, science, poli-tics, and power. In contrast, the categorical and institutional closures of modernism are clearly part of a political struggle in which modernity's regime of sexual truth reflects a heterocentric and male-dominated divi-sion of desire.

As the body enters history through sex, contemporary notions of coming out can be seen as a way of *speaking sex out loud,* over, above, through, and against historically given categories of containment. On a personal level, category-driven narrations of our sexual selves may seem forever incomplete as we come to see how contingent or (un)settled our identity formations may be. Certainly, the addition of bisexual politics to the civil struggles of the 1990s begins to widen our cultural ontologies of sex. On a community level we create discursive spaces for sexual kinds often perimetered by various definitions of who can be a member in a sex-ual shelter or what values and actions define a given sexual kind. In such communities, whether real or virtual, contestation at the border becomes a normal state of affairs.[33] Within these community-based social practices where identity hybridization and contestation are alive and lively, we as a species are creating and renewing a more diverse erotics of life on earth. The desire of sexual orientation enters this scene not as an extended phe-notype but as an extended shelter in a material struggle for meaning, sur-vival, and identity.

Sexual desire in the contemporary world is not easily contained, yet its anarchic frenzy is persistent. Through the momentum of desire, pleasure, and sensual life, we collectively create new forms of erotic hybridity and individual variation. This life inhabits different communities of meaning that articulate a politic of survival for different sexual kinds. The ontolo-gies of this politic do not necessarily call for a modernist search for causal truth in the body's matter. *The call to an ontology* in this new multiplic-itous politic of sex is a call for less oppressive social/sexual relations of power. In this sense sex comes to matter as a deeply political and histori-cal category. In contrast to the dream of sexual modernity, where there may have been an *end-all gene* to hold our sexual selves in place, there is now an evolution of sex in the production of erotic hybridities and in the multiplication of narratives and categories available for making sense of sex. Hamer's *science of desire*, cast in the language of sexual phenotypes and their genes, is just one such story, perhaps a remindful nostalgia of modernity's body and its need for origin, stability, dichotomy, and unity. In the postmodern world another way of thinking sex is emerging. On the horizons of various sexual communities, there are many new ways of *coming to terms* and *coming out loud* in bodies unminding the rules of modernity.

Three   **Rearticulations**

At this point it may appear as though I am committed to the belief that the categories of sex, gender, race, and other significant identities are discursive and cultural productions that in turn give meaning and final form to matters of the body. Certainly a great deal of contemporary social construction and performativity theory commits us to the view that the "materialization" of bodies—their specific meanings, values, identities, kinds, as well as their disciplined and developed skills—are produced within the social practices of a specific culture. However, there must be something there for bodies to materialize as cultural bodies. What then is the matter of bodies?[1]

In this final section, *Rearticulations*, I explore attempts to return matter to the physical body in various contemporary theories. Matters of the body are neither completely culturally unmediated nor completely culturally mediated. Several distinctions are necessary to understand this. The body is a *materialization*, a social formation lived as a personally unique embodiment. This is a cultural production that brings discipline, meaning, and means of agency to the body. *Materialization* is *the second corpus* of the body. *Matter* is that which is there for the materialization to materialize; the body's matter is the physically structured, living thing, the physical organism of the body itself. *Materialism* refers to an ensemble of cultural forces and institutions that bear down on the body, enhancing or diminishing its life, what I have previously referred as *the third corpus* or the extension of the body beyond itself. *Historical materialisms* suggest that this materialism is historical, changed by human labor and changing in time and location. Historical materialisms give structure to large-scale narratives of social struggle that criss-cross the desires and interests of individuals, their communities and cultures. Historical materialisms, unlike sheer natural forces, can destroy and nurture human life by heaving humanity and death in directions that often favor selected human intentions and interests. *Returning the physical body* to theory is a challenge that requires reflection on all three domains—*matter, materialization*, and *materialisms*.

In the four essays in this section, I attempt to understand how theorists have *returned matter to the physical body* by exploring how the body matters in writing. Though this analysis remains local, it is in the body writing that the body can be reflexively theorized. In the first essay in this section, "Hard Traits/Fluid Measures," I explore a scientific writing that pursues the existence of hard traits to explain the body's sexual desires and a poetic writing that creates the body's erotic trail. Both Simon LeVay in *The Sexual Brain* and Monique Wittig in *The Lesbian Body* engage a strategy of resistance to heterosexual normativity. The body in LeVay's work becomes a recalcitrant object unable to comply with heterosexual norms because of molecular structures that determine a material truth in gay desire. The body in Wittig's work becomes a resource for creative refiguring and rewriting as female desire resists the heterosexual terms of male dominance. Both Wittig and LeVay seek in the anatomies and vocabularies of bodily substance a way to talk back to power. Their solutions in writing are rather typically gendered, not only in LeVay's commitment to hard mechanism and Wittig's commitment to fluid poetics but also in their final political alliances with and against the brother's polity.

In the second essay, "Anzaldúan Body," I explore how Gloria Anzaldúa's writing moves beyond Cartesianized notions of the body's matter to an odyssey of corporeal resistance, healing, and historical transformation. In Anzaldúa's world, the body is not a biological machine, separate from spirit, but an infusing of the two, discursively implicated in history, geography, and location. To write the body is to create a radically redemptive strategy for survival. Materialization and historical materialism converge in Anzaldúa's writing: in the pressure of her ink against the page, the force of her body against the norm, and the power of her people against the colonizing North. Given Anzaldúa's perspective, the Cartesian dream of *a body from nowhere* and a mind freed from bodily encumbrance appear as a privilege of imperialism and isolate philosophical trouble.

The third essay in this section, "Venus: The Looks of Body Theory," raises the question of who controls the theoretical gaze of contemporary body theory. Starting with Jenny Livingson's "Paris Is Burning,"a video documentary on the ballroom cultures in Harlem's black and Latino gay and transgender drag communities, I explore the intensely emotional responses of theorists to Livingston's documentary and situate these ways of looking at the body. In this process I became interested in the significance of Venus Extravaganza, whose death occurred during the making of the documentary. In the body of Venus there is a convergence of bodily matter, desired materialization, and brutal annihilation. My own looking at Venus reflects how bodily matters in theory are related to the location of looking. I pursue a hunch that contemporary theoretical fascination with the body as performativity can be recast as a minstralization of materialism.

The final essay, "A Suite for the Body," was written as an experimental dialogue on bodies, power, and knowledge. It attempts to get at some of the ineffable moments of bodily connection and disconnection in the ways we come to know our bodies. I explore these issues at a level of sexual and medical intimacy where the body is opened up or shared outside itself. Both of these excursions into the body's interior play across the differences of inner and outer in a search for what matters to philosophers, lovers, and other experts. This motion continues, sometimes at odds, but always in a process of coming to know the bodies we are through one another.

J/e te cherche m/a rayonnante à travers l'assemblée.
—Monique Wittig, *Le Corps lesbien*[1]

What are human bodies made of . . . an assembly of skin, internal organs, tissues, fluids, mineral traces, cells, molecules, atoms, free radicals, neuronal currents, energy, heat? Living bodies are also materialized and assembled in cultures, histories, and languages, and continuously represented by laws, ideologies, media, and various regimes of knowledge. The body is a critical nexus serving the effects of power, as well as an inner sanctum of human agency and erotic desire. Desire's persistence and necessity can fill the body, even define it, if words are put to this. In what follows, I explore the material philosophies in two very different contemporary projects: Simon LeVay's investigations of the gay male body and Monique Wittig's explorations of the lesbian body.[2] I consider each of their endeavors a quest for love's body, a quest in re/figuring love's mattering on the body. Both of these theorists explore the body from the inside out to "figure out" the felt persistence and vagaries of sexual desire and to "refigure" the body's mirroring in the self-truth of sex. In the work of LeVay and Wittig, bodies are suspended in matters of biology and language, providing an opportuntity for us to explore how desire can be figured in the meaning of tissues and in the physicality of words. LeVay and Wittig start at different ends of this blending: LeVay begins with the dead weight of postmortem brain matter and Wittig with the weightful power of words. Both seek to refigure desire in matters of difference: for LeVay, in the difference that makes men gay, and for Wittig, in the differences that can make a body lesbian. Both are mavericks of material weight in an increasingly disembodied postmodern world, and both are lovers of a different sort, seeking a special radiant one across the throng.

Incisions

> *The Lesbian Body THE JUICE³ THE*
> *SPITTLE THE SALIVA THE SNOT*
> *THE SWEAT THE TEARS THE WAX*
> *THE URINE THE FAECES THE*
> *EXCREMENTS THE BLOOD THE*
> *LYMPH THE JELLY THE WATER*
> *THE CHYLE THE CHYME THE*
> *HUMOURS THE SECRETIONS THE PUS*
> *THE DISCHARGES THE SUP-*
> *PURATIONS THE BILE THE JUICES*
> *THE ACIDS THE FLUIDS THE*
> *FLUXES THE FOAM THE SULPHUR*
> *THE UREA THE MILK THE*
> *ALBUMEN THE OXYGEN THE*
> *FLATULENCE THE POUCHES THE*
> *PARIETES THE MEMBRANES THE*
> *PERITONEUM, THE OMENTUM,*
> *THE PLEURA THE VAGINA THE*
> *VEINS THE ARTERIES THE VESSELS*
> *THE NERVES*   —MONIQUE WITTIG, *The Lesbian Body*

First Incisions

In 1990 Simone LeVay's lover died of AIDS complications. Trained as a neuroanatomist, LeVay turned to research on the biological causes of sexual orientation. His research targeted the lower brain stem and a neuroendocrine component of that system—the hypothalamus—as a possible link for explaining sexual orientation. His assumption was based on previous research suggesting that the interstitial nuclei in the anterior hypothalamus may have some determining role in animal sexual behavior.[4] At least in some male monkeys, damage to these nuclei results in impaired heterosexual behavior, where the affected males mount females less readily or persist in mounting other males. Similar to ablation studies in rats and ferrets,[5] the affected monkey sex drive remains intact, but its aim is "off" as indicated by same-sex behaviors. Such behavior is depicted as homosexual and as a "default position,"[6] so-named because hypothalamic alteration apparently causes these animals to engage in sexual behaviors with the same sex.

To see if hypothalamic interstitial nuclei might have a bearing on human sexual orientations,[7] LeVay collected the brains of forty-one subjects who had died at metropolitan hospitals in New York and California. Eighteen of the deceased were identified as gay men who had died of AIDS complications. Sixteen of the other subjects were presumed heterosexual men, six of whom died of AIDS complications and ten from other causes. Six of the deceased subjects were women, all presumed heterosexual, one of whom died of AIDS complications and five from other causes. One bisexual man was included. His death was related to AIDS. LeVay includes him in the cohort of gay men, increasing the number of homosexually responsive male brains to nineteen subjects, all of whom died of AIDS complications.

The forty-one brains were fixed by immersion for one to two weeks.

First Incisions: I discover that your skin can be lifted layer by layer, I pull, it lifts off, it coils above your knees, I pull starting at the labia, it slides the length of the belly, fine to extreme transparency, I pull staring at the loins, the skin uncovers the round muscles the trapezii of the back, it peels off up the nape of the neck, I arrive under your hair, m/y fingers traverse its thickness, I touch your skull, I grasp it with all m/y fingers, I press it, I gather the skin over the whole of the cranial vault, I tear off the skin brutally beneath the hair, I reveal the beauty of the shining bone traversed by blood-vessels, m/y two hands crush the vault and the occiput behind, now m/y fingers bury themselves in the cerebral convolutions, the meninges are traversed by cerebrospinal fluid flowing from all quarters, m/y hands are plunged in the soft hemispheres, I seek the medulla and the cerebellum tucked in somewhere underneath, now I hold all of you silent immobilized every cry blocked in your throat your last thoughts behind your eyes caught in m/y hands, the daylight is no purer than the depths of m/y heart m/y dearest one (Wittig).[8]

In the late 1970s Monique Wittig stood before the academic world and argued that lesbians are not women.[9] For Wittig, "lesbian" names a location outside an implicit heterosexual contract that grounds the social reality of "women" in relations of sexual oppression and heteroerotic conscription. When a lesbian refuses that contract—sexually, emotionally, economically, politically, and ideologically—she enters a zone outside the political regime of the phallus and its appropriation of the female sex as sexual property. For Wittig, "lesbian" becomes a site of resistance to cultural formations that "heterosexualize" the female flesh and prohibit the possibilities of outlawed desire and subversive female community.[10]

According to Wittig, the heterosexual contract[11] and its political regime create "woman" as a fragmented, fetishized, expropriated, psychoanalyzed, and commodified object of exchange. The "woman" of this contract is, however, a political category, not a natural given. As such the concept of sex difference "has nothing ontological about it."[12] Its reification in the straight mind as a natural fact is *in fact* an historical interpretation of a particular form of culturally mediated male dominance. A female can enter this scene at the level of language and social contract, resisting many aspects of representation and social relation that "heterosexualize" and appropriate her sexual interest and pleasure.

Unlike LeVay's inquiry into the biological causes of gay male desire, Wittig begins her quest for the lesbian body by disassembling "heterosexualized" bodies at the level of symbolic and social contract. For Wittig, the body is a physical thing but also an inscribed matter of language and law; as she argues, "there is a plasticity of the real to language."[13] Just as heterosexual bodies are partially constituted through discursive effects, so lesbian bodies are a *matter inscribed* and thus partially produced through language and discursive practices that can mobilize and create new life forms and new social relations. Language becomes a vehicle of liberation: "the movement back and forth between the levels of reality (the conceptual reality and the material reality of oppression, which are both social realities) is accomplished through language."[14]

In disassembling the sexual ontologies of sex difference that ground the heterosexual contract, Wittig attempts to construct a lesbian difference in a place beyond heterosexual meanings and realities. However, there is no real place to go. "There is no escape (for there is no territory, no other side of the Mississippi, no Palestine, no Liberia for women). The only thing to do is to stand on one's own feet as an escapee, a fugitive slave, a lesbian."[15] For Wittig, this lesbian space is the body, "lesbianized"[16] through the violence and creative work of new languages, forbidden desires, and transgressive acts between impassioned lovers. Her path toward transcendence is in-the-body-becoming-lesbian and through a convolution of its parts and meanings. Unlike the traditional Eurocentric notions of transcendence based on an abhorrence of the flesh, Wittig's "lesbian-transcendentalism" intimately mixes with the sensuous textures and tissues of the female body—its innumerable parts, fluids, and structures; its innumerable limits, pleasures, and pains; its innumerable encounters, positions, and possibilities. These explorations of the body, reinscribed as sexual acts, reconstitute the body as lesbian in an erotic extravaganza. In Wittig's writing, this lover relation is transferred to the reader as the pronominal spaces of *j/e* and *tu* are filled up and "lesbianized," and refilled literally in the *j/e* of the writer and the *tu* of the reader, who as intertextual lovers create *"tant je l'aimais qu'en elle encore je vis."*[17] Whether these two bodies have the correct hypothalamic nuclei for committing these acts makes no difference to Wittig and is overshadowed by the need for excessive passion, revulsion, rage, grief, and peace between the *j/e* (lover) and the *tu* (lover). The reader like the lovers traverses these tumultuous scenes.[18]

Wittig's experimental writing creates a corporeal space outside the sexual economies of the straight mind, a space where lesbian embodiment can find its territory—its blood, bone, urine, lymph, muscle, vomit, excreta, teeth, skin, tears—its bodily matters of life and death. This is also a territory of motion, charged by the desire to escape, to find a mythic elsewhere, often referred to in *The Lesbian Body* as an island where lesbians dwell.[19] However, the mythic dimension of this transcendence returns to the immanence of flesh and its yearning for metamorphosis beyond the sexual duality and ontologies defining "woman" and "man." A Wittigian lesbian can thus exist but not as a "woman." Her body is a dismembered and a discovered land. She is a biological atrocity in ecstasy.

Second Incisions

LeVay fixes the brains by immersion for 1 to 2 weeks in 10 to 29% buffered formalin and then slices by hand at a thickness of about 1 cm. in, or close to the coronal plane (LeVay, p. 1035). . . . *J/e run light fingers down the length of your spine or else my hands bury themselves in your coat. J/e touch your firm breasts, squeeze them in m/y hand.* (Wittig, p. 20).

LeVay dissects the tissue blocks containing the sliced hypothalamus and stores them for 1 to 8 weeks in 10% buffered formalin (LeVay, p. 1035). . . . *J/e remove the muscles cautiously so as not to damage them, j/e take each one between m/y fingers the long muscles the round muscles the short muscles, j/e pull, j/e tear them by their fibres from their bones, j/e pile them in a heap each fragment moving slightly quivering when j/e put it down. J/e gradually extract the bone, j/e see it appear pearly white with reddish shreds, j/e lick it, j/e caress it, j/e pumice it to polish it, j/e wait till it has a pleasing shine, j/e watch it in its silence ... j/e am seized with desire for you.* (Wittig, p. 29)

LeVay assigns each block of tissue a code number so that all subsequent processing and morphometric analysis is done without knowledge of the subject group to which the brain tissue belonged. (LeVay, p. 1035). . . . *J/e have access to your glottis and your larynx red with blood voice stifled. J/e reach your trachea, j/e embed m/yself as far as your left lung, there m/y so delicate one j/e place m/y two hands on the pale pink bland mass touched it unfolds somewhat, it moves fanwise, m/y knees flex, j/e gather into m/y mouth your entire reserves of air.* (Wittig, p. 66)

LeVay serially mounts sections of the frozen brain slices infiltrated with 30% sucrose and mounts them serially on slides, dried, defatted in zylene, stained with 1% thionin in acetate buffer (for 15 to 30 min.), and differentiated with 5% rosin in 95% aclohol (LeVay, p. 1035). . . . *J/e succeed thus in making your eyeball topple out, j/e watch it hanging, j/e am gripped simultaneously by emotion in the throat and by the pleasure of seeing behind your eye. At once j/e test the elasticity of the optic nerve by pulling on your eyeball with m/y fingers but without letting go.* (Wittig, p. 74)

With the aid of a compound microscope equipped with a camera lucida attachment, LeVay traces the outlines of four nuclei in every section at a linear magnification of x85 (LeVay, p. 1035). . . . *J/e announce that you are here alive though cut to pieces, j/e search hastily for your fragments in the mud, m/y nails scrabble on the small stones and pebbles, j/e find your nose a part of your vulva your labia your clitoris, j/e find your ears one tibia then the other, j/e assemble you part by part, j/e reconstruct you, j/e put your eyes back in place. . . . J/e begin a violent dance around your body.* (Wittig, p. 78)

LeVay draws the outline of each nucleus (LeVay, p. 1035). . . . *The surest of m/y fingers the index insinuates itself along your rectum, uncompressed as far as the colon it forces a passage through the faeces, it reaches the bend of the intestine, it enlarges, it turns twice on itself, it descends the length of the ascending intestine making*

almost a complete circle girdling the small intestine like a lasso. . . .
J/e pursue my slow inexorable invasion of you. (Wittig, p. 88)

LeVay determines the areas of the traced outlines representing the
hypothalamic nuclei with a digitizing tablet, in which the volume of
each nucleus is calculated as the summed area of the serial outlines
multiplied by the section thickness (LeVay, p. 1035). . . . *You say it is*
unbearable to see m/e vomit you up, j/e am overcome by greater
pity than ever, j/e begin to eat you again as fast as j/e can m/y so
adored one j/e lick the last scraps on your belly, j/e get rid of the
traces of blood, j/e absorb you m/y very precious one, j/e retain you
within m/e. (Wittig, p. 120)

In these passages I have rewritten Simon LeVay's actions in an active singular voice, transforming the anonymous passive voice of the scientific
text to parallel the transitive actions in Wittig's writing. By placing these
texts back to back, one can immediately feel the difference between the
objective, descriptive mode of LeVay's writing and the subjective performative mode of Wittig's writing. These two ways of writing reflect a difference in writing, body, and desire. LeVay's subject(ification) is disciplined by the methods of science, as he remains outside the frame, emotionally detached from the slices of postmortem brain tissue. He
manipulates matters of the body to determine their morphometric truth.
LeVay's subjectivity is present in the precisions of cutting, labeling, trac-
ing, measuring, analyzing, and writing, but he is not an undisciplined
bodily presence. His is a unified subject sequestering secrets from organic
matter. The object of his inquiry is in the traces of what remains of name-
less lovers, understandably not his own.

Wittig's subjectivity is openly present and less unified. She inten-
tionally splits her subject position, an act signified in the French text by a
bar splitting the first person pronouns, the *j/e*. Some critics have suggested that this split pronoun indicates a female lack in relation to the
symbolic, as the female subject marked by sex difference is always already
constructed as an object even as she assumes and occupies the position of
a writing and speaking subject.[20] She is in this way cut off and split as the
j/e, never fully the subject of pure objective disembodiment as is the *j/e*,
the subject position unproblematically occupied by LeVay.[21] Wittig
explains the positivity of the *j/e* as a sign of female excess. She suggests
this in the following passage where she translates her French "*j/e*" as an
English "I":

A sign that helps to imagine an excess of "I," an "I" exalted. "I" has become so powerful in *The Lesbian Body* that it can attack the order of heterosexuality in texts and assault the so-called love, the heroes of love, and lesbianize them, lesbianize the symbols, lesbianize the gods and the goddesses, lesbianize the men and women. This "I" can be destroyed in the attempt and resuscitated. Nothing resists this "I" (or this *tu*, which is the same, its love), which spreads itself in the whole world of the book, like a lava flow that nothing can stop.[22]

My own reading of Wittig's pronomial incision of the subject is based on my comparative exploration of Wittig's and LeVay's writing on the body. LeVay's subject position is that of the scientifically trained disembodied *je*, a disciplined self that acts upon matter but is not significantly acted upon in return. This *je* disappears behind the passive and anonymous descriptions of how the brain tissues were manipulated. As LeVay would describe this: *the brains were fixed, tissue blocks were dissected, sections were mounted, four nuclei were traced* [emphasis mine]. Obviously in my previously reversed transcription of LeVay's actions into transitive voice, I place LeVay as the agent for what he and other members of his research group did to the brain tissues. I find that this effectively puts LeVay back in the picture as an agent of scientific and sexual intimacies and as the subject who is always already present in these intimate incisions and dissections but who disappears behind the passive voice of scientific writing. He is positioned outside, as the looker or knower, a solidified *je*, the unobtrusive self separate from the thing worked upon and studied for its truth. However, this thing he interrogates is also his own truth, if there is, in fact, biological cause for his loving.

In contrast, Wittig's subject is profoundly affected, reshaped, and refigured in the actions she initiates with her lover's body. The movement between the lovers, no matter how violent or grotesque, is usually returned to the lover who initiates in one scene and receives in the next. The *j/e* acts and is acted upon, both subject and object, in her intimate encounters with love's body, the *tu*. In her immersion, dismemberment, dissection, mastication, incorporation, regurgitation, and the reassembly (the *rassemblage*) of love's body, the subject exists continuously on both sides of the verb in an active/acted-upon dynamic. This seems to signify for Wittig the impossiblity of knowing love's body from the perspective of a unified *je*, untouched and unmoved by the object of passion, by a lover's body.

This rhythm—the to and fro—in Wittig's writing is reflected in numerous passages where the microscopic intimacies of the body are disassembled and reassembled in a tortured tension between love and hate, presence and absence, near and far, and life and death:

> Having absorbed the external part of your ear *j/e* burst the tympanum, *j/e* feel the rounded hammerbone rolling between m/y lips, m/y teeth crush it *j/e* find the anvil and the stirrup-bone, *j/e* crunch them, *j/e* forage with my fingers, *j/e* wrench away a bone, *j/e* fall on the superb cochlea bone and membrane all wrapped round together, *j/e* devour them, *j/e* burst the semicircular canals, *j/e* ignore the mastoid, *j/e* make an opening into the maxilla, *j/e* study the interior of your cheek, *j/e* look at you from inside yourself, *j/e* lose m/yself, *j/e* go astray, *j/e* am poisoned by you who nourish m/e, *j/e* shrivel, *j/e* become quite small, now *j/e* am a fly, *j/e* block the working of your tongue, vainly you try to spit m/e out, you choke, *j/e* am a prisoner, *j/e* adhere to your pink sticky palate, *j/e* apply m/y suckers to your delicious uvula. (p. 22)[23]

> *J/e* liquefy within and without. . . . M/y muscles separate from each other in sodden masses. M/y entire body is overwhelmed. First to fall is m/y anus. Some glutei soon follow. M/y biceps abandon m/y arms. The arms themselves fall entire to the ground. Only m/y cheeks remain intact. A very strong smell of moist earth spreads around. *J/e* see plants rooted in the fibres of m/y muscles. *J/e* lose heart, *j/e* submit m/yself to your will m/y deplorable one *j/e* have no share in this systematic transformation you impose on m/e. (p. 70)

> J/e announce that you are here alive though cut to pieces, J/e search hastily for your fragments in the mud, m/y nails scrabble at the small stones and pebbles, *j/e* find your nose a part of your vulva your labia your clitoris, *j/e* find you ears one tibia then the other, *I* assembly you part by part, *j/e* reconstruct you. (p. 78)

> *J/e* gather you up piece by piece, *j/e* reassemble you. *I* lick each of your parts sullied by the earth. *J/e* speak to you. *J/e* am seized by vomiting, *j/e* choke, *j/e* shriek, *j/e* speak to you, *j/e* yearn for you with such marvelous strength that all of a sudden the pieces fall together, you don't have a finger or a fragment missing. (p. 112)

It is then, changing your target divining what *j/e* am about to do, that you turn the barrel of your weapon against m/e fierce silent casting m/e out into the silence of the infinite spheres sole bearer of the secret of your name along with you m/y most unknown now and for ever, so be it. (p. 129)

While clearly some of Wittig's in/cisions are parodic gestures of dissection, she destroys the disinterested positioning of the scientific subject by eroticizing and animalizing her hunger for anatomy in her passionate desire to touch, feel, taste, stretch, detach, consume, and glorify each and every autonomously and aesthetically perceived part of her lover's body. In this violent re-writing of the female body, there is no special priority given to primary and secondary sex characteristics, the highly privileged and eroticized parts of the female body as represented by and for the straight mind. In contrast, Wittig's lust and hunger focus on all parts, just as her eight lists of body parts interspersed between 112 poetic explorations in *The Lesbian Body* rather incidentally include "vagina," "clitoris," "vulva," "labia," and "breast." These parts are not erotically privileged but placed at the same level as other less well-known parts and territories attracting Wittig's voracious lust.[24] All these anatomies and corporeal terrains become visible and adored in the pleasurable displasias of severed tissues and refracted fluids. In all of this, Wittig calls out to her lover, *"j/e am seized with desire for you."*[25] Desire has its epistemology in the flesh, *"you m/y most unknown now and forever, so be it."*[26]

Findings

LeVay Discovers the Markers of Sexual Difference

LeVay's research group studied four interstitial anterior hypothalamic nuclei(INAH) in the tissue samples from forty-one brains. Since previous studies reported that INAH 2 and 3 were significantly larger in men than in women, LeVay surmised that these two nuclei were perhaps involved in the generation of male-typical heterosexual behavior. Thus the sex dimorphism in these two nuclei might be related to sexual orientation behaviors. He divided his samples into three subject groups, females (F), presumed heterosexual males (M), and homosexual males (HM). Individuals who died of AIDS complications were symbolized by ●; those who died of non-AIDS related causes by ▲; and a singular bisexual male who died of AIDS complications by ○. The bisexual was given a ○ rather than a ● and statistically included with the homosexual males rather than the heterosexual males, though his micrometric nuclei volumes more closely resemble those of heterosexual males. The spread of volume in the four INAH nuclei in all the subject groups were compared and measured down to .10 mm.

As can be seen in the results presented below, only INAH 3 seems to indicate a sex and sexual orientation dimorphism. Heterosexual females and homosexual males have in general (though not universally) smaller INAH 3 nuclei than heterosexual males. One could infer that a smaller INAH may be involved in the generation of sex-typical female sexual attraction to men. Likewise, the larger INAH 3 in heterosexual men may be causally related to sex-typical male sexual attraction to women. Thus, male homosexual brains can be said to resemble female heterosexual brains in their smaller INAH 3—a gendering of body parts in which the distinction between gender (sex-typical behaviors) and sexual orientation (as sexual object choice) collapses into a hard trait. The sexual body becomes a mechanics of solids biologically marking sex difference.[27]

Wittig Uncovers the Mark of Gender

The body as conceived by Monique Wittig is both a physical thing with parts, structures, and functions but also a cultural construction produced through language practices, epistemic and social objectification, and social relations of oppression and power. Wittig's search for lesbian body does

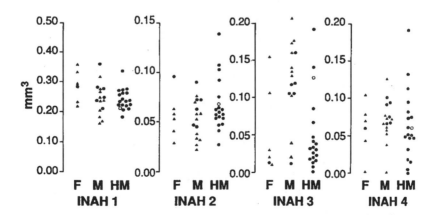

LeVay Study of 41 Brains

Source: Excerpted with permission from Simon LeVay, "A Difference in Hypothalmic Structure
Between Heterosexual and Homosexual Men," *Science* 253:1036; copyright 1991 American
Association for the Advancement of Science.

not assume a static essentialism—a biological hard trait or biochemical cause in the lesbian body. Her writing is a dynamic interaction between two lovers who "lesbianize" body parts and desires, which are named and pulled out for inspection and adoration. At the same time, *the whole of this body* is unnamable and not easily contained by language, since lesbian body is a process between lovers, who are underway, leaving the confines of a male-termed heterosexual contract where women's bodies and their parts are fetishized, fragmented, commodified, and consumed in the bio-power relations of heterosexual life.

For Wittig, lesbian desire and pleasure cannot be explained by genetic cause since the project of creating lesbian from a straight mind seems to require a metaphorically violent and brutal transmutation in which body parts are reassembled in the dense territories of extreme emotional turmoil between the lovers *j/e* and *tu*. This is not the biochemical spark of a small hypothalamic nucleus. For Wittig, the body's anatomy provides the material text for expressing the raw emotive explosions and vulnerabilities between the lovers *j/e* and *tu*. These emotional states are without limit, achieving levels of purity and extremism in rage, fear, grief, and ecstasy that erase more ordinary and assumed boundaries of mind and body. The result is a new psycho/somatic space (in embodiment and in a community of female sociality, the *elles*). Lesbian body as a language-in-relation (between self, other, and community) creates potentially new ways of living beyond the heterosexual contract. This is a body always (be)coming in its devouring, ravaging, and desiring, and a body never fully captured by measure or method. The sexual body becomes a poetics of unquiet fluidity establishing the mark of gender.

LE CORP LESBIEN . . . ARTÉRIEL LE SANG AORTIQUE LES VEINULES LES ARTÉRIOLES LES VAISSEAUX CAPILLAIRES L'AORTE LA CAROTICE LA CÉPHALIZQUE LA JUGULAIRE LA CORONAIRE L'OESOPHAGIENNED LA PULMONAIRE LA FACIALE LA TERPORALE LA SOUS-CLAVIERE LA MAM-MAIRE LA BRACHIALE LA MÉSENTÉRIQUE LA RÉNALE LA LOMBAIRE L'ILIAQUE LA SACRÉE LA RADIALE LA SAPHENE LES TIBIALES LA VEINNE CAVE LA VEINE PARTE LA PUL-MONAIRE LES COAGULATIONS LES FIGEMENTS LES CON-CRÉTIONS LES GELS LES CAILLOTS LES SOLIDIFICATIONS LES . . . LE CORP LESBIEN.[28]

THE LESBIAN BODY . . . THE ARTERIAL BLOOD THE AORTIC
BLOOD THE VENULES THE ARTERIOLES THE CAPILLARY
VESSELS THE AORTA THE CAROTID THE CEPHALLIC THE
JUGULAR THE CORONARY THE OESOPHAGEAL THE PUL-
MONARY THE FACIAL THE TEMPORAL THE SUBCLAVIAN
THE MAMMARY THE BRACHIAL THE MESENTERIC THE
RENAL THE LUMBAR THE ILIAC THE SACRAL THE RADIAL
THE SAPHENOUS THE TIBIALS THE VENA CAVE THE POR-
TAL VEIN THE PULMONARY THE COAGULATION THE
CLOTTING THE CONCRETIONS THE GELS THE CLOTS THE
SOLIDIFICATIONS THE . . . THE LESBIAN BODY.[29]

Sex Anatomies

According to Simon LeVay, to have sex, "one hardly needs a brain" (p. 47).
The reason for this is that many of the neuronal circuits triggering the
reflexes in human sexual response are mediated through the spinal cord
and can bypass the brain.[30] The brain and especially the hypothalamus do,
however, control and regulate some of these reflexes, and obviously, the
subjective experience of sexual pleasure requires a brain, at least of some
sort. In his thinking about desire and sex, LeVay wants a body that
accounts for this, where one thing leads to another. Using a biological
model, he lists the basic components in human sexual response:

1. erection of the penis;
2. engorgement of the walls of the vagina and the labia majora, lubri-
   cation of the vagina by glandular secretions and transudation, and
   erection of the clitoris;
3. insertion of the penis into the vagina (intromission);
4. pelvic thrusting by one or both partners;
5. elevation of the uterus, with a consequent forward and upward
   rotation of the mouth of the cervix;
6. ejaculation of semen into the vagina;
7. orgasm, the intensely pleasurable sense of climax and release,
   often accompanied by increases in heart rate, flushing of the skin,
   muscle spasms, and involuntary vocalizations. (p. 47)

LeVay resorts to coitus in nonhuman mammals for a paradigm of
mating behavior. In many of these nonhuman mammals, the male enters
the female from the rear and coordinates with a female flexing her back

into a U-shape (lordosis) to expose her genital area readied for rear intromission (p. 47). The male assumes the top position, mounting her from
behind, grasping the fur on her back, and thrusting with his penis and
pelvic muscles until he ejaculates. These two behaviors—lordosis and
mounting—are considered prototypical female and male sex-motor patterns in the copulation behaviors of rats and other lower mammals.

In rat studies these copulatory mechanics have been traced back to
the presence or absence of testosterone in rat pups during a critical period
a few days before and five days after birth. Female pups exposed to testosterone during this period have a propensity in adult life to display male-
typical mounting behaviors, and male pups deprived of their testosterone
effects during this critical period are likely to display female-typical lordosis behaviors.[31] In this scene, the affected females mount, grasp, and
hump other rats while affected males rear their rumps into the air for
potential offers. For scientific observers, this has inspired a renaming of
rat body parts: the muscles and spinal motor neurons in the affected
female rat are described as "masculinized," and the counterparts in the
affected male rat are said to be "feminized." As LeVay describes this,
blocking the effects of testosterone in the male pup, "causes the muscles
and neurons to atrophy and die, leaving the female pattern" (p. 49). This
is a default position, where male brain tissue is "feminized" and rat
behavior turns "homosexual." Thus, top and bottom—mounting and lordosis—in the sex action of rats determines not only how we perceive their
sexual orientation but also the gendered nature of their body parts and
tissues.

Research has also shown that sex-typical patterns in rats can be correlated with differences in the nuclei of a rat hypothalamus.[32] This
remarkable anatomical feature may also be related to the rat's critical
postnatal testosterone period. One could then reasonably surmise that
the persistence of desire in human homosexual patterns might result
from a "feminized" hypothalamus in the male homosexual and a "masculinized" hypothalamus in the female homosexual. As in rat sex, a
human heterosexual script—the mounting male animal and the submissive female animal—is used as a reference point for determining human
sexual kinds. While in contemporary human life, sexual orientation categories are based on sexual object choice rather than style, the specter of
humping females and males in anal surrender to members of their own
sex amplifies a scientific anomaly and mammalian analog calling for
explanation. Such a category of deviance is apparently based on misplaced

sex parts.[33] This is exactly what LeVay is suggesting: feminized hypo-thalamic interstitial nuclei in the homosexual male brain correlate with homosexual desire.[34] It makes a difference how it is determined that a part is "misplaced," "dysfunctioning," or "misused." On a deeper level, one wants to know how language determines the parts, places, and pleasures of the sexually normative body?[35]

In contrast to LeVay's work, none of the anatomical parts explored in Wittig's *The Lesbian Body* is feminized or masculinized. This is because Wittig is attempting to write the lesbian body beyond the straight mind. As Elaine Marks has suggested, "[Wittig's] texts go beyond idiosyncratic sexual preferences toward the creation of a new mythology in which the female body is undomesticated."[36] In contrast to LeVay's writing, which closes the interior of the gay male body, Wittig's writing opens up and exposes body parts and tissues to the lesbian lover's/reader's eye. The causal linearity of LeVay's thinking is in Wittig replaced by an explosive effusion of desire and erotic acts that transgress a simple definition of a sexual orientation. LeVay's reliance on a mechanics of sexual response as a sign of ordered sexual orientation is in Wittig displaced by multiple dis-orientations and disordered acts, many involving violence and sado-masochistic extremes that shift back and forth between *j/e* and *tu*.[37] For LeVay some anatomical parts in the gay body become transgendered, as feminized hypothalamic nucleii in the male body are evoked to explain male homosexual desire. In Wittig's work anatomy is a matter of drama in the raw emotional intensity between two lovers, and desire is often a directionless persistence, randomly eroticizing any part of the body. Anatomy is clearly an imaginary facticity, and, part by part, it is freed from its articulation under the sign of heterosexual relation. LeVay's fluid mechanics—of micro to macro, of cause to effect, of brain nuclei to erec-tile tissues—are replaced by a poetics of a multifaceted and unnamable unity—the unknowable generic of the lesbian body.[38]

Sexual Identities

Unlike the homosexual body in LeVay's work, Wittig's lesbian body unsettles the unities of sex and gender meaning as these are culturally designated to fit the terms of heterosexual power relations. Body parts in *The Lesbian Body* are not gendered, as they are in rat sex. Instead her writing is an enactment, an attempt "to lesbianize" the female body, by transforming its matter and colonized interior into a palatial and some-

times macabre and almost Baktinian celebration of blood, saliva, and bone
in the viscosities and fluidities of lesbian sexual pleasures. The body's lush
and fetid interior becomes a lover's text, not the object of solid mechanics
or Cartesian dread. With the force of poetic rather than scientific writing,
Wittig figuratively loves her lover to pieces, as she also appropriates the
language of medical anatomy for her sordid transcendence.

Of course, Wittig does not really tear her lover's body to pieces, can-
nibalize and vomit back the parts, reassemble and sanctify them into
majestic constellations. In contrast, LeVay actually does engage, although
modestly, in some such acts—the cutting, slicing, freezing, magnifying,
and measuring of body matters. Both, however, are in pursuit of the
body's secret in desire, as love comes to matter in different ways:
For LeVay:

Although the gene itself has not yet been isolated and sequenced, it
probably will be found within a few years. When this happens, it will
be possible to ask how and when the gene works. Does it, for example, influence the development of those brain regions—hypothalamus in particular—that are believed to play a role in generating our
sexual feelings and behavior? (p. 140)[39]

For Wittig:

[M]/y hands are plunged in the soft hemispheres, *j/e* see the
medulla and cerebellum tucked in somewhere underneath, now *j/e*
hold all of you silent immobilized every cry blocked in your throat
your last thoughts behind your eyes caught in my hands. (p. 15)

Both LeVay and Wittig seek to hold love's body long enough to create
an instant of meaningful unity. For LeVay this unifying moment reflects
the body's basic dimorphic ontology; for Wittig it represents a sudden stability in the wildness of emotional unrestraint and morphic recomposition
transfiguring the intersubjectivity of lovers. Occasioned by the artificial
stillness of words—*you silent immobilized*—and the temporary solidity
of meaning, lovers often struggle to create an identity in desire. We speak
of discovering or becoming lesbian, gay, bisexual or heterosexual, as if to
name this as a state of being is to secure its identity in unity. For Wittig, I
surmise that the construction of this kind of "sexual orientation identity,"
though obviously a category of contempory being, constitutes an act of

self assembly in the *manque* of language and imagination. Her anatomical poetics attempt to fill this void as she seeks to write the female body beyond the terms of straight-minded categories of sexual orientation.

For LeVay, "sexual orientation identity" is a discovered truth of the body, an emergent property of matter, providing an ontology of hard traits and biological fact that reinforces the heterosexual contract (its categories of gender, parts, acts, and rules of pleasure and identity formation) and calls for gay equity. In civil rights struggles in the United States, this science of hard traits has been used to bring gay bodies to the social contract of the brother's polity and to ignore the polity's commitment to straight thinking. Wittig resists this, as she also seeks a new polity and place for lesbians, even though there is no place to go. There is, however, the body—her only country. On the level of political struggle, her writing on the lesbian body forges a place beyond the brother's polity as the nascent moments of lesbian desire provide for Wittig an opportunity for biological recomposition and political transformation. Hers is an ontology of creation rather than a biology of fact.

Given these different political ends, both LeVay and Wittig are insurrectionary lovers and material philosophers of different sorts. Both bring science and passion to writing. The passions of LeVay in *The Sexual Brain* appear in the beginning of each chapter with a passage from Shakespeare as a preface to his more dispassionate review of scientific research and its implications. The reader will discover that LeVay dedicated his work to the memory of Richard George Hersey, his lover who died from AIDS complications and who continues to inhabit the literary corners and the inspiration for LeVay's science. While LeVay refuses to merge his scientific writing with love poetics, a confluency that Wittig cavalierly celebrates, he holds them tenuously apart by function and font on the pages of his text. In Wittig's writing, she crosses passion and biology quite freely. In her anato-poetics, she "gallops night by night through lovers' brains, and then they dream of love."[40] In finding this beloved across the throng, a lover finds a small personal truth in the hidden interiors of love's body, in the *tu* that is the same as *j/e*. This mirroring of the self trespasses on ordinary science and sex, defying the borders and words that keep them apart.

Matters of Love

I have compared the writing of LeVay and Wittig to reflect on contemporary body theory as it is now somewhat influenced in the United States by postmodernist thinking. The influence of postmodernism theory on corporeal theory often encourages theorists to accept *en bloc* the assumptions of antifoundationalism, anti-essentialism, and a variety of revisions on our notions of identity, race, sexuality, and gender. This results in a tendency to reshape the categories of identity politics and to render the ontologies of gender and race as performativities and citationalities—both maneuvers having a profound effect on our metaphysical and physical assumptions about the body, as well as our survival.[41] Criticisms of such postmodernist theory frequently point to the lack of a materialist theory of the body that can effectively anchor and delimit the ludic playfulness of postmodernist musing. This seems to me a basically sound criticism of the way postmodernism frequently represents the body as if it is endlessly fluidic and multiply fragmentable. Too often the postmodern body seems exclusively a function of language and representation, suspended in discourse as rhetorical effect, performative substance or fanciful narration.

Both LeVay and Wittig return bodily matters to the contemporary postmodern scene by re-mattering desire, even as they offer two very different ways of rethinking the materiality of the body. In their work, the postmodern body-as-rhetorical-effect returns to the felt materiality of desire—its palpable persistence and direction, its intensity, recurrent need, and stubborn autonomy. In theorizing about the gay male body and the lesbian body, LeVay and Wittig seem to posit an anchor in bodily matters. For LeVay, one *figures out* gayness from the matter of the body.[42] For Wittig, one *figures out* lesbian from matters both inside and outside the body, in the material of language and cultural practices, and in the body's seething substance.

LeVay's essentializing strategy is reductionist and biological.[43] He seeks in the body of gay men, more specifically in their anterior hypothalamic tissues, a misplaced part, a node of difference, which will explain the persistence of same sex desires. Hypothalamic matter gives directionality to desire.[44] LeVay's strategy is to put sexual desire into the language of science, to seek its origin, measure its content, and explain its fate.[45] Science is used as a weapon for epistemic and political survival as sexual desire is *figured out* from the body. In his research the lesbian body is remarkably absent, although by the logic of his analysis, one would predict that lesbian hypothalamic nodes would be closer in size to those of heterosexual men rather than heterosexual women. However, both lesbians and the poetics of writing are marginalized in LeVay's work, where deceased lesbian brains are not studied and where the poetic of writing is displaced to the margins in Shakespearian excerpts that frame and title his chapters. This language of the heart is superseded by the language of science that grounds his strategy for re-mattering desire in science and politics.

Between the extremes of LeVay's materialism and postmodernist immaterialism, Wittig's work is curiously situated. Using the language of anatomy, she evokes her lover's body, turning it inside out by the power of word and in/cision. In this turning she creates a new direction in desire that makes a lesbian of mind and body. Ironically, she represents lesbian sex as fantastical, if not revolting and, above all, public, breaking open the skins of feminine purity as she breaks through the boundaries of the body and its Cartesian guardian, the straight mind. In her writing Wittig seeks a lesbian public, who can see in their desire a politics of resistance to straight materializations of woman. This is a pragmatic and anti-essentialist strategy aimed toward separatism and other dangerous pleasures.

Wittig understands lesbian body not as a function of misplaced parts (such as cross-gendered hypothalamic nuclei) and as more than a rhetorical construction of discourse. The persistence of lesbian desire is used by Wittig as an opening into an unknown territory and an orientation that allows lesbians to move the body's vocabulary and its ontology to another place. Wittig's project clearly recognizes corporeal location, the persistence of desire, a sexual politics of male domination, and the weight of heterosexual contract on the bodies of women. In poetic voice she speaks for a revolutionary violence necessary to break from the trajectory of sexual desire and its pseudopromise of a liberation while still committed to heterosexual ontologies and meanings. She re/minds us of a more animalistic craving for liberation as she dis/members and re/members our minding of the body. She creates a positivity that defines lesbian as a place to go *in the body* and as a strategy of survival against the regimes of power, whose conservative dream has always been one of death to lesbians and whose new postmodern dreamer calls for the dissolution of matter into words and the elimination of lesbian as a mark of difference. While LeVay seeks a return of the body to the contemporary body politic of the brother's polity, Wittig reconvenes a more radical politic of the body in her corporeal poetics. Both seek their beloved across the assemblies of matter.

THE MOUTH THE LIPS THE JAWS
THE EARS THE RIDGES OF THE EYE-
BROWS THE TEMPLES THE NOSE

THE CHEEKS THE CHIN THE FORE-
HEAD THE EYELIDS THE COM-
PLEXION THE ANKLE THE THIGHS
THE HAMS THE CALVES THE HIPS
THE VULVA THE BACK THE CHEST
THE BREASTS THE SHOULDER-
BLADES THE BUTTOCKS THE
ELBOWS THE LEGS THE TOES THE
FEET THE HEELS THE LIONS THE
NAPE THE THROAT THE HEAD THE
INSTEP THE GROINS THE TONGUE
THE OCCIPUT THE SPINE THE
FLANKS THE NAVEL THE PUBIS
THE LESBIAN BODY (Wittig).[46]

I am lost in a frenzy, unable to find where I am.
                    —René Descartes, *Meditations*

The struggle is always inner, and is played out in the
outer terrains.
                    —Gloria Anzaldúa, *Borderlands/La Frontera*[1]

Sitting in his small study over three centuries ago, René Descartes developed a foundation for scientific knowledge that required the separation of mental discipline from the chaotic passions of the body, as if mind and body constituted distinct and mutually exclusive substances. Anglo-European philosophy is indelibly marked by this Cartesian dualism, requiring a separation of the secular from the divine and the body's matter from an inner self. Much of Anglo-European philosophy has attempted to mediate the relations between these two substances: to reconcile the gap, explain their relations or reduce one to the other. In such thinking, the desire to overcome what appears to be an unbridgeable dualism—the gulf between mind and body—became an obsession that paid homage to the Cartesian knife as it sought to heal the wound.[2]

In Cartesian writing the disciplining of the mind is encumbered by the body's unruly passion. By training the mind to pursue none but clear and distinct ideas, the Cartesian dream voids the messiness of corporeal life.[3] Epistemic objectivity, as the purifying telos of Cartesian philosophy, is determined by a view from no particular body or from no particular location, "a view from nowhere."[4] This apositionality of the knower warrants that any mind, through proper discipline and training, can more effectively grasp objective truth.[5] In the scene of this grand inquiry, the particularities of the inquirer's body or personal experience ideally disap-

pear from the path of reason. Matters of the body are stationed in opposition to the knower as *the body*, an object of knowledge, becomes a
mechanically enclosed substance different from the inquiring mind.
Descartes inscribed upon the body this modernist trope of a mechanically
structured extended substance reducible to itself.

This is only one way to write the body's matter. Such writing may be
a function of genre and method, since philosophical writing aims toward
high-level abstraction, normative analytics, and a logic of generalizations,
as opposed to open-ended personal narrative or emotive effects. However,
in reconsidering Descartes' social location and his manner of writing,
even where he wrote—in a lonely chamber, longing for release from the
body's encumbrance—his corporeal location in history, social relation,
and culture may be reflected in how the body mattered to Descartes.[6]
Naomi Scheman has characterized our obsessive inheritance of Cartesian
philosophical tradition as neuroses of privilege:

> Those problems—notably the mind-body problem, problems of ref-
> erence and truth, the problem of other minds, the scepticism about
> knowledge of the external world—all concern the subject's ability or
> inability to connect with the split off parts of itself—its physicality,
> its sociability. Such problems are literally and unsurprisingly
> unsolvable so long as the subject's very identity is constituted by
> those estrangements. A subject whose authority is defined by his
> location on one side of a gulf cannot authoritatively theorize that
> gulf away. Philosophers' problems are the neuroses of privilege; dis-
> cipline makes the difference between such problems and the psy-
> chosis of full-blown paranoia.[7]

Scheman's analysis of Cartesian dualism both pathologizes its pater-
nal transmission and suggests that the problem itself may be a function
of social privilege, reflecting the willful interests and less conscious
investments of Descartes' class, race, and gendered privileges. How this
may be reflected in Cartesian writing on the body is suggested in the following sketch:

1. *Cartesianized writing demands a theoretical separation of the
   thinking mind from the writing body.*
2. *Cartesianized body seems to be suspended in an extended substance, metaphorically understood as a machinelike structure,*

> *lacking any significant memory of a collective history, geographic
> location, messy maternal birth, or ancestral bloodbaths.*
>
> 3. *Cartesianized body seems to lack a race or ethnicity, a recogniz-
>   able class identity, a traceable sexuality or any overtly gendered
>   dimension—it is "the body" in abstraction and of a substance dif-
>   ferent from "the mind."*
> 4. *Cartesianized body remains deeply immersed in this dualism, sep-
>   arating mind (or soul) from body and creating an ontic gulf that
>   establishes philosophical problems to be resolved or reproduced in
>   the disciplining of new philosophers.*

The academically trained philosopher often remains a loyalist to the
obsessions of Anglo-European cultural memory. While this loyalty may
be a matter of academic survival, disciplinary identity, and even genuine
interest, what would happen if we followed Scheman's hunch and
explored the ways in which Cartesian dualism may be related to social
privilege and the loss of responsive connection to physicality and socia-
blity—a neurotic state of affairs? In this chapter I will explore a completely different way of writing the body found in Gloria Anzaldúa's
mythopoetic work,[8] a writing that is deeply contextual, historically and
geographically located, and decidedly raced, sexed and gendered, and a
writing that hybridizes various ways of returning matter to theory. In my
reflections on what I call *Anzaldúan body* (as opposed to *Cartesian body*),
I pursue a slightly different hunch: that Cartesian dualism and Cartesian
body may have functioned historically to foster a cultural mentality that
supported European imperialism and the massive race genocides of
indigenous peoples of the Americas and throughout the world. The
philosopher's gulf that he wishes to theorize away is inflected in the splitting of land by war, theft, murder, and rape, leaving behind on the Continent the abstraction of philosophy's dualism and elsewhere in the world
the open wounds that ravaged "native" bodies and severed continuities of
life into metabolic continents of colonized pain and suffering.

The work of Gloria Anzaldúa provides a compelling voice from the south-
ern edge of a north Americanized and Cartesianized hemisphere. She
writes from where she stands at the threshold of these borders. I read
Anzaldúa as a philosopher, experimenting with forms that allow for
abstraction and metaphysical thinking without erasing her body or her
writing practices and her constantly changing locations.[9] She writes in

opposition to Cartesian thinking by giving to concrete events of daily life a space for larger reflective truths that do not require the disappearance of the thinker's body. Her writing constitutes a disassembly of Cartesianized writing practices, forcing us to question what is meant by "the body" or "the mind" and their relationship to a Euro-American colonizing of the body's matter.

Gloria Anzaldúa's *Borderlands/La Frontera* is a text that draws on her experience as a mestiza queer woman, born in Cargill Texas, in the borderlands between the United States and Mexico. The text compiles experiences, various identities, and cross currents of her life into a multi-linguistic writing *of the body*. She enters the text generously, drawing on history, memory, and personal narrative. In what follows I will trace the ways in which Anzaldúa's writing *of the body* brings us to a *body as activity* in resistance, survival, and historical transformation. Anzaldúan body, unlike the Cartesian body, breaks into history, geography, race memory, political struggle, and ancient practices of the flesh. Her writing returns to matters of the body through an evolution of non-Cartesianized discourse. I will follow this movement with her text close to us through five distinct images: open wound, face, skin, bone, and blood.

Herida Abierta: Open Wound

> *North Americans call this return to the homeland a silent invasion.*
>
> —GLORIA ANZALDÚA, *Borderlands/La Frontera*

In the opening chapter of *Borderlands/La Frontera* Anzaldúa tells the story of Mexican-American relations from a viewpoint of someone south looking north toward the Rio Bravo border. This is a view from somewhere. This perspective allows the author and reader to come from the history of Indian people, specifically the Cochise, and to bear witness to their subsequent subjugation and genocide: a loss of over twenty-four million bodies. In 1521, as a result of much bloodshed, intermarriage, and rape, a new race was born, *el mestizo, el mexicano,* a people of mixed Indian and Spanish blood, able to survive smallpox, measles, and typhus introduced by *los conquistadores*. This history of sex, disease, and war, created a geography of unsteady boundaries and changing landowner-ship, a specific location where Gloria Anzaldúa emerges in the late twentieth century as *una mestiza, una Chicana,* a woman displaced in a territory that first belonged to her ancestors, the Cochise, and further displaced by the homophobia and misogyny of her Mexican-American communities.

Born in Cargill, Texas, Anzaldúa describes herself in the Preface of *Borderlands/La Frontera* as a "border woman," who grew up between two cultures: "the Mexican (with a heavy Indian influence) and the Anglo (as a member of a colonized people in our own territory)."[10] Straddling the *Tejas*-Mexican border, the border becomes *una herida abierta* (an open wound) "where the Third world grates against the first and bleeds" (p. 13).[11] Instead of a mark, "a dividing line, a narrow strip along a steep edge" (p. 3), this open wound marks the border as a place of bodily suffering and historical violation. Such a border is not understood in its material bluntness—a chainlink fence crowned with rolled barbed wire—but in the life which hovers in the borderland, a vague and undetermined place created by the emotional residue of an unknown boundary, and in a constant state of transition. This is the place where the dominant culture contains its misfits: "The prohibited and forbidden are its inhabitants. *Los atravesados* live here: the squint-eyed, the perverse, the queer, the troublesome, the mongrel, the mulatto, the half-breed, the half dead; in short, those who cross over, pass over, or go through the confines of the "normal" (pp. 3–4). The purity of dominance is mired here.[12]

Many of the inhabitants of this borderland are named by verbal substantives related to border travel, *los atravesados* (*atravesar* = to cross over) and *los mojados* (*mojar* = to soak), making one an outsider on the other side, a "wetback" in the body traffic moving North. Anzaldúa writes, "the only 'legitimate' inhabitants are those in power, the whites and those who align themselves with the whites" (p. 3).[13] But the right to be there, to police the border, reveals its violent past in Anzaldúa's retelling of the land wars that wounded and slayed her original Indian ancestry. This open wound still cuts her body as it divided the land.

Bodies in the border culture are historically located in the intersections of cultures, histories, genetic mixing, divided families, and economic class struggle. "Tension grips the inhabitants of the borderlands like a virus. Ambivalence and unrest reside there and death is no stranger" (p. 4). Anzaldúa brings all of this into the hologram of her body poetry, first pressing a child's hand against the barbed wire and then transfiguring this touch into stakes of fence rod that split her body in two:

> *1,950 mile-long open wound*
> *dividing a* pueblo, *a culture,*
> *running down the length of my body,*
> *staking fence rods in my flesh,*
> *splits me splits me*
> me raja me raja
> *This is my home*
> *this thin edge of*
> barbwire. *(pp. 2–3)*

The body surviving here cannot easily escape its historical location, an experience of violence that splits the body just as a thick edge of barbwire cuts into the northward exodus. Conversely, metaphors of the flesh are impressed upon these struggles of shifting geographies. Gringos stripping the land from Indians and Mexicans are described through violent body metaphors. "*Con el destierro y el exilo fuimos desuñados, destroncados, destripados*—we were jerked out by the roots, truncated, disemboweled, dispossessed, and separated from our identity and our history" (pp. 7–8).[14] Such a history is re/membered as the body becomes a sensate resource for understanding the horrific magnitude of pain and grief in this violent geographic dislocation and genocidal assault. Anzaldúa names this history *el destierro,* a word that means exile as well as having the land taken from you. In turn, she uses body metaphor and memory to enable a crossing over of the living to the dead, transforming the body into an historical hologram that holds this past in the present.

One of the ways history and geography bear down on the body is in language policing. Born into a world where growing up female meant to hold her tongue, to remain silent, Anzaldúa transgresses this gender prohibition when she raises the question of which language to use in her writing: *que voz?* standard English, working-class and slang English, standard Spanish, standard Mexican Spanish, North Mexican Spanish dialect, Chicano Spanish in any number of regional variations, Tex-Mex, or Pachuco (pp. 58–59).[15] Languages and dialect are evidence of historical location and ethnicity figured in the disciplined tongue (speaking) and in the trained hand (writing), a close and intimate union when tongue mounts the hand of the writer. (Anzaldúa borrows from Margo Glantz, "*La lengua se monta sobre la mano y produce la escritura.*")[16] In this vision of language, the body is not seen as a rhetorical effect in theoretical space but as the tissued living and organic origin of language itself, which in turn creates the intimate interiors of life. Anzaldúa's writing *Borderlands/ La Frontera* in mixed languages and assorted styles reflects her ability to cross the borders of different language worlds with the radical felicity of *una atravesada*. Each language becomes a different point of interior and remembered connection.

These multiple tongues and the border talk of Chicano Spanish—*"un lenguaje que corresponde a un modo de vivir"* (p. 55)—retain the memory of colonial attempts to force English onto Chicano children or to shame children for their "inferior" Spanish. This history—*"el Anglo con cara de inocente nos arrancó la lengua"*—which placed a *"candados en la boca"* (padlocks on the mouth) (p. 54) is contrasted with the ease and pleasure Anzaldúa finds in her mix of languages and dialect. Anzaldúan body is a body in the process of nomadic decolonization. However, the history of cultural imperialism reappears in the intimacies of her writing, in the struggle to take pride in one's language and in the crossing from one lingua-culture to another. "If you want to really hurt me, talk badly about my language. Ethnic identity is twin skin to linguistic identity—I am my language" (p. 59).[17]

The border—*una herida abierta*—tears at the hearts and skins of a displaced people and fragments the bodies of the borderlands. The wound requires healing, but it also brings into awareness a self-relatedness to one's own body and its liminality when located at the threshold of various cultures and identities. Surviving there, oppressions directly affect the body, "the bruises throwing her back on herself and her feminine rhythm" (p. 23). This body, surviving the physical dis/integrations and subjective annihilations of literal torture and lethal wounding,[18] can become a resource for decolonization, for creating new meanings and border-crossings. For Anzaldúa writing the body resists the white Anglo colonizer as much as it transgresses the enforced silencing of her gender. She attends to her body with words and images:

> For silence to transform into speech, sounds and words, it must first traverse through our female bodies. For the body to give birth to utterance, the human entity must recognize itself as carnal—skin, muscles, entrails, brain, belly. Because our bodies have been stolen, brutalized or numbed, it is difficult to speak from/through them. *No hables de esas cosas, de eso no se habla. No hables, no hables! Cállate! Estáte quieta.* Seal your lips, woman! When she transforms silence into language, a woman transgresses.[19]

Cara: Face

> *Her face caught between* los intersticios
>   —Gloria Anzaldúa, *Borderlands/La Frontera*

Anzaldúan writing *of the body* produces soul. In her introduction to
Making Face/Haciendo Cara, she begins with the face:

> "Face" is the surface of the body that is the most noticeably
> inscribed by social structure, marked with instructions on how to be
> *mujer,* macho, working class, Chicana. As mestizas—biologically
> and/or culturally mixed—we have different surfaces for each aspect
> of identity, each inscribed by a particular subculture. We are "writ-
> ten" all over, or should I say, carved and tattooed with the sharp nee-
> dles of experience. (p. xv)

The "face, which is perhaps "the most naked, most vulnerable,
exposed and significant topography of the body" (p. xv) becomes a location for survival, resistance, accommodation, and self-creation. In the
English language one speaks of "making a face," "making faces," "saving
face," "losing face," or "making up" a face—linguistic expressions that
place the face inside our interactions with and against power. The face
shows with its whole surface and is constantly read for messages that support or undermine its speaking or its silence. "Face" is a medium of culture, a bodily surface where muscle and skin express nuances and shape
the feelings of finely tuned resistance and connection. Living within conflicting cultural tensions, Anzaldúa survives by *haciendo cara,* a phrase
(*hacer cara*) that also means "to face an enemy" and thus to have courage.
Anzaldúa survives with her faces traversing many daily worlds, making
her body not just an obstacle or mere object of contemplation but a vehicle of survival and crafty travel. In the "interfacing" of these various
worlds (p. 20), Anzaldúa seeks out those places where it is possible to
carve a face of one's own, a soul-making that is motion *from the outside
in* (from face) and *from the inside out* (from soul):

> In sewing terms, "interfacing" means sewing a piece of material
> between two pieces of fabric to provide support and stability to a col-
> lar, cuff, yoke. Between the masks we've internalized, one on top of
> another, are our interfaces. . . . it is the place—the interface—

between the masks that provides the space from which we can thrust out and crack the masks. (pp. xv–xvi)

Making face for Anzaldúa is a means of making soul. *"Usted es el moldeador de su carne tanto como el de su alma"* (p. xvi). This works not by assuming a Cartesian separation of soul from body but by assuming their inseparable intermingling and coexistence in the living flesh. Each area of the body becomes a possible morphic space for making soul or for masking its protection. In this experience of self-protection, the outer is split from the inner and thus creates the experience of the inner with a face that hides what is less visible and perhaps more precious to its inward side. The body both hides and makes the soul. In other words, only through the body can the human soul be created, transformed, and protected. To capture this power Anzaldúa appeals to the Nahuatl concept of *la Coatlicue*, which she describes as an ancient Indian spirit power for transforming one thing into another. Writing is for Anzaldúa such a power:

> When I write it feels like I'm carving bone. It feels like I'm creating my own face, my own heart—a Nahuatl concept. My soul makes itself through the creative act. It is constantly remaking and giving birth to itself through my body. It is this learning to live with *la Coatlicue* that transforms living in the borderlands from a nightmare into a numinous experience. It is always a path/state to something else. (p. 73)

Piel: Skin

> *Every time she makes "sense" of something, she has to "cross over," kicking a hole out of the old boundaries of the self and slipping under or over, dragging the old skin along, stumbling over it.*
>
> —GLORIA ANZALDÚA, *Borderlands/La Frontera*

The human skin is thought to separate the inside of the body from the outside world. Wounding the skin causes a blending of inner with outer and outer with inner—at times a matter of life and death. In Anzaldúa's writing, skin is also a border through which many things pass, such as blood, fluids, metaphors, images, sounds, and spirits. As a Chicana, she must defend her skin, but this skin is not a mute or simple surface. It is both permeable and ruggedly enduring. Her skin can become the skin of a cactus, a turtle, a serpent, a coyote, a rattlesnake in alternate states of metaphorical consciousness supplying her body with the power to move on. "*Soy nopal de castilla* like the spineless and therefore defenseless cactus that Mamagrande Ramona grew in back of her shed. I have no protections. So I cultivate needles, nettles, razor-sharp spikes to protect myself from others" (p. 45). As a cactus, her skin signifies protection against race hatred, imperialist greed, misogyny, and homophobia.

The serpent, a second metaphorical skin for Anzaldúa, provides the surface for another meditation. Anzaldúa begins with her mother's warning not to go to the outhouse at night. "A snake will crawl into your *nalgas*, make you pregnant" (p. 25). This is followed by an incident where the family was chopping cotton at the Jesus Maria Ranch and Anzaldúa is bitten by a rattlesnake. Her mother killed the snake with her hoe and cut it to pieces. "When Mama had gone down the row and was out of sight, I took out my pocketknife. I made an X over each prick. My body followed the blood, fell into the soft ground. I put my mouth over the red and sucked and spit between the rows of cotton" (p. 26). That night Anzaldúa's body is transformed into the serpent, as she "dreamed rattler fangs filled my mouth, scales covered my body" (p. 26). This metamorphosis introjects *Coatlicue*, the Serpent goddess, into the body:

> In the morning I saw through snake eyes, felt snake blood course through my body. The serpent, *mi tono*, my animal counterpart. I was immune to its venom. Forever immune. . . . Forty years it's taken me to enter into the Serpent, to acknowledge that I have a body, that I am a body and to assimilate the animal body, the animal soul. (p. 26)

Coatlicue—"a consuming internal whirlwind" (p. 46)[20]—allows Anzaldúa to slow down, to leave the everyday world, and to exit the demands of a literal-centered Anglo-European reality. She enters a *Coatlicue* state through a *susto*, a sudden jolt that frightens the soul out of the body, allowing her to rest and recuperate without interference or condemnation. From there she can get beyond the *embrujadas* that hold her from her destiny and keep the soul arrested. "Frozen in stasis, she perceives a slight movement—a thousand slithering serpent hairs, *Coatlicue*. It is activity (not immobility) at its most dynamic stage, but it is an underground movement requiring all her energy. It brooks no interference from the conscious mind" (p. 47). She describes the process of descent and self recovery through the layerings of serpent skins:

When I reach bottom, something forces me to push up, walk toward the mirror, confront the face in the mirror. But I dig in my heels and resist. I don't want to see what's behind *Coatlicue*'s eyes, her hollow sockets. I can't confront her face to face; I must take small sips of her face through the corners of my eyes, chip away at the ice a sliver at a time. Behind the ice mask I see my own eyes." (p. 48)

Miro que estoy encabronada, miro la resistencia—resistance to knowing, to letting go, to that deep ocean where once I dived into death. I am afraid of drowning. Resistance to sex, intimate touching, opening myself to the alien other where I am out of control, not on patrol. The outcome of the other side unknown, the reins falling and the horses plunging blindly over the crumbling path rimming the edge of the cliff, plunging into its thousand foot drop. (p. 48)

It is only then that her consciousness expands a tiny notch, another rattle appears on the rattlesnake tail and the added growth slightly alters the sounds she makes. (p. 49)

Every increment of consciousness, every step forward is a *travesiá*, a crossing. . . . I am no longer the same person I was before. (p. 48)

In this place Anzaldúa reaches another state of awareness through a deep transformation in figurative consciousness. The shame and terror that can hold her life in stasis or to the constant and frenzied repetitions of daily life give way to a new level of awareness, as she sheds the old skin and crosses over into a new life form. In her journey through the body she crosses many such borders, not only the literal external borders separating one land from another, one language from another, but also an internal border that separates one self from another. Crossing a border, she becomes a different person. In this inward journey she is assisted by the historical retrieval of *Nahual* that crafts her transformations into coyote, cactus, serpent, or other forms that strengthen her self-knowledge and inner transformation. In making this body with her words, she is making soul. In making this soul, she introjects a labyrinth of borders, mappings, histories, and spiritual powers from the outside. Her skin is a border between inner and outer, but a border to be crossed; her body *una bocacalle* (p. 80).

To be a mouth—the cost is too high—her whole life enslaved to that devouring mouth. *Todo pasaba por esa boca, el viento, el fuego, los mares y la Tierra.* Her body, a crossroads, a fragile bridge, cannot support the tons of cargo passing through it. She wants to install "stop" and "go" signal lights, instigate a curfew, police Poetry. But something wants to come out. (p. 74)

Hueso: Bone

As her book *Borderlands/La Frontera* begins to take shape, emerging in "a weaving pattern, thin here, thick there" (p. 66), Anzaldúa often finds the bones or the deep structure of the text emerging in the writing process, not from a linear method of thinking the deep structure first and then moving to the surface. Rather, she is more preoccupied with textures and the slippage of one category into another:

> Too, I see the barely contained color threatening to spill over the boundaries of the object it represents and into other "objects" and over the borders of the frame. I see a hybridization of metaphor, different species of ideas popping up here, popping up there, full of variations and seeming contradictions, though I believe in an ordered, structured universe where all phenomena are interrelated and imbued with spirit. This almost finished product seems an assemblage, a montage, a beaded work with several leitmotifs and with a central core, now appearing, now disappearing in a crazy dance. (p. 66)

In this birthing, a thing with a life of its own emerges. "It is a rebellious, willful entity, a precocious girl-child forced to grow up too quickly, rough, unyielding, with pieces of feather sticking out here and there, fur, twigs, clay. My child, but no for much longer. This female being is angry, sad, joyful, is *Coatlicue*, dove, horse, serpent, cactus" (pp. 66–67). Talking back to Anzaldúa as she talks with it, this physical and psychic offspring becomes a book, an essay, or a poem. They make greedy demands on her life, calling her talents to the yoke of writing while they struggle to be liberated into a world of readers.

In her writing process Anzaldúa's body becomes both encumbrance and resource. In the inner screen of her mind, stories and images emerge, an experience that is especially available to her when she is alone and in a state of sensory-deprivation that induces a trancelike experience. "I am held prisoner to it. My body is experiencing events" (p. 70). She enters these scenes from outside the frame as a director, and from inside as an actor, constantly crossing these boundaries of inner and outer in the subjective theaters of her body. "Sometimes, I put imagination to a more rare use. I choose worlds, images, and body sensations and animate them to impress them on my consciousness, thereby making changes in my belief system and reprogramming my consciousness" (p. 70). This involves facing her "inner demons" and deciding which to nourish and which to starve. "This is harder to do than to merely generate 'stories.' I can only sustain this activity for a few minutes" (p. 71).

Anzaldúa's writing is fed by this pleasure and pain. The pain Anzaldúa describes as a cactus needle embedded in the flesh, that digs deeper, delivers more pain as she pokes at it, and finally breaks her surface skin with a festering sore. She must dig deeper to pluck it out, a pain that is transformed into pleasure, "playing it like a musical instrument—the fingers pressing, making the pain worse before it can get better" (p. 73).[21] Her writing cycle, which carries her through cultural blocks and psychic unrest, is "an endless cycle of making it worse and making it better"— eventually transforming her own soul and perhaps that of her readers. In this way her writing body crosses over to the body of the reader, "piercing tongue and ear lobes with a cactus needle, are my offerings, are my Aztecan blood sacrifices" (p. 75). The reader must stay open to what Anzaldúa calls the "crazy dance" in order to be recarved to the bone.

There is clearly no separation of body from mind in Anzaldúa's work. The body's interferences, grieved as a nuisance in Cartesian writing, become occasions for continuous shape-shifting and creative process for Anzaldúa. This process is best grasped by metaphor, a style of pictorial writing that links the writing body, the body-written, and the reading body, in a flesh-to-flesh connection. As Anzaldúa suggests, "images are more direct, more immediate than words, and closer to the unconscious. Picture language precedes thinking in words; the metaphorical mind precedes the analytical" (p. 69). Unlike Cartesian meditation that splits the mind from the body, Anzaldúa's thinking stays connected to and located in her body. Her use of metaphor reverses Cartesian dualities, to "concretize the spirit" and to "etherealize the body" (p. 75).

Sangre: Blood

> *I am a turtle, wherever I go I carry "home" on my back.*
> —GLORIA ANZALDÚA, *Borderlands/La Frontera*

Like many women, Anzaldúa leaves her home to find her way as *una Chicana con consciencia, una chingada,* and *una joteriá.* Departing from home because she is no longer welcome as a critic of her culture, as a sexual deviant in her community, and as a defiled woman among her people, Anzaldúa takes a geographic but not a spiritual leave. She carries with her the "homeground," the ancestral roots of her mestiza heart. The figure of the turtle body gives her a strength to carry what is most precious under the protection of her hardened skin: "Being Mexican is a state of soul—not one of mind, not one of citizenship" (p. 62). In this journey away from home, she spirals toward an inner reclamation of her own body as a place where her fragments can be re-formed and made into her own territory.

This inner journey requires a way of seeing through the colonized body and its Western dualisms, Catholic shame, and suffered violations. In both the Anglo-European and Mexican-Catholic culture, Anzaldúa finds a cultural loathing of the body, especially the body of women, queers, and *la chingada.* "The Catholic and Protestant religions encourage fear and distrust of life and of the body; they encourage a split between the body and the spirit and totally ignore the soul; they encourage us to kill off parts of ourselves" (p. 37). For Anzaldúa the female body is no more safe in Mexican-Catholic environments—"*esta raza vencida, enemigo cuerpo*" (p. 22)—where women's bodies are traditionally required to fulfill one of two functions, to serve man or to serve God. Moving from a world where women are placed in the name of these protectors, Anzaldúa seeks new survival strategies and new ways of respecting the intelligences and creative powers of her body. "We are taught that the body is an ignorant animal; intelligence dwells only in the head. But the body is smart. It does not discern between external stimuli and stimuli from the imagination. It reacts equally viscerally to events from the imagination as it does to "real" events (pp. 37–38). This journey into and through her body happens at least in part in her writing as she traverses worlds attempting to split her body into categorical fragments; *Me raja!* In this travel she seeks a third way in her own body where oppositional dualisms are rendered coexisting tendencies and potentials in the core of her flesh. Her body becomes a place expanding and contracting oppositional and contradictory tendencies.

> The new mestiza copes by developing a tolerance for contradictions,
> a tolerance for ambiguity. She learns to be an Indian in Mexican cul-

ture, to be Mexican from an Anglo point of view. She learns to juggle cultures. She has a plural personality, she operates in a pluralistic mode—nothing is thrust out, the good the bad and the ugly, nothing rejected, nothing abandoned. Not only does she sustain contradictions, she turns the ambivalence into something else.

From this perspective, mestiza blood and mestiza consciousness merge two cultural and physical blood worlds, just as Anzaldúa experiences her queerness as a merging of both sexes. Male and female in one body become capacities of her singular flesh. "I am the embodiment of the *hieros gamos*: the coming together of opposite qualities within" (p. 19).[22] With the ancient alchemic term "*hieros gamos*," Anzaldúa reclaims her body in all of its morphic forms—a body despised for its queerness in both Anglo-American and Catholic Mexican cultures, but powerful in its capacity to merge the dualities of modernist sex ontology. For Anzaldúa this is a "*loqueriá*, a way of balancing and mitigating duality." Just as her mestiza blood runs *mita' y mita'*, so in her sex, she is *mita' y mita'* (p. 19). "The soul makes use of whatever comes its way" (p. 46)—"a blending that proves that all blood is intricately woven together, and that we all spawned out of similar souls" (p. 85). To leave home as a sexual exile is to venture this different path of knowledge.

All of these connections are corporeal as her writing folds back onto her body making and re-making her soul. For Anzaldúa, images, words, and stories can have this transformative power on the writer and the reader only when, they "arise from the human body—flesh and bone—and from the Earth's body—stone, sky, liquid, soil" (p. 75). Anzaldúa writes with *tlilli, tlapalli*, the black and red inks found in the ancient Aztec codices, inks that signify *escritura* (writing) and *sabiduriá* (wisdom). She converts these inks into her blood: "*Escribo con la tinta de mi sangre*. I write in red. Ink. Intimately knowing the smooth touch of paper, its speechlessness before I spill myself on the insides of trees" (p. 71).

Una mestiza is a struggle of flesh, a struggle of borders, an inner war. Anzaldúa describes her border-life as a morphogenesis, a changing of forms in the flesh, created through writing and daily survival in the borderlands. "In our very flesh, (r)evolution works out the clash of cultures. It makes us crazy constantly, but if the center holds, we've made some kind of evolutionary step forward. *Nuestro alma el trabajo*, the opus, the great alchemical work; spiritual *mestizaje*, a 'morphogenesis,' an inevitable unfolding. We have become the quickening serpent movement" (p. 81).

The power of the body is not its sheer mechanism but its *meta*-physical ability to deconstruct the polarities of dualism by physically blending and kneading (*"soy un amasamiento,* I am an act of kneading," p. 81) the fragmented body. In making and remaking her body, her soul is *fleshed out* in and through her body. Anzaldúa resists a North-American academic insistence that she sever the head from the body, soul from the flesh, man from woman, human from animal, animal from vegetable, Anglo from Mexican, heterosexual from homosexual, spiritual from sexual, living from dead, and the inner from the outer.

In this resistance a bleeding border between North and South reappears. For Anzaldúa the apparent dualities of the North are not completely derivable from a philosophical separation of mind from body in Anglo-European philosophy. They can also be read as dualities originating in an imperialist division of conscience and consciousness emerging at the open wound of history—*una herida abierta*—and calling forth *el susto* and resistance in the still-living survivors. From an Anzaldúan horizon, the Anglo-Cartesian-disciplined body exists in its displacement from history and in its complicity with continuing political atrocities. This is preconditioned by an abstract separation of body from mind that feeds a capital-driven historical amnesia—a dislocation of bodies from their concrete locations in social and historical life. In its contemporary form, such a body is reduced to capital gains, quick fixes, and metric means in a materialism of self-redundancy and isolation.

This body was first prefigured in how bodies mattered to Descartes. His was a body that seldom left home, that sat alone in secluded libraries and contemplated the familiar as terrifying. He experienced his body as nuisance, sloth, and lethargy (interrupting the work of philosophy). His was a body unified by skin and isolated from the external world, from other bodies, and from all that flows between bodies (substances otherwise causing great pollution and disturbance to his reason). His was a body lacking in intelligence (since the mind was thought separable from the mindless body). His was a body that housed what it was alien—a soul that longed for the purity of a Godhead and that loathed ambiguity and the weight and mess of matter. *His way* was inward and then *out of the body*.

Anzaldúa's way is different—a constant motion-in-relation *moving out in the body*. Her morphogenesis creates non-Cartesian ways of writing and figuring the body as deeply mediated in historical, geographic, and personal narratives. A body not incited by capital or by the social privileges of race, sex, and culture, Anzaldúan body becomes a resilient agent and resource and her means of survival. Her writing develops a sixth sense, a sensual long-distance capacity that connects her body to history, to the race struggles of her ancestry, and to the lived experiences of *los olvidos*: this sixth sense receives by means of a story:

> "Drought hit South Texas," my mother tells me. *"La tierra se puso bien seca y los animales comenzaron a morirse de se. Mi papá se murío de un* heart attack *dejando a mamá* pregnant y *con ocho huercos,* with eight kids and one on the way. *Yo fuí la major, tenía diez años.* The next year the drought continued y *el ganado* got hoof and mouth. *Se calleron* in droves en *las pastas y el* brushland, *pansas blancas* ballooning to the skies. *El siguiente año* still no rain. *Mi pobre madre viuda perdió* two-thirds of her *ganado.* A smart *gabacho* lawyer took the land away when *mamá* hadn't paid the taxes. *No hablaba inglés,* she didn't know how to ask for time to raise the money." My father's mother, Mama Locha, also lost her *terreno.* For a while we got $12.50 a year for the "mineral rights" of six acres of cemetery, all that was left of the ancestral lands. Mama Locha had asked that we bury her there beside her husband. *El cemeterio estaba cercado.* But there was a fence around the cemetery, chained and padlocked by the ranch owners of the surrounding land. We couldn't even get in to visit the graves, much less bury her there. Today, it is still padlocked. The sign reads: "Keep out. Trespassers will be shot." (p. 8)

History of the land returns through Anzaldúa's body, through her senses, feelings, pleasures, and pains. She makes her history concrete by facing the life and death issues of historical trauma.[23] Although hers is a body immersed and inseparable from history, it is not completely overwhelmed by history. Hers is a nomadic but located body insisting on survival, memory, and transformation by writing always in motion and in relation. Whereas the Anglo-European body haunted by Cartesian dualism relies on the pure interiority of the mind, cut off from the physicality of the body and from social/historical relation, Anzaldúan body transgresses these boundaries "writing the gulf away" and articulating "truths" from a variety of shifting perspectives.[24]

Anzaldúan mestiza morphogenesis begins literally with the physical mix of blood and blended sexes and progresses through the emergence of a creative bricolage—collecting what she needs from histories, cultures, geographies and from her body's creative energies. "And suddenly I feel everything rushing to a center, a nucleus. All the lost pieces of myself come flying from the deserts and the mountains and the valleys, magnetized toward that center. *Completa*" (p. 51). As such, Anzaldúan body is not a mere surface or a tabula rasa; not a sheer mechanism; not the muted flesh of victimism; it is a place where powers "metaphorize" against ruling dualisms and against the deadly stasis of domination and servitude. This *meta-morph*ing moves the body into a radical aesthetic and political space filled with a growing consciousness of history, connection, Cargill, Texas, woodsmoke, homemade white cheese sizzling in the pan, hot steaming tamales, and red pieces of panza and hominy floating on top of a spicy *menudo* (p. 61). Moving *outward in her own body*, Anzaldúa's writing is a constant motion *incorporating the memory and meanings of shifting geographies and historical struggle*.

Returning Matters

> *Stubborn, persevering, impenetrable as stone, yet possessing the malleability that renders us unbreakable.*
> —Gloria Anzaldúa, *Borderlands/La Frontera*

I have closely followed Anzaldúa's writings to explore another way to return the body to philosophy. Unlike the reductionism of many materialist philosophies, Anzaldúa's way of *mattering the body* challenges the discursive construction of matter reflected in Cartesian extensions of European conquest. For Anzaldúa the division between the body's inner and outer is not a clear distinction, as the skin becomes a border for crossing and a means of historical survival and shape-shifting. Her corporeal writing is based on metaphor and memory, energy and suffering, introspection and connections—unlike Cartesian doubt, which seems to be based on enduring isolation and a continuous logic of the present. Anzaldúa's figurations of her body draw from the outer world (from other living and nonliving forms of matter) to re-make her body and its powers, just as her body provides metaphors for bringing her surroundings and past into different foci and perspectives. Soul-making and identity-making do not result in insular or singularly split identities (the Cartesian *je* or the Wittigian *j/e*)[25] but in a multiplication of blending identities with many interconnections to life and matter, dissolving into *"no hay más que cambiar"* (p. 49) and condensing at various points into the tentative and potent jolts of *susto*:

She can be jarred out of ambivalence by an intense, and often painful, emotional event which inverts or resolves the ambivalence. I'm not sure exactly how. The work takes place underground—subconsciously. It is work that the soul performs. The focal point or fulcrum, that juncture where the mestiza stands, is where phenomena tend to collide. It is where the possibility of uniting all that is separate occurs. This assembly is not one where severed or separated pieces merely come together. Nor is it a balancing of opposing powers. In attempting to work out the synthesis, the self has added a third element which is greater that the sum of its severed parts. That third element is a new consciousness—a mestiza consciousness—and though it is a source of intense pain, its energy comes from continual creative motion that keeps breaking down the unitary aspect of each new paradigm. *En unas pocas centurias,* the future will belong to the *mestiza.* (pp. 79–80)

This new mestiza consciousness is experienced by Anzaldúa by writing through and in the body. Anzaldúan embodiment resides in a space of Cartesian negation: not as the body of pure mechanism; not as the body isolated from social relation and historical location; not as the mind separated from body, emotion, and suffering; not as the mind relocating itself in the pure interiority of reason; not as the self relocated in the ahistoricity of an objective, universal voice of authority. In mestiza consciousness perspectivism shifts and orchestrates a larger voice coming together from centuries past and from the other side of landed, gendered, and sexual borders. In this new mestiza framing, the body's matter incorporates the memory and suffering of ancestors and family, rearticulated in the many particular voices emerging through a body that is local, specific, and living. This is a view from somewhere. This way of returning bodily matters to the scene of philosophy recasts what Scheman has couched as Cartesian neuroses of privilege into a violence perpetrated by the Anglo-European colonizing mind, unable to read the gulf between mind and body as the *herida abierta* of human suffering and as the arrogant tyranny of reason's race against the body.

Venus: The Looks of Body Theory[1]

"Whatever you want to be, you can be.

"You can become anything and do anything and it won't be questioned."   —An MC voice at the ballrooms

When I first saw Jennie Livingston's documentary film *Paris Is Burning*, I was sitting in a mostly white and gay audience in a movie theater located near the lake district of a fairly well-to-do urban area in Minneapolis. I had gone across town to see the film because it was a "must see" event, adulated as "incredible," "wonderful," and "out of this world" by many of my film-going friends. I was not disappointed. Jennie Livingston's *Paris Is Burning* documents a New York City black and Latino culture found in the drag balls of Harlem, where gay men, transvestites, and transsexuals congregate to compete against each other as they walk the runway before an assembly of enthusiastic lookers and judges. The walks are various, not just female impersonations but drags of Military Realness, Executive Realness, Going to School, Real Man, and other categories, where black and Latino bodies perform the images and identities of contemporary commercialism on Harlem's runways. To win a trophy at a drag ball is to come the closest to the Real, a word that darts throughout this documentary, accompanied by Cheryl Lynn's seventies tune, "Got To Be Real." To win a category is to be better than the others according to the rules. It is for that split second, to be real, a mending of the social rift between desire and reality. From where I sat, the mood that inhabited the theater was filled with visual delight and enthusiasm.

I will speak only from my own experience. I loved it. I was swept away by the intense pleasures of the drag ball participants whose lives seemed to circulate around the ball competitions. I was saddened by the death of Venus extravaganza, a preoperative transsexual Latino fem who was "presumably" murdered by a john during the two years of filming. My pleasure was twisted by a sense of wistfulness and premonition that inhabited each scene, the clairvoyant wisdom of the older queens, and the joyous moments of staged life. My pleasure was also voyeuristic. I felt what I had felt before, sitting behind the scenes with a lover years ago who was cross-dressing for her performance of Michael Jackson at a local Sunday night drag show. I was the only white person backstage, listening to the joys of transgender dishing, watching female impersonators get ready, and catching sight of a woman, who would perform Billy Ocean, binding her breasts and applying a mustache. I remember then wishing I could make a documentary of this. What was this fascination? What was my "white look" doing there?

Since my first enthusiastic viewing of *Paris Is Burning*, the documentary has become somewhat of an academic cult film, where the work finds a lively currency in gender performance theories and current academic fascination with transgender experience. Why, I must ask, after my first viewing of the documentary, did I too feel the urge to write about this piece? In what follows I will explore several gender and race analyses that have emerged from *Paris Is Burning* as a function of viewer identities, especially the race perspective of the viewer, and as a function of "receiving contexts"—whom you sat with, whom you talked to, who talked back, who listened, and who controlled the conversation. While *Paris Is Burning* was made by a white lesbian filmmaker, Jenny Livingston, and while many commentators have pointed out the lack of any interrogation of the race/racist components of the film's making and viewing, I find this lack energetically addressed in the space that has opened up since the film's appearance, namely "the talk back space" where theorists and critics have engaged a new kind of theory-making that brings theory back to the body, to social location and identity, and to the self-reflective process of visual literacy. In what follows I explore the looks of body theory.

Black Straight Looks[2]

My own visual pleasure in viewing *Paris Is Burning* was first challenged when bell hooks's essay "Is Paris Burning?" appeared in her collected writings, *Black Looks: Race and Representation*.[3] Reading hooks's essay was disturbing. It caused me to reflect on the constructed subjectivity of the camera and the spectator looking at *Paris Is Burning*. After reading hooks, I had to reconsider my own experience: "Was the gaze in *Paris Is Burning* white?" Originally the documentary was named after the most important drag ball of the season—Paris Is Burning—and hooks changes this title into a question as she interrogates the politics of black drag as well as the documentary's production and use. She locates a body trouble in both the aspirations of a vulnerable black community and its worship of whiteness and in the relationship of the filmmaker, Jennie Livingston, a white lesbian documenting a black underclass. It is Livingston who captures these ghetto images for commercial circulation in a white America. As hooks writes:

> And no, I didn't just love it. For in many ways the film was a graphic documentary portrait of the way in which colonized black people (in this case black gay brothers, some of whom were drag queens) worship at the throne of whiteness, even when such worship demands that we live in perpetual self-hate, steal, lie, go hungry, and even die in its pursuit. (p. 148)

> What could be more reassuring to the white public fearful that marginalized disenfranchised black folks might rise any day now and make revolutionary black liberation struggle a reality than a documentary affirming that colonized, victimized, exploited, black folks are all too willing to be complicit in perpetuating the fantasy that ruling-class white culture is the quintessential site of unrestricted joy, freedom, power, and pleasure. (p. 149)

In *Paris Is Burning*, where hooks saw internalized oppression, I saw resistance. Where hooks experienced anger and displeasure, I experienced delight and exuberance. Where I felt the death of Venus was present in the tragic underside of the documentary, hooks saw a superficial treatment. Where I felt the presence of the filmmaker as transparent, hooks found her whiteness problematic and her work a colonizing appropriation of black experience converted into a colorful ethnicity for the white consumer. Where I felt entertained by and had some identification with the subversive body performances, hooks felt ripped off and pandered to with thinly veiled images of white conformity and black self-hatred. Apparently, hooks and I saw and experienced very different documentaries, something that seems to emerge from our different locations and identities, from where we sat, with whom, and how the images affected us.

However, didn't hooks see that there were other categories besides the glamorous white ruling class *female* body pursued by these drag artists? Didn't she see that there was a haughty ridicule and irony in this staging of white femininity? Didn't she see the community of "houses," "mothers," and "sisters," as the older mother-positioned mavericks created an ambience of care and resistance in a hostile and brutally homophobic and race-hating world? Didn't she see the lamentations for the murdered Venus expressed by mother Angie Extravaganza and the looming sense of danger and tragedy that frames the images of the documentary? Didn't hooks see that the pleasure experienced by the black and Latino brothers was real and life affirming for them? Didn't the brothers say that this *was* their entertainment? Was this really false consciousness?

I agree with hooks that there was no direct interrogation of the whiteness in the documentary: neither the whiteness of the idealized drag nor the whiteness of the filmmaker nor the complacent "whiteness" of a white spectator. The bodies in the documentary in no way gave me a direct "read" on the race of my own gaze. But why didn't I see that whiteness was represented as the quintessential site of liberatory pleasure? Why didn't I see the pain and despair of race imitation? Why didn't I feel the presence of Livingston, a white woman screening across the top of a culture and socioeconomic world very different from her own reality? Why did I feel safe watching these images? Why did I feel in good company? What was my "white look" doing there? What was Jenny doing there? Certainly my own gaze is widened and challenged by hooks talking back to her readers, but I am more like Jenny in other ways. Wasn't Octavia Extravaganza Jenny's kind of girl?[4]

Queer Black Looks

My thinking was given another spin when I encountered Jackie Goldsby at the Outwrite Conference in Boston, where she mentioned that she had written an essay on *Paris Is Burning*. She warned me that she had written her essay before reading bell hooks's essay. When I found it, Jackie Goldsby's "Queens of Language: *Paris Is Burning*" was a pleasure to read.[5] As a reader, I experienced a different perspective from a writer who owns among her other identities, African-American and queer. At that same conference I listened to Robert Reid-Pharr present an impressive paper. Later I came across his essay "The Spectacle of Blackness."[6] Both of these essays written by queer theorists of color created a new "talk back space," that adds to the voice of hooks. Again my own white look was challenged.

Goldsby and Reid-Pharr both had very complex viewing experiences of *Paris Is Burning*. Goldsby's overall experience was highly positive: she thanks Livingston for making a documentary that gave voice to the drag queens: "I am thankful that she did, because never has speech, as performance and oral text, been so irresistible to my eyes and ears" (p. 115). Reid-Pharr describes two experiences in his viewing of Livingston's work:

> Black gay New York had come out *en masse* to see its own. Waiting in line was itself a lesson in the intricacies of black speech, dress, hair, gossip, attitude and camp. Our reaction to the film was nothing less than outrageous. People were doubled over laughing in their seats as Pepper LaBeija held forth on the intricacies of House Life. We squealed our approval as "sisters" vogued their way across the screen. We talked back to the characters, even read them, while at the same time openly yearning that one, just one, might trick fate and snatch up the crown of glory." (p. 62)

At a second viewing in a Soho theater, Reid-Pharr had a completely different experience sitting in an almost completely white audience:

> This time the atmosphere seemed thoroughly domesticated. Laughter came on cue. The only spontaneous responses I heard were the whispered complaints of a lesbian couple who found the queens' gender politics offensive. This time my focus was not on myself. I didn't wonder what I would do if I were up there. Didn't care what category I would walk in at the ball. I was forced instead to consider how very tragic what I was seeing actually was. The narrative seemed entirely too played and tired: the Black subjects caught up in a dream of whiteness, sacrifice their ties to reality and end in tragedy and despair." (p. 62)

It would seem that in looking at *Paris Is Burning*, it does matter where you come from, where you sit, with whom, who determines how you look, who talks back, who laughs, who listens, who gets printed, who gets forgotten, and who controls the conversation. Theory is at some level just that: a prolonged conversation helping us get clear on what happened and what we can do about it. "We" is the most important pronoun. As hooks commented, "I reflected on why whites could so outspokenly make their pleasure in this film heard and why the many black viewers who express discontent, raising critical questions about how the film was made, is seen, and is talked about, have not named their displeasure publicly" (p. 153). The polyphony of voices from hooks, Goldsby, and Reid-Pharr creates an array of possibilities.

What surprised me was Goldsby's claim that Jennie Livingston's whiteness provides an uncanny optic advantage. She contrasts Livingston's treatment of drag queens with that of director Marlon Riggs in *Tongues Untied* (1989): "that Riggs silences drag queens is the obverse of Livingston's authority to accord them speech" (p. 115). To Goldsby, the drag queens in Livingston's work were not silenced or wistfully drawn; in fact they seemed to love the camera with its promised eye to a larger public. Riggs's silencing of queens Goldsby explains as a possible conflict of his own race and gender identities with that of the black queens. His hesitance, perhaps even embarrassment, results in a closed image, a tragic portrayal of queens, whereas Livingston's distance in class and race privilege opened a playful and loquacious queeny space. Is hooks's identity likewise implicated along the lines of race and gender in the visible presence of black queen subjectivity? Or is the figuration of white femininity in the black male body differently problematic for Riggs and hooks? Where hooks experienced anger and displeasure, did Riggs produce a "shade"? Are these displeasures displaced by the play of desire?

Goldsby's look at *Paris Is Burning* recaptures the fragile vulnerability of the Harlem drag ball culture, its crafted personages, spectacles, and ball world lexicon as a culture of resistance, a resistance to what has most devastated the stability and security of this life world, namely the violence of capitalism and white racism. Bypassed by the cybernetic world of white transnational capitalism, these neighborhoods of poverty are still flooded with advertised images of opulence and wealth. Cut off from the capital resources for acquiring such a lifestyle, the "children" of the ball culture make up their own legends from white cultural fantasy. To win trophies in the ball world is to become a legend. Rich and famous designer fantasies become a playground of liminal possession on the runways of Harlem's ball culture. As Goldsby reviews this, the oppressive oppositions, "male/female, colored/white, power/disenfranchisement, margin/center, the aisle-cum-run-way at the Imperial Elks Lodge (where many of the competitions were filmed) becomes a path into the psyche of ball culture; its logic unfolds in subversive splendor" (p. 110).

To Goldsby, the "legendary children" of the Houses "take consumerism to its logical conclusion: identity is nothing so much as commodity fetish," performed before the approving gaze of the House "mothers," the "sisters," and an eubullient audience of admirers and lookers (p. 111). To make it Real is to find status and security in these communities of survival. As one young man expressed it in the documentary, "I went to a ball. I got a trophy. And now everybody wants to know me."[7] A trophy, a parodic equivalent to an Oscar, creates a sense of real glory and social status. As Goldsby comments,

> That the children, legendary or not, want what these life-styles represent is entirely explicable; indeed, their desires are wholly logical within the scheme of consumer capitalism. They should want to be Alexis Colby and Blake Carrington (or Ronald and Nancy Reagan, for that matter) precisely because they are of color, poor, and queer, living in one of the most class-conscious cities in the country. Why shouldn't they want out of their reality? (p. 111)

What could otherwise be construed as a *Bluest Eye*[8] problem for hooks is (re)versed in Goldsby's vision as subversion and salvation: "Drag, for these black and Latin queens (*haute femme* and butch alike), disrupts the economy of desire and difference, the identification of self with an object meant to represent self, that fuels consumerism" (p. 111). The fantasy becomes instantly the Real, sliding past the violence that keep the "legendary children" from obtaining their dreams. This is most clearly seen in the class cross-overs, in categories such as High Fashion Evening Wear, Town and Country, Opulence, and Executive Realness. In *Paris Is Burning*, Dorian Corey, an older queen, explains the political content of these cross-overs: "You're not really an executive, but you look like an executive, and therefore you're showing the straight world that I can be an executive. If I had the opportunity to be one, I could be one because I can look like one."[9] These resignifying bodies run the gamut of transcapital's spin-off imagery, a mimesis that makes the Real near and accessible, inciting desire, pleasure, applause, and status. On the runways, freedom in performance stages the excesses of race, class, and sexual oppression. Bodies live the fantasy! The moment is the Real.

These performances, together with ballroom categories and lexicons, make up the life of the runway: the Houses, the families, the ball competitions, and the trophies for the "legendary children." The framing is, however, momentary. A young man in the film who does military drag comments on the struggle between Realness and reality: "The ballroom tells me that I'm somebody, but when a ballroom is over and you come home, you have to convince yourself that you are somebody, and that's where they [the "legendary children"] get lost."[10] As Goldsby reviews this, "the trope of "realness" derives its charge from the gesture of erasure precisely because the marks of race, class, and sexuality limn these image(s) indelibly and cannot be suppressed no matter how hard the children try" (p. 110).

In Goldsby's "black queer look" at *Paris Is Burning*, she appreciates the subversive role of resignifying dominant cultural practices in vulnerable and oppressed communities of black and Latino queens and drag artists. Commercialized images that can be oppressive and offensive to the poor and the underclass are reversed in the rituals of these Harlem drag balls, redeployed by the community to constitute its own culture of value and status. Goldsby also sees the erotic intensity in these transgender and transclass crossings, transferring the appearance of gender, race, and class privilege through the execution of style and performance. She worries protectively about the cultural genius of this community, invaded by the callous death-sweep of capitalism that leaves its scuff marks of poverty and returns again to steal whatever aesthetics seem marketable, as in Madonna's white girl raids of the vogue and voguing's popularity in Manhattan *haute couture*. Who profits, asks Goldsby. This involuted capitalism also belies the filmmaker's subtle betrayal of queens and transsexuals who really wanted to make it—to make it really Real—in the straight white fashion world. As Goldsby observes, Livingston reveals their performance as dissimulation for all to see, perhaps dashing their dreams against her cinematic gains. What was her white look doing there?

Reid-Pharr's analysis, influenced by his reading of bell hooks, also emphasizes the imperialistic greed of white looks visiting Harlem's ghetto. According to his critique, Livingston's camera gives us a "surface read" devoid of any historical or power analysis, erasing the long history of balls and transvestism in Harlem life, including the history of passing and gender reassignment and the meaning of "good face" as a survival strategy for African Americans. As Reid-Pharr comments:

> Jenny Livingston has created in *Paris Is Burning* a product that is quite similar to the minstrel show. Her whiteness is never demonstrated. Instead we only see it creep in around the edges of the Black

mask that she has constructed for herself. Just like the minstrel show, moreover, *Paris Is Burning* operates via a narrative that lampoons Black pretensions to whiteness and consigns the Black body to the realm of the farcical, the grotesque, and the tragic. Indeed it is no mistake that the last major move in the film is the death of Venus Extravaganza followed closely by more outrageous singing and dancing, shucking and jiving. Like their Nineteenth and Early Twentieth Century minstrel counterparts these characters rarely feel pain or remorse; they just keep step to the music and prepare themselves for the next show. (p. 64)

The tragedy of Venus's murder reframes questions of gender, race, and sex in *Paris Is Burning*. Jennie Livingston gives considerable attention to Venus Extravaganza, a preoperative male-to-female Latino transsexual, blonde, light skinned, petite fem with green eyes, who shares with us her desire to become a spoiled rich white girl. The distance between her desire and her reality seems cavernous, yet she apparently passes and continues to hope. When Venus is introduced in the documentary, we see her primping in front of a mirror, while on the soundtrack an older queen, Dorian Corey, comments on fem realism: "When they're undetectable, when they can walk out of that ballroom into the sunlight and get home and still have all their clothes and no blood running off their bodies, those are the fem realist queens, and usually it's a category for young queens."[11] To be really Real is to pass and to make it home in the white world. This was the dream of the young Venus.

Because she could be found out, however, her performance of white femininity carried a double edge: it probably incited desire as well as a possible murderous hatred in her unknown killer. The double-speak in the pleasures of gender cross-over is inscribed by sheer danger. Venus had carried the logic of commodity capitalism and gender performance beyond the ball world. Perhaps hooks is right: in not giving central attention to these tragic edges, "these televised images of black men in drag were never subversive; they helped sustain sexism and racism."[12]

To an extent I can understand some of the anger hooks and her friend experienced watching *Paris Is Burning* with an audience of many white folks seemingly "entertained" and "pleasured" by scenes that for hooks and her friend were tragic and infuriating. As hooks describes her experience, "Several times I yelled out in the dark: 'What is so funny about this scene? Why are you laughing?' The laughter was never innocent."[13] Her anger emerges in watching whites watch *Paris Is Burning,* especially whites who supposedly had little knowledge of African-American cultures, let alone black sexual minority communities in Harlem. Whites laughing at Pepper Labeija, Angie Extravaganza, Willi Ninja, Octavia St. Laurant, and Venus Extravaganza seem not at all wholly innocent. The pleasure of whites looking at color seems based on a yearning for a resolution of tragic race history, but the looking often erases what it longs to put behind.

White Looks[14]

> Black skin splits under the racist gaze, displaced into
> signs of bestiality, genitalia, grotesquerie, which reveal
> the phobic myth of the undifferentiated whole white
> body.   —Homi Bhaba

As Laura Mulvey has suggested in her analysis of the cinematic gaze in "Visual Pleasure and Narrative Cinema,"[15] the gaze *is* never neutral. While focused on relations of gender, Mulvey analyzes the subjectivity in screen images and in the spectator as valanced by the cultural unconscious of a heteropatriarchal society. In Mulvey's view, the subject addressed by the diagetic world of film and in the auditorium is male subjectivity. This is reflected in the marginalization of female characters from a film's narrative, the punishment and succumbing of strong women, and the "phallicization" of the female body as nonnarrative spectacles within the film's story. In these moments of spectacle the male sexual subject takes active possession and desire in "the look"—looking at the "other" in a way that assures phallic pleasure and denies the threat of castration represented by the female body. The race of the subject addressed by these cinematic representations is absent from Mulvey's analysis. Surely this matters in viewing pleasures.

A critique of to "white looks" is formulated in Tania Modleski's analysis of *Crossing Delancey,* where she focuses on the spectacle of two black women in a sauna, a scene gratuitously inserted into the film's otherwise white, Jewish narrative. At this point in the film's story, Izzy, a thirty-three-year-old white Jewish woman, who works in a bookstore where she has access to the glittery self-enamored world of Manhattan's literati, is contemplating whether or not to call up Anton Mass, a writer who has shown some sexual interest in her. She is definitely taken by him. The scene that ensues involves Izzy meeting her white girlfriend

Candace at the gym for a workout. Their mildly anorexic bodies hit the indoor track where they discuss Izzy's incipient relationship with Anton while jogging. This is followed by a cut to the sauna, where the two white women literally over/hear and over/look a conversation between two black women who are positioned below them inside the sauna. As Modleski describes this scene:

> While the women recline in their towels, the camera pans down to reveal two black women, one of whom, a very large woman whose ample flesh spills out of a tight bathing suit, loudly recounts to her friend an anecdote about lovemaking in which while performing fellatio ("I'm licking it, I'm kissing it, he's moaning") she discovers a long—"I mean long"—blonde hair, which the man rather lamely tries to explain away. The camera tilts back up, as Izzy, having listened intently to the conversation, thoughtfully remarks, "Maybe I *will* call him."[16]

In this specular scene, gratuitously inserted into the film's narrative, the white woman Izzy is *pushed over the edge* in her desire to ask Anton out. The black female bodies are there to incite that desire in Izzy and for the spectator to infuse black nonanorexic flesh with the meanings of sex and transgression. To symbolize this, the disciplined white female body on top looks down on the ample flesh that "spills out of the tight bathing suit." Likewise, in a film that makes no direct mention or display of sexuality elsewhere, the conversation between the black women is explicitly sexual in contrast to the white women's discussion on the innuendos of possible romance between Izzy and Anton. The two black female bodies, seemingly "out of bounds," are there to be "looked at" and to incite desire through the difference of race. As Modleski suggests, "The function of the fat, sexually voracious black women in *Crossing Delancey* is to enable the white Jewish subculture, through its heterosexual love story, to represent itself in a highly sentimentalized, romanticized, sublimated light, while disavowing the desires and discontents underlying the civilization it is promoting" (p. 86). In this scene from *Crossing Delancey*, the address to the spectator is to a white female subjectivity that is in control and safely distanced from the meanings reinscribed on black skin. White look yearns to exceed its innocence at the expense of racism.

White viewers of *Paris Is Burning* may have experienced this kind of sensual excess—displacing the pleasures of transgender erotics on the bodies of racialized "others," in a way of looking that incites pleasure rather than guilt, despair, sympathy, or grief. While this looking may be white in what it desires to see, it is also, as Judith Butler reminds us, phallic. Behind the camera is Jennie Livingston, a white *lesbian*. Butler analyzes this as a double transsexualization of lesbian desire in *Paris Is Burning*:

> The one instance where Livingston's body might be said to appear allegorically on camera is when Octavia St. Laurent is posing for the camera, as a moving model would for a photographer. We hear a voice tell her that she's terrific, and it is unclear whether it is a man shooting the film as a proxy for Livingston, or Livingston herself. What is suggested by this sudden intrusion of the camera into the film is something of the camera's desire that motivates the camera, in which a white lesbian phallically organized by the use of the camera (elevated to the status of disembodied gaze, holding out the promise of erotic recognition) eroticizes a black male-to-female transsexual—presumably preoperative who "works" perceptually as a woman. What would it mean to say that Octavia is Jennie Livingston's kind of girl?[17]

In this analysis Butler has disrupted the traditional cinematic gaze by the presence of lesbian desire, refigured as the phallic camera in the campy scene of queer girl talk. Race reappears as an area Butler briefly interrogates: what is this desire to feminize black and Latino men in a filmatic transubstantiation of a race economy? In the dominant culture the camera, which trades on the masculine privilege and maneuvers, produces these bodies while it is itself of apparently no body—producing the notion of viewer innocence or inobtrusiveness. Butler reminds us that the gaze in *Paris Is Burning* is more honest. It does have a body, a white lesbian body in phallic possession of the camera, calling out to Octavia "hey, terrific!," giving her the completeness of the feminine form and frame, and interpellating the Real with desire. Is the lesbian pleasure had in the usurpation of male authority or in the less-spoken-of transgressions of transgender desire? Is Jenny's marginal kinship with Octavia enough? Or is this again "white looks" fascinated with the other side of excess? Does it matter that white Jenny looks at black Octavia and Octavia looks back? Wanting what from each other? Who gains?

Venus: Who's Looking?

> *Oppositional representation of the black male body that*
> *does not perpetuate white supremacist capitalist patri-*
> *archy will not be highly visible unless we change the way*
> *we see and what we look for. More important than the*
> *race, gender, class, or sexual practice of the image maker*
> *is the perspective, the location from which we look and*
> *the political choices that inform what we hope these*
> *images will be and do.*   —BELL HOOKS, *Black Male*

I leave the theaters of *Paris Is Burning* more easily as a white than as a woman or a lesbian—since my queerness and my femaleness have always been more first-emergency identities on the streets. However, as I have suggested this has a lot to do with how far I am willing to travel, with who sits next to me, who looks, who talks, who listens, and who walks with me. I remember running scared from *Boyz N' the Hood* late at night . . . down-town . . . the only two white women in the theater, heading for the ramps and being followed as a tease. Yet, in all my looking at white looks, my "whiteness" has become more fragile, more destabilized, more visible, and more suspect, less willing to take up residence on one side of the scene. White figuration is an especially troubled site in *Paris Is Burning*.

I will conclude this chapter with some reflections on what hooks describes as "the position from which we look" and explore how whiteness may inform some of the visual pleasures or displeasures in viewing *Paris Is Burning*, as well as how we theorize bodies, pleasure, and power. I will offer a few thoughts on how one's "looking position" may affect contem-porary ways of thinking about the body. My viewing of *Paris Is Burning* along with that of hooks, Goldsby, Reid-Pharr, and Butler suggests a panoply of perspectives and differently nuanced ways of looking at Liv-ingston's documentary. Clearly, who one is, where one is sitting, with whom one is sitting and identifying, as well as how one expresses deeply felt visceral and emotive responses to *Paris Is Burning* reflect a synergis-tic personal and political relationship between the body, image, location, and audience. Conflicting positionalities of the gaze reveal a complex intersection of social relations in the theater as in life, just as my intense pleasure and bell hooks's intense displeasure mark such a distinction.

It is Venus Extravaganza who draws me most deeply into my own inward looking. While reclined on a bed in her adoring feminine pose, she talks directly into the camera: "I don't think there's anything mannish about me except maybe what I might have between me down there . . . which is my little personal thing. I guess that's why I want my sex change to make myself complete." She desires her own castration to become a natural woman. She, like others of the "legendary children," also has a dream of someday having it all. In the words of Venus:

> I want to be a spoiled rich white girl. . . . I want a car. I want to be with the man I love. I want a nice home away from New York. . . . I want my sex change. . . . I want to get married in a Church in white. . . . I want to be a complete woman, and I want to be a professional model . . . in the high fashion world.[18]

> *Venus was found dead, apparently strangled to death and left for three days under a bed in a New York hotel. At the morgue Angie Extravaganza identified the body for the police just in time, before the body was to be consigned to the Unidentified.*

> I'm so petite and little. When they hold my hand, the client's hand will be bigger than mine. They liked feeling that I was something perfect and little and not someone bigger than them, because I guess that kind of disturbed them.[19]

Venus in many ways represents the tragic underside, the demivisible material world represented in *Paris Is Burning*. Her murder during the making of the documentary is marked by Angie's testimony as the death of Venus becomes one more event inflecting life on the Harlem runways. Butler comments on her death in a more theoretically inclined, eulogistic passage. Interpreting Venus's fantasy as a phantasmatic pursuit that mobilizes identities and hopeful promises, Butler writes:

> A fantasy that for Venus, because she dies—killed *apparently* by one of her clients, *perhaps* after the discovery of those remaining organs—cannot be translated into the symbolic. This is a killing that is performed by the symbolic that would eradicate those phenomena that require an opening up of the possibilities for the resignification of sex. . . . The painfulness of her death at the end of the film suggests as well that there are cruel and fatal social constraints on denaturalization. (pp. 131, 133, emphasis mine)

The words "perhaps," "apparently," and "presumably" tip the reader to Butler's way of viewing *Paris Is Burning*, as Butler has no exact notion of what motivated the killer. However, the "perhaps" mistaken identity of sex supports many of Butler's assumptions about sex and gender. According to Butler, gender is always an *imitation for which there is no original*. In other words, gender is constituted by a series of reiterative discursive practices that enact or produce what is named, in this case gender and sex, in accordance with regulative norms and discursive practices that give privilege to some bodies and not others. What I have referred to in earlier chapters as a modernist sex/gender ontology is according to Butler achieved by "imitation that produces the very notion of the original as an effect and consequence of the imitation itself."[20] Gender is then not necessarily biologically locked into one sex or other but is a performative practice that can migrate across different bodies, producing different materializations and configurations of sex and gender. For Butler, drag displays gender's radical contingency.

> In imitating gender, drag implicitly reveals the imitative structure of gender itself—as well as its contingency. Indeed, part of the pleasure, the giddiness of the performance is in the recognition of a radical contingency in the relation between sex and gender in the face of cultural configuration of causal unities that are regularly assumed to be natural and necessary.[21]

The migratory aptitude of gender and sex presents a challenge to modernist sex/gender ontology, one that questions the "realness" in which heterosexual and straight alignments of sex and gender seem *the original* while all else appears to be an imitation or deviation. For Butler the conceit of *the original* is to be understood as an artifice that works or as a performative achievement incorporating regulative norms in a regime of heterosexualized power and truth that dissimulates its production, contingency, and citational dependency. When Butler views *Paris Is Burning*, she sees life on the runways calling into question the normativity and *the origin*-ality that grounds the realness of gender and sexuality. Not all drag can do this, but all drag necessarily sports the denaturalization and destabilization of "normalized" body categories in a way that can subvert the norm as it can serve its perpetual reidealization. Reading Venus, Butler invests her with this theoretical promise; she suspects that Venus's killer has also read her, but quite differently as her killer destroys her life in a brutal return of normalizing hatred and ontic conceit. Perhaps Venus was murdered for other reasons, but the "perhaps" in Butler's writing on the death of Venus seeks a theoretical keepsake in the remains of her crumpled body—"*apparently* . . . *perhaps* after the discovery of those remaining organs . . . a killing that is performed by a symbolic."[22]

The position from which Butler looks is theoretically self-interested, desiring that the bodies in the white-no-tresspass zone of Harlem's runways—bodies that matter less (if at all) to the dominant white culture, except perhaps as signs of danger and entertainment—perform her theory and constitute its truth. She spectates from afar as the artifice dies. In contrast the views of Goldsby and Reid-Pharr articulate a race alliance reading of *Paris Is Burning*, highlighting cultural style, survival, and defiance emanating from the floor of material poverty. As a cultural critic bell hooks charges behind the scenes to call into question the ethnographic practices of a white Jenny Livingston, demanding more attention to the material destitution and hardship in the lives of Livingston's interpellated subjects and more interrogation of our exoticizing white gaze. Butler also turns to Jenny Livingston, superseding her race identity with an interest in her phallically charged camera, at once usurping male prerogative and transsexualizing lesbian desire, making Octavia a woman, a *Jenny's kind of girl*, as race dissolves to sex.

Looking is a way of making *the seen* intelligible. Different ways of looking make different kinds of sense. In making sense of bodies, our looking often determines what matters by how bodies matter. In the different ways that Butler, hooks, Reid-Pharr, and Goldsby view *Paris Is Burning*, one finds different ways of seeing the matter of bodies. Butler insists on the discursivity of matter and its materialization through practices conscripted to the regulatory norms of bodily intelligibility; she sees the drag of Harlem's runway culture as a statement about the performative and contingent aspects of gender and other privileged social identities. The death of Venus explodes on this scene. Goldsby, Reid-Pharr, and hooks insist, albeit in different ways, on seeing the effects of material poverty on bodily matters; they more readily look beyond the performative body to the historical weight of hunger, poverty, and early death that hang beside Jenny's scenic camera. What Goldsby, Reid-Pharr, and hooks more readily see is the contingency of history's materialism as it renders these bodies invisible. The death of Venus becomes a matter of political economy. The bodies they see are in *sheer survival mode* as they are *in style*. What this brief comparison of viewpoints elicits is the risk in looking back: how bodies matter or the priorities given to gender, race, sex, and class and how bodies come to matter in gender, race, sex, and class reveal the tricks of power inhabiting the location from which we look.

Looking Back

What does it mean to me as a white woman to see a desire for white privileged femininity refigured in a Latino transsexual body—a figuration of feminine "whiteness" that has often historically meant *death* for the phallus of color and *prized possession* for the white master? What does it mean to see *her*, white and female, refigured there on the body of Venus. Venus has vanished, but *she* is left everywhere, this ghost of white figuration. *She* stares at me as I watch *Paris Is Burning*. Venus is dead because of *her*. Thousands of dark men were lynched and mutilated because of *her*. Many of the "legendary children" will fall because of *her*. What are you doing there, I ask. *She* silently asks the same of me. *She* says *she* is taking care of the children. I play a game of mirrors in pleasure, pain, and mutual recognition with this vicious white nanny. *"What are we doing there? . . . Where is your leather daddy?" I ask. Wanting what?*

. . . What was my "sexual look" doing there? . . . disowning *her* violence, enjoying the show, living the promise of racism's happy resolution, feeling a fierce queerness in the life force, sitting mostly with whites, looking at what *she* and Jenny made, feeling safe enough to go home, feeling pleasure and tragedy as we deliberately forget about *her*, but also sensing how *her* white figuration cleans up the scene.

. . . I am looking again. Venus is gone. Her dreams concluded. *She*, on the other hand, is still at large seeking more skins from children of all colors. *She* the dream-maker. Who should rise up against *her* and in the name of what? Who will see *her*? Who will look away? What is my sexual look doing there? My looking sees *her* and looks *her* over, always remembering white Venus, the runways, and the subverting pleasures of all the "legendary and the almost legendary children." *She* will always be there—a simmering image white-faced and female—dancing among the souls who may desire the pleasure of *her* smiling promise or fall through the death grip of *her* small petite hands. Who made *her* up? I am not *she* but *she* occupies me as I wear on *her* seams: to name *her* crimes, stop *her* violence, deconstruct *her* image, and teach the truth of who created *her* and what was done to *her*. *She* also has histories and stories to be told though *she* represents an ideal of frequent panic and failure.

There is space for ambiguity here. And pleasure. Still I want to look away. HEAD home.

By FOOT(note): The problem with some "white looks" is in what we may overlook. We may wish to in scenic color: sex as a technical act, race as an incitement, gender as a reiterative performance, color as a style; we forget the violence done in e-racing what matters in this scene/seeing. A privilege of some white looks is that looking only gives us the present, the intensity of visual matters; we neglect to ask where the bodies come from, and fail to comprehend the historical gravities of poverty, homelessness, and hunger. A privilege of some white looks is that wherever we light there is assumed a shiny consent underneath a surface of different skins. A privilege of some white looks is that we wish to look away if historical truth means displeasure or loss of profit or theoretical error. A privilege of some white looks is that we adjust our sites to the world, within shooting distance, and decide from there what matters and what pleasures. This is an epistemology of visual massacre. A problem with some white looks is in the pleasure of translating Revolution into sex and ludic eulogy.

Part One

"What classically distinguishes knowledge is its
essential thrust away from the body: its ambition to transcend the carnal.
Mind is not simply immanent in matter; it is transcendent over it. All
visions of knowledge must accordingly struggle with the dialectic
between immanence and transcendence."[1]

> To theorize is to create and elaborate on names for things and their
> relations. Making theory is not usually making up the world but
> making up a map of what the world might be made of. Theory can,
> however, make up the world when "constructed unities" of dis-
> parate things and relations become, like *sexuality*, an a object of
> knowledge and pleasure.[2]

> *"Theoria"* in Greek refers to contemplation, spectacle, mental concep-
> tion and is derived from *"theoros"* (spectator) and *"thea"* (sight). In
> contemporary universities "theory" is often separated from daily
> practices, a place where the body has needs and persistence, and
> from theater, a place where the spectator looks at performing bod-
> ies. Such theory is born between the everyday and theatrical illu-
> sion, making "the body" a theoretical spectacle.

> The body of the theory-maker performs well when it keeps "the intru-
> sive self" under its skin. "Objectivity consists in so fully realizing
> the countless intrusions of the self in everyday thought and the
> countless illusions that result—illusions of sense, language, point
> of view, value, etc.—that the preliminary step to every judgment is

the effort to exclude the intrusive self."[3] This "intrusive self" was too poetic for Plato, too carnal for Descartes, and too womanly for Augustine. In the modern world, she is still a problem.

I have noticed when contemplative men discuss theory the talk takes place between heads, above tables, behind podiums, and over neckties. Rarely is a gaze of the whole body invited by positions and posturing. They look at the face, the head, the lips, the hidden labor of the tongue, divining a mind inside the skull. The gaze does not move below the neck as it might with a woman speaking theory.

Foucault once started a lecture in Uppsala on top of a table lying on his side with his head propped up by his elbow on the table, presenting a full frontal and feminine pose to the audience—a teasing inversion of pedagogical erotics, where he might have had boys at his feet rather than Swedes at his sideways.[4]

Theory-making is a labor of the body. Who looks after the logistics of the theory-maker's body? Where are all the parts when the body writes? Theory-making is a labor of hands and fingers, fine and tiny work at the busy ends of skins and pen tips. Theory-making is a labor of tongue, well-behaved. Where is the tongue when the fingers write? Matter in motion circulates in the spaces where this writing touches my finger tips against this page. How should I touch this body in writing? My hands are seldom idle for the page or for you, for that matter. My tongue rests as thoughts skid off from other parts. My hands hanging loose, out in the open, transcending the carnal in theory-making. Wanting you. Finding thighs.

Schultz has argued that when we enter a conceptual mode of labor and become absorbed in it, attention to the body becomes "horizontal" not thematic and focal.[5] When writing theory, attention to bodily habits taxes only the most superficial aspects of our awareness; if more, it grabs momentarily at our full attention, demanding relief. Eventually the body intrusively tires from fatigue and drags down the thinker's suspended flesh. Historically, the flesh has delayed this fall with the help of other bodies who take care of the bodily needs of the theory-maker: wives, slaves, lovers, housekeepers, maids, nannies, mothers, cooks, doctors, custodians, house boys, secretaries, gardeners, prostitutes, nurses, lawmakers, and the police. Western theory-making requires two important omissions: that we overlook the intrusive body and ignore the bodily labor of others who make the suspension of the body possible for the theory-maker.[6]

When theorizing about the body, does anything change? Does the presence of the body in writing theory about the body make the body more focal and thematic, singular or plural or otherwise exposed? Is such theory-making for men like sex, only holy? Is lesbian theory a perversion?

Part Two

Since Augustine, the body, as an object of theory, has been reflected through categories that abhor its impulsive frailty and unbearable opacity. The body is too disgusting for the purity of theory, and when referred to, it is with distaste, denial, and subtle death threats. Can we change that?

> The body is always in theory and is always already deferred to. How may I theorize your body? Does my touch defer like words, pointing to what is there and not there, thought to be "in nature" as a thought?

> "For descriptive purposes, the body is separated into cavities. The cranial cavity contains the brain and its boundaries are the skull bones."[7] Your mouth is a body cavity I know. Are there others? Historically charted? According to Lacquer, your gendered port of entry was not your skull but a cave of inverted male genitalia to be explored by the extroverted organs of the male sex.[8] I have also explored this-the-written-masculine text of your inverted body— re/marking on their text the out/lines of other cavities, divisions, meanings, and pleasures. How to theorize this without the discourse of male anatomists? without an archaeology of ancient clitographies? without a genealogy of female desire?

> Which is closer to your body, the (dis)course of my touch or the (dis)course of the surgeon's knife? Our solutions are different, as I erase in my micro-labors centuries of text and tissue of your body. In the contemporary world, both tongue and knife touch your body with different destinations and sciences. The right to touch or to cut confers an authority (all) over your body.

> Of these acts, only you can name the "pleasure" or "pain," once the words are learned . . . from others. We circle terminally through

language believing in the commonality of feeling words, as we touch.

In learning these words, "pleasure," "pain," "cold," "hot," "sweet," "bitter," "soft," "hard," my body opened to a world felt through the flesh. Through the screens of meaning and theory-making, my body fleshed out a knowing self—a body suspended in meanings. If these should vanish, this "I" [that I am] would disappear. Change their meanings and "I" change, a chemical modification in brain cells and a matter of words. Theory is then a living conversation, but historically and with time, bodies may become inhabited and in-flexible resisting *the new*. So I tell you—*we must die* along with the other unintelligibles.

In living, the *real* referent of "I" is as inaccessible as the *real* referent of "my body." "We thus have no "direct" innocent or unconstructed knowledge of our bodies: rather we are always reading our bodies through various interpretive schemas."[9] Even theories of medical science rest on unsteady histories and paranoid anxieties, just as the surgeon may find the node without deeply knowing it. How much of Western medical theory rests on the authority of a knife that guards its professional boundaries like a weapon? The right to cut marks the right to speak a truth about the body, while also castrating the tongues of witches, midwives, pagans, tribads, and nuns . . . mother-tongues. In other words, theories matter by brutal means.

Theory makes "the body" and constantly defers to it as the always-already-there "in nature." Thinking about this . . . *since we have been together* . . . has shown this practice to be primarily a male affair. Should we speak to this?

Part Three

The body is most concrete and present to us in our lived daily experience which is, in some sense, antithetical to the labor of abstraction in theory-making. At the same time the body seems most accessible to us through the lenses of abstraction, generalization, and reorganization of sense data—the *very* tools of theory-making. The body is both more than its meanings in any particular theory and is also a discursively constituted object of many different theories.

How do I know this?

Explanandum. She touches me. The touch itself moves through me. This is a palpable physical event and she has the ability to do this from afar. I can sense it when my flesh opens.

Knowledge. I know her touch. That "she" is doing this, that "she" is similar to "her," that the touch is friendly, that it portends or settles, that she is present, that I am invited into her, that this is sex, that this is notice, that she wants . . . these are knowings that require generalization, risk, trust, and repetition. I come to know the language she speaks through her touch. This is a theory, not a controlling prediction. The action can change. I *will to know* her surprise, over and over, and again.

Unknown anonymous touch in the absence of knowing *who you are* is high-risk and open-ended. The first small touch of a potential killer or a future lover—perhaps indistinguishable. Theory-making is a shelter for the body when it comes to touch. But theory-making collapses when one day he sprays the crowd with a semi-automatic. Words failed. Bodies turned into pools of blood, crushed like roses in a funeral march. (Can you trust what I will do next with these hands?) Home has always been a fragile idea. (Is theory a home one that denounces this impulse to violate or murder, foreclosing the unpredictable?) "It is amid these ruins that we look for ourselves."[10]

First Touch. What does an infant "know" about touch? Is "touch" known immediately before theory or is this the beginning of theory-making, in trusting the touch? trusting the body next to me? the enigma that could violate or feed me? What is the relationship between theory-making and trusting the body, my own and that of another? Is a falling body merely a habit of thought or a matter of trust?

First Words. Theory-making need not exclude moments of in-articulation, of intuition and subconscious access moving toward words. These ways of knowing feel immediate: we commonly say I knew it "at once," "in my bones," "in my gut," "in my heart," or "at first sight." We place these ways of knowing in an infallible metaphorical body, one we can trust. The body's theory-making includes these intuitions as anchors for more elaborate theoretical constructions *of the body* in its many disciplines: microbiology, biochemistry, immunology, histology . . . ( )ology. With this sliding in and out from one language to another, my body becomes even more a phantasm, theoretically slouched in a house of mirrors, ( ) ( ) ( ) ( ) . . . reflecting back parts that total no sum. At last, they say a molecule can tell me what I am!

Touching Words. In this passing contingency called life, is there a theory-making that is closer to the body I want to live in and with? Which gives more comfort to this brief duration of flesh? Which theory feels more like the crystal warmth of the sun on my spring-hungry skin or the luscious heat of my lover's pressing body? Can theories become warm and wet with certainty? Verification, a renewable pleasure? Satisfying and complete? At least for now? Where is the body in this longing for the trust in knowledge?

Taboo. A body touches her and she returns this touch. This is not a mirror stage. Children must learn the difference between "good" and "bad" touch. Touchings portend. There is danger. There is warmth. When do we know? Theory-making creates a shelter for the body and an armor/*amor* of taboo. The origin of the word "taboo"—*n' touches pas!*—maps a body topography of danger and pleasure. In our past, female body substances have been at variously perceived as a danger to men and to theory. It is said of women who yearn for theory: *n'touches pas!* In practice: we are told to *remain silent!* These actions have been theorized as a sign of woman's nature.

Crossing the (K)not. I have discovered this touch is good. I have discovered that thought is good. My knowledge for this is as fierce and as forceful as the sex that explodes between us when we act on our desires. This serves as a context of discovery, shelving centuries of theories that forbid this: outlawing our desires, our bodies, and our ways of knowing.

Theory and Practice. The relationship between theory and practice is in all that passes between our bodies, from the primal fears, pains, and angst of animal consciousness to the ecstasies en-fleshed in our out-of-daily skins. We have learned the words "pleasure" and "pain," "love" and "hate," "life" and "death," "you" and "I," "possession," and "theft." With these words we move into the outer terrains, from inner to outer, from our lips to the streets with resistance remodeling our bones and recharging our molecular muscles.

Part Four

Theory is one of many inner windows.

> *Love.* Since we have been together, we have made theory over and over—to our heart's content. We have become less afraid to face the enemy. We are bolder because of it.

> *Theoros.* Theories are word-tools for navigating history, directing movements, defining enemies, predicting the future, getting specific, exploring connections, and moving through the hard places. Theories are word-tools for saying what you mean and meaning what you say. Theories are community builders—some divide and exclude, and some invite and incite. Theories also have smaller journeys between lovers, between minds. Some theories are deadly.

> *Bodies.* Theory-making, like touch, can open the body. Which theories do you live in? What kind of words shelter you? Turn you? Give you courage? Guide your way?

> *Spirit.* "In these obsessional, fortified systems of defense, *the articulation* and *the order* work to keep out the pain, despair, and the chaos caused by transcendent ineffables."[11] Most likely our weighted anchors and celestial arrogance will fall short.[12]

> *Ordinary Pleasures.* The body is a *poetics* of fluid, touch, surrender. The body is a *methodics* of control, limit, division. You decide. I will wait for you *over there, but remember much of this may take us by surprise.*

Theory is one of many inner windows.

Notes

Articulations

1. The social construction of "the practical body" understands culture to be incorporated into the body through discipline, routine, and daily practices. Pre-Foucault, these ideas were developed by Marcel Mauss, "Body Techniques," in *Sociology and Psychology* (London: Routledge and Kegan Paul, 1936). Current theoretical work on "the practical or disciplined body" includes Michel Foucault, *Discipline and Punish* (New York: Vintage, 1979); Pierre Bourdieu, *Outline of a Theory of Practice* (Cambridge: Cambridge University Press, 1977); Susan Bordo, "The Body and the Reproduction of Femininity: A Feminist Appropriation of Foucault," in Alison Jaggar and Susan Bordo, eds., *Gender/Body/Knowledge: Feminist Reconstructions of Being and Knowing* (New Brunswick: Rutgers University Press, 1989) and Bordo, *Unbearable Weight: Feminism, Western Culture, and the Body* (Berkeley: University of California Press, 1993); Frigga Haug et al., eds., *Female Sexualization* (London: Verso, 1987); Paul Connerton, "Bodily Practices," in *How Societies Remember* (Cambridge: Cambridge University Press, 1989).

2. This social constructionist theory understands "the body" as a product of semiotic or symbolic meaning incorporated through the body, bodily parts, functions, and surfaces. It has most recently has been articulated in performativity theories of sexuality and gender, where such meanings are constructed through semiotically infused and reiterative performative practices. See Judith Butler, *Gender Trouble: Feminism and the Subversion of Identity* (New York: Routledge, 1990); "Imitation and Gender Insubordination," in Diana Fuss, ed., *Inside/Out: Lesbian Theories, Gay Theories* (New York: Routledge, 1991); and *Bodies that Matter: On the Discursive Limits of "Sex"* (New York: Routledge, 1994). Elizabeth Grosz in *Volatile Bodies: Toward a Corporeal Feminism* (Bloomington: Indiana University Press, 1994) provides an elucidating exploration of the philosophical foundations for this model of discursive body construction. See also Elizabeth A. Meese, *(Sem)Erotics: Theorizing Lesbian: Writing* (New York: New York University Press, 1992).

3. In *Bodies that Matter*, Butler describes this process very lucidly in her introduction.

1. The Magic of the Pan(eroto)con

1. Earvin "Magic" Johnson has played for the Los Angeles Lakers since 1979. He was selected the NBA's Most Valuable Player (MVP) for three years (1987, 1989, 1990), named to the All-NBA First Team (1983–1991), and participated in the MVP Playoff in 1980, 1982, and 1987. He was a member of NBA championship teams in 1980, 1982, 1985, 1987, and 1988. He holds numerous records in the NBA and played on the All-Star Olympic Team in 1991. He was given the nickname "Magic" by Fred Stabley, Jr., a sportswriter for the *Lansing State Journal*, who asked Magic if he could use this nickname in an article on Magic's astounding performance for the Everett High School team in Lansing, Michigan. Magic was fifteen years old when this exchange occurred, and the nickname stuck with him over time. For an overview of Magic's life, I recommend P. Pascarelli, *The Courage of Magic Johnson* (New York: Bantam, 1992) and Earvin "Magic" Johnson (with William Novak), *My Life* (New York: Random House, 1992).

2. Johnson, *My Life*, pp. 266–267.

3. For an excellent review of the representations of Rock Hudson's body, see Richard Meyer, "Rock Hudson's Body," in Diana Fuss, ed., *Inside/Out: Lesbian Theories, Gay Theories* (New York: Routledge, 1991), pp. 258–288. A further elaboration on these ideas can be found in David Rappaport's video "Rock Hudson Home Movies," 1991.

4. News Services, "The World has Magic on its Mind," *Minneapolis Star Tribune*, November 9, 1991, p. C5 (emphasis mine).

5. Barbara Kantrowitz with Emily Yoffe, Patricia King, Anthony Duignan-Cabrera, "From Hero to Crusader: Activists Debate What Magic Should Do Next," *Newsweek*, November 18, 1991, p. 69.

6. Paula A. Treichler, "AIDS, Gender, and Biomedical Discourse: Current Currents for Meaning," in Elizabeth Fee and Daniel M. Fox, eds., *AIDS: The Burdens of History* (Berkeley: University of California Press, 1988), p. 200.

7. I have borrowed this phrase from Alycee J. Lane, who has written with direct clarity about sexual racism in "What's Race Got to Do with It?" *Black Lace* (Summer 1991).

8. Foucault's "panopticon" is referenced both to Jeremy Bentham's new prison model, which had a circular building enclosing a central inspection tower, and to Foucault's metaphor for a new discursive power that operates on individuals as a continuous observation system with an unknown, norm-setting observer, whose presence (or unknowable absence) influences and structures the behaviors of the observed individual, creating a docile and productive body. I borrow this term to evoke Magic's spectators as hidden observers and Magic's many visual re/presentations in numerous theaters in which he is displayed. This multirepresentational system, produced through millions of screens and images, constructs

the meaning, content, and value of Magic's public body. For more analysis of the panopticon, see Foucault's *Discipline and Punish: The Birth of the Prison* (New York: Vintage, 1979).

9. I realize that I am twisting Elizabeth Meese's term, since she is specifically interested in the (sem)erotics of the lesbian body in lesbian writing. See Elizabeth Meese, *(Sem)Erotics: Theorizing Lesbian: Writing* (New York: New York University Press, 1992). However, I have found her thinking useful in trying to understand the magic of Magic. "(Sem)erotics is the energy of the excess produced by the substitutive quality of words, where word stands (in) for a 'thing,' and word substitutes for word, slides into word, as in metonymy. The elision of sex/textuality fuels the project of desire" (Meese, p. 98). I understand this as a passage between reader and writer that "makes the body present" for both. What I see in the construction of Magic's body is an energy of excess at play between Magic and his spectators who watch Magic with "muscled eyes"—allowing for a transfer of energy and sensate physicality in the flow of body transference energy. I do consider such erotics of intense sports spectatorship *a process* internal to the libidinal gaze of sports fans and their sports heroes. The hybrid term "pan(eroto)con" combines the productive power of the panopticon and the erotic power of (sem)erotics—both aspects of the construction of Magic's body in the specular economy of adored men.

10. In many ways the fragmented, dispersed, and mutable constructions of Magic's body fit a postmodern framework. See Susan Bordo "Postmodern Subjects, Postmodern Bodies, *Feminist Studies* 18, no. 1 (1992): 159–175. See also Arthur and Marilouise Kroker, *Body Invaders: Panic Sex in America* (New York: St. Martin's, 1987).

11. Cited in John Gallagher, "Johnson Disclosure Brings AIDS Issues to Middle America," *The Advocate*, December 17, 1991, p. 16.

12. Cheryl Cole and Harry Denny III, "Visualizing Deviance in the Post-Reagan America: Magic Johnson, AIDS, and the Promiscuous World of Professional Sport," *Critical Sociology* 20, no. 3 (1994): 129.

13. Margaret Whitford, *Luce Irigaray: Philosophy of the Feminine* (New York: Routledge, 1991), p. 151.

14. Ibid.

15. Rumor circulated that Isiah Thomas, a boyhood friend of Magic's, supposedly leaked the rumor that Magic was bisexual. Thomas later vehemently denied this. The story was attributed to Thomas's hurt feelings in not being chosen to play on the All-Star Olympic Team and his disappointment that Magic did not pressure Chuck Daley (coach of the Detroit Pistons and coach of the All-Star Olympic Team) to put Thomas on the Olympic Team. There was also a great deal of press coverage when Magic kissed Thomas on the cheek in public before the NBA Finals in 1988 and 1989. As several columnists have noted, players with less stature than Magic would not as easily rebuff the gay-baiting thrown at Magic if their HIV-positive status was made public. Magic's ability to rebound from these

accusations was because of his sports celebrity status. See Jay Weiner, "Teams in State Discuss AIDS Testing, Awareness," *Minneapolis Star Tribune*, November 5, 1991, pp. C1, C5. See also Lorrain Kee Montre, "Magic Flap," *St. Louis Post-Dispatch*, October 24, 1992, p. C1.

16. Wiley A. Hall III, "Some of Wilt's Bedroom Tales are Really Incredible," *Minneapolis Star Tribune*, November 16, 1991, p. E9.

17. Johnson, *My Life*, p. 244.

18. "Magic: How He Got the AIDS Virus—His Wild Sex Life with More than 1,000 Women," "The Untold Story—A 5-page *Enquirer* Special," *National Enquirer*, November 26, 1991, pp. 30, 31, 33, 36, and 37.

19. E. M. Swift, "Dangerous Games: In the Age of AIDS Many Pro Athletes are Sexually Promiscuous, Despite the Increasing Peril," *Sports Illustrated*, November 18, 1991, p. 43.

20. Boeck, "Women Support Martina's Stand," p. C2. See also Associated Press, "Navratilova: AIDS Double Standard Exists," *Minneapolis Star Tribune*, November 21, 1991.

21. Johnson, *My Life*, p. 228.

22. Ibid., p. 229.

23. Ibid., p. 230.

24. Ibid.

25. Johnson, *My Life*, p. 234.

26. Todd W. Crosset, James Ptacek, Mark A. McDonald, Jeffrey R. Benedict, "Male Student-Athletes and Violence against Women: A Survey of Campus Judicial Affairs Offices" *Violence Against Women* 2, no. 2 (June 1996): 163–179; Wray Vamplew, *A View from the Bench: Coaches and Sports Violence in Australia* (Canberra: Australian Sports Commission, 1991); Jack Tatum, *Final Confessions of NFL Assassin Jack Tatum* (Coal Valley, Ill.: Quality Sports Publications, 1996); Arnold Goldstein, *Violence in America: Lessons on Understanding Aggression in Our Lives*, 1st ed. (Palo Alto, Calif.: Davies-Black, 1996); Jackson Katz, "Reconstructing Masculinity in the Locker Room: The Mentors in Violence Prevention Project" *Harvard Educational Review* 65, no. 2 (Summer 1995): 163–174; Mary Pat Frintner and Laurna Rubinson, "Acquaintance Rape: The Influence of Alcohol, Fraternity Membership, and Sports Team Membership" *Journal of Sex Education & Therapy* 19, no. 4 (Winter 1993): 272–284; Garland F. White, Janet Katz, Kathryn E. Scarborough, "The Impact of Professional Football Games upon Violent Assaults on Women" *Violence and Victims* 7, no. 2 (Summer 1992): 157–171.

27. Merrill Melnick, "Male Athletes and Sexual Assault," *Journal of Physical Education, Recreation, and Dance* (May/June 1992): 32.

28. Larry Gross, "Is Tyson Case Helping the Stereotype?" *Chicago Defender*, February 1, 1992, p. 48.

29. Ellen Goodman, "Un-Magic Moment," *Boston Globe*, November 12, 1992, p. 19.

30. Frank Deford, "Is There No More Magic?" *Newsweek*, November 16, 1992, p. 91.

31. Magic's lawyers managed a confidential settlement of the AIDS-exposure suit of Waymer Moore of Lansing, Michigan. See Eric Freedman, "Confidentiality Clause in Johnson HIV Suit Not Unusual, Lawyers Say," *Detroit News*, December 13, 1993, p. B5.

32. Swift, "Dangerous Games," p. 41

33. Ibid., p. 43.

34. Ibid., p. 42.

35. Evelyn Hammonds, "Missing Persons: African American Women, AIDS, and the History of Disease," *Radical America* 24, no. 2 (1992): 7–24.

36. Ibid., p. 22.

37. In 1992, 12,881 AIDS cases in the United States were contracted through heterosexual contact. This constituted 3 percent of the men with AIDS (5,100) and 34 percent of the women with AIDS (7,781) (*HIV/AIDS Surveillance Report*, Centers for Disease Control, April, 1992). In the United States, the ratio of male-to-female and female-to-male transmissions through heterosexual contact is 1.5:1; in areas of the world such as sub-Saharan Africa this ratio is 1:1. Heterosexual transmission accounts of 80 percent of AIDS in Zaire but only 5 percent in the United States. (Robert W. Ryder, et al., "Heterosexual Transmission of HIV-1 among Employees and their Spouses at Two Large Businesses in Zaire," *AIDS* 4 [1990]: 725–732.) See also Tedd Ellerbrock, et al., "Epidemiology of Women with AIDS in the United States, 1981 Through 1990," *Journal of the American Medical Association* 265, no. 22 (June 12, 1991): 2971.

38. "Tale of Revenge Stirs AIDS Furor: Woman Claims She's Trying to Infect Men, Prompting a Surge of Concern," *New York Times*, October 1, 1991, p. A16.

39. For a parallel exploration of how the German male Nazi psyche condensed its misogyny by reducing women to an image of amorphous mass, see Klaus Theweleit, *Male Fantasies*, vol. 1 (Minneapolis: University of Minnesota Press, 1987).

40. Cheryl Cole and Harry Denny provide an excellent analysis on how Magic's post-HIV representation was framed by a commitment to family values. See Cole and Denny, "Visualizing Deviance," pp. 127–137. Samantha King has also developed an analysis of how representations of Magic's HIV-positive body reinforce social relations, myths, and stereotypes of sexism and homophobia, justifying many people's fears of marginalized groups. See Samantha King, "The Politics of the Body and the Body Politic: Magic Johnson and the Ideology of AIDS," *Sociology of Sport Journal* 10 (1993): 270–285. Douglas Crimp has made similar arguments about how representations of Magic in *Playboy* and *Ebony* reinforce homophobic constructions of AIDS. See Douglas Crimp, "Accommodating Magic," in J. Matlock and L. Walkowitz, eds., *Media Spectacles* (New York: Routledge, 1994), pp. 254–266.

41. According to Sarah Schulman, Magic said he had been infected by a sexual encounter two months prior to his appearance on the Arsenio Hall Show. At that time, he also said that he had offered his wife a divorce after eight weeks of marriage but she had refused and that his wife and their seven-week-old fetus had tested negative. Schulman has pointed out that antibody detection two months after a transmission is quite rare and that there is no way to test a seven-week-old fetus. Magic made these statements before it would have been possible to test his wife's HIV status, which generally requires a waiting period of three to six months for an accurate Elisa Test. Sarah Schulman, "Laying the Blame: What Magic Johnson Really Means," in *My American History: Lesbian and Gay Life During the Reagan/Bush Years* (New York: Routledge, 1994), pp. 223–225.

42. Johnson's characterization of the issues, in *My Life*, p. xiv. As Magic's life continued, he returned to the NBA for the 1994–1995 season after a four-year retirement. *Life Magazine* reported that he had "adopted a child, donated $5 million to a church, and opened a multiplex theater in south-central L.A., providing jobs and entertainment for the inner city," (July 15, 1996, p. 21).

43. This could be compared with Rock Hudson's three-year sham marriage with Phyllis Gates. See Richard Myer, "Rock Hudson's Body," pp. 258–288.

44. Johnson, *My Life*, pp. 238–239.

45. Cindy Patton, "Heterosexual AIDS Panic: A Queer Paradigm," *Gay Community News*, February 9, 1985, p. 6.

46. Cindy Patton, *Inventing AIDS* (New York: Routledge, 1990), p. 160.

47. Patton, *Inventing AIDS*, p. 55.

48. "Heterosexually acquired AIDS" was not a new category in 1991; it has been used since the mid-1980s. For an interesting analysis of the history of this category of AIDS transmission, prior to Magic's public exemplification, see Treichler, "AIDS, Gender, and Biomedical Discourse" and Cindy Patton, "Heterosexual AIDS Panic," p. 263.

49. The idea of the "border case" was first brought to my attention in Mary Poovey's "Speaking of the Body: A Discursive Division of Labor in Mid-Victorian Britain" in Mary Jacobus, Evelyn Fox Keller, and Sally Shuttleworth, eds., *Body/Politics: Women and the Discourses of Science* (New York: Routledge, 1990), pp. 29–46. In Poovey's analysis of nineteenth-century prostitutes, she sees women who both own property and have sexual relations as border cases. They violate two normative constructions of "womanhood"—that single women who own property should not have sex or that married women who have sex should not own property. She analyzes the discourse generated to restore and stabilize these dichotomous categories of normative femininity. In many ways Poovey's border body resembles the ambiguously situated bodies in Susan Bordo's analyses of anorexia nervosa, agoraphobia, and bulimia, as bodies that seek to resolve the antinomies of conflicting social demands. See Susan Bordo, *Unbearable Weight: Feminism, Western Culture, and the Body* (Berkeley: University of California Press, 1994). Other analyses of bodies in "border crossings" and in "border existence" can be found in

Gloria Anzaldúa's *Borderlands: La Frontera: The New Mestiza* (San Francisco: Spinsters/ Aunt Lute, 1987) and in Maria Lugones, " 'Playfulness,' 'World'-Traveling, and Loving Perception," in Jeffner Allen, ed., *Lesbian Philosophies and Cultures* (New York: State University of New York Press, 1990). In *Bodies that Matter: On the Discursive Limits of "Sex"* (New York: Routledge, 1993), Judith Butler develops the Freudian and Kristevian notions of abjection as a way to elucidate political and corporeal strategies that force certain bodies to the margins, outside of normative borders of bodies that matter. I develop the idea of border bodies in more detail in chapter 2, "Heterosexual Anti-Biotics."

50. The gay press has made ample reference to this distinction. See Randy Schilts, "Speak for All, Magic: In His Fight Against HIV, Magic Johnson Should Not Confine His Concerns to Heterosexual Victims," *Sports Illustrated*, November 18, 1991, p. 130; see also the *Equal Time* editorial, "No Magic Bullet," *Equal Time*, November 22, 1991.

51. Gay, lesbian, and bisexual press, rumor, and conversation have occasionally focused on whether or not Magic should "come out." Even those who think Magic is bisexual argue that coming out may do more harm than good because he would lose his authority to speak on AIDS to the American pubic who would not otherwise believe gay or bisexual AIDS activists. Bart Casamir, a gay, black, and HIV-positive AIDS educator, wrote Magic a thank-you letter: "he can address the issue better than anyone I can think of. God couldn't have picked a better spokesman" (cited in Kantrowitz, "From Hero to Crusader," p. 69).

52. The softness and vulnerability of Magic Johnson signify Magic's honesty, innocence, light-heartedness—a sign of his willingness to accommodate the many women who desire him and his credibility as a reformed father. He comes across as providing a humanizing voice for the "womanizing" of heteromasculine promiscuity. As one columnist stated: "Magic Johnson was an athlete with no hostile audiences. He was and is an athlete of such rare intuitive ability, and a human being with so much unarguable good will and effervescence, that people applauded even when he was beating their team. He was basketball, circus and concert. His very movement, his inviting face told us: How can you not love this guy?" (Jim Klobuchar, "Reactions to Magic Show How Much Our Attitudes Have Changed," *Minneapolis Star Tribune*, November 9, 1991, p. B3).

53. Suzanne Kessler and Wendy McKenna, "Gender Construction in Everyday Life," *Gender: An Ethnomethodological Approach* (Chicago: University of Chicago Press, 1978), pp. 112–141. Given the thinning process of AIDS, bulk is also important for Magic's image. In 1996 news stories reported that Magic came back thirty pounds heavier than before and still strong. See Mike Lopresti, "Magic Takes Last Chance to Hold Court," *USA Today*, January 31, 1996, p. C4.

54. Kantrowitz, "From Hero to Crusader," p. 69.

55. Cole and Denny point out that Magic used to endorse a number of products including Disneyland, Pepsi Cola, Converse, Kentucky Fried Chicken, Spalding, Nintendo, Nestle Crunch, Magic Johnson T's, Magic's 32, and an electronic

video game ("Magic Johnson's Fast Break") for Tradewest, Nintendo. According to Cole and Denny, this added approximately 9 to 12 million dollars to his 3.1 million dollar annual salary with the Lakers (Cole and Denny, "Visualizing Deviance," pp. 133, 143). Already as early as 1992 the *New York Times* reported that endorsers were beginning to shy away from Magic: "Advertisers Shying from Magic's Touch," January 1, 1991, *New York Times*, p. 44.

56. Cole and Denny point out that Johnson's body "was placed under an immediate retroactive surveillance that attempted to make visible earlier evidence of HIV." Such surveillance alleged that Magic suffered from shingles in 1985, from flu-like symptoms in the 1991–1992 season, and from an illness in 1991 that caused him to miss exhibition games. Cole and Denny, "Visualizing Deviance," p. 133.

57. "In 1992 the *majority* of new AIDS cases in the United States was reported among people of color. Blacks account for 12 percent of the population, but more than 25 percent of total reported cases of full-blown AIDS. More than half of all women with AIDS are black. Three out of four women with AIDS are black or Hispanic. Nine out of ten children with AIDS and over half the teenagers with AIDS are black or Hispanic." Douglas Crimp (reporting from the April 1992 statistical report from the Center for Disease Control in Atlanta), "Accommodating Magic," in Matlock and L. Walkowitz, eds., *Media Spectacles*, p. 262.

58. For an analysis of the gendered and militaristic metaphors used in representation of the body immune system, see Emily Martin, "The End of the Body?" *American Ethnologist* 19, no. 1 (1992): 121–141, and Donna Haraway, "The Biopolitics of Postmodern Bodies: Determinations of Self in Immune System Discourse," *differences* 1, no. 1 (1989): 3–43.

59. The following excerpts are taken from Johnson, *My Life*, p. 285.

60. Johnson, *My Life*, p. 288.

61. Ibid., p. 292.

62. Many gay AIDS activists watched Magic's every move to see if he would only "play a ceremonial role in AIDS education, spending his days posing for photo opportunities" (Randy Schilts, "Speak for All, Magic," p. 130).

63. Richard Majors, "Cool Pose: Black Masculinity and Sports," in Michael A. Messner and Donald F. Sabo, eds. *Sport, Men, and the Gender Order: Critical Feminist Perspectives* (Champaign, Ill.: Human Kinetics Books, 1990), pp. 109–114. For other readings on racism in sports, see Harry Edwards, "The Collegiant Athletic Arms Race: Origins and Implications of the 'Rule 48' Controversy," *Journal of Sport and Social Issues* 8 (1984): 4–22; Harry Edwards, "Race in Contemporary American Sports," *National Forum* 62 (1984): 19–22; Forrest J. Berghorn et al., "Racial Participation in Men's and Women's Intercollegiate Basketball: Continuity and Change, 1958–1985," *Sociology of Sport Journal* 5 (1988): 107–124; Noel Cazenave, "Race, Socioeconomic Status, and Age: The Social Context of American Masculinity," *Sex Roles* 11 (1984): 639–657.

64. In "Epilogue: A Message for Black Teenagers," Magic urges young African American males to seek out other professions besides basketball: "the black community already has enough basketball players" (*My Life*, p. 328). Cole and Denny have eloquently argued that Magic's return to African-American communities to promote his education work associates black communities with AIDS and functions as a containment, eliminating white contamination with race and AIDS ("Visualizing Deviance," p. 131). A similar point is made by Samantha King, "The Politics of the Body."

65. Majors, "Cool Pose," pp. 113–114.

66. There are a number of articles that analyze the relationship between physically constructed masculinity and its relationship to violence in sport and the maintenance of male hegemony. See Michael A. Messner, "Sports and Male Domination: The Female Athlete as Contested Ideological Terrain," *Sociology of Sport Journal* 5 (1988): 197–211; Michael A. Messner, "When Bodies are Weapons: Masculinity and Violence in Sport," *International Review of Sociology of Sport* 25, no. 3 (1990): 203–219; Lois Bryson, "Sport and the Maintenance of Masculine Hegemony," *Women's Studies International Forum* 10, no. 4 (1987): 349–360; Michael Messner and Donald Sabo, eds., *Sport, Men and the Gender Order* (Champaign, Ill.: Human Kinetics Books, 1990). For feminist analyses on the social containment and exclusion of women from sport, see Katherine MacKinnon "Women, Self-Possession, and Sport" *Feminism Unmodified: Discourses on Life and Law* (Cambridge: Harvard University Press, 1987); Mary Jo Kane, "Resistance/Transformation of the Oppositional Binary: Exposing Sport as a Continuum," *Journal of Sport and Social Issues* 19, no. 2 (1995): 191–218; and Lisa Disch and Mary Jo Kane, "When a Looker is Really a Bitch: Lisa Olson, Sport, and Heterosexual Matrix," *Signs* 21, no. 2 (Winter 1991): 278–308.

67. Alan Clarke, and J. Clarke, "Highlights and Action Replays—Ideology, Sport, and the Media," in J. Hargreaves, ed., *Sport, Culture, and Ideology* (London: Routledge and Kegan Paul, 1982), p. 63.

68. The term "buck" has often been used in reference to black male sexual prowess. See Michael Mullen, *Africa in American: Slave Acculturation and Resistance in the American South and the British Caribbean: 1736–1831* (Urbana: University of Illinois Press, 1988).

69. Michael Eric Dyson, "Be Like Mike? Michael Jordan and the Pedagogy of Desire," *Reflecting Black: African American Cultural Criticism* (Minneapolis: University of Minnesota Press, 1993), p. 67.

70. Nelson George, *Elevating the Game: Black Men in Basketball* (New York: Harper Collins, 1992), p. xix.

71. "Trash-talking"—as defined by Mark Starr when a person, usually an athlete, talks to an opponent in an excessively boastful and scornful manner—has become a black-generated stylistic (*in your face, running your mouth, your*

mama), now commonly part of basketball court jest and spirit. See Mark Starr, "Yakety-Yak: Do Talk Back," *Newsweek*, December 21, 1992, p. 60.

72. There has been ample discussion on the association of the black male with saturated hypersexual powers. See Franz Fanon, *Black Skin, White Masks* (New York: Grove, 1967); Homi Bhabha, "The Other Question: The Stereotype and Colonial Discourse," *Screen* 24 no. 6 (1983): 18–36; Abdul Jan Mohammed, "Sexuality on/of the Racial Border," in Domna C. Stanton, ed., *Discourses of Sexuality: From Aristotle to AIDS* (Ann Arbor: University of Michigan Press, 1992), pp. 94–116; Kobena Mercer, "Just Looking for Trouble: Robert Mapplethorpe and the Fantasies of Race," in Lynne Segal and Mary McIntosh, ed., *Sex Exposed: Sexuality and the Pornography Debate* (New Brunswick: Rutgers University Press, 1993), pp. 92–110.

73. Toni Morrison's analysis of the charges against Clarence Thomas and the *racial stain of blackness* in Thomas's Senate confirmation hearings bear a relationship to the re-racing of Magic's body in my analysis. Morrison writes of Thomas, "the stain need only be proved reasonably doubted, which is to say, if he is black, how can you tell if that really is a stain? Which is also to say, blackness is itself a stain, and therefore unstainable. . . . the search for the racial stain turned to Anita Hill. . . . Her character. Her motives. Not his?" Toni Morrison, "Introduction: Friday on the Potomac," in Toni Morrison, ed., *Race-ing, Justice, En-gendering Power: Essays on Anita Hill, Clarence Thomas, and the Construction of Social Reality* (New York, Pantheon, 1992), pp. xviii–xix.

74. I have coined the term "fluidophobia" to refer to fear of HIV transmission in bodily fluids other than blood, ejaculate, or vaginal secretions. These more "peripheral" bodily fluids, such as tears, perspiration, urine, and saliva, have been shown to carry the virus in minute quantities, but most experts claim that the virus is not found in quantities high enough in these fluids to permit transfer from one body to another through such daily encounters. For a superb analysis of how bodily fluids are related to constructions of gender, see Elizabeth Grosz, "Intensities and Flows," *Volatile Bodies: Toward Corporeal Feminism* (Bloomington: Indiana University Press, 1994), pp. 160–183. Note that my notion of "strategies of restoration" are also consolidating to emphasize the need to keep Magic from dissolving and slipping away, another fear of fluidity.

75. Karl Malone played basketball with Magic on the All-Star Olympic Team. He raised this objection to playing on the same court with Magic after he had left the Olympics and returned to his home team, Utah Jazz. Many read Malone's intention as a reflection of an adversarial tactic rather than a real fear based on fluidophobia.

76. *Dallas Morning News*, February 4, 1996.

77. *Detroit News*, February 1, 1996.

78. Klobuchar, "Reactions to Magic," p. B3 (emphasis mine).

79. Crimp, "Accommodating Magic," pp. 261–262.

80. According to Patton, "symbolically, AIDS has collapsed gay sexuality and straight sexual anxiety under the sign of anal sex. Somewhere deep in our repre-

sentational scheme, the anus is constructed as the quintessential forbidden organ of male/male desire, calling into question the sexuality of straight aficionados of anal sex" (Patton, *Inventing AIDS*, p. 118). For other references on the anxiety of male desire and the anus, see Eve Kosofsky Sedgwick, *Between Men: English Literature and Male Homosocial Desire* (New York: Columbia University Press, 1985); Guy Hocquenghem. *Homosexual Desire* (London: Allison Busby, 1978); and Leo Bersani "Is the Rectum a Grave?" in Douglas Crimp, ed., *AIDS: Cultural Analysis, Cultural Activism* (Cambridge: Massachusetts Institute of Technology Press, 1988). Empirical studies have found that anal sex is a lively practice among heterosexual couples and not universally practiced in gay male communities. In one study 39 percent of heterosexuals reported performing anal sex (June Reinish et al. "The Study of Sexual Behavior in Relations to the Transmission of HIV," *American Psychologist* 43, no. 1 [November 1988]: 921–927), and in another study of teenagers at an urban clinic, 26 percent had performed anal sex (*Siecus Report* [December 1988]). In a more recent study of youth in Minnesota, approximately one third of a gay and bisexual male adolescent client sample did not practice anal sex (Gary Remafedi, "Predictors of Unprotected Intercourse among Gay and Bisexual Youth: Knowledge, Beliefs, and Behaviors," *Pediatrics* 94, no. 2 [1994]: 163–168).

81. For an analysis of racism in the association of AIDS with Africa, see Richard Chirimuuta and Rosalind Chirimuuta, *AIDS, Africa, and Racism* (London: Free Association Books, 1989); Cindy Patton, "Inventing "African AIDS," in *Inventing AIDS*; and Simon Watney, "AIDS, Language, and the Third World," in E. Carter and S. Watney, eds., *Taking Liberties* (London: Serpent's Tail, 1989), pp. 183–192.

82. Earvin "Magic" Johnson, *What You Can Do to Avoid AIDS* (New York: Times Books, 1992). Johnson and Arsenio Hall have also produced a video tape "Straight Talk about Sex" for adolescent youth. The practical effect of Magic's work can be found in the two following studies: Deborah Rugg, "Changes in Behavioral Intentions Among Adolescents Following HIV National Sports Celebrity Disclosure," AIDS International Conference on AIDS, Amsterdam, July 19–24, 1992; and Bruce Rapkin "Do You Believe in Magic? The Public Health Consequences of Magic Johnson's Announcement for Inner City Women," North American Society for Sociology of Sport, November 1993. Only the Rugg study indicated positive changes in behavioral intentions among sexually experienced youth.

83. Magic reflects on his experience on the Arsenio Hall show: "When I said that I wasn't gay the audience broke into applause. It was a strange moment, and I felt a little awkward when it happened. And yet it didn't really occur to me that gay viewers would be offended by that applause. Today, of course, I understand their outrage. But I had to be sensitized on this whole topic, and I'm still working on it" (Johnson, *My Life*, p. 226).

84. Magic has been inclusive in his efforts to foster compassion in the American public's attitudes toward people living with AIDS (PLA). In his role as

spokesman for the virus, he considers one of his responsibilities to make sure that PLAs are treated with dignity and compassion. He writes: "AIDS is not about 'us' and 'them.' People don't get HIV because they're 'bad,' and they don't not get it because they're 'good.' *You don't get HIV because of who you are. You get it because of what you do.*" (Johnson, *My Life,* p. 292) While many critics have attacked Magic for his homophobia, I understand this statement as an anti-homophobia strategy.

85. In some ways I feel very moved and affirmed by Magic's public pronouncements and the actions he has taken. He has not completely retreated into a campaign for sexual abstinence. He has not dumped his anger and pain on "groupie sluts," and he has not directly displayed homophobia to his American public. He did pose for Bush when he served on the AIDS Commission, but he cut this connection in a grandly public way when Bush failed to deliver. Magic moves carefully between the anti-sex agendas of Right Wing conservatives and the pro-safe sex education agendas of political liberals and sex-ed activists. He does not go as far as to promote promiscuity, noncoital sex, or sexual pluralism. He articulates well-crafted *semiotic and political compromises* between these extremes. Magic's body resides in a zone of ambiguity.

86. While I am drawn to Foucault's analysis of modern modalities of power that are theorized as productive rather than repressive, with local origins "from below," I still do not fully embrace his belief that micropractices aggregately accumulate into recognizable asymmetries of power (I share the critique developed by Vikki Bell in her *Interrogating Incest: Feminism, Foucault, and the Law* [New York: Routledge, 1993]). The micropractices that constitute Foucault's theory of power are readily reinforced by military and police state brutalities and other sanctioned aggressions that hold the micropractices in place. It is perhaps Foucault's position of relative privilege and prestige that permits these ever-present and everyday violences to recede from his analysis of power.

87. Dyson, "Be Like Mike?" p. 72.

2. Heterosexual Anti-Biotics

1. This approach to defining homophobia can be found in George Weinberg, *Society and the Healthy Homosexual* (New York: St. Martin's, 1972) and G. K. Lehne, "Homophobia among Men," in D. David and R. Brannon, eds., *The Forty-Nine Percent Majority: The Male Sex Role* (Reading, Mass.: Addison-Wesley, 1976), pp. 66–88.

2. Celia Kitzinger, "Heteropatriarchal Language," *Gossip: A Journal of Lesbian Feminist Ethics* 5: 15–20.

3. See in particular Gregory Herek, "On Heterosexual Masculinity: Some Psychical Consequences of the Social Construction of Gender and Sexuality," *American Behavioral Scientist* 29, no. 5 (May/June 1986): 563–577, and Suzanne Pharr, *Homophobia: A Weapon of Sexism* (Inverness, Calif.: Chardon, 1988).

4. Audre Lorde, "Age, Race, Class, and Sex: Women Redefining Difference," *Sister Outsider: Essays and Speeches* (Trumansburg, N.Y.: Crossing Press, 1984), pp. 114–123.

5. Joseph Neisen, "Heterosexism: Redefining Homophobia for the 1990s," *Journal of Gay and Lesbian Psychotherapy* 1, no. 3 (1990): 21–35.

6. For a particularly lucid analysis on how social relations of oppression interpolate and transform one another, see Elizabeth Spelman, *Inessential Woman: Problems of Exclusion in Feminist Thought* (Boston: Beacon, 1988).

7. The term "homophobia" became popular in the 1970s, primarily conceptualized as a psychological term; as Herek has noted, it was variously labeled as *homoerotophobia, heterosexism, homosexphobia, homosexism, homonegativism, antihomosexualism*, and *antihomosexuality*. See Gregory Herek, "Stigma, Prejudice, and Violence Against Lesbian and Gay Men," in John Gonsiorek and James Weinrich, eds., *Homosexuality: Research Implications for Public Policy* (Newbury Park, Calif.: Sage, 1991), pp. 60–80. In the early 1970s Weinberg and Smith coined the more enduring term "homophobia." See K. T. Smith, "Homophobia: A Tentative Personality Profile," *Psychological Reports* 29 (1971): 1091–1094, and George Weinberg *Society and the Healthy Homosexual* (New York: St. Martin's, 1972). This depiction of "homophobia" reversed the pathologization, making the homophobe a problem rather than the homosexual. As a discursive strategy, this reversal raised new questions and social concerns about the negative attitudes and personality formations supporting homophobia. However, the psychological bent of this reversal tended to obscure several levels of analysis, namely the structural and material domains of homophobia, its more widely nuanced forms of expression in different social, ethnic, racial, and economic contexts, and its relationship to various deployments of power and social relations that intersect and transform manifestations of homophobia.

8. Julia Kristeva, *Powers of Horror: An Essay on Abjection*, trans. Leon S. Roudiez (New York: Columbia University Press, 1982), p. 9.

9. Some readers may immediately react to what appears to be an essentialist reading of heteromasculinity, but I want to provide a few caveats to dissuade such a reading. My reflections on straight repulsion and heteromasculinity entail generalizations about the normative components of heteromasculinity as a social formation. This can be considered a "grand text" of relational sexual gender identity formation, which is forced upon most boy children. As a social formation, some adult men will embody its truth, some more loyally than others, and some will resist its influence, convert its thematics, question its necessity, and come to embody a sexual masculinity that is non-normative, reformist, or transgressive. These locations are all available but are indexed by a normative view of privileged heteromasculinity. My claims about heteromasculinity refer to these normative aspects of a social formation and not to all men. Second, my analysis rests upon the notion of a hegemonic heteromasculinity available to socially privileged males. This disciplining of masculinity is most easily embodied by men who are white,

heterosexual, economically advantaged, able-bodied, etc. It can be embodied as a compensatory or exemplary identity formation to make up for the lack of power in other domains of male life. Finally, I have not attempted to add detailed historical, ethnic, class, racial specificity to my template of normative, white, Euro-American heteromasculinity, although I have suggested that differently stationed masculinities may be at least partially influenced and relationally interpreted (especially in a racist context) with respect to the hegemonic heteromasculinity described by Herek. A closer study of heteromasculinities would add more detail and specificity, revealing conditions of differentiation and meaning in the lived embodiments of heteromasculinities. As a privileged form of power played off against other bodies, hegemonic heteromasculinity's definition will reflect tactics that define it as different from or better than other kinds of sex and gender formations. Heteromasculinities are particular social formations of power that may change over time, place, and context but seek to stabilize an identity in power through relational sexual practices and relational identity formations. Hegemonic heteromasculinity as a social formation is a constructed dispersion of relational power. I am writing about the nomic and the material formations of masculinity, not about all men. I suggest ways in which these formations are interpolated through class, race, and other relations, but I resist the postmodern call for a disarticulation of grand power narratives and social totalities. I share Vikki Bell's critique of Foucault's notions of power in *Interrogating Incest: Feminism, Foucault, and the Law* (New York: Routledge, 1993) and, to an extent, Teresa Ebert's critique of ludic feminism in *Ludic Feminism and After: Postmodernism, Desire, and Labor in Late Capitalism* (Ann Arbor: University of Michigan Press, 1995)

10. The notion of "border body" was first brought to my attention in Mary Poovey's "Speaking of the Body: A Discursive Division of Labor in Mid-Victorian Britian," in Mary Jacobus, Evelyn Fox Keller, and Sally Shuttleworth, eds., *Body/Politics: Women and the Discourses of Science* (New York: Routledge, 1990), pp. 29–46. Subsequent development of this notion can be found in Judith Butler, "Introduction," *Bodies that Matter: On the Discursive Limits of "Sex"* (New York: Routledge, 1993), p. 1–23.

11. I refer the reader to the grid I develop in chapter 4, "Male Lesbians and the Postmodern Body," p. 95.

12. I realize that I am playing with the ambiguity of this term: "antibiotic" or "antibody" as an induced or injected response to what is *not self* and "anti-biotic" as a cultural formation of attitudes and beliefs about bodies that is decidedly anti-body or rejecting of certain kinds of bodies.

13. The use of the masculine pronoun is purposive, if only to further the course of my speculations on the heteromasculine origins of straight repulsion. I discuss female straight repulsion subsequently. My decision to adopt the term "straight repulsion" may appear as though I am abandoning the specificity of lesbian feminist analyses of gender, sexism, and heterosexism by using an umbrella term that seems to belong to queer theory, thus blurring the issues of male vio-

lence and male power. However, I analyze straight repulsion by focusing on the construction of heteromasculine embodiment and its different race and class locations in an attempt to revise lesbian feminist analyses. Lesbian feminist analyses of gender, sexism, and heterosexism that I have found helpful in formulating my own ideas can be found in Audre Lorde *Sister Outsider* (Trumansburg, N.Y.: Crossing Press, 1984); Adrienne Rich "Compulsory Heterosexuality and Lesbian Existence, *Signs* 5, no. 4 (Summer 1980): 631–600; Marilyn Frye "A Lesbian Perspective on Women's Studies," *Sinister Wisdom* 14 (Fall 1980): 3–7; Sarah Hoagland "Separating from Heterosexualism," *Lesbian Ethics: Toward New Value* (Palo Alto, Calif.: Institute of Lesbian Studies, 1988); Claudia Card "Homophobia and Lesbian/Gay Pride," *Lesbian Choices* (New York: Columbia University Press, 1995) pp. 151–168; Suzanne Pharr, *Homophobia: A Weapon of Sexism* (Inverness, Calif.: Chardon, 1988).

14. This *will to violence* exists along a continuum that in the extreme erupts into queer-bashing or other brutalities. Along this continuum there are various degrees of negative and defensive posturing, including a willful ignorance toward the unknown, disregard, malice, ill-meaning acts, name-calling, discriminations, and other harms associated with hate speech and hate crimes. I have decided to use the the term "will to violence" to refer to an ensemble of dispositions that incites a variety of different responses that violate the boundaries and possibilities of a life form different from heteronormativity.

15. Similarly to the conceptual tactic used by Tamsin Wilton in *Lesbian Studies: Setting the Agenda* (New York: Routledge, 1995), p. x, I consider this ontic space best depicted by the word "queerness," since the word "queer" carries with it a provocative and negative history (though subject to playful reversal), while "queerness," like "richness" and "loveliness," holds a more flexible set of meanings. Wilton makes a similar distinction between "lesbian" and "lesbianness." I would further argue that sex/gender identity formations are a kind of enfleshed discursive space infused with power relations and productive of meaning. "Queerness" refers to an enfleshed discursivity that challenges the heterocentric sex and gender categories and the epistemic commitments of hegemonic heteromasculinity. It is a discursive space open to multiple formations and loosened categories. Queers are, however, what is hated, while aspects of queerness and its practices are appropriated as "the wild and fringey" by the colonizing capital interests of the dominant heterocentric culture, eg., male earrings previously signifying gay status.

16. In this approach I borrow and reshape some conceptual tools from Arthur W. Frank who has done extensive theoretical writing on the body. I adapt Frank's notion of "recursive structuration" to open up a way of understanding the body as constituted by institutions, discourses, and corporeality. The corporeality of the body provides both a resource and limit for embodiment—what I refer to as the body's physicality. Discursive practices provide cognitive mappings of the body's possibilities and limitations, which embodied subjectivities experience as if

already there by nature. Institutions are constituted in and through discursive practices that secure their sites of enunciation, transformation, and legitimation through embodied social relations. As institutions and discursive practices emerge through bodies or through the labor of bodies, institutions and their discursive practices can be studied "from the body up." However, this body is always already constituted in and through cultural discursivities and institutional practices. Thus all three aspects—discursivities, institutions, corporealities—are in a relationship of mutual structuration that is always in the process of constituting itself. Hence the action and effects of bodies are recursive, moving through and continuously re-constituting all three levels, as social structures both inform and make possible embodiments that in turn inform and make possible social structures and relations. This materially recursive process is the body. See Arthur W. Frank, "For a Sociology of the Body: An Analytical Review" in Mike Featherstone, Mike Hepworth, and Bryan S. Turner, eds., *The Body: Social Process and Cultural Theory.* (Newbury Park, Calif.: Sage, 1991), pp. 37–102 and Anthony Giddens, *The Constitution of Society* (Berkeley: University of California Press, 1984).

17. Though this may signal the reader that I am heading towards a Lacanian reading of sex/gender formations, I am not. I will, however, use the notion of phallus is a quasi-Lacanian manner similar to Gayle Rubin's analysis "Traffic in Women" in Rayna Reiter, ed., *Toward an Anthropology of Women* (New York: Monthly Review Press, 1975), pp. 157–210. The phallus is understood as the mythic signifier that establishes the binary divide of sex/gender identity formations, hence I refer to it as *the cultural phallus*. My arguments rest upon the now customary distinction between penis (as the actual male genitalia) and phallus (as the mythic, omnipresent, invulnerable signifier of the binary divide). See Charles Bernheimer, "Penile Reference in Phallic Theory," *differences (the Phallus Issue)* 4, no. 1 (Spring 1992): 116–132. My attempts to understand the racialization of the Phallus are implicit in the power analysis that assumes white phallic power as "better endowed" by virtue of its privileged economic and cultural capital, as well a race privilege. Nonwhite racialized phallic constructions inflect this power differential, as well as what Bordo has called the threat of the penis to the phallus. See Susan Bordo, "Reading the Male Body," *Michigan Quarterly Review* 32, no. 4 (Fall 1993): 696–737; Richard Fung, "Looking at My Penis: The Eroticized Asian in Gay Video Porn," in Bad Object Choices, eds., *How Do I Look? Queer Film and Video* (Seattle: Bay, 1991); and Kobena Mercer, "Imaging the Black Man's Sex" in Pat Holland, Jo Spence, and Simon Watney, eds., *Photography/Politics: Two* (London/New York: Comedia Publishing Group, 1986), pp. 61–69.

18. Carrigan, Connell, and Lee define "hegemonic masculinity" "as a particular variety of masculinity to which others—among them young and effeminate as well as homosexual men—are subordinated" (Tim Carrigan, Bob Connell, and John Lee "Toward a New Sociology of Masculinity," in Harry Brod, ed., *The Making of Masculinities* [London: Allen and Unwin, 1987], p. 86). In seeking to depict an *origin* of straight repulsion in the sex/gender formations of hegemonic heteromas-

culinity, I am not identifying a metaphysical or physical origin or even an origin understood as "temporally prior to" or "more authentic than." My sense of *origin* draws attention to where power seems most invested in fomenting and strengthening the fervor and abuses of its power. This notion of *origin* is not subject to a Butlerian critique, since it is an origin within the performativity of heteromasculinities. In my use of "origin," I view this as a power analysis, where privileged heteromasculinities require straight repulsion as a means of securing and holding power and privilege, even though white, straight, relatively privileged men may espouse liberal attitudes and beliefs about homosexuality. However heterosexism and homophobia are not as widely recognized by white male liberals as is racism and the need to eliminate racial oppressions. The current lack of high-level support in the United States for gay marriage or the "don't ask, don't tell, don't pursue" policy in the military reveals a willful lack of clarity on these issues—if not outright abhorrence—and an interest in allowing the abuses and violence against queer bodies to continue.

19. A similar point is well argued in Bordo, "Reading the Male Body," pp. 696–737.

20. Herek, "On Heterosexual Masculinity," pp. 563–577. For popular press critical analyses of white masculinity, see K. Druck and J. Simmons, *The Secrets Men Keep* (Garden City, N. Y.: Doubleday, 1985) and C. W. Franklin, *The Changing Definition of Masculinity* (New York: Plenum, 1984).

21. Though I do not pursue an analysis of different racialized or class-based constructions of masculinity, my assumption is that masculinities solidify a stylized presentation or a performativity that marks a difference from the feminine in specific cultural contexts. See Richard Majors and Janet Mancini Billson, *Cool Pose: The Dilemmas of Black Manhood in America* (New York: Macmillan, 1992); Paul Breines, *Tough Jews: Political Fantasies and the Moral Dilemma of American Jewry* (New York: Basic Books, 1990); Harry Brod, ed., *A Mensch Among Men* (Freedom, Calif.: Crossing Press, 1988); Fred Pfeil, *White Guys: Studies in Postmodern Domination and Difference* (London: Verso, 1995); and J. M. Carrier "Family Attitudes and Mexican Male Homosexuality," *Urban Life* 5, no. 3 (October 1976): 359–375. For a good review of research on how African American masculinities are different from white middle-class, Euro-American masculinities, see George Roberts, "Brother to Brother: African American Modes of Relating to Men, *Journal of Black Studies* 24, no. 4 (June 1994): 379–390, and Don Belton, ed., *Speak My Name: Black Men on Masculinity and the American Dream* (Boston: Beacon, 1995).

22. Through the lens of social psychology, both Gregory Herek and Erwin Goffman seem to provide a bridge for thinking about straight repulsion as an ensemble of psychological attitudes that have social anchors and everyday manifestations. Jonathan Dollimore and Kaja Silverman have further deployed psychoanalysis as a way of understanding the deep structures the homophobic self. While I find these approaches helpful, I do not use a psychoanalytic model, preferring to develop a theory of embodiment that integrates into a multitiered

analysis of embodied identity formations and the social relations of power in class, race, state, and police economies that reify those differences in a total recursive production. Thus my particular approach to theorizing straight repulsion seems to be compatible with a constructivist psychoanalytic application, although I do not pursue that venue of theory. See Jonathan Dollimore, *Sexual Dissidence: Augustine to Wilde, Freud to Foucault* (New York: Oxford University Press, 1991); Kaja Silverman, *Male Subjectvity on the Margins* (New York: Routledge, 1992); and Erving Goffman, *Stigma: Notes on the Management of Spoiled Identity* (Englewood Cliffs, N.J.: Prentice Hall, 1963).

23. Dollimore, *Sexual Dissidence*, p. 245.

24. Ibid., p. 244.

25. I realize that this analysis is very hastily covered and requires a more sustained analysis. For a narrative that exemplifies my point, see Cherríe Moraga, *Loving During the War Years: lo que nunca pasó por sus labios* (Boston: South End, c. 1983).

26. In most research that is not conscious of its race assumptions, nonwhite groups are indicated by a qualifying adjective such as "black" or "Asian-American." When these qualifiers are absent, researchers often assume they are studying men in general; this is usually a pseudogeneric claim, however, since such studies are invariably based on studies of mostly white male subjects or socially privileged white male subjects, such as college students.

27. These studies can be found in Gregory Herek, "Heterosexuals' Attitudes Toward Lesbians and Gay Men," *Journal of Sex Research* 25, no. 4 (1988): 451–477, and "Beyond 'Homophobia': A Social Psychological Perspective on Attitudes Toward Lesbians and Gay Men," *Journal of Homosexuality* 10, nos. 1/2 (1984): 1–21.

28. Homophobic attitudes have been correlated with authoritarian personality structure: Gregory Herek, "Beyond 'Homophobia' " and "Heterosexuals' Attitudes"; B. Altemeyer, *Enemies of Freedom: Understanding Right-Wing Authoritarianism* (San Francisco: Jossy-Bass, 1988); racist attitudes: M. M. Bierly, "Prejudice Toward Contemporary Outgroups as a Generalized Attitude," *Journal of Applied Social Psychology* 15, no. 2 (1985): 189–199; N. M. Henley and F. Pincus, "Interrelationships of Sexist, Racist, and Antihomosexual Attitudes," *Psychological Reports* 42 (1978): 83–90; intolerance based on religious beliefs: Gregory Herek, "Religion and Prejudice: A Comparison of Racial and Sexual Attitudes," *Personality and Social Psychology Bulletin* 13, no. 1 (1976): 56–65; cognitive rigidity: K. T. Smith, "Homophobia: A Tentative Personality Profile,"*Psychological Reports* 29 (1971): 1091–1094; and stronger sex-stereotype beliefs: Suzanne Harper, "Subordinating Masculinities/Racializing Masculinities: Writing White Supremacist Discourse on Men's Bodies," *masculinities* 1, no. 4 (1994): 1–20, Gregory Herek, "Psychological Heterosexism and Anti-Gay Violence: The Social Psychology of Bigotry and Bashing," in Gregory Herek and Kevin Berril, ed., *Hate Crimes: Confronting Violence Against Lesbians and Gays* (Newbury Park, Calif.: Sage, 1992): 149–169.

These studies suggest a composite of the homophobic heterosexual male as rigid in categorical thinking, dependent on authority, and invested in sexual conservativism and sexual stereotyping as well as racist and xenophobic beliefs.

29. Herek, "Beyond 'Homophobia' "; "Heterosexuals' Attitudes."

30. Herek, "Heterosexuals' Attitudes."

31. I take this to mean that women may move in circles that overlap with the feminine-identified interests of some gay men or that they encounter the services of gay men, e.g., hair-dressing, gourmet classes, gardening, and interior design, which may have higher numbers of gay men than other kinds of work. To some extent the comment is based on stereotypes.

32. See Adrienne Rich, "Compulsory Heterosexuality"; and Lillian Faderman, *Surpassing the Love of Men: Romantic Friendship and Love Between Women from the Renaissance to the Present* (New York: Morrow, 1981).

33. Marshall Forstein, "Homophobia: An Overview,"*Psychiatric Annals* 18, no. 1 (January 1980): 33–36.

34. Gregory Herek and J. H. Pleck, *The Myth of Masculinity* (Cambridge: Massachusetts Institute of Technology Press, 1981).

35. Dollimore, *Sexual Dissidence.*

36. G. K. Lehne, "Homophobia among Men." In D. David and R. Brannon, eds., *The Forty-Nine Percent Majority: The Male Sex Role* (Reading, Mass.: Addison-Wesley, 1976), pp. 66–88.

37. Leslie Feinberg, *Stone Butch Blues* (Ithaca: Firebrand, 1993).

38. Joyce Trebilcot, "Taking Responsibility for Sexuality." In *Dyke Ideas: Process, Politics, Daily Life* (Albany: State University of New York Press, 1994), pp. 97–109. Originally published in Elaine Barton, Kristen Watts-Penny, Barbara Hillyer Davis, eds., *Women and Mental Health: Conference Proceedings* (Norman: University of Oklahoma Women's Studies Program, 1982), pp. 55–62.

39. Eridani, "Is Sexual Orientation a Secondary Sex Characteristic?" in Elizabeth Reba Weise, ed., *Closer to Home: Bisexuality and Feminism* (Seattle, Wash.: Seal, 1992), pp. 173–181.

40. See Gough's analysis discussed in Rich, "Compulsory Heterosexuality."

41. By "class-privileging capitals," I have in mind easier access to higher education, jobs and positions of power, styles of literacy, comportment, self-management, and the embodied assumptions of superiority over "lower" socioeconomic classes in a life-world that seemingly configures this reality as the way the world is. I have found the following helpful in thinking about the *embodiment of class*: Joanna Kadi's *Thinking Class: Sketches from a Cultural Worker* (Boston: South End, 1996) and Robert Hanke's "Hegemonic Masculinity in *thirtysomething*," *Critical Studies in Mass Communication* 7 (1990):231–248.

42. See n. 21.

43. Pleck, *Myth of Masculinity.*

44. This point has been made by a number of theorists: Leo Bersani, "Is the Rectum a Grave?" in Douglas Crimp, ed., *AIDS: Cultural Analysis, Cultural*

Activism (Cambridge: Massachusetts Institute of Technology Press, 1988); John Stoltenberg, *Refusing to be a Man: Essays on Sex and Justice* (Portland, Ore.: Breitenbush, 1989); Brian Pronger, *The Arena of Masculinity: Sports, Homosexuality, and the Meaning of Sex* (New York: St. Martins, 1990); Richard Mohr, " 'Knights, Young Men, Boys': Masculine Worlds and Democratic Values," *Gay Ideas: Outing and Other Controversies* (New York: Beacon, 1992); and Naomi Scheman, "Though This Be Method, Yet There Is Madness in It: Paranoia and Liberal Epistemology," *Engenderings: Constructions of Knowledge, Authority, and Privilege* (New York: Routledge, 1993), pp. 75–105.

45. Eve Kosofsky Sedgwick's analysis of homophobia between men is handsomely explored in *Between Men: English Literature and Male Homosocial Desire* (New York: Columbia University Press, 1985).

46. Jacquelyn N. Zita, "The Feminist Philosopher's Revolutionary Toolbox and the Unavoidability of Queerness." Paper presented at the American Philosophical Association, Central Division, Kansas City, Missouri, May 4–7, 1994.

47. Luce Irigaray, *This Sex Which Is Not One*, trans. Catherine Porter with Carolyn Burke (Ithaca: Cornell University Press, 1985).

48. There are extenuating circumstances, such as prisons where homosexual behaviors are described as temporary and not necessarily essential to those engaged in such sexual behaviors. Sexual identity formation seems to require a sense of individual free determination, rather than the coercion of need or other unwanted factors.

49. Susan Bordo has provides an analysis of the female body in heterosexual male pornography as "a willing construction of the self in gestures of total receptivity to the male" that transform the "embarrassed penis into proud phallus—the point of pornography" (Bordo, "Reading the Male Body," pp. 706–707). This supports my notion that heteromasculinity requires the open and objectified female body to maintain the fantasy of the invulnerable phallus. This fantasy of the open female body accompanies the shadow of the closeted (and soft) queer body that together triangulate with the hard, aggressive, and possessive heteromale body. This privileged hard sex is reified in propertied extensions and class relations colonizing a bodily domain secured by heterosexual class, gender, and heterosex privileges. An astute reader will notice that lesbians have disappeared from this scene. That's right.

50. Susan Bordo has stated the need for an armored heteromasculinity quite aptly: "Indeed, the penis—insofar as it is capable of being soft as well as hard, injured as well as injuring, helpless as well as proud, emotionally needy as well as cold with will, insofar as it is a vulnerable, perishable *body*—haunts the phallus, threatens its undoing. Patriarchal culture generally wants it out of sight" (Bordo, "Reading the Male Body," pp. 698–699).

51. I encourage the reader to understand my use of the terms "origin" and "derivative" in terms of a larger analysis of social relations of power, intersecting oppressions, and recursive formations of embodied subjectivity. Just as I argue

that straight repulsion has its *origin* in privileged heteromasculinity, I do not impute to this origin an essence, an authenticity, a temporal priority, or a mono-causal trajectory. It is an origin in that its locus of concentrated and recursively constructed power requires straight repulsion as it requires the subjugations and oppressions of race, class, gender, disability, etc. The collective exploitation and oppression of women *in different ways* is required by the social formations of het-eromasculinities. I argue that heterofemale straight repulsion is, therefore, *deriv-ative* to the extent that a woman carries out the mandates of heteromasculinity in her sexual loyalty to men. It may be experienced as originating in herself, as very real, as a booster to her own self-esteem and identity as a heterosexual. It can be just as intense and violent or as soft and muted as heteromasculine straight repul-sion. My analysis of its *origin* and *derivations* rests on the unanswerable question of what would happen if straight men no longer abjected queers. Holding straight women in place and as the preferred sexual object choice are critically important to the validation of heteromasculine identity and desire.

52. Marilyn Frye, "Some Reflections on Separatism and Power," *Politics of Reality: Essays in Feminist Theory* (Freedom, Calif.: Crossing Press), 1983, pp. 95–109.

53. Bersani, "Is the Rectum a Grave."

54. Frye, "On Separatism."

55. Mary Douglas, *Natural Symbols: Explorations in Cosmology* (New York: Pantheon, 1970) p. vii.

56. The best analysis of this can be found in Carole Pateman, *The Sexual Contract* (Stanford: Stanford University Press, 1988).

57. Pateman, *Sexual Contract*, pp. 5–6.

58. Gerda Lerner, *The Creation of Patriarchy* (New York: Oxford, 1986).

59. John Wrathall, *Take the Young Stranger by the Hand: Same Sex Relations in the YMCA, 1868–1920* (Chicago: University of Chicago Press, 1998); Anthony Rotundo, *Journal of Social History* 23 (Fall 1989): 1–25; George Chauncey, "Christian Brotherhood or Sexual Perversion? Homosexual Identities and the Construc-tion of Social Boundaries in the World War One Era," *Journal of Social History* 19 (Winter 1985): 189–212.

60. Michael Messner and Donald Sabo, eds., *Sport, Men, and the Gender Order* (Champaign: Human Kinetics, 1990).

61. Michel Foucault, *History of Sexuality*, vol. 1, trans. Robert Hurley (New York: Pantheon, 1978).

62. George Chauncey Jr., "From Sexual Inversion to Homosexuality: Medi-cine and the Changing Conceptualizations of Female Deviance." *Salmagundi* 58–59 (Fall/Winter 1983): 114–146; Lillian Faderman, *Surpassing the Love of Men*; Michel Foucault, *History of Sexuality*, vol. 1.

63. Leonard Duroche, "Men Fearing Men: On the Nineteenth-Century Ori-gins of Modern Homophobia," *Men's Studies Review* 8, no. 3 (Summer 1991), pp. 3–7.

64. Wrathall, *American Manhood.*

65. I have found Omni and Winant's notion of racial formations extremely helpful in thinking about about the social formations of race, gender, and sexuality emerging in class relations of contemporary North America. Omni and Winant provide both a semantic and materialist account of racial formations as "an unstable and 'decentered' complex of social meanings constantly being transformed by political struggle" (Michael Omi and Howard Winant, *Racial Formation in the United States: From the 1960s to the 1980s* (New York: Routledge, 1986).

66. For a clarification of the term "sex-gender ontology," see chapter 4, "Male Lesbians and the Postmodern Body."

67. Douglas, *Natural Symbols,* p. viii.

68. Cindy Patton, *Sex and Germs: The Politics of AIDS* (Boston: South End, 1985). Francis Barker, *The Tremulous Body: Essays on Subjection* (Ann Arbor: University of Michigan Press, 1995).

69. Judith Butler, *Bodies that Matter: On the Discursive Limits of "Sex"* (New York: Routledge, 1993).

70. The racist implications of AIDS imagery are always present. See Simon Whatney, "AIDS, Language, and the Third World," in E. Carter and S. Watney, eds., *Taking Liberties* (London: Serpent's Tail, 1989), pp. 183–192; Richard C. Chirimuuta and Rosalind Chirimuuta, *AIDS, Africa, and Racism* (London: Free Association Books, 1989); Cindy Patton, "Inventing African AIDS," in *Inventing AIDS* (New York: Routledge, 1990).

71. For analyses of the immunological metaphors and the AIDS crises, see Emily Martin, *Flexible Bodies: The Role of Immunity in American Culture from the Days of Polio to the Age of AIDS* (Boston: Beacon, 1994) and "The End of the Body?," *American Ethnologist* 19, no. 1 (1992): 121–141; Donna Haraway, "The Biopolitics of Postmodern Bodies: Determinations of Self in Immune System Discourse," *differences* 1, no. 1 (1989): 3–34.

72. For a suggestive parallel on white nurses in German fascist male fantasy, see Klaus Theweleit, *Male Fantasies,* trans. Stephan Conway in collaboration with Erica Carter and Chris Turner (Minneapolis: University of Minneapolis Press, 1987). See also Timothy Landers, "Bodies and Anti-bodies: A Crisis in Representation," *The Independent* 11, no 1 (January/February 1988): 133–145.

73. Lisa Duggan, "Making It Perfectly Queer," *Socialist Review* 22, no. 1 (1992): 11–31.

74. Judith Butler, *Gender Trouble: Feminism and the Subversion of Identity* (New York: Routledge, 1990); *Bodies that Matter.*

75. Celia Kitzinger, *Social Construction of Lesbianism* (London: Sage, 1987). While Kitzinger bemoans the loss of difference occasioned by "sameness" arguments, the studies she critiques are not those currently being used to mark a difference biologically in brain structures, hormones, or genes. In the latter kind of studies, evidence is marshalled to organize for equal civil and familial rights for sexually different kinds of people.

76. Urvashi Vaid, *Virtual Equality: The Mainstreaming of Gay and Lesbian Liberation* (New York: Anchor, 1995).

77. Iris Young, "The Scaling of Bodies and the Politics of Identity," in *Justice and the Politics of Difference* (Princeton: Princeton University Press, 1990), pp. 122–155.

78. See June M. Reinish and Ruth Beasley, *The Kinsey Institute New Report on Sex: What You Must Know to be Sexually Literate* (New York: St. Martin's, 1990).

79. Naomi Goldenberg, *Returning Words to Flesh: Feminism, Psychoanalysis, and the Resurrection of the Body* (Boston: Beacon, 1990) pp. 62–64.

80. Michel Foucault, *Power/Knowledge: Selected Interviews and Other Writings 1972–1977*, trans. and ed. Colin Gordon (New York: Pantheon, 1980) p. 55.

81. Mary Douglas, *Purity and Danger: An Analysis of the Concepts of Pollution* (New York: Praeger, 1966), p. 115.

82. Tim Carrigan, Bob Connell, and John Lee, "Toward a New Sociology of Masculinity." In Harry Brod, ed., *The Making of Masculinity* (London: Allen and Unwin, 1987), p. 81.

83. Robert Mapplethorpe, "Untitled 1972," in *Robert Mapplethorpe* (Whitney Museum of Art, New York: Bullfinch, 1988), p. 22. What I found in my own first experience of this image was that I was drawn to the bordered kiss by virtue of Mapplethorpe's use of color; only secondarily did I notice that the beloved bodies were male with one positioned in a typical female sexual presentation with a frontal view of the body lying down, relaxed in the arms of a male lover, disclosing the visible genitals and spread-legged openness of the beloved. This image celebrates the soft and fluid body image as a male trespass on feminine domain.

84. Michel Foucault, "Friendship as a Way of Life." In *Foucault Live (Interviews, 1966–1984)*, trans. John Johnson and ed. Sylvère Lotringer (New York: Semiotext, 1989), pp. 203–209

85. John Stoltenberg, *Refusing to be a Man: Essays on Sex and Justice* (Portland, Ore.: Breitenbush, 1989).

86. At the 1993 gay, lesbian, bisexual, and transgender march in Washington, D.C., I saw several people standing alongside the long march with signs bearing "Proud to be a Homophobe." This inversion of the gay pride motif seemed oddly placed in the passing scene. Similar placards, such as "Proud to be a Racist" or "Proud to be a Rapist" seem to elicit more intolerance among the liberal-minded.

3. Prozac Feminism

1. Emphasis and interpolation mine. All references to page numbers listed in the text in parentheses hereafter refer to Peter Kramer, *Listening to Prozac: A Psychiatrist Explores Antidepressant Drugs and the Remaking of the Self* (New York: Viking Penguin, 1993).

2. Prozac is the common proprietary (trade) name for a chemical substance originally designed as an antidepressant drug and first synthesized in 1974 by

employees of Ely Lilly (David Wong, Frank Bymaster, and Eric Engleman, "A Selective Inhibitor of Serotonin Uptake: Lilly 11014, 3-(p-Trifluoromethylphe-noxy-)-N-Methyl-3-Phenylpropylamine," *Life Sciences* 15 [1974]: 471–479). Prozac is also known by its chemical or generic name, fluoxetine. Prozac belongs to a group of engineered drugs called SSRIs or *selective serotonin reuptake inhibitors* because the structural design of these drugs is specifically created to bond with chemical receptors in the brain cells involved in the uptake of sero-tonin. Because of Prozac's blocking action, the levels of serotonin in the synaptic spaces between brain cells increases, allegedly causing an increased firing of nearby postsynaptic nerves. This can be experienced as an elevation of mood, allowing Prozac to be classified as an antidepressant. Since the appearance of Prozac, several other copycat SSRIs have been manufactured, including Zoloft (sertraline), Praxil (paraxetine), and Luvox (fluvoxamine). Given the multimillion dollar profits made from SSRIs, Fortune 500 companies are racing for a corner on the market. See Milt Freudenheim, "Merck and Lilly Post Strong Earnings and Sales, *New York Times*, October 19, 1994, p. D3; Milt Freudenheim, "The Drug Makers Are Listening to Prozac," *New York Times*, January 9, 1994, sec. 3, p. 7; Elyse Tanouye, "Critics See Self-Interest in Lilly's Funding of Ads Telling the Depressed to Get Help," *Wall Street Journal*, April 15, 1993, sec. B, p. 1.

3. The FDA gave initial approval to Prozac in 1985, with final approval given to Lilly in 1987, after two years of testing. Lilly's marketing of Prozac began in January 1988. By 1993 annual sales of Prozac peaked at $1.2 billion, and by the end of 1993 an estimated 6 million Americans and another 4 million people world-wide were using Prozac. Peter Kramer's book, which was published in 1993 and at least partially financed by Eli Lilly, appeared one year after Lilly had encountered approximately 170 law suits seeking recovery from Prozac-related damages. See Peter and Ginger Breggin's *Talking Back to Prozac: What Doctors Won't Tell You about Today's Most Controversial Drug* (New York: St. Martin, 1994). The pro-motion of Kramer's *Listening to Prozac* by Eli Lilly echoes a similar incident in the 1960s when Robert A. Wilson's book *Feminine Forever* was largely financed by drug companies for the promotion of Estrogen Replacement Therapy to women seeking a fix for their aging process. See K. I. MacPherson, "Menopause as Disease: The Social Construction of a Metaphor," *Advances in Nursing Science* 3, no. 2 (1981): 95–113.

4. The media hysteria on Prozac reached a peak in 1991, two years before the appearance of Kramer's book. The Phil Donahue Show (February 27, 1991) ran a program entitled "Prozac—Medication That Makes You Kill"; *Newsweek* fol-lowed with a special article "A Prozac Backlash" (April 1, 1991); and on May 6, 1991 *Time* ran a cover exposé of the Church of Scientology's attack on Prozac. Prozac horror stories flooded the media—stories of drug-induced paranoia, depression, violence, and suicide—as lawsuits mounted against Ely Lilly. See Paula Span, "The Man Behind the Bitter Pill Debate: Lawyer Leonard Finz Presses the Case Against Eli Lilly and Prozac," *Washington Post*, August 14, 1991, pp.

C1–C3. In the midst of these perverse and out-of-control stories, Peter Kramer's *Listening to Prozac* appears in 1993 in a professional calm with his Prozac poster-child, Tess, promising a return to middle-class normality.

5. Markie Robson-Scott ("Who is the Real Ms. Prozac? *The Guardian*, September 21, 1993, p. 16) has estimated that women take Prozac more than men in a ratio of five to one, a gender trend that is roughly matched by Kramer's sample of clinical cases: Allison, Gail, Hillary, Jerry, Julia, Lucy, Sally, Sam, Sonia, and Tess. Although Kramer includes men among his happy Prozac patients, he is primarily marketing his idea to and for women, especially with his notion of Prozac feminism. More specifically, Prozac is marketed to and for middle-class "self-accelerated" and privileged women, who can afford both Prozac and its diagnostic expense and who experience loss in efficiency and energy as a terrifying turn in personality requiring medical intervention. Studies show that middle-class women are more inclined to adopt the medical model and the reductionist metaphysic of psychotropic medicine, while working-class women remain more suspicious of the pharmaceutical remedies. See Emily Martin, *The Woman in the Body: A Cultural Analysis of Reproduction* (Boston: Beacon, 1989); Michael Calnan, "Lay Evaluation of Medicine and Medical Practice: Report of a Pilot Study," *International Journal of Health Services* 18 (1988): 311–322; and Michael Calnan and S. Williams, "Images of Scientific Medicine," *Sociology of Health and Illness* 14, no. 2 (1992): 233–254.

6. "Hyperthymia" is derived from the Greek term for sanguine temperament. Kramer describes "hyperthymia" as "distinct from mania and hypomania, the disorders in which people are grandiose, frenetic, distractible, and flawed in their judgment. Hyperthymics are merely optimistic, decisive, quick of thought, charismatic, energetic, and confident" (*Listening*, p. 17).

7. For more discussion on the commodification of psychopharmaceutical cosmetics and its new disciplines for the body, see D. Concar, "Design Your Own Personality" *New Scientist* 141 (March 1994): 22–26; Michiko Kacutani "The Examined Life Isn't Worth Living," *New York Times*, September 20, 1994, p. B2; David Rothman, "Shiny Happy People: The Problem with 'Cosmetic Psychopharmacology'," *New Republic*, February 14, 1994, pp. 34–38; "The New You," *Psychiatric Times* (March 1990): 45–46.

8. This notion of panic in the postmodern body can be explored in the works of Kathy Aker, *Empire of the Senseless* (New York: Grove, 1988); Jackie Orr, "Theory on the Market: Panic, Incorporating," *Social Problems* 37, no. 4 (November 1990): 460–484; and Stephen Pfohl, *Death at the Parasite Cafe: Social Science (Fictions) and the Postmodern* (New York: St. Martin's, 1992).

9. While I elaborate more carefully on the notion of postmodern bodies elsewhere in this book, I refer the reader to the several key sources I have found most helpful in comprehending the dissolution of boundaries and refictioning of organic/cultural unities marking the postmodern body as a new cultural formation: Gilles Deleuze and Felix Guattari, *Anti-Oedipus: Capitalism and Schizo-*

phrenia, trans. R. Hurley, Mark Seem, and Helen Lane (New York: Viking, 1977); Barbara Duden, *Disembodying Women: Perspectives on Pregnancy and the Unborn* (Cambridge: Harvard University Press, 1991); Arthur and Marilouise Kroker, "Thesis on the Disappearing Body in the Hyper-Modern Condition," in *Body Invaders: Panic Sex in America* (New York: St. Martin's, 1987), and *The Postmodern Scene: Excremental Culture and Hyper-Aesthetics* (New York: St. Martin's, 1986); Donna Haraway's "A Cyborg Manifesto" and "The Biopolitics of Postmodern Bodies: Constitutions of Self in Immune System Discourse," both in *Simians, Cyborgs, and Women: The Reinvention of Nature* (New York: Routledge, 1991); and Elizabeth Grosz, *Space, Time, and Perversion: Essays on the Politics of Bodies* (New York: Routledge, 1995).

10. Donna Haraway suggests that the older more familiar form of domination, that of *white capitalist patriarchy*, has been replaced by an *informatics of domination*, which is a new way of recrafting bodies through communication technologies and biotechnologies and of translating the world into a problem of coding. "Communications technologies and biotechnologies are the crucial tools recrafting our bodies. These tools embody and enforce new social relations for women world-wide. Technologies and scientific discourses can be partially understood as formalizations, i.e., as frozen moments, of the fluid social interactions constituting them, but they should also be viewed as instruments for enforcing meanings. . . . Furthermore, communications sciences and modern biologies are constructed by a common move—the translation of the world into a problem of coding, a search for a common language in which all resistance to instrumental control disappears and all heterogeneity can submitted to disassembly, reassembly, investment, and exchange" ("Cyborg Manifesto" p. 164).

11. Noticeably, Kramer's Prozac women are described by their relationships, heterosexual practices, career functions, and body image—concerns that seem to be located in a middle-class and sometimes upper-class context. Other kinds of differences, such as differences in race, sexuality, physical disabilities, ethnicity, etc., seem to fall away from Kramer's diagnostic vision or remain unmarked. Among the "substantial minority" (*Listening*, p. 11) of Kramer's women who respond positively to Prozac, most of these are homogenized by class, heterosexual, and gender norms. Only seldom does he make explicit this sex bias among his clients, and he repeatedly fails to offer any analysis of the social and historical factors affecting women's oppression and depression. Kramer's Prozac feminism relies on these omissions and oversights.

12. While Kramer does express his horror that Prozac might be perceived as another "mother's little helper pill," such as valium, prescribed for frustrated housewives in the 1950s, he can disclaim this only in so far as Prozac enables women to experience a drug-induced kick towards liberation and away from the prefeminist domestic set-up. His promotion of Prozac feminism is his only guarantee that Prozac is not another drug-induced fog to keep women going. Some studies of advertising suggest that contemporary advertising of psychotropic

drugs for women conveys a striking contrast to the pathetically depressed and miserable images of the 1950s' housewife. More recent advertising studies reveal the go-getter, versatile, drug-sparked psychotropic woman of the 1990s as a shift in advertising strategy and audience. See Elizabeth Ettorre and Elianne Riska, "Advertising as a Representation of Gendered Moods" in *Gendered Moods: Psychotropics and Society* (London/New York: Routledge, 1995), pp. 65–88.

13. The rhetorical strategies I am referring to grow out of the 1970s when the slogan "the personal is political" spawned a number of performative and rhetorical practices: *breaking silence, finding your voice, telling your story, listening to another woman's story, refusing to be a victim, letting the victim speak, listening to your body, creating support and survivor groups, raising consciousness, fighting back,* and *naming the problem*. I will later analyze how Naomi Scheman engenders a different analysis of the emotions through a philosophical analysis of consciousness raising in the 1970s. In the meantime I find that Kramer's appropriation of these rhetorical flourishes creates a surface of liberation talk while riding on Prozac's molecular promise—the material conditions of his feminist liberation. In 1995 Prozac testimonials again appear on the market in Debra Elfenbein ed., *Living with Prozac and Other Selective Serotonin Reuptake Inhibitors (SSRIs): Personal Accounts of Life on Antidepressants* (San Francisco: Harper San Francisco, 1995), with a foreword writing by Peter D. Kramer, M.D.

14. The metaphors of *margin to center* and *talking back to power* are deeply and historically embedded in African-American feminisms, as exemplified in the work of bell hooks. See specifically bell hooks, *Talking Back: Thinking Feminist, Thinking Black* (Boston: Southend, 1989).

15. Originally approved by the FDA as an antidepressant, Prozac was soon thereafter prescribed for obsessive-compulsive disorder, seasonal affective disorder, obesity, anorexia, chronic fatigue syndrome, premenstrual syndrome, postpartum depression, drug and alcohol addiction, migraine headaches, arthritis, body dysmorphic disorder, and behavioral and emotional problems in children and adolescents (cited in Breggin and Breggin, *Talking Back to Prozac.*, p. 4).

16. According to the Breggins, the FDA's studies indicated that Prozac was not a very effective drug as an antidepressant, and a few more recent studies have shown that antidepressants in general may be no more effective than placebos ("The Real Story Behind Prozac's Approval by the FDA," *Talking Back to Prozac*, pp. 41–66)

17. The Breggins focus on the tragic victims of Prozac and the oversights of drug testing that allowed Prozac to go onto the market too quickly without careful protocols for screening and dosages. They ultimately develop a homey critique of the evils of capitalism and the fast profits made from the drug's promotion. The Breggins call for a return to the traditions of therapy and family values with an understanding of mental illness as caused by dysfunctional family dynamics. As Judith Kegan Gardiner has pointed out, the terrain of the debate between Kramer and the Breggins commits Prozac to liberal feminism: "Kramer treats contempo-

rary professional women who love too much and who are liberated by Prozac. Breggin describes devoted wives and mothers, who under the influence of the same drug, want to divorce their husbands and kill their children. Both thus portray the drug as acting like liberal feminism in detaching women from traditional roles and fitting them for contemporary corporate life" (Gardiner, "Can Ms. Prozac Talk Back? Feminism, Drugs, and Social Constructionism," *Feminist Studies* 21, no.3 [Fall 1995]: 508). See also "The Oprah Winfrey Show: Everything You Wanted to Know about the Happy Pill" (Chicago: Harpo Productions, March 7, 1994), Burrelle's Information Services, Livingston, N. J. The debate is also stylized for the popular press in "Ordinary Pleasures and Prozac for All," *Psychology Today* 27, no. 4 (July/August 1994): 44–49, 72, 80–81, which includes a sideboard article written by Peter Breggin.

18. Serotonin is found in the serum, the intestinal mucosa, and the central nervous system; only 1–2 percent of the body's serotonin is found in the brain. The serotonin found in the brain is synthesized by neurons mostly located in the midline region of the pons and upper brain stem. These neurons have projections that extend into the limbic system, the cerebral and cerebellar cortices, and the thymus. The serotonergic system is positioned to coordinate complex sensory and motor patterns during varied behavioral states. It is most active in periods of waking arousal, reduced in slow-wave sleep, and absent during REM sleep. Its activity seems to be altered in depression, hyperaggressive states, and schizophrenia. Both Prozac and LSD are effective in blocking serotonin receptors in the brain. See Jack Cooper, Floyd Bloom, and Robert Roth, *The Biochemical Basis of Neuropharmacology* (New York: Oxford University Press, 1991).

19. Much of the argument that Prozac and other SSRIs act as anti-depressants is based on the a few studies that show that there are lower levels of serotonin and its breakdown products in the brains of people who die of suicide rather than heart attack. See Peter Kramer, *Listening to Prozac*, pp. 328, 61n. It is also believed that there are lower levels of serotonin in clinically depressed patients. That this is the direct effect of one transmitter is far from conclusive. Heather Ashton has argued, "It may be vain to search for an explanation of depression . . . in terms of any single transmitter or its receptors. . . . The delayed effect of antidepressant drugs may result from the establishment of a number of mechanisms, of greater overall stability at synapses for several monoamine transmitters, and/or an alteration of balance between them, resulting in greater efficiency in synaptic transmission through critical brain pathways," (*Brain Function and Psychotropic Drugs* [New York: Oxford Medical Press, 1992], p. 247).

20. For Kramer's discussion on the differences between *clean* and *dirty* drug action, see *Listening*, pp. 57–66.

21. In Kramer's work, people are portrayed as victims of neurochemical onslaught or of expensive and time-consuming psychotherapy; in the Breggins' work, people are portrayed as victims of Prozac who swing wildly and sometimes fatally out of control. The Breggin list includes many who commit or attempt

suicide; batter, abuse, and murder their friends, children, and family members; or find themselves obsessed with maniacal fantasies. For example, a sixty-one-year-old university professor found herself suddenly taking bone-deep bites out of her elderly mother after taking Prozac for two weeks. These monstrous victims of Prozac, transformed from the ordinarily depressed into violent and impulsive psychopaths, share some similarities with Kramer's clients who suffer endless violence to self caused by neurochemical imbalance. In both scenarios the dissolution of the self and the ontology of leaky brains engender a postmodern panic that haunts both the lived experience of the body and the contemporary body politic. For a more scientific review of the side effects of Prozac, see Maurizio Fava and Jerrold Rosenbaum, "Suicidality and Fluoxetine: Is There a Relationship?" *Journal of Clinical Psychiatry* 52, no. 3 (March 1993): 108–111, and Joy Martyniuk *Adverse Effects of Fluoxetine (Prozac): January 1987 through June 1991* (Bethesda, Md.: U.S. Department of Health and Human Services, 1991).

22. This state of being is particularly well-described in Stephen Phohl's *Death at the Parasite Cafe: Social Science (Fictions) and the Postmodern* (New York: St. Martin's, 1992).

23. This notion that the body as the only place where an individual can seek control over her life is echoed in the work of Susan Bordo, *Unbearable Weight: Feminism, Western Culture, and the Body* (Berkeley: University of California Press, 1993); Wendy Chapkis, *Beauty Secrets: Women and the Politics of Appearance* (Boston: South End, 1986); and Kim Chernin, *The Obsession: Reflections on the Tyranny of Slenderness* (New York: Harper and Row, 1981). This physical body-centered solipsism seems particularly relevant in female experiences of obsessive dieting, body sculpting, fitness mania, eating disorders, and various kinds of scripted fetishism and s/m practices. From this perspective these forms of body cathexis shape and discipline the body for intensified commodification, exchange, and the pursuit of pleasure and pain along an axis of *in-control/out-of-control*, a distinguishing mark of *cyborgian homo ludens*.

24. In "A Cyborg Manifesto," Donna Haraway introduces the idea of the cyborg as a fictional mapping of our bodily and social reality. The cyborg is a cybernetic organism, a hybrid of machine and organism, which has a real social reality and a common commerce in our cultural fantasies and fictions. Haraway sees the recrafting our bodies as cyborgs as a challenge to boundaries that have hitherto held the human body in place as an imagined organic unity. These boundaries include the boundary between human and animal, the boundary between animal/human (organism) and machine, and the boundary between physical and nonphysical. While there are frightening consequences of the cyborg becoming the future of human physicality on earth, Haraway urges oppressed groups to embrace the cyborg rather than retreat into body fantasies of greater purity or an imagined organic unity. Entering the age of the informatics of domination requires a different way to organize oppositional resistance and liberatory imagination.

25. I have in mind here the phases of scientific practice that tend toward description and cataloguing, an amassing of data that can be shifted into any number of discursive theoretical formations. See Michel Foucault, *Birth of the Clinic* (New York: Pantheon, 1973) and *The Archaeology of Knowledge* (London: Routledge, 1992).

26. I am modifying somewhat Gramsci's notion of *hegemony*, understood as a *collective popular will* that adheres to and supports the dominant group. In hegemonic relations social dominance of the ruling group is secured by coercion and consent from those below and is accomplished through control over basic resources and institutional powers as well as the control over the meanings and metanarratives used to understand self, identity, and community. See Antonio Gramsci, *Selections from the Prison Notebooks*, ed. Quintin Hoare and Geoffrey Nowell-Smith (New York: International Publishers, 1971) p. 57.

27. "Prozac nation" plays off of Elizabeth Wurtzel's rambling and self-absorbed, but clairvoyant *Prozac Nation: Young and Depressed in America* (Boston and New York: Houghton Mifflin, 1994). Wurtzel argues that with twelve million depressed people in the United States, the condition has ceased to be a unique tragic secret and has become somewhat trendy. Obviously, Prozac as a public sign for depression assists in this conversion of a shameful pathology to a new fashioning of the emotionally disciplined self.

28. See Michel Foucault, "Technologies of the Self: The Political Technology of the Individual" in Luther H. Martin, Huck Gutman, and Patrick Huttons, eds., *The Technologies of the Self* (Amherst: University of Massachusetts Press) and *Discipline and Punish: The Birth of the Prison*, trans. Alan Sheridan (New York: Pantheon, 1979).

29. Sandra Lee Bartky, *Femininity and Domination: Studies in the Phenomenology of Oppression* (New York: Routledge, 1990), which includes "Foucault, Femininity, and the Modernization of Patriarchal Power," originally published in Irene Diamond and Lee Quinby, eds. *Feminism and Foucault: Reflections on Resistance* (Boston: Northeastern University Press, 1988). See also Susan Bordo, *Unbearable Weight*, and "Feminism, Foucault, and the Politics of the Body," in Caroline Ramazanoglu, ed., *Up Against Foucault: Explorations of Some Tensions Between Foucault and Feminism* (New York: Routledge, 1993).

30. Kramer clearly states that only a "a few, a substantial minority"(*Listening*, 11) of his patients are transformed by Prozac, which cautions against overgeneralizing "the Prozac miracle" and entices the patient/consumer with hopes of becoming one of the few. Likewise, its modest success may inspire patients and consumers with the hope of becoming one among this substantial minority. Kramer does not talk about the thousands of people who have taken Prozac without successful result. Could this be *an insubstantial majority*?

31. I surmise that communities of meaning endorse either explicitly or implicitly metanarratives of the self or prescribed ways in which the story of the self can be told and validated. These metanarrative structures establish rules of

intelligibility and empathic identification consolidating a sense of self and a sense of belonging to various groups.

32. Naomi Scheman, "Anger and the Politics of Naming," in *Engenderings: Constructions of Knowledge, Authority, and Privilege*. (New York: Routledge, 1993), pp. 22–35. All references hereafter to Scheman's essay will be marked by parenthesis and page number, unless otherwise indicated.

33. Mryna Weissman and Mark Olfson, "Depression in Women: Implications for Health Care Research," *Science* 269 (August 11, 1995): 799–801; Ellen McGrath, ed., *Women and Depression: Research, Risk Factors, and Treatment Issues: Final Report of the American Psychological Association Task Force on Women and Depression* (Washington, D.C.: American Psychological Association, 1990).

34. Various feminist theories of women's depression often focus on one or several variables of a multivariable model for explaining women's depression. For an early version of feminist analysis, see Pauline Bart, "Depression in Middle-Aged Women" in Vivian Gornick and Barbara Moran, eds., *Women in Sexist Society: Studies in Power and Powerlessness* (New York: Basic Books, 1971). For more current views on women and depression, see Dana Crowley Jack, *Silencing the Self: Women and Depression* (Cambridge: Harvard University Press, 1991) and Ellen McGrath, ed., *Women and Depression*. Excellent analysis and methodological considerations for developing gender-sensitive frameworks for studying women's mental health and psychotropic drug use can be found in K. Pugliesi, "Women and Mental Health: Two Traditions of Feminist Research," *Women and Health* 19, nos. 2/3 (1992): 43–68 and in Elizabeth Ettorre and Elianne Riska, *Gendered Moods*

35. Susan Faludi, *Backlash: The Undeclared War Against American Women* (New York: Crown, 1991).

36. I understand this kind of cultural feminism as a mobilized resistance to the dominant culture's ideation grounded by a strategic essentialism of the body's organic unity that articulates a collective action. For further discussion on "strategic essentialism," see Diana Fuss, *Essentially Speaking: Feminism, Nature and Difference* (New York: Routledge, 1989), pp. 30–33. See Gayatri Chakrovorty Spivak, "Subaltern Studies: Deconstructing Historiography," in *Other Worlds: Essays in Cultural Politics* (New York: Methuen, 1987), pp. 197–221.

37. Obviously, this is not to say that emotions are floating willy-nilly from context to context and emerging as apples or oranges depending on the communities of meaning one enters. However, even strong emotions such as knowing that one is angry or furious can be rearticulated into different aims and intensities in different communities of meaning. What Scheman's work suggests is that there may be no particular biochemical constellation that sufficiently causes a particular emotional state, nor can these states be thought of as discovered rightly or wrongly by the subject, as if there is a truth at the bottom of the silt. She is also not suggesting that emotions float free from a biology that may shape

aspects of our emotional life. She is suggesting, and I consider this right, that how we eventually come to name and more intimately shape our emotions has a lot to do with how we produce the meaning of "what's inside" and a narrative of the self that makes that meaning intelligible and valid. Communities of meaning provide these self-constitutive metanarratives and a language of emotions that affect our sense of who we are and our sense of belonging to a particular group.

38. Donna Haraway, "Cyborg Manifesto," p. 152. I borrow here from Haraway's notion of the cyborg.

39. Ibid., p. 151.

40. Ibid., p. 164.

41. After reading David Roediger's *The Wages of Whiteness* (London: Verso, 1991), I am understanding "whiteness" as a social category partially implicated in the racialization of certain kinds of work most associated with middle-class internalizations of the clock and a concomitant disdain toward the body. Those excluded from the work ethic because of enslavement, lack of property, sex, gender, or disability are also seen as excluded from the American dream. The induction into whiteness through the internalization of the work ethic, but only as it applies to certain kinds of work, seems important in understanding the body panic occurring with increased white-collar lay-offs and the perceived threat of affirmative action to white male jobs. For women in careers, there is increased pressure to perform at the level of superwomanism, again producing a racialized white image of the successful career woman. The role of Prozac in keeping the overworked middle class in full gear seems related to a fear of falling. This is discussed in Barbara Ehrenreich, *Fear of Falling: The Inner Life of the Middle Class* (New York: Pantheon, 1989) and exemplified in the movie "Falling Down," starring Michael Douglas, where the male anti-hero goes violently over the edge after losing his job. Perhaps his female counterpart might have fallen quite differently—into depression.

42. Haraway, "Cyborg Manifesto," p. 180.

43. Both Donna Haraway and Kathryn Morgan have suggested that a self-determined production of nondocile or nonnormative bodies may be a new form of resistance to the informatics and biotechnologies of domination. See Kathryn Morgan, "Women and the Knife: Cosmetic Surgery and the Colonization of Women's Bodies," *Hypatia* 6, no. 3 (Fall 1991): 25–53, and Donna Haraway, "The Promises of Monsters: A Regenerative Politics of Inappropriate/d Others," in Grossberg, et al., *Cultural Studies* (New York: Routledge, 1992), pp. 295–337.

4. Male Lesbians and the Postmodern Body

This essay was originally published in Hypatia: A Journal of Feminist Philosophy 7, no. 4 (1992): 106–127.

1. David Halperin, *One Hundred Years of Homosexuality and European Greek Love* (New York: Routledge, 1990).

2. Alan Bray, *Homosexuality in Renaissance England* (London: Gay Men's Press, 1982), p. 114.

3. Michel Foucault, *History of Sexuality*, vol. 1, trans. Robert Hurley (New York: Pantheon, 1978); Judith Butler, "Critically Queer," in Butler, *Bodies that Matter* (New York: Routledge, 1994), pp. 223–242.

4. Susan Suleiman. "(Re)Writing the Body: The Politics of Female Eroticism," in S. Suleiman, ed., *The Female Body in Western Culture: Contemporary Perspectives* (Cambridge: Harvard University Press, 1986), pp. 7–29.

5. Susan Bordo, *Unbearable Weight: Feminism, Western Culture, and the Body* (Berkeley: University of California, 1993), p. 226.

6. Radicalesbians, "The Woman-Identified Woman." in Anne Koedt, Anita Rapone, and Ellen Levine, eds., *Radical Feminism* (New York: Quadrangle, 1973), p. 245.

7. This point is explored by Pamela J. Olano, "Throw Over Your Man, I Say, and Come: Reading Virginia Woolf as a Lesbian" (manuscript, 1992).

8. Jan Clausen, "My Interesting Condition," *Out/Look* (Winter 1990): 10–21.

9. I am indebted to Julia Penelope's development of a grid from which mine is derived. Several of the ideas developed in this paragraph were influenced by her "Heterosexual Semantics: Just Two Kinds of People in the World' " *Lesbian Ethics* (Fall 1986): 58–80, and "The Patriarchal Universe of Discourse" in J. Penelope, ed., *Speaking Freely: Unlearning the Lies of the Father Tongue* (New York: Pergamon, 1990).

10. John Stoltenberg, *Refusing to Be a Man: Essays on Sex and Justice* (Portland, Ore.: Breitenbush, 1989), p. 112.

11. Ibid., p. 32.

12. Michel Foucault, preface to Richard McDougal, trans., *Herculine Barbin: Being the Recently Discovered Memoirs of the Nineteenth Century French Hermaphrodite* (New York: Pantheon, 1980), pp. vii–xvii.

13. Kessler and McKenna are using "gender" in a different way from my usage. This quotation aligns with my definitional system if the reader substitutes "sexes" for "genders." Suzanne Kessler and Wendy McKenna, *Gender: An Ethnomethodological Approach* (Chicago: University of Chicago Press, 1978), pp. 113–114.

14. Ibid.

15. Foucault, *History of Sexuality*, vol. 1..

16. Sarah Lucia Hoagland, *Lesbian Ethics: Toward New Value* (Palo Alto, Calif.: Institute of Lesbian Studies, 1988), p. 9.

17. Kessler and McKenna, *Gender*, p. 166.

18. Joan Nestle, *A Restricted Country* (New York: Firebrand, 1987), p. 132.

19. Ashby Janis, "Festival Forum." *Lesbian Connection* 14, no. 4 (1992): 12.

20. Quoted in Eileen Myles, "Gender Play" *Outweek* 5 (December 1990): 49.

5. FemFire: A Theory in Drag

1. Mary Daly, *Gynecology: The Metaethics of Radical Feminism* (Boston: Beacon, 1978), p. 336. Daly writes as follows: "Thus the doubly/triply tokenized woman, the multiply Painted Bird, functions in the antiprocess of double-crossing her sisters, polluting them with poisonous paint, making them less and less real in their own eyes and in the eyes of others. For unknowingly, she is herself a carrier of the paint disease, an intensifier of the common condition of women under patriarchy. Those women strong enough to resist the paint infection carried by this token torturer are carrying on a battle of will power, of gynergetic force, on a deep psychic level" (p. 336).

2. Andrea Dworkin, *Woman Hating* (New York: E. P. Dutton, 1974), pp. 113–114.

3. Radicalesbians, "The Woman-Identified Woman," in Anne Koedt, Ellen Levine, and Anita Rapone, eds., *Radical Feminism* (New York: Quadrangle, 1973), p. 244

4. Dworkin, *Woman Hating*, p. 115.

5. Daly, *Gynecology*, p. 336.

6. Sandra Lee Bartkey, *Femininity and Domination: Studies in the Phenominology of Oppression* (New York: Routledge, 1990).

7. Taken from a La Prairie Cellular Skincare Preparations advertisement, cited in Wendy Chapkis, *Beauty Secrets: Women and the Politics of Appearance* (Boston: Southend, 1986), p. 10.

8. Alice Walker, "Coming Apart," *You Can't Keep a Good Woman Down* (New York: Harcourt Brace Jovanovich, 1981), p. 42.

9. Patricia Hill Collins, *Black Feminist Thought: Knowledge, and the Politics of Empowerment* (New York: Routledge, 1990), p. 177.

10. Daly, *Gynecology*, p. 336.

11. Monique Wittig, *Les Guerrillères*, trans. David Le Vay (London: Owen, 1971).

12. Mary Daly, *Gynecology*.

13. Marilyn Frye, *Willful Virgin: Essays in Feminism, 1976–1992* (Freedom, Calif.: Crossing Press, 1992).

14. Janice G. Raymond, *A Passion for Friends: Toward a Philosophy of Female Affection* (Boston: Beacon, 1986).

15. Atkinson, Ti-Grace, *Amazon Odyssey: Collection of Writings* (New York: Links, 1974).

16. Marilyn Frye, "Willful Virgin or Do You Have to be a Lesbian to be a Feminist?," in *Willful Virgin*, p. 133.

17. Frye, *Willful Virgin*, p. 134.

6. Fiddling with Preference

1. Most of these models begin with experiences of erotic attractions and identity confusions and end with a wholly integrated monosexual identity for-

mation, usually established in good community affiliations or an enduring love relationship. Vivienne Cass's model ends with an interpersonal congruency in cognitive and affective levels of self mediated by others (Vivienne Cass, "Developmental Stages of the Coming Out Process," *Journal of Homosexuality* 7, no. 2/3 [1981/1982]: 313–43). The final stage in Troiden's model is defined by an internal integration of sexuality and emotions and a shift in the values and satisfactions assigned to homosexual identity; and externally by same-sex love relationships, coming out to nonhomosexuals, and changes in stigma management (Richard R. Troiden, "The Formation of Homosexual Identities," *Journal of Homosexuality* 17 [1989]: 43–73). In many of these models bisexuality is depicted as an aspect of early identity confusion. For example, in Troiden's analysis bisexual identity is an attempt to define one's homosexual desires along conventional lines, what he calls the ambisexual strategy of redefinition. See also Vivienne Cass, "The Implications of Homosexual Identity Formation for the Kinsey Model and Scale of Sexual Preference," in D. McWhirter, S. Sanders, and J. Reinisch, eds., *Homosexuality/Heterosexuality: Concepts of Sexual Orientation,* (New York: Oxford University Press, 1990) and Eli Coleman, "Developmental Stages of the Coming Out Process, *Journal of Homosexuality* 7, no. 2/3 (1981–1982): 31–43.

2. "Kinship selection" is the notion that a nonreproductive individual can still promote his or her reproductive fitness (the transmission of similar alleles to offspring) by promoting the reproductive success of relatives. The apparent loss of personal reproductive fitness is counterbalanced by the increases in reproductive success among close relatives, such as brothers, sisters, and cousins. A nonreproductive homosexual displaying this behavior is surmised to have inherited an altruistic gene that selects for kin rather than for the self. Edward Osborne Wilson promoted this notion in *Sociobiology: The New Synthesis* (Cambridge: Harvard University Press, 1975), and in his popular work *On Human Nature* (Cambridge: Harvard University Press, 1978) in which he argued that homosexuals carry some of the more altruistic genes of the human species. For an analysis supporting this view see Michael Ruse, "Are There Gay Genes? Sociobiology and Homosexuality," *Journal of Homosexuality* 6 (1981): 5–34, and for a critique of this theoretical approach to homosexuality, see Douglas Futuyma and Stephen Risch, "Sexual Orientation, Sociobiology, and Evolution," *Journal of Homosexuality* 9, no. 2/3 (Winter 1983/Spring 1984).

3. The search for a biological cause for homosexuality is not a new venture. See W. Byne and B. Parsons, "Human Sexual Orientation: Biological Theories Reappraised," *Archive of General Psychiatry* 50(1993): 228–239.

4. Dean Hamer and Peter Copeland, *The Science of Desire: The Search for the Gay Gene and the Biology of Behavior* (New York: Simon and Schuster, 1994). Although the book is co-authored, Dean Hamer takes full responsibility for all the scientific content and interpretation, relying on his friend and journalist Peter Copeland as a co-writer to help translate Hamer's thoughts to a wider public readership (p. 6). Hereafter, I refer to Hamer as the sole author/researcher.

5. Hamer's research group adopts Kinsey's categories for establishing sexual orientation based on self-identification, attraction, fantasy, and behavior. Because there was a greater polarization among his subjects in the internal categories of attraction and fantasy than in actual behavior, he marks the discreteness of the sexual orientation as an internal state: "Since we were more interested in what goes on above the neck than below the belt, it seemed that our definition of sexual orientation as an 'attraction' rather than an 'action' was a good one" (*Science of Desire*, p. 66).

6. This critique can be followed in R. C. Lewontin, S. Rose, and L. J. Kamin, eds., *Not in Our Genes* (New York: Pantheon, 1984).

7. The term "phenotype" refers to the outward appearance of an organism, its observable characteristics, which may include anatomical form and function and even certain aspects of psychological traits or behaviors. Because it it not possible to give a complete description of a person's total phenotype, it is common in genetic science to partition the body into contrasting or variegated "traits," such as differences in eye color, skin color, blood type, etc. The term "genotype" refers to the sum total of genes or the inherited genetic make up of an organism. A "gene" is thought to be a primary or necessary cause for a phenotypic trait, such as the genes for eye color, skin color, blood type, etc. For a discussion on the extension of phenotypes to include human behaviors, see R. Dawkins, *The Selfish Gene* (Oxford: Oxford University Press, 1976) and *The Extended Phenotype* (San Francisco: W. H. Freeman, 1980). The attempt to explain various patterns of human behavior to genetic determinism is a critical strategy in sociobiological thinking. In sociobiology, arguments against such bioreductionist explanations are almost completely disregarded in the effort to find correlations between genes and identifiable forms of human behavior.

8. Hamer and Copeland, *Science of Desire*, pp. 53–54.

9. Ironically, Hamer uses the rather antiquated scale developed by Alfred Kinsey in 1948 and 1953, a scale for human sexuality that at the time was one of the first major challenges to thinking of sex orientation as an absolute dichotomous polarization, meaning more of one way means less of the other way. See Alfred Kinsey, Wardell Pomeroy, and Clyde Martin, *Sexual Behavior in the Human Male* (Philadelphia: W. B. Saunders, 1948) and Alfred C. Kinsey, Wardell Pomeroy, Clyde Martin, and Paul Gebhard, *Sexual Behavior in the Human Female* (Philadelphia: W. B. Saunders, 1953). Hamer uses Kinsey's measures to further his own assumptions that human sexuality is expressed in two exclusive and alternative forms of sexual orientation.

10. Hamer and Copeland, *Science of Desire*, p. 59.

11. Though these correlations were studied thirty years ago, Hamer refers to them to support his claim that the Kinsey scale is reliable. See K. W. Freund, "Diagnosing Homo- or Heterosexuality and Erotic Age-Preference by Means of a Psychophysiological Test," *Behavior Research and Therapy* 5 (1967): 209–228.

12. Hamer and Copeland, *Science of Desire*, p. 66.

13. "Biphobia" is defined as the fear and hatred of bisexual people and bisexuality; sometimes indicated by an intolerance for sexualities that do not fit neatly into the mutually exclusive and oppositional monosexual categories of the hetero/homo divide, i.e., homosexuality or heterosexuality.

14. Hamer and Copeland, *Science of Desire*, p. 66.

15. I refer the reader back to pp. 120–121 where I make a distinction between strongly and weakly determining models of genetic determinism.

16. Barbara Ponse, *Identities in the Lesbian World* (Westport, Conn.: Greenwood, 1978).

17. E. Sagarin, "The Good Guys, the Bad Guys, and the Gay Guys," *Contemporary Sociology* 2, no. 1 (1973): 10.

18. Given that Hamer could not avoid the essentialist and social constructionist debate, it is interesting to note how he responds to what he calls "the trendiest of the behaviorist schools . . . called social constructionism." He discusses social constructionist theory as follows: "It postulates that there is no such thing as heterosexuality or homosexuality; only definitions of sexuality that are imposed by culture. Proponents of this theory are fond of pointing out, at every opportunity, that prior to 1892 the word 'homosexuality' did not even exist in English. Therefore, they argue, homosexuality (without the quotes) is merely a cultural label; it has no universal meaning, much less any biological component. Ironically, the strongest advocates of social constructionism in sexuality are the *Journal of Homosexuality* and certain academic gay studies centers, institutions that, if their theories about the unreality of homosexuality were correct, would not even exist. Fortunately for them, the social constructionist theory is not likely to be disproved any time soon, since its content is too amorphous to ever be tested rigorously" (pp. 176–177).

19. My analysis in the next few passages is strongly influenced by Foucault's epistemic theories.

20. Michel Foucault, *History of Sexuality*, vol. 1, trans. Robert Hurley (New York: Pantheon, 1978), p. 43.

21. Ibid., pp. 47–48.

22. I refer the reader to chapter 4, "Male Lesbians and the Postmodern Body," and to chapter 2, "Heterosexual Anti-Biotics," for a more detailed elaboration on the matter of sexual kinds.

23. To support their claim that sexual orientation is a phenotype expressing a real state of desire, Hamer has this to say about constructionist theory: "This kind of thinking in other areas would have left us in the dark, literally. There wasn't really a unified theory of 'electricity' until James Clark Maxwell came up with one in 1864, and electricity has been well understood and harnessed only during the past one hundred years. So, taking social constructionism to the extreme, electricity did not 'exist' until quite recently and even now has no 'real' meaning. Try that theory on someone who's been struck by lightning" (p. 177).

24. I do not have in mind here the notion of "genetic mosaics." The reader may find this confusing, but I am using the notion of mosaic as an aesthetic metaphor for the personal creative and collecting process in which the pieces of erotic life are placed into a definitive pattern that can be more or less settled or changing in the every increasing complexity of an erotic signature unique to an individual.

25. Eve Kosofsky Sedgwick, *Tendencies* (Durham: Duke University Press, 1993).

26. Ibid., p. 8.

27. Criticisms of the Kinsey scale emerged in the late 1970s. The Kinsey scale purported to measure sexuality along a continuum, with seven ratings (0 = exclusively heterosexual and 6 = exclusively homosexual). Critics pointed out that Kinsey scale commits researchers to a bipolar unidimensional measure where the more the subject moves toward a 6 (homosexual) the less the individual has of the other orientation (heterosexual). The either/or bipolarity on the Kinsey scale does not allow a person to score high on both homosexuality and heterosexuality, or low in both, or any number of other possibilities. The middle section remains very obscure and oversimplified. The scale also appears to make sexual desire a static quality, since there is no attempt to measure temporal distinctions beyond a five-year period. In 1978 Storms argued that heterosexuality and homosexuality may be separate orthogonal dimensions rather than a single bipolar continuum. Unlike the perfect Kinsey bisexual, who is half hetero- and half homosexual (a perfect Kinsey 3), Storms argued that a two-dimensional model could represent bisexuals having a high degree of homosexuality and heterosexuality, not necessarily in moderate balance. Using Storms's scale, an individual does not lose degrees in one orientation by scoring high in the other. Obviously, this opens the possibility of different kinds of sexualities based on various degrees and intensities. See M. Storms, "Theories of Sexual Orientation," *Journal of Personality and Social Psychology* 38, no. 5 (1980): 783–792. Storms's critique of the old Kinsey continuum set the stage for the new Klein Sexual Orientation Grid (KSOG), which included the Kinsey traditional measures of sexuality orientation (sexual behavior, attraction, and fantasies) and added the new categories of emotional preference, social preference, and lifestyle preference. See F. Klein, B. Sepekoff, and T. Wolf, "Sexual Orientation: A Multi-Variable, Dynamic Process, *Journal of Homosexuality* 11, nos. 1/2 (1985): 35–39. Subsequently, the Multidimensional Scale of Sexuality (MSS) developed by Berkey, Perelman-Hall, and Kurdek (1990) was even more innovative in incorporating Klein's behavioral and cognitive/affective components and also six categories for bisexualities. Unlike the assumptions of stasis in the Kinsey scale, the MSS allows an individual to identify changing sexual orientations over time. See Branden Robert Berkey, et al., "The Multidimensional Scale of Sexuality," *Journal of Homosexuality* 19, no. 4 (1990): 67–87.

These new scales prevent researchers from simple-mindedly dichotomizing sexuality orientation in any absolute way. They engender a notion bisexualities differentiated by behavioral, cognitive, and affective categories and by a variety of time variables. Following the recognition this temporal dimension, the MSS depicts bisexuals as "sequential" or "contemporaneous"; or "serial" or "concurrent" along with various gradations mapped over a number of variables. See discussions in Jay Paul, "The Bisexual Identity: An Idea Without Social Recognition," *Journal of Homosexuality* 9 (1983/1984): 45–63; in G. Zinik, "Identity Conflict or Adaptive Flexibility? Bisexuality Reconsidered," *Journal of Homosexuality* 11 (1985): 7–19.

While these scales have increased the complexity how sexual orientation is operationalized, they are still based on a genitocentric notion of orientation. What may be needed in the future is a scale that measures sexual orientation with possible desires and behaviors unlinked to the biological sex of the preferred partner. Bisexual responsiveness begins to open up such categories of erotic feeling where affinities, attractions, and complementarities could be mapped in a wider terrain of human desire. This would entail a redefinition of the erotic that lifts it beyond the genitocentric reduction; for an inspired reading of such an erotic, see Audre Lorde's "Uses of the Erotic," in her *Sister Outsider: Essays and Speeches* (Trumansburg, N.Y.: Crossing Press, 1982]). It would also require a new kind of sexual cultural formation that would foster a more complex notion of erotic expression.

From a slightly different perspective, Eridani has argued that the entire notion of sexual orientation as defined in contemporary society may be based on male experience or on male patterns of sexual response that tend to be far more narrowly channeled than those of women. She considers sexual orientation a male "secondary sex characteristic," a characteristic that more men than women have. Though Eridani couches sexual orientation as a secondary sex characteristic, its genetic manifestation is perhaps best taken up at the level of the erotic directivity in the male body (enculturated to release in or upon another body when possible), in contrast to the clitoral directivity, female erotic receptivity, female proceptivity and multi-orgasmic capacities open a variety of articulations in a female-centered erotic. See Eridani, "Is Sexual Orientation a Secondary Sex Characteristic?" in Elizabeth Reba Weise, ed., *Closer to Home: Bisexuality and Feminism* (Seattle, Wash.: Seal, 1992). For continued discussion on the possibilities of opening up erotic categories beyond the genitofocused categories of "same" or "opposite" sex, see G. Kaplan and L. Rogers, "Breaking Out of the Dominant Paradigm: A New Look at Sexual Attraction," *Journal of Homosexuality* 10 (1984): 71–76 and M. Ross, "Beyond the Biological Model: New Directions in Bisexual and Homosexual Research," *Journal of Homosexuality* 10 (1984): 63–70.

28. As Ronald Fox has pointed out: "Bisexual identify formation has not been conceptualized as a linear process with a fixed outcome, as in theories of lesbian and gay identity formation. The development of bisexual identities has been viewed as a more complex and open-ended process in light of the necessity of considering patterns of homosexual and heterosexual attractions, fantasies, behav-

iors, and relationships that occur during any particular period of time and over time" ("Bisexual Identities," in A. R. D'Augelli and C. J. Paterson, eds., *Lesbian, Gay, and Bisexual Identities Across the Lifespan* [New York: Oxford University Press, 1995]. p. 57).

29. I refer the reader to chapter 4, "Male Lesbians and the Postmodern Body" and chapter 2, "Heterosexual Anti-Biotics" for analysis of modernist sex ontologies. I consider the application of bio-evolutionary sociobiological theory to modernist sex ontology a grand theory of modernist sex.

30. Many of the contemporary political strategies for gay civil rights rely on a biological argument that often rests on modernist assumptions. The "intransigent nature" of human sexual orientation is often used as an axis for equal rights struggles. It should be noted that I am not arguing that all people are bisexual, but I am suggesting we would be better off to participate in a struggle for social justice that can incorporate more than monosexuality identities, more than a few sparse categories of erotic life, and more than reductionist explanations for the directivity and intensity of human sexual desires.

31. Shane Phelan, *Getting Specific: Postmodern Lesbian Politics* (Minneapolis: University of Minnesota Press, 1994).

32. For a discussion on the construction of criteria for membership to a given sexual orientation category, see chapter 4, "Male Lesbians and the Postmodern Body." I have always wondered how the genetic theory would fare at the door: will those people having the wrong genes for a sexual orientation shelter/category be denied entrance? will they become the transgressive resisters—those who have such desires without the right genetic make-up? This might create a new category of *transerotics* . . . as the struggle continues. It could also create two categories of passing: passing with desire but with the wrong genes and passing without desire (with feigned desire) with the right or wrong genes.

33. For more recent discussions on these border struggles, see Jacob Hale, "Are Lesbians Women?" *Hypatia* 11, no. 2 (1996): 94–121; Jacob Hale, "Blurring Boundaries, Marking Boundaries: Who Is Lesbian?" (A Claudia Card Symposium) *Journal of Homosexuality* 32, no. 1 (1996): 21–42; Kate Bornstein, *Gender Outlaw: Our Men, Women, and the Rest of Us* (New York: Routledge, 1994).

Rearticulations

1. Jacquelyn N. Zita, review of *"Making Bodies, Making History: Feminism and German Identity* by Leslie Adelson; *Unbearable Weight: Feminism, Western Culture, and the Body* by Susan Bordo; *Bodies That Matter: On the Discursive Limits of "Sex"* by Judith Butler; and *Volatile Bodies: Toward a Corporeal Feminism* by Elizabeth Grosz, *Signs: Journal of Women in Culture and Society* 21, no. 3 (1996): 786–795.

7. Hard Traits/Fluid Measures

1. Monique Wittig, *Le Corps lesbien* (Paris: Les Editions de Minuit, 1973), p. 188. I know of two significant English translations of this sentence, "J/e te cherche m/a rayonnante, à travers l'assemblée." In his translation of Wittig's *Lesbian Body*, David Le Vay (no relation to Simon LeVay) translates this sentence as "I see you m/y radiant one across the throng," rendering *"l'assemblée"* into a word that suggests a romantic sighting across the nondescript sea of others. Shaktini translates the sentence as "I look for you m/y radiant one, across the assembly" to invoke the contingency of individuals assembled (however playfully or anarchistically) in Wittig's lesbian society. Shaktini's translation furthers the project of a lesbian intertextuality in a composite of many perspectives emerging beyond heterosexual mindedness. See Namascar Shaktini, "The Revolutionary Signifier: The Lesbian Body," in Karla Jay and Joanne Glasgow, eds., *Lesbian Texts and Contexts: Radical Revisions* (New York: New York University Press, 1990), pp. 299, 302. Given my own interpretation of Wittig's work, I find "assembly" closer to Wittig's project and a term bearing closer resonance with the radical scenes of Paris 1968 and the revolutionary feminist movements in France in the early 1970s. However, "assembly" in the English language seems to connote a governing body structured by rules of order, while "throng" carries a more erotic sense.

2. In this chapter I will refer to two primary texts by Simon LeVay: his popular text *The Sexual Brain* (Cambridge: Massachussets Institute of Technology Press, 1993) and his research article "A Difference in Hypothalamic Structure Between Heterosexual and Homosexual Men," *Science* 253 (1991): 1034–1037. I will be directly comparing these two writings with Monique Wittig's *The Lesbian Body*, trans. David Le Vay (New York: Avon, 1975), originally published as *Le Corps lesbien*. I also include my reflections on Monique Wittig's collected essays from the late 1970s through the 1980s, recently republished in *The Straight Mind and Other Essays* (Boston: Beacon, 1992).

3. Shaktini has pointed out that the word "cyprine" is a politico-poetic neologism derived by Wittig from the island of Cyprus where Aphrodite/Cyprine was honored. Wittig uses the term "cyprine" to refer to the sexual substances produced by the female body. The phallic subject produces ejaculate, and the lesbian subject produces cyprine. David Le Vay translates "cyprine" as "juice" in the second word in the first list of body parts (Wittig, *Lesbian Body*, p. 26) missing the significance of Wittig's original term. See Shaktini, "Revolutionary Signifier," p. 294.

4. Y. Oomura, A. Aou, Y. Koyama, and H. Yoshimatsu, "Central Control of Sexual Behavior, *Brain Research Bulletin* 20 (1988): 863–870; J. C. Slimp, B. L. Hart, and R. W. Goy, "Heterosexual, Autosexual, and Social Behavior of Adult Male Rhesus Monkeys with Medial Preoptic-Anterior Hypothamic Lesions," *Brain Research* 142 (1978): 105–122.

5. J. A. Cherry and M. J. Baum, "Effects on Lesions of a Sexually Dimorphic Nucleus in the Preoptic/Anterior Hypothalamic Area on the Expression of

Androgen- and Estrogen-Dependent Sexual Behaviors in Male Ferrets," *Brain Research* 522 (1990): 191–203; A. C. Hennessey, K. Wallen, and D. A. Edwards, "Preoptic Lesions Increase Display of Lordosis by Male Rats," *Brain Research* 370 (1986): 21–28.

6. LeVay often refers to the prenatal development of the female fetus as "the default position," since prenatal development in the absence of a sufficient amount of circulating testosterone is programmed toward femaleness. "Thus one can say that female development is the default pathway, the one that is followed in the absence of specific instructions to the contrary" (LeVay, *Sexual Brain*, p. 29). LeVay also speaks of the brain's intrinsic developmental program as female: "It takes a specific external signal, the presence of sufficient circulating levels of androgens, to reprogram development in the male direction" (LeVay, *Sexual Brain*, p. 86). In this model of sexual maturation, intersex becomes an anomaly of hormonal or genetic mishap. Sex difference is represented as a polarity of female or male, where female development is represented as an intrinsic default position and male development is represented as a hormonally mediated nondefault position. In contrast to this polarity model, Fausto-Sterling has recently offered an analysis that favors a continuum of several different sexes.

7. This hunch is based on previous research. L. S. Allen, M. Hines, J. E. Shryne, and R. A. Gorski, "Two Sexually Dimorphic Cell Groups in the Human Brain," *Journal of Neuroscience* 9 (1989): 497–506; D. F. Swaab and E. Fliers, "A Sexually Dimorphic Nucleus in the Human Brain, *Science* 228 (1985): 1112–1114.

8. Wittig, *Lesbian Body*, p. 15.

9. Wittig moved to the United States in 1976 after her political involvement in May 1968 and the subsequent struggles of radical feminists in Paris. According to Ann Rosalind Jones, "Writing the Body: Toward an Understanding of *L'Ecriture feminine*," *Feminist Studies* 7, no. 2 (1981): 247–263. "One Is Not Born a Woman" was first presented as a speech at City University of New York, Graduate Center, in September 1979. "The Straight Mind," was first presented as a speech at the "Feminist as Scholar Conference" in May 1979, at Barnard College, New York. However, according to Hélène Vivienne Wenzel, "The Text as Body/Politics: An Appreciation of Monique Wittig's Writings in Context," *Feminist Studies* 7, no. 2 (1981): 264–287, "The Straight Mind" was a paper first delivered at the 1978 Modern Language Association convention and dedicated to American lesbians.

10. New critics of Wittig's work have been largely influenced by the postmodern project to rid theory of its cumbersome essentialist notions. Diana Fuss has criticized Wittig for homogenizing lesbians into a category of sameness that erases material and ideological differences. See Diana Fuss, "Monique Wittig's Anti-Essentialist Materialism," *Essentially Speaking: Feminism, Nature, and Difference* (New York: Routledge, 1989), pp. 39–53. Judith Butler has argued that Wittig's deconstruction of the binary categories of gender and sex is grounded on an appeal to a radically pure construction of lesbian and a prediscursive field of

plenitude upon which the binaries of the straight thinking are imposed as universals. At both ends of this project Butler finds essentialist symptoms, in Wittig's preontic plenitude of being and in her drive toward telic purification, which again commits "lesbianization" to a reified binary of negation, i.e., "lesbian" as not heterosexual. See Judith Butler, "Monique Wittig: Bodily Disintegration and Fictive Sex," *Gender Trouble: Feminism and the Subversion of Identity* (New York: Routledge, 1990), pp. 111–128.) Judith Roof agrees with Butler's critique of Wittig's work and emphasizes what she calls the "utopian gap" in Wittig, where the elimination of gender from writing is an assumed equivalent to surmounting gender. Roof also places Wittig's work within the modernist project, where the pursuit of identity, certitude, and legitimation structure the trope of Wittig's transcendental lesbian. See Judith Roof, "Lesbians and Lyotard: Legitimation and the Politics of the Name," in Laura Doan, ed., *The Lesbian Postmodern* (New York: Columbia University Press, 1994), pp. 45–66. My own position on Wittig's essentialism is that she is not committed to a substantive essentialism but to a community redefinition of body/erotic/lesbian, a strategic essentialism that opens into a territory not committed to heterosexual terms. This exploration is not exhaustive, containable, or essentializable, but for Wittig it constitutes a radical politics of erotic being. Wittig's project is "u-topic" in the classic sense of having "no place," since there is no literal territory or boundary containing the meaning of "lesbian," except as a semantic expanse and erotic reorganization beyond the constraints of the heterosexual contract and its ontologies of straight thinking.

11. The "heterosexual contract" is a concept that is central to Wittig's and other analyses supporting the notion that "woman" is a cultural construction, not fixed by biology but by the force of social relations determined by an implicit heterosexual contract. As I understand this concept, there are three levels of contract-like relationships between the sexes: (1) semantically, "woman" is understood as a relational term or as the counterpart of "man," and both gender terms are dependent on the circulation of meanings in a heterosexual and male-dominated episteme; (2) "woman" is a sign/object of sexual and labor exchange within the economies dominated by heterosexual male erotic and reproductive need; (3) "woman" is a category of social meaning and status primarily determined by a heterosexual/sexual contract that marginalizes the position of women within a larger social contract defining rights, obligations, entitlements, and special powers and authorities in the public sphere. In Wittig's work the "straight mind" is a consciousness that perceives these relationships between "woman" and "man" as natural. Deconstructing the historically contingent binary division of "man" and "woman" challenges the essentialism of a gender ontology that anchors the erotics and politics of heterosexuality.

12. Monique Wittig, "The Straight Mind," in *The Straight Mind and Other Essays* (Boston: Beacon, 1992), p. 29.

13. Wittig, "On Social Contract," in *Straight Mind*, p. 44.

14. Wittig, "One is not Born a Woman," in *Straight Mind*, p. 19.

15. Wittig, "Preface," in *Straight Mind*, p. xiii.

16. "Lesbianizing" as a verb refers to writing strategies that attempt to transform heterosexual writing practices relying on conventional sex and gender alignments and the inferiorization of women. Through a variety of experimental strategies, Wittig disrupts these practices. Shaktini refers to this as a process of *overwriting* the phallogocentric metaphors of contemporary symbolic systems by *displacing* the symbolic order without falling back into the default position of the unmarked subject. See Namascar Shaktini, "Displacing the Phallic Subject: Wittig's Lesbian Writing," *Signs: Journal of Women in Culture and Society* 8, no. 1 (Autumn 1982): 29–44. A much more extensive analysis of this can be found in Karin Cope, "Plastic Actions: Linguistic Strategies and *Le Corps lesbien,*" *Hypatia* 6, no. 3 (Fall 1991): 75–96. Cope defines "lesbianization" as a practice of the *détournement* of the presumptions and the designative and appropriative powers of thought and language (p. 76) and as a strategic weapon for "the dispersal and differentiation of subjectivity of multiple kinds and occasions of revolt against the status quo" (p. 79). For a closer examination of some of the specific writing strategies deployed by Wittig in *Le Corp lesbien*, see Marthe Rosenfeld, "The Linguistic Aspect of Sexual Conflict: Monique Wittig's *Le Corps lesbien,*" *Mosaic: A Journal for the Interdisciplinary Study of Literature* 17, no. 2 (Spring 1984): 235–241. See also Wenzel, "The Text as Body," and Jones, "Writing the Body," for closer textual analyses of Wittig's fantastical neologisms, mocking takeovers of traditional culture, revision of conventional genres, and provocative use of pronouns.

17. "I loved her so that in her I still lived" translation by Wittig in "The Mark of Gender" in *Straight Mind*, p. 88. Wittig notes that this comes from a poem by Maurice Scève, which she uses at the end of her first novel, *Opononax* to mark the occasion of emerging lesbian subjectivity. I have found this an interesting thematic for *The Lesbian Body*, as the body becomes an occasion for the emergence of lesbian subjectivities positioned beyond the heterosexual episteme. Essentialism vanishes in this notion of the body as a material occasion for the intersubjective *rassemblage* of lesbian. The body provides the "speaking anatomies" for this *u-topic* fragmentory exploration cast by a dynamic erotic immersion between lesbian lovers.

18. Hélène Wenzel captures the parallel between writer and lover: "The lover *j/e* in *Le Corps lesbien* is also the writer, whose violent lovemaking, both as subject and as object, is a metaphor for the craft of the writer. Just as the lover enters, dismembers, and reassembles the body of the beloved, so the writer must enter and deconstruct patriarchal language/ideology to reconstruct new possibilities. *J/e* is at once the lover and the writer who must cut into body/text to create a new body/text, a new erotic discourse." (See "The Text as Body/Politics: An Appreciation of Monique Wittig's Writings in Context," *Feminist Studies* 7, no. 2 [Summer 1981]: 264–287, 284.)

19. For an analysis of the island metaphor and its opposition to the dark continent (a reference to Freud's opacity on women), see Shaktini, "Revolutionary Signifier," pp. 294–298.

20. The split pronoun *"j/e"* in Wittig's writing has received considerable attention from theorists. In the introduction to *The Lesbian Body* Wittig writes, "If, in writing *je*, I adopt this language, this *je* cannot do so. *J/e* is the symbol of the lived, rending experience which is m/y writing, of this cutting in two which throughout literature is an exercise of the language which does not constitute m/e as subject. *J/e* poses the ideological and historic question of feminine subjects. . . . If I [*j/e*] examine m/y specific situation as subject in the language, I [*J/e*] am physically incapable of writing 'I' [*je*], I [*j/e*] have not desire to do so" (p. x). For a studied interpretation on the meaning of the split j/e in Wittig's writing see Namascar Shaktini, "Revolutionary Signifier." Judith Butler understands the *j/e* "not as a split subject, but as the sovereign subject who can wage war linguistically against the 'world' that has constituted a semantic and syntactic assault against the lesbian" (p. 120). Engelbrecht finds the split *j/e* bearing a phallic intention that is antithetical to Wittig's lesbian project. See her " 'Lifting Belly Is a Language': The Postmodern Lesbian Subject," *Feminist Studies* 16, no.1 (Spring 1990): 85–114. Lynn Higgins has made the interesting suggestion that the "/" splitting the *je* functions as the sign of a stutter or a hiccup that indicates a somatic unconscious desire from the noisome body to break through the symbolic order. See Higgins, "Nouvelle Nouvelle Autobiography: Wittig's *Le Corps lesbien*," *Substance* 14 (1976): 160–166.

21. While Wittig uses the split *j/e* to challenge the Lacanian dismissal of women from the speaking/writing subject position, she sometimes refers the split pronoun to "the minority subject." The status of the minority subject is, however, not further developed in her own writing as a mark of race, class, or other eccentric positionalities. See Wittig, "The Point of View: Universal or Particular?" in *Straight Mind*, pp. 61–62. Likewise, color is rarely politicized in Wittig's writing, except as an epiphenomenon of cultural exchange as women cease to be exchanged as objects and enter into their own aesthetic exchange of colors among themselves. See also Shaktini, "Revolutionary Signifier," pp. 292–293, 296–297 for an analysis of Wittig's use of color. Attempts to apply Eurocentric French feminist philosophy to the marginal experiences of women of color in the United State are rare, but intriguing. See Emma Perez, "Irigaray's Female Symbolic in the Making of Chicana Lesbian *Sitio y Lenguas* (Sites and Discourses)" in Doan, *Lesbian Postmodern*, pp. 104–117.

22. Wittig, "Mark of Gender," p. 87.

23. This and the following quotations are all taken from Wittig, "Mark of Gender."

24. As Cathy Linstrum has pointed out, "throughout *Le Corps lesbien*, both form and content are profoundly governed by fracture and heterogeneity: the juxtaposition of two separate, intercutting 'texts' breaks up the continuity of both, so that the uppercase passages which catalogue the female body interrupt the flow of the lowercase ones which recount the events between the two figures, and at the same time it is the lowercase ones which interrupt the upper-

case pages" (Cathy Linstrum, "L'Asile des Femmes: Subjectivity and Femininity in Breton's *Nadja* and Wittig's *Le Corps lesbien*," *Nottingham French Studies* 27, no. 1 [1988]: 35–45). In this uppercase script, Wittig lists numerous bodily parts and processes, each at the same level, with no part more eroticized or fetishized than any other, and with each part disarticulated from its structural or biological function and rendered an autonomous, aesthetic, and erotic object, word, and sound. In this list, "THE LESBIAN BODY" appears as the first and last term (Wittig, *Lesbian Body*, p. 26, where the list begins, and p. 150 where the list ends). Such an arbitrary linguistic closure in writing the body creates a temporary unity of the fractionated and heterogeneous parts and perspectives. This leveling of the heterosexual erotic colonization and fetishization of female body parts and sex differences is also referenced in Wittig's earlier work *Les Guerrillères*, where her female warriors, after refusing the valorize the phallus, in turn reject the vulva as their own self-determining and tribal symbol: "The women say that they perceive their bodies in their entirety. They say that they do not favor any of its parts on the grounds that it was formerly a forbidden object. They say that they do not want to become prisoners of their own ideology" (Wittig, *Les Guerrillères*, trans. David Le Vay [New York: Avon, 1976], p. 57).

25. Wittig, "Mark of Gender," p. 29.

26. Ibid., p. 129.

27. While Simon LeVay's reductionist strategy is directed toward finding biological markers that correlate with differences in sexual orientation, he wants these biological markers to be a genetic consequence of the organizational effects of hormones in the prenatal formation of the brain's hypothalamic nodes. "The effect of testosterone on the development of the SDN is called *organizational* because it permanently influences the organization of the brain in away that affects behavior much later in life" (p. 85). What counts as a "biological marker" for nonheterosexual orientation includes (1) a marker that distinguishes a nonheterosexual body from a heterosexual body; (2) a marker that is *organizational* in two senses: it is the *organizational* effect of a gene or hormonally mediated genetic effect, and it is further *organizational* in its far-reaching effects on the body's structure, function, and neuro-experiential potential. While other researchers such as Döerner have looked for endocrinological biological markers in homosexuals, LeVay is looking for sex-atypical brain markers in the hypothalamus that bear this organizational effect. LeVay's "postnatal organizational genetic effect" is similar to Dawkins' notion of "the extended phenotype." See R. Dawkins, *The Extended Phenotype* (San Francisco: W. H. Freeman, 1981) and G. Dörner, W. Rohde, F. Stahl, L. Krell, and W. G. Masius, " A Neuroendocrine Predisposition for Homosexuality in Men," *Archives of Sexual Behavior*, vol. 4: pp. 1–8.

28. Wittig, *Corps lesbien*, pp. 22, 80–81, 175.

29. Wittig, *Lesbian Body*, pp. 26, 74, 150.

30. LeVay does concede that it is important to have a brain for the experience of sex, but he still represents sex as mechanical stimulation or psychogenic factors that cause hemodynamic effects on erectile tissue. The symbolic and cultural practices of courtship, love, poetry, and romance are subsumed under "psychogenic causes" of hemodynamic phenomena. LeVay also concedes that there are elements in human sexual courtship that are strongly influenced by culture, but in typical sociobiological fashion he is prone to reinterpret these cultural elements in terms of sociobiological forces (*Sexual Brain*, p. 61). By this rhetorical move, what he offers as a *possible interpretation* for human sexual behaviors comes to be *an explanation for* the phenomena. In LeVay's framework sexuality is best represented as a physiological function mediated by sociobiological forces.

31. S. M. Breedlove. "Cellular Analysis of Hormone Influence on Motorneuronal Development and Function," *Journal of Neurobiology* 17 (1986): 157–166; S. M. Breedlove and A. P. Arnold, "Hormonal Control of the Developing Nueromuscular System: I. Complete Demasculinization of the Male Rat Spinal Nucleus of the Bulbocavernosus Using the Antiandrogen Flutamide. II. Sensitive Periods for the Androgen Induced Masculinization of the Rat Spinal Nucleus of the Bulbocavernosus," *Journal of Neuroscience* 3 (1983): 417–423, 424–432.

32. R. E. Dodson, J. E. Shryne, and R. A. Gorski, "Hormonal Modification of the Number of Total and Late-Rising Neurons in the Central Part of the Medial Preoptic Nucleus of the Rat," *Journal of Comparative Neurology* 275 (1988): 623–629.

33. For more discussion on this misplacement and an "auto parts conception of personhood," see Helen Longino, "Gender, Sexuality, and the Flight from Complexity," *Metaphilosophy* 25, no. 4 (1994): 285–292.

34. This has been expertly covered in Rob Brookey, "Reinventing the Male Homosexual: The Rhetoric and Power of the Gay Gene," (Ph.D. diss., University of Minnesota, 1998).

35. The gendering of body parts is also reflected in the vocabulary LeVay uses to name his "biological markers" as sex-typical and sex-atypical structures in the brain. The assumption is that the heterosexual body provides the norm for a binary schema for all bodies: what is perceived as male-typical or female-typical (or what is most commonly found in one sex or the other) is found in heterosexual bodies. In LeVay's discussion of his findings, what is sex atypical in the gay male hypothalamus, the smaller size of the INAH III, is sex-typical in the female brain, reinforcing the notion that these body parts are transgendered "misplacements" of bodily matter. Such misplaced sex parts reinforce the commonly held ideological assumptions that gay men are more like women than heterosexual men. Rob Brookey (*Reinventing the Male Homosexual*) has pointed out that the rhetorics of gender used to construct the gay male body in LeVay's research theory reinforce our status quo notions of gender attribution to male homosexuals. On a biological level, the discovery of a biological marker defines a difference that makes (and marks) the homosexual body as sex-atypical and thus protects the

heterosexual male body from cross-over desires and sexual desire for other men. I refer the reader to chapter 2, "Heterosexual Anti-Biotics," for an analysis of how this is related to the articulation of the heterosexually normative body.

36. Elaine Marks, "Lesbian Intertextuality," in George Stambolian and Elaine Marks, eds., *Homosexualities and French Literature: Cultural Contexts/Critical Texts* (Ithaca: Cornell University Press, 1979), p. 372.

37. Marthe Rosenfeld points out that Wittig's way of writing the body shows how feelings reside in the body. This is, however, not predicated on the template of heterosexual coital sex as it is in LeVay's science of desire. In "The Linguistic Aspect of Sexual Conflict," Rosenfeld writes: "Since lesbian bodies can unite any-where, penetration has no constricted meaning: swallowing, chewing, digesting, vomiting become acts of interpenetration and union. In this imaginary world, the richness of floral, animal, liquid, anatomical terms suggests the existence of a cosmic sexual desire which enables women to love or to become another self, a flower, an animal, a stream or the sea. The sensuous language, describing woman's physical longing in the passages where her lover is absent or dead, indicates that Wittig never intellectualizes deep emotions; on the contrary her visceral descriptions show that all our feelings reside in the body" (239).

38. In writing the lesbian body, Wittig cleverly avoids a substantive essentialism as she creates a somatic/semantic space governed by a negative dialectic or a movement away from heterosexual body ontologies. I do not agree with Butler's analysis ("Monique Wittig") that this creates a commitment to binarism; rather, it creates a new territory for erotic and corporeal exploration that is open-ended in its semantic and sexual landscapes. Rather than A and not-A as exhaustive categories, Wittig creates a space for not-A that is open-ended. This parallels Marilyn Frye's analysis of categorical distinctions ("The Necessity of Difference"). Marthe Rosenfeld ("The Linguistic Aspect...") captures this in a rather lively passage: "The dominant culture's obsession with penetration and intercourse has been replaced with a multiplicity of amorous encounters in which the lesbian lovers now heal and give birth to each other; now pursue, kidnap, devour, peel and dissect one another. In the absence of a vocabulary that would express the infinite depth of feeling between women, Wittig uses anatomical descriptions as the way of achieving this intensity" (p. 240). Karin Cope makes a similar point: " 'lesbian' becomes the mark of Wittig's practice of appropriating, opening up, and redeploying language. In *The Lesbian Body* what 'lesbian' is or does changes at every turn. At best we may see only *how* it does, not what it is" (Cope, "Plastic Actions," p. 86).

39. LeVay seems to reject other kinds explanation of homosexuality rather casually. For example, on pp. xiii-xiv of *The Sexual Brain*, he simply rejects the notion that his parents are to blame for his homosexuality: "it became harder and harder to see them, or myself, as the products of defective parenting; we just seemed too normal" (p. xiii). In response to Döerner's research, he makes a personal note on maternal stress theory: "I may be biased away from believing that

something as cool as homosexuality could be caused by something as uncool as stress" (p. 126). While LeVay does not close out the explanatory potential of these "environmental theories," he is inclined to reject them with his rhetorical asides.

40. William Shakespeare, *Romeo and Juliet*, cited by LeVay in his opening to *The Sexual Brain*.

41. LeVay's work is historically consistent with the modernist grand theory of sex's origin. This grand theory is a modified bioevolutionary explanation of the origin of sex and sex differences. It operates on two levels of closure—the origin of individual geno/phenotype is determined by genetic causes (mediated by pre- and postnatal environmental influences) that are determined by the mechanisms of natural or environmental selection affecting the survival, reproduction, and viability of progeny, and ultimately the viability of genes. This grand theory assumes a modernist construction of the body, that is *linear* in its casualities, *hierarchical* in its deep organizational structure, *integrated* in the totality of its parts, and a *unified structure* that bears multiple and synergistic functions shaped by evolutionary forces and heritable matters. In this modernist framework the body is an organic unity, telically aimed toward survival and reproduction of its kind. Heterosexual reproduction becomes not only its motor of generation but also its major metaphysical modus operandi, an organizing telos for interpreting the body's structures, functions, behaviors, and erotic mechanics.

42. Homosexuality is incorporated into the grand theory of modernist sex evolution through its kinship alliance with the heterosexual project. It is countenanced as a helper for the active force of evolution—the genetically driven phallus that continuously pursues opportunity for impregnation and genetic transmission. Adopting this belief, LeVay endorses all the assumptions of sociobiological theory, even to the point of explaining gay male promiscuity and the tendency of men to seek more different sex partners than lesbians as an ironic function of the genetically driven heterosexual phallus (free at last from the bonds of women). LeVay writes, "This tendency has its origin in the fact that males are biologically capable of having more offspring than are females . . . this sex difference is exaggerated among homosexual men and women, because gay men, unlike heterosexual men, are not constrained by women's reluctance to have sex with them" (LeVay, *Sexual Brain*, p. 127). For a review and critique of the construction of homosexuality as "an evolved trait," see Douglas Futuyma and Stephen Risch, "Sexual Orientation, Sociobiology, and Evolution," in John De Cecco and Michael Shively, eds. *Bisexual and Homosexual Identities: Critical Theoretical Issues* (New York: Haworth, 1984), pp. 157–168.

43. For a critique of LeVay's reductionist research assumptions, see Anne Fausto-Sterling, " 'The Sexual Brain' " (book review), *Biological Science* 44 (February 1994): 102–104.

44. Ironically, LeVay does not have enough evidence to completely make his case for this reductionist explanation, but he makes the case by "writing the body" as he wants it to be. In other words, he makes the case for his reduction-

ist explanations by a strategy of linguistic locutions, phrases, and nuanced transitions. He opens *The Sexual Brain* with a plea to move the study of sexual behavior feelings from the domain of psychology to the biological brain sciences. He first states that "even the most nebulous and socially determined states of mind are *a matter of* genes and brain chemistry too" (p. xii, emphasis mine), implying that all psychological states have a biological substate. A few pages later, however, the phrase "a matter of" is recast as "in terms of" in LeVay's introductory comments: "In this book, I have not totally ignored psychological studies of sex, even though I am a neurobiologist by training and sympathy. But the emphasis is on understanding sex *in terms of* the cellular processes that generate it" (p. xiii, emphasis mine). This is a significant shift in meaning, since the latter phrase suggests more than a correlative biological substrate; it suggests that the substrate provides a causal explanation of what generates these feelings. This is followed by a metaphorical style of writing that is typically found in sociobiological theory, where the alleged cause of biological behavior—the genes—begin to take on anthropomorphic qualities of intention and directionality and hence the ability to control human behavior or its psychogenic ideation. LeVay's reductive explanation in *The Sexual Brain* of sexual desires rests heavily on this metaphorical writing that ascribes human agency to our genes. For example, in his discussion on the cunning sexual behaviors of female and male languors, LeVay writes: "Of course, we do not have to ascribe conscious thought to this behavior, either on the part of the gullible male and the devious female. *Their genes see to it* one way or another that they behave the way they do" (p. 15, emphasis mine). For a critique of this anthropomorphic metaphorical writing in sociobiology, see R. C. Lewontin, S. Rose, and L. J. Kamin, *Not in Our Genes* (New York: Pantheon, 1984).

45. The causal linkages from genes to sexual behavior are rhetorically created by LeVay as he writes how he wants the body to be in *The Sexual Brain*:

"The aim of this book is to focus more precisely on the brain mechanism that are responsible for sexual behavior and feelings" (LeVay p. xi).

"The hormones are able to modulate the degree to which a neuron responds to an incoming input, such as the potentially exciting olfactory signal" (LeVay p. 75).

"It is more likely that prenatal events lead to sex-distinct patterns of synaptic connections in the ventromedial nucleus" (LeVay p. 79).

"Thus one can think of the cortex-hypothalamus-cortex circuit (actually it probably includes the structures such as the amygdala) whose activity as a whole is the key to sexual life. The medial preoptic area and the entromedial nucleus may well be the prime nodes in this circuit: the nodes whose activity most purely represented the general level of sexual arousal" (LeVay p. 81).

"There are intrinsic, genetically determined differences in the brain's hormone receptors or in the other molecular machinery that is interposed between the circulating hormones and their actions on brain development" (LeVay p. 127).

46. Wittig, *Lesbian Body*, p. 150.

8. Anzaldúan Body

1. Gloria Anzaldúa, *Borderlands/La Frontera: The New Mestiza* (San Francisco: Spinsters/Aunt Lute, 1987), p.87. All subsequent references to this book will be indicated by page numbers in the text.

2. Feminist philosophical theorizing on the body often takes up this antidualism project in denouncing the gendered nature of Cartesianized masculinity as a function of mind and femininity as a function of body. See Genevieve Lloyd, *The Man of Reason: "Male" and "Female" in Western Philosophy* (Minneapolis: University of Minnesota Press, 1984.) Some feminist philosophers have taken up both the question of how the philosopher's engendered male body has influenced the emergence of western dualisms and how the female body can engage in a philosophy that no longer mandates of her exclusion from the profession (Naomi Scheman, "Introduction: The Unavoidability of Gender," in *Engenderings: Constructions of Knowledge, Authority, and Privilege* [New York: Routledge, 1993], pp. 1–8, and "Undoing Philosophy as a Feminist," ibid., pp. 239–249). Many philosophers involved in this challenging project agree with Elizabeth Grosz, that "new terms and different conceptual frameworks must also be devised to be able to talk of the body outside or in excess of binary pairs" (Elizabeth Grosz, *Volatile Bodies: Toward a Corporeal Feminism* [Bloomington: Indiana University Press, 1994]). See also Susan Bordo, *Unbearable Weight: Feminism, Western Culture, and the Body* (Berkeley: University of California Press, 1993); and Judith Butler, *Bodies That Matter: On the Discursive Limits of "Sex"* (New York: Routlege, 1993).

These academic feminist philosophers of the body have given us a number of metaphors for thinking our way out of Western mind/body dualism. Susan Bordo (1993) introduces the notion of cultural "chrystalizations," as a way of reading anorexia nervosa and market-driven pursuits of thinness as a lattice of intersecting cultural forces structuring the female flesh. The body is no longer a self-enclosed material thing, but a socially produced medium of culture. Elizabeth Grosz offers a Lacanian metaphor—the moebius strip, a twisted three-dimensional figure eight—as a means for thinking our way out of dualism. Traversing the outer surface of the moebius, it eventually folds over into the inner, and traversing along that inner surface eventually brings us back the outer. According to Grosz, just as the inner mind inscribes boundaries, unities, and functionalities on the body—creating an inner awareness of a seemingly coordinated and quasi-autonomous organism—so the cultural labor inscribed on the surface of the body creates the feeling of inner depth, unity, and identity in what we experience as the inner self. The point of origin for mind and body is the body's surface—inner folding into the outer and back again. This inner/outer problematic is also reflected in Judith Butler's work (1993), where repetition and reiteration of body performances constitute an inner experience of subjectivity as a more or less stabilized subjectivity. Mind and body are figured as significant effects of reiterative performativities and citationalities. For all three theorists the body, which is socially inscribed upon, constitutes a surface or a disciplining potential generative of an embodied subjectivity. At the same time this inner sanctum *is* only in its enfleshing. In various ways the mind-body dualism is refigured as the inner and outer processes of chrystalization (Bordo), infolding process of surfaces (Grosz), and reiterative performativities (Butler). In contrast to Anzaldúa's work, these three theorists reproduce a semi-Cartesianized dislocation from geography, historical location, and anti-imperialist struggle.

3. For further discussion on sex, class, and gender in Descartes' *Meditations,* see Jacquelyn N. Zita, "Transsexual Origins: Reflection on Descartes' *Meditations,*" *Genders* 5 (1989): 86–105.

4. See Susan Bordo, "The View from Nowhere and the Dream of Everywhere: Heterogeneity, Adequation, and Feminist Theory," *APA Newsletter on Feminism and Philosophy* 88, no. 2 (March 1989): 19–25. The notion of "a view from nowhere" was first coined by Thomas Nagel, *A View from Nowhere* (New York: Oxford University Press, 1986).

5. Academic feminist critiques of this Enlightenment subject can be found in Scheman, *Engenderings;* Susan J. Hekman, *Gender and Knowledge: Elements of a Postmodern Feminism* (Boston: Northeastern University Press, 1990); and Jane Flax, *Thinking Fragments: Psychoanalysis, Feminism, and Postmodernism in the Contemporary West* (Berkeley: University of California Press, 1990). Women of color have also delivered a critique of monolithic constructions of feminism from a perspective and experience of exclusion and silenced voices, a critique first articulated in various anthologies and in confrontations at various feminist conferences. See, most notably, Patricia Hill Collins, *Black Feminist Thought: Knowledge, Consciousness, and the Politics of Empowerment* (New York: Routledge, 1990) and Patricia Williams, *The Alchemy of Race and Rights* (Cambridge: Harvard University Press, 1991.)

6. See Bordo, *The Flight to Objectivity: Essays on Cartesianism and Culture* (Albany: State University of New York Press, 1987); Scheman, "Though This Be Method, Yet There Is Madness in It: Paranoia and Liberal Epistemology," in *Engenderings;* Zita, "Transsexual Origins."

7. Scheman, "Though This Be Method," p. 96.

8. While most of my analysis focuses on two texts by Anzaldúa: *Borderlands/ La Frontera,* and "Haciendo caras," in Gloria Anzaldúa, ed., *Making Face,* pp. xv–xviii, I have also consulted other writings and interviews to bring the wide breadth of her work into view. See also Anzaldúa, "Speaking in Tongues: A Letter to Third World Women Writers," in Cherríe Moraga and Gloria Anzaldúa, eds., *This Bridge Called My Back: Writings by Radical Women of Color* (Watertown, Mass.: Persephone, 1981) and in Anzaldúa, "To(o) Queer the Writer: *Loca, escritoria, y chicana,*" in Betsy Warland, ed., *Inversions: Writings by Dykes, Queers, and Lesbians* (Vancouver: Press Gang, 1991), pp. 249–264. Interviews with Anzaldúa include AnaLouise Keating, "Writing, Politics, and *las Lesberadas: Placticando con Gloria Anzaldúa,*" *Frontiers: A Journal of Women's Studies* 14, no. 1 (1993):

105–130 and Donna Perry, "Gloria Anzaldúa," *Backtalk: Women Writers Speak Out* (New Brunswick: Rutgers University Press, 1993), pp. 19–42.

9. For an analysis of Anzaldúa's work in the context of Chicana women's writing, see Eden Torres, *Caras vemos, corazones no sabemos: Their Faces We See, Their Hearts We Don't Know*, Ph.D. diss., University of Minnesota, 1997; AnaLouise Keating, *Women Reading Women Writing: Self-Invention in Paula Gunn Allen, Gloria Anzaldúa, and Audre Lorde* (Philadelphia: Temple University Press, 1996); and Tey Diana Rebolledo, *Women Singing in the Snow: A Cultural Analysis of Chicana Literature.* (Tucson: University of Arizona Press, 1995).

10. Anzaldúa continues to describe the Borderlands as a place where the space between races, classes, and cultures and between two individuals shrinks with intimacy, altering this space in ways that challenge the rigid binaries of difference separating individuals locked away from one another by distance and the immunities of power. In an interview with Donna Perry, Anzaldúa revisits her experience as a border woman: "When you are right in the middle, your identity and your language partake of both sides. I consider Chicanas and Chicanos, my people, as in-betweens. We mediated between the Mexican side and the American side, speaking both languages, Chicano Spanish, especially Tex-Mex, is made up of both. I extended the physical Borderlands to the psychological metaphor. Border people are in an in-between state, able to have two or three points of view because we've been in all these other spaces, worlds, and cultures." See Perry, "Gloria Anzaldúa," p. 21.

11. Sidonie Smith argues that Anzaldúa's *Borderlands/Frontera* constitutes an autobiographical manifesto through a rhetorical focus on the geographical subject. The geographic trope is at once psychological, physical, metaphysical, spiritual, creating a space where the complexities, splittings, and sutures of a mestiza self can be articulated. Smith further describes this self as reflected through the histories of shifting geographies. According to Smith, Anzaldúa thus engages borderland people in a project of anamnesis: a recollection or remembrance of the past in order to move past the obfuscations and misinterpretations of United States and global history. Sidonie Smith, "The Autobiographical Manifesto: Identities, Temporalities, Politics," in Shirley Neuman, ed., *Autobiography and Questions of Gender* (London: Cass, 1992), see esp.pp. 200–201. The Anzaldúan self is perhaps best described as a histo-geographic self in which the Cartesian process of isolatory disconnection from location, community, and body appears as an alien and alienating cultural practice of rational stupefication.

12. This concept of purity is analyzed as a political construct of domination in Maria Lugones, "Purity, Impurity, and Separation," *Signs* 19, no. 2 (1994): 458–479.

13. Kate Adams emphasizes that Anzaldúa's use of Aztec history and lyrics of Mexican corridos is an attempt to articulate a generations-deep, oppositional reading of the "nation building" events of the Southwest in order to challenge the legitimacy of whites in the Borderlands. See Kate Adams, "Northamerican

Silences: History, Identity, and Witness in the Poetry of Gloria Anzeldúa, Cherríe Moraga, and Leslie Marmon Silko," in Elaine Hedges and Shelley Fisher Fishkin, eds., *Listening to Silences: New Essays in Feminist Criticism* (New York: Oxford University Press, 1998), pp. 130–145.

14. Eden Torres has best articulated a review and analysis of how this historical trauma is incorporated into Chicana writings. See Torres, "Historic Trauma: *Donde hay amor, hay dolor," Caras vemos*, pp. 89–150..

15. This decision regarding language is carefully considered by Anzaldúa. In her interview with Perry she describes the language in *Borderlands* as follows: "Mostly . . . it's the kind of Borderland dialect that I grew up with, talking both Spanish and English. But I also wanted the readers to start thinking about the myth of a monocultural U.S. There are people of other cultures that speak Italian, the different Jewish languages, Native American dialects, black English, plus all the Asian languages. By speaking and writing both languages, I wanted to force that awareness that this country is not what those in power say it is. It's a *mestizanation* (Perry, "Gloria Anzaldúa," p. 22). Barbara Christian has also noted the the importance (though perhaps not the necessity) of Anzaldúa's selection of presses. In her contrast of Henry Louis Gates's anthology *Reading Black, Reading Feminist*, published in a New York mainstream press (Meridian), and Anzaldúa's small press (Aunt Lute on the West Coast), Christian observes "Gates's selections tend to privilege an East Coast mainstream view, while Anzaldúa's choices indicate a literary landscape beyond the mainstream of publishing (Barbara Christian, "A Rough Terrain: The Case Shaping an Anthology of Caribbean Women Writers," in David Palumbo-Lui, ed., *The Ethnic Canon: Histories, Institutions, and Interventions* (Minneapolis: University of Minnesota Press, 1995), pp. 251–252.

16. Anzaldúa, *Haciendo cara*, p. xxiv.

17. The importance of language in radical Chicana identity formation is also explored in Cherríe Moraga's *Loving in the War Years: Lo que nunca pasó por sus labios* (Boston: South End, 1983). Moraga's experience of language and identity involves her enrollment in a Berlitz school to return to her mothertongue; "Paying for culture. When I was born between the legs of the best teacher I could have had," *Loving in the War Years* (Boston: South End, 1983), p. 141. Anzaldúa is surrounded by her Chicana culture early in life and the mestiza blendings of Spanish language. While both Anzaldúa and Moraga use a mix of Spanish and English in their writing, their life experiences leading to language as identity are different but connecting. In the Preface to *Borderlands/La Frontera*, Anzaldúa announces her intention to use a variety of Spanish dialects as a way for Chicanos to "no longer feel that we need to beg entrance, that we need always to make the first overture—to translate to Anglos, Mexicans and Latinos, apology blurting out of our mouths with every step. Today we ask to be met halfway." The presence of untranslated passages of Spanish in *Borderlands/La Frontera* creates for the non-Spanish reader a sense of exclusion, imprecisely replicating

the exclusion that is sometimes experienced by Chicanos and Latinos in reading feminist texts written in English and exacting the challenge that Anglo readers come "halfway."

18. Elaine Scarry, *The Body in Pain: The Making and Unmaking of the World* (New York: Oxford University Press, 1985).

19. Anzaldúa, *Haciendo cara*, p. xxii. One important border that Anzaldúa tranverses is the gender and sexuality norms in her culture, a transgression that many Chicana feminist writers use as a location for oppositional and transformative writing. Norma Alarcón's writing is especially helpful in articulating the cultural reinvention involved in such radical Chicana writing. See Norma Alarcón, "The Theoretical Subject(s) of *This Bridge Called My Back* and Anglo-American Feminism," in Anzaldúa, ed., *Making Face*, and *"Traddutora, Traditora*: A Paradigmatic Figure of Chicano Feminism," in Jo Whitehorse Cochran, Donna Langston, and Carolyn Woodward, eds., *Changing Our Power: An Introduction to Women's Studies* (Dubuque, Iowa: Kendall-Hunt, 1988), pp. 195–203.

20. *Coatlicue* is a pre-Azteca-Mexica great goddess—a symbol of the fusion of opposites, containing and balancing the dualities of males and female, light and dark, and life and death. See Anzaldúa, *Borderlands*, p. 32. Sidonie Smith points out that once Anzaldúa recovers her relationship to Coatlicue, she proceeds to rewrite the history of the Azteca-Mexica nation and to historicize her own geographic location. (See Smith, "Autobiographical Manifesto," pp. 186–212.) The use of archetypal images in Chicana writing is fully analyzed in Torres, *Caras vemos*. As Alarcon and Torres have pointed out, this rewriting of history from a Chicana perspective often involves a rewriting of the way Chicanas have been traditionally portrayed as *malinches*, *vendidas*, or *chingadas* (Alarcón, "Theoretical Subject(s)"; Torres, *Caras vemos*), a project that Anzaldúa also takes up in *Borderlands*.

21. For a deeper analysis of how historical trauma is fundamental to radical Chicana writing, see Torres, *Caras vemos*, and Reuman's comparative analysis of Moraga and Anzaldúa, in Ann S. Reuman, " 'Wild Tongues Can't Be Tamed': Gloria Anzaldúa's (R)Evolution of Voice," in Deirdre Lashgari, ed., *Violence, Silence, and Anger: Women's Writing as Transgression* (Charlottesville: University of Virginia Press, 1995), pp. 305–319.

22. For Anzaldúa's discussion on sexual identity and her rejection of the identity "lesbian," see Keating, "Writing, Politics, and *las Lesberadas*," p. 32 and Anzaldúa, "To(o) Queer the Writer," pp. 249–261. Sternbach has written a particularly lucid account of the personal and political traumas of lesbian Chicana identity formation as reflected in the works of Cherríe Moraga. See Nancy Saporta Sternbach, " 'A Deep Racial Memory of Love': The Chicana Feminism of Cherríe Moraga," in Asuncion Horno-Delgado, et. al, eds., *Breaking Boundaries: Latina Writing and Critical Readings* (Amherst: University of Massachusetts Press, 1989), pp. 48–61.

23. Torres, *Caras vemos*, pp. 89–150.

24. This idea of many multiple perspectives is fundamental to Anzaldúa's project and a strategy of attack on monolithic Ango-American constructions of "woman" as well as the Enlightenment construction of "man." The strategy is not aerial but grounded and written through the body. A similar analysis of this is developed by Keating in "Writing, Politics, and *las Lesberadas*." In this interview with Keating, Anzaldúa comments: "There are many personalities and subpersonalities in *you*, and your identity shifts every time you shift positions. . . . In just the forehead area there are literally millions of little organisms that live in your skin, and the root of each eyelash has a particular different organism from the ones in your forehead. So that you, AnaLouise, are not just AnaLouise. You're all the different organisms and parasites that live on your body and also the ones that live in symbiotic relationship to you. And then the animals, too. You look at the cows and there'll be little birds picking the ticks off the cows, and there'll be a water buffalo with a little bird sitting on its back. So who are you? You're not a single entity. You're a multiple entity" (p. 111).

25. I refer the reader back to my analysis of the *je* and *j/e* in chapter 7, "Hard Traits/Fluid Measures."

9. Venus: The Looks of Body Theory

1. Originally this essay was drafted as a critique of the notions of gender developed by Judith Butler in *Gender Trouble: Feminism and the Subversion of Identity* (New York: Routledge, 1990). Her subsequent publication of *Bodies that Matter: On the Discursive Limits of "Sex"* (New York: Routledge, 1993) addressed many of the criticisms that I was developing, and I was delighted and surprised to find that she had also selected *Paris Is Burning* to elucidate her notions of gender performativity and social materiality. I do not think that she carries this analysis far enough, although her new concept of how bodies matter is a move in the right direction. I also find that she pays too little attention to who looks, from where, with whom—questions directly addressed in this chapter. I experiment in this chapter with a theorizing that tries to stay on location.

2. My notion of "looks" used in this chapter is not meant to essentialize the content or parameters of a particular looking or viewing. Although indexed by race, class, and sexuality, I do not adopt such locutions as *the* black look, *the* queer look, *the* black straight look or various other renditions of *the* gaze. Nor do I believe that the race, gender, sexuality, and class vectors that I explore in this chapter exhaust all the relevant or significant aspects that create different ways of looking or viewing. I am suggesting that how we self-identify and where we are situated may serve as starting points for how we view *Paris Is Burning*. I keep "looks" in the plural to include multiple fields of contestation.

3. bell hooks, "Is Paris Burning?" in *Black Looks: Race and Representation* (Boston: South End, 1992), pp. 145–156.

4. See Butler, "Gender Is Burning: Questions of Appropriation and Subversion," in *Bodies that Matter*, p. 135.

5. Jackie Goldsby, "Queens of Language: *Paris Is Burning*," in Martha Gever, Pratibha Parmar, and John Greyson, eds., *Queer Looks: Perspectives on Lesbian and Gay Film and Video* (New York: Routledge, 1993), pp. 108–115..

6. Robert Reid-Pharr, "The Spectacle of Blackness" in *Radical America* [this issue subtitled "Becoming a Spectacle: Lesbian and Gay Politics and Culture"] 24, no. 4 (1990): 57–65.

7. From *Paris Is Burning*, dir. Jennie Livingston (Facets Video, 1990).

8. Toni Morrison, *The Bluest Eye* (New York: Washington Square, 1972).

9. *Paris Is Burning*, dir. Livingstone.

10. Ibid.

11. Ibid.

12. hooks, *Is Paris Burning?*, p. 146.

13. Ibid., p. 154.

14. I have not included in this chapter white radical lesbian feminist analyses of male drag (Frye, Hoagland, Raymond, Daly) for a number of reasons: (1) the topic was very cleverly addressed in Butler's analysis in "Gender Is Burning" in *Bodies that Matter*; (2) the inquiry I am developing demands a multi-vectored analysis of drag that is absent from earlier radical feminist analyses of drag as misogyny and male imperialism; and (3) though I have written within the paradigms of radical lesbian analysis in my earlier philosophical work, such an analysis seemed extremely *out of synch* with performativity approaches to gender. See Zita, "Lesbian and Gay Studies: Yet Another Unhappy Marriage," in Linda Garber, ed., *Tilting the Tower* (New York: Routledge, 1994). As Butler points out, hooks's theoretical alliance with white lesbian writing on drag is an odd affinity.

15. Laura Mulvey, "Visual Pleasure and Narrative Cinema," *Screen* 16, no. 3 (Autumn 1975): 6–18.

16. Tania Modleski, "Cinema and the Dark Continent: Race and Gender in Popular Film," in Linda Kauffman, ed., *American Feminist Thought at Century's End: A Reader* (Cambridge: Blackwell, 1993) p. 85.

17. Butler, "Gender Is Burning," pp. 134–135.

18. From *Paris Is Burning*, dir. Jennie Livingstone.

19. Ibid.

20. Butler, "Imitation and Gender Insubordination," p. 21.

21. Butler, *Gender Trouble*, pp. 137–138.

22. Butler, "Gender Is Burning," p. 131. The passage where this interpolation occurs is framed by hypothetical qualifiers: "A fantasy that for Venus, because she dies—killed *apparently* by one of her clients, *perhaps* after the discovery of those remaining organs—cannot be translated into the symbolic" (emphasis mine).

10. A Suite for the Body

1. Evelyn Fox Keller, *Reflections on Gender and Science* (New Haven: Yale University Press, 1985), p. 18.

2. Michel Foucault, *History of Sexuality*, vol. 1, trans. Robert Hurley (New York: Pantheon, 1978).

3. Jean Piaget, *The Child's Conception of the World* (Totawa, N.J.: Littlefield, 1972), p. 34.

4. A description of this event was given to me in a personal conversation with Gudrun Ekeflo many years ago.

5. Alfred Schultz, *Reflections on the Problem of Relevance* (New Haven: Yale University Press, 1970).

6. Dorothy Smith, "The Standpoint of Women Is Outside the Extralocal Relation of Things," in *The Everyday World as Problematic: A Feminist Sociology* (Boston: Northeastern University Press, 1987), pp. 78–88. Smith writes as follows: "The place of women, then, in relation to this mode of action is where the work is done to facilitate men's occupation of the conceptual mode of action. Women keep hours, bear and care for children, look after men when they are sick, and in general provide for the logistics of their bodily existence. But this marriage aspect of women's work is only one side of a more general relation. Women work in and around the professional and managerial scene in analogous ways. They do those things that give concrete form to the conceptual activities. They do the clerical work, giving material form to the words or thoughts of the boss. They do the routine computer work, the interviewing for the survey, the nursing, the secretarial work. At almost every point women mediate for men the relation between the conceptual mode of action and the actual concrete forms on which it depends" (p. 83).

7. Jeanette Winterston, "The Cells, Tissues, Systems, and Cavities of the Body," in "The Body," special issue, *Granta* 39 (Spring 1992): 128.

8. Thomas Laqueur, *Making Sex: Body and Gender from the Greeks to Freud* (Cambridge: Harvard University Press, 1990).

9. Susan Bordo, *Unbearable Weight: Feminism, Western Culture, and the Body* (Berkeley: University of California Press, 1993).

10. Celeste Olalquiaga, *Megalopolis: Contemporary Cultural Sensibilities* (Minneapolis: University of Minnesota Press, 1992), p. 14.

11. Jane Gallop, *Thinking Through the Body* (New York: Columbia University Press, 1988), p. 14, emphasis mine.

12. Particia J. Williams, *The Alchemy of Race and Rights* (Cambridge: Harvard University Press, 1991), see Preface Preamble.

References

Adams, Kate. "Northamerican Silences: History, Identity, and Witness in the Poetry of Gloria Anzaldúa, Cherríe Moraga, and Leslie Mormon Silko." In Elaine Hedges and Shelley Fisher Fishkin, eds. *Listening to Silences: New Essays in Feminist Criticism*. New York: Oxford University Press, 1994, pp. 130–145.

Adler, Jerry, Mary Hager, Jeanne Gordon, Emily Yoffe, Patricia King, and Lucille Beachy. "Living With the Virus." *Newsweek* (November 18, 1991): 63–64.

"Advertisers Shying from Magic's Touch." *New York Times*, January 1, 1991, p. A44.

Aker, Kathy. *Empire of the Senseless*. New York: Grove, 1988.

Alarcón, Norma. "The Theoretical Subject(s) of This Bridge Called My Back and Anglo-American Feminism." In Gloria Anzaldúa, ed., *Making Faces, Making Soul: Creative and Critical Perspectives by Feminists of Color*. San Francisco: Aunt Lute, 1990, pp. 356–369.

——. "*Traductora, Traditora*: A Paradigmatic Figure of Chicano Feminism." In Jo Whitehorse Cochran, Danna Langston, and Carolyn Woodward, eds., *Changing Our Power: An Introduction to Women's Studies*. Dubuque, Iowa: Kendall-Hunt, 1988, pp. 195–203.

Allen, L. S., M. Hines, J. E. Shryne, and R. A. Gorski. "Two Sexually Dimorphic Cell Groups in the Human Brain." *Journal of Neuroscience* 9 (1989): 497–506.

Angier, N. "Zone of Brain Linked to Men's Sexual Orientation." *New York Times*, August 30, 1991a, pp. A1, 18.

——. "The Biology of What It Means to Be Gay." *New York Times*, September 1, 1991b, pp. A1, 4.

Anzaldúa, Gloria. "To(o) Queer the Writer: *Loca, Escritora, y Chicana*." In Betsy Warland, ed., *Inversions: Writings by Dykes, Queers, and Lesbians*. Vancouver: Press Gang, 1991, pp. 249–264.

——. "*Haciendo Caras, una Entrada*: An Introduction." *Making Face, Making Soul: Creative And Critical Perspectives by Feminists of Color*. San Francisco: Aunt Lute, 1990, pp. xv–xviii.

——. *Borderlands/La Frontera: The New Mestiza.* San Francisco: Spinsters/Aunt Lute Press, 1987.

——. "Speaking in Tongues: A Letter to Third World Women." In Cherríe Moraga and Gloria Anzaldúa, eds., *This Bridge Called My Back: Writings by Radical Women of Color.* Watertown, Mass: Persephone, 1981.

Ashton, Heather. *Brain Function and Psychotropic Drugs.* New York: Oxford Medical Press, 1992.

Associated Press. "Navratilova: AIDS Double Standard Exists." *Minneapolis Star Tribune*, November 21, 1991, p. C3.

Atkinson, Ti-Grace. *Amazon Odyssey: Collection of Writings.* New York: Links Books, 1974.

Barker, Francis. *The Tremulous Private Body: Essays on Subjection.* Ann Arbor: University of Michigan Press, 1995.

Barondes, Samuel. "Thinking About Prozac." *Science* 263 (1994): 1102–1103.

Bart, Pauline. "Depression in Middle-Aged Women." In Vivian Gornick and Barbara Moran, eds., *Women in Sexist Society: Studies in Power and Powerlessness.* New York: Basic Books, 1971, pp. 163–186.

Bartky, Sandra Lee. *Femininity and Domination: Studies in the Phenomenology of Oppression.* New York: Routledge, 1990.

——. "Foucault, Femininity, and the Modernization of Patriarchal Power." In Irene Diamond and Lee Quinby, eds. *Feminism and Foucault: Reflections on Resistance.* Boston: Northeastern University Press, 1988.

Bell, Vikki. *Interrogating Incest: Feminism, Foucault, and the Law.* New York: Routledge, 1993.

Belle, Deborah, ed. *Lives in Stress: Women and Depression.* Beverly Hills: Sage Publications, 1982.

Belton, Don, ed. *Speak My Name: Black Men on Masculinity and the American Dream.* Boston: Beacon Press, 1995.

Berghorn, Forrest J. et al. "Racial Participation in Men's and Women's Intercollegiate Basketball: Continuity and Change, 1958–1985." *Sociology of Sport Journal* 5 (1988): 107–124.

Berkey, Branden Robert et al. "The Multidimensional Scale of Sexuality." *Journal of Homosexuality* 19, no. 4 (1990): 67–87.

Bernheimer, Charles. "Penile Reference in Phallic Theory." *differences: A Journal of Feminist Cultural Studies: The Phallus Issue* 4, no. 1 (Spring 1992): 116–132.

Bersani, Leo. "Is the Rectum a Grave?" In Douglas Crimp, ed., *AIDS: Cultural Analysis, Cultural Activism.* Cambridge: MIT Press, 1988.

Bhabha, Homi. "The Other Question: The Stereotype and Colonial Discourse." *Screen* 24, no. 6 (1983): 18–36.

Boeck, Greg. "Public Attitude Seems to Be 'Good Guys' vs. 'Bad Guys.' " *USA Today*, November 21, 1991, p. 2C.

———. "Women Support Martina's Stand." *USA Today,* November 21, 199, p. 2C.

Bordo, Susan. "Reading the Male Body." *Michigan Quarterly Review* 32, no. 4 (Fall 1993): 696–737.

———. "Feminism, Foucault, and the Politics of the Body." In Caroline Ramazanoglu, ed., *Up Against Foucault: Explorations of Some Tensions Between Foucault and Feminism.* New York: Routledge, 1993, pp. 179–202.

———. *Unbearable Weight: Feminism, Western Culture, and the Body.* Berkeley: University of California Press, 1993.

———. "Postmodern Subjects, Postmodern Bodies." *Feminist Studies* 18, no. 1 (1992): 159–175. Reprinted in Bordo. *Unbearable Weight,* pp. 277–300.

———. "Feminism, Postmodernism, and Gender-Skepticism." In Linda Nicholson, ed., *Feminism/Postmodernism.* New York: Routledge, 1990, pp. 133–156. Reprinted in Bordo, *Unbearable Weight,* pp. 215–244.

———. "Reading the Slender Body." In Mary Jacobus, Evelyn Fox Keller, and Sally Shuttleworth, eds., *Body/Politics: Women and the Discourse of Science.* New York: Routledge, 1990. Reprinted in Bordo, *Unbearable Weight,* pp. 185–212.

———. "The Body and the Reproduction of Femininity: A Feminist Appropriation of Foucault." In Alison Jaggar and Susan Bordo, eds., *Gender/Body/Knowledge: Feminist Reconstructions of Being and Knowing.* New Brunswick: Rutgers University Press, 1989, pp. 13–33. Reprinted in Bordo, *Unbearable Weight,* pp. 165–184.

———. "The View from Nowhere and the Dream of Everywhere: Heterogeneity, Adequation, and Feminist Theory." *APA Newsletter on Feminism and Philosophy* 88, no. 2 (March 1989): 19–25.

———. *The Flight to Objectivity: Essays on Cartesianism and Culture.* Albany: State University of New York Press, 1987.

Bornstein, Kate. *Gender Outlaw: Our Men, Women, and the Rest of Us.* New York: Routledge, 1994.

———. "Transsexual Lesbian Playwright Tells All!" In Amy Scholder and I. Silberberg, eds., *High Risk.* New York: Plume Press, 1991, pp. 259–261.

Bourdieu, Pierre. *Outline of a Theory of Practice.* Cambridge: Cambridge University Press, 1977.

Bray, Alan. *Homosexuality in Renaissance England.* London: Gay Men's Press, 1982.

Breedlove, S. M. "Cellular Analysis of Hormone Influence on Motorneuronal Development and Function." *Journal of Neurobiology* 17 (1986): 157–166.

Breedlove, S. M. and A. P. Arnold. "Hormonal Control of the Developing Neuromuscular System: I. Complete Demasculinization of the Male Rat Spinal Nucleus of the of the Bulbocavernosus Using Antiandrogen Flutamide. II. Sensitive Periods for the Androgen Induced Masculinization of the Rat Spinal Nucleus of the Bulbocavernosus." *Journal of Neuroscience* 3 (1983): 417–423, 424–432.

Breggin, Peter R. and Ginger Ross Breggin. *Talking Back to Prozac: What Doctors Won't Tell You About Today's Most Controversial Drug*. New York: St. Martin's Press, 1994.

Breines, Paul. *Tough Jews: Political Fantasies and the Moral Dilemma of American Jewry*. New York: Basic Books, 1990.

Brookey, Rob. *Reinventing the Male Homosexual: The Rhetoric and Power of the Gay Gene*. Ph.D. diss., University of Minnesota, 1998.

Bryson, Lois. "Sport and the Maintenance of Masculine Hegemony." *Women's Studies International Forum* 10, no. 4 (1987): 349–360.

Butler, Judith. "Gender Is Burning: Questions of Appropriateness and Subversion." In *Bodies that Matter: On the Discursive Limits of "Sex."* New York: Routledge, 1993, pp. 121–140.

———. "Imitation and Gender Insubordination." In Diana Fuss, *Inside/Out: Lesbian Theories, Gay Theories*. New York: Routledge, 199l, pp. 13–31.

———. *Gender Trouble: Feminism and the Subversion of Identity*. New York: Routledge, 1990.

———. "Monique Wittig: Bodily Disintegration and Fictive Sex." In Butler, *Gender Trouble: Feminism and the Subversion of Identity*, pp. 111–128.

Byne, W. and B. Parsons. "Human Sexual Orientation: Biological Theories Reappraised." *Archive of General Psychiatry* 50 (1993): 228–239.

Calnan, Michael. "Lay Evaluation of Medicine and Medical Practice: Report of a Pilot Study." *International Journal of Health Services* 18 (1988): 311–322.

Calnan, Michael and S. Williams. "Images of Scientific Medicine." *Sociology of Health and Illness* 14, no. 2 (1992): 233–254.

Card, Claudia. "Homophobia and Lesbian/Gay Pride." *Lesbian Choices*. New York: Columbia University Press, 1995.

Carlson, Alison. "When Is a Woman Not a Woman?" *Women's Sports and Fitness* (March 1991): 24–29.

Carrier, J. M. "Family Attitudes and Mexican Male Homosexuality." *Urban Life* (October 1976): 359–375.

Carrigan, Tim, Bob Connell, and John Lee. "Toward a New Sociology of Masculinity." In Harry Brod, ed., *The Making of Masculinities*. London: Allen and Unwin, 1987, pp. 63–100.

Cass, Vivienne. "The Implications of Homosexual Identity Formation for the Kinsey Model and Scale of Sexual Preference." In D. McWhirter, S. Sanders, and J. Reinisch, eds., *Homosexuality/Heterosexuality: Concepts of Sexual Orientation* (The Kinsey Institute Series, Vol. 2). New York: Oxford University Press, 1990, pp. 239–266.

———. "Developmental Stages of the Coming Out Process." *Journal of Sexuality* 7, nos. 7/8 (1981/1982): 313–343.

———. "Homosexual Identity Formation: A Theoretical Model" *Journal of Homosexuality* 4 (1979): 219–235.

Cazenave, Noel. "Race, Socioeconomic Status, and Age: The Social Context of American Masculinity." *Sex Roles* 11 (1984): 639–657.

Chapkis, Wendy. *Beauty Secrets: Women and the Politics of Appearance.* Boston: South End Press, 1986.

Chauncey, George Jr. "Christian Brotherhood or Sexual Perversion? Homosexual Identities and the Construction of Social Boundaries in the World War One Era." *Journal of Social History* 19 (Winter 1985): 189–212.

——. "From Sexual Inversion to Homosexuality: Medicine and the Changing Conceptualizations of Female Deviance." *Salmagundi* 58–59 (Fall/Winter 1983): 114–146.

Chernin, Kim. *The Obsession: Reflections on the Tyranny of Slenderness.* New York: Harper and Row, 1981.

Cherry, J. A. and M. J. Baum. "Effects on Lesions of a Sexually Dimorphic Nucleus in the Preoptic/Anterior Hypothalamic Area on the Expression of Androgen and Estrogen-Dependent Sexual Behavior in Male Ferrets." *Brain Research* 522 (1990): 191–203.

Chirimuuta, Richard and Rosalind Chirimuuta. *AIDS, Africa, and Racism.* London: Free Association Books, 1989.

Christian, Barbara. "A Rough Terrain: The Case Shaping an Anthology of Caribbean Writers." In David Palumbo-Lui, ed., *The Ethnic Canon: Histories, Institutions, and Interventions.* Minneapolis: University of Minnesota Press, 1995, pp. 251–252.

Clarke, Alan and J. Clarke. "Highlights and Action Replays: Ideology, Sport, and the Media." In J. Hargreaves, ed., *Sport, Culture, and Ideology.* London: Routledge and Kegan Paul, 1982: 62–87.

Clausen, Jan. "My Interesting Condition." *Out/Look* (Winter 1990): 10–21. Reprinted in *Journal of Sex Research* 27, no. 3 (1990): 445.

Cohen, Cheryl H. "The Feminist Sexuality Debate: Ethics and Politics." *Hypatia* 1, no. 2 (1986): 71–86.

Collins, Patricia Hill. *Black Feminist Thought: Knowledge, Consciousness, and the Politics of Empowerment.* New York: Routledge, 1990.

Cole, Cheryl L. and Harry Denny III. "Visualizing Deviance in the Post-Reagan America: Magic Johnson, AIDS, and Promiscuous World of Professional Sport." *Critical Sociology* 20, no. 3 (November 1994): 123–147.

Coleman, Eli. "Developmental Stages of the Coming Out Process." *Journal of Homosexuality* 7, nos. 2/3 (1981/1982): 31–43.

Concar, D. "Design Your Own Personality." *New Scientist* 141 (March 12, 1994): 22–26.

Connell, Robert. "Theorizing Gender." *Sociology* 19 (May 1988): 260–272.

Connerton, Paul. *How Societies Remember.* Cambridge: Cambridge University Press, 1989.

Cooper, Jack, Floyd Bloom, and Robert Roth. *The Biochemical Basis of Neuropharmacology.* New York: Oxford University Press, 1991.

Cope, Karin. "Plastic Actions: Linguistic Strategies and *Le Corps Lesbien*." *Hypatia* 6, no. 3 (Fall 1991): 75–96.

Cope, Lewis. "AIDS Line Busy after Johnson's Revelation." *Minneapolis Star Tribune*, November 9, 1991: B1.

Cowley, Geoffrey, with Karen Springen, Jeanne Gordon, and Carla Koehl. "The Prozac Backlash." *Newsweek* (April 1, 1991): 64–67.

Crabb, C. "Are Some Men Born to Be Homosexual?" *U.S. News and World Report* (September 9, 1991): 58.

Crimp, Douglas. "Accommodating Magic." In J. Matlock and L. Walkowitz, eds., *Media Spectacles*. New York: Routledge, 1993, pp. 254–266.

———. "Portraits of People with AIDS." In Lawrence Grossberg, Cary Nelson, and Paula Treichler, eds., *Cultural Studies*. New York: Routledge, 1992, pp. 117–133.

Crosset, Todd W., James Ptacek, Mark A. McDonald, and Jeffrey R. Benedict. "Male Student-Athletes and Violence Against Women: A Survey of Campus Judicial Affairs Office." *Violence Against Women* 2, no. 2 (1996): 163–179.

Daly, Mary. *Gyn/Ecology: The Metaethics of Radical Feminism*. Boston: Beacon Press, 1978.

Daumer, Elisabeth. "Queer Ethics; or, The Challenge of Bisexuality to Lesbian Ethics." *Hypatia* 7, no. 4 (1992): 91.

Dawkins, R. *The Extended Phenotype*. San Francisco: W. H. Freeman, 1981.

———. *The Selfish Gene*. Oxford: Oxford University Press, 1976.

DeCecco, John and M. Shively, eds. *Bisexual and Homosexual Identities: Critical Theoretical Issues*. New York: Haworth Press, 1984.

———. "From Sexual Identity To Sexual Relationships: A Contractual Shift." *Journal of Homosexuality* 9 (1983/4): 1–26.

Deford, Frank. "Is There No More Magic?" *Newsweek* (November 16, 1992): 91.

de Lauretis, Teresa. *Technologies of Gender: Essays on Theory, Film, and Fiction*. Bloomington: Indiana University Press, 1987.

———. "Feminist Studies/Critical Studies: Issues, Terms and Contexts." In Teresa de Lauretis, ed., *Feminist Studies/Critical Studies*. Bloomington: Indiana University Press, 1986, pp. 1–19.

Deleuze, Gilles and Felix Guattari. *Anti-Oedipus: Capitalism and Schizophrenia*. Trans. R. Hurley, Mark Seem, and Helen Lane. New York: Viking Press, 1977.

Disch, Lisa and Mary Jo Kane. "When a Looker Is Really a Bitch: Lisa Olson, Sport, and Heterosexual Matrix." *Signs* 21, no. 2 (1991): 278–308.

Dodson, R. E., J. E. Shryne, and R. A. Gorski. "Hormonal Modification of the Number of Total and Late-Rising Neurons in the Central Part of the Medial Preoptic Nucleus of the Rat." *Journal of Comparative Neurology* 275 (1988): 623–629.

Doll, L., L. Peterson, C. White, E. Johnson, J. Ward, and the Donor Study Group. "Homosexually and Nonhomosexually Identified Men Who Have Sex with Men: A Behavioral Comparison." *Journal of Sex Research* 29, no. 1 (1992): 1–14.

Dollimore, Jonathan. *Sexual Dissidence: Augustine to Wilde, Freud to Foucault.* New York: Oxford University Press, 1991.

Dörner, G., W. Rhode, F. Stahl, L. Krell, and W. G. Masius. "A Neuroendocrine Predisposition for Homosexuality in Men." *Archives of Sexual Behavior* 4 (1975): 1–8.

Douglas, Mary. *Natural Symbols: Explorations in Cosmology.* New York: Pantheon Books, 1970.

———. *Purity and Danger: An Analysis of the Concepts of Pollution and Taboo.* New York: Praeger, 1966.

Druck, K. and J. Simmons. *The Secrets Men Keep.* Garden City, N.Y.: Doubleday, 1985.

Duden, Barbara. *Disembodying Women: Perspectives on Pregnancy and the Unborn.* Cambridge: Harvard University Press, 1991.

Duggan, Lisa. "Making It Perfectly Queer." *Socialist Review* 22, no. 1 (1992): 11–31.

Duroche, Leonard L. "Men Fearing Men: On the Nineteenth-Century Origins of Modern Homophobia." *Men's Studies* 8, no. 3 (Summer 1991): 3–7.

Dworkin, Andrea. *Intercourse.* New York: Free Press, 1987.

———. *Women Hating.* New York: E. P. Dutton, 1974.

Dyson, Michael Eric. "Be Like Mike? Michael Jordan and the Pedagogy of Desire." *Reflecting Black: African American Cultural Criticism.* Minneapolis: University of Minnesota Press, 1993, pp. 64–75.

Earl, W. "Married Men and Same-Sex Activity: A Field Study on HIV Risk Among Men Who Do Not Identify as Gay or Bisexual." *Journal of Sex & Marital Therapy* 16, no.4 (1990): 251–257.

Ebert, Teresa. *Ludic Feminism and After: Postmodernism, Desire, and Labor in Late Capitalism.* Ann Arbor: University of Michigan Press, 1995.

Edwards, Harry. "Race in Contemporary American Sports." *National Forum* 62 (1984): 19–22.

———. "The Collegiant Athletic Arms Race: Origins and Implications of the 'Rule 48' Controversy." *Journal of Sport and Social Issues* 8 (1984): 4–22.

Ehrenreich, Barbara. *Fear of Falling: The Inner Life of the Middle Class.* New York: Pantheon Books, 1989.

Elfenbein, Debra, ed. *Living with Prozac and Other Selective Serotonin Reuptake Inhibitors (SSRIs): Personal Accounts of Life on Antidepressants.* San Francisco: Harper, 1995.

Ellerbrock, Tedd et al. "Epidemiology of Women with AIDS in the United States, 1981 through 1990." *Journal of the American Medical Association* 265, no. 22 (June 12, 1991): 2971.

Englebrecht, Penelope. " 'Lifting Belly Is a Language': The Postmodern Lesbian Subject." *Feminist Studies* 16, no. 1 (Spring 1990): 85–114.

Eriadani. "Is Sexual Orientation a Secondary Sex Characteristic?" In Elizabeth Reba Weise, ed., *Closer to Home: Bisexuality and Feminism.* Seattle: Seal Press, 1992.

Ettorre, Elizabeth and Elianne Riska. "Advertising as a Representation of Gendered Moods." In *Gendered Moods: Psychotropics and Society*. New York: Routledge, 1995, pp. 65–88.

Faderman, Lillian. *Surpassing the Love of Men: Romantic Friendship and Love Between Women from the Renaissance to the Present*. New York: Morrow, 1981.

Faludi, Susan. *Backlash: The Undeclared War Against American Women*. New York: Crown, 1991.

Fanon, Franz. *Black Skin, White Masks*. New York: Grove Press, 1967.

Fausto-Sterling, Anne. " 'The Sexual Brain' " (book review). *Biological Science* 44 (February 1994): 102–104.

Fava, Maurizio and Jerrold Rosenbaum. "Suicidality and Fluoxetine: Is There a Relationship?" *The Journal of Clinical Psychiatry* 52, no. 3 (March 1993): 108–111.

Feinberg, Leslie. *Stone Butch Blues*. Ithaca, N.Y.: Firebrand Books, 1993.

Ferguson, Ann, Illene Philipson, Irene Diamond, Lee Quinby, Carole S. Vance, and Ann Barr Snitow. "Forum: The Feminist Sexuality Debates." *Signs* 10, no. 1 (1984): 106–135.

Flax, Jane. *Thinking Fragments: Psychoanalysis, Feminism, and Postmodernism in the Contemporary West*. Berkeley: University of California Press, 1990.

Forstein, Marshall. "Homophobia: An Overview." *Psychiatric Annals* 18, no. 1 (January 1980): 33–36.

Foucault, Michel. "Friendship as a Way of Life." In *Foucault Live (Interviews, 1966–1984)*. Trans. John Johnson and Sylvere Lotringer, ed., New York: Semiotext, 1989, pp. 203—209.

——. "Technologies of the Self: The Political Technology of the Individual. In Luther H. Martin, Huck Gutman, and Patrick Huttons, eds., *The Technologies of the Self*. Amherst: University of Massachusetts Press, 1988.

——. *Herculine Barbin: Being the Recently Discovered Memoirs of the Nineteenth Century French Hermaphrodite*. Trans. Richard McDougal. New York: Pantheon, 1980.

——. *Power/Knowledge: Selected Interviews and Other Writings 1972–1977*. Trans. and ed. Colin Gordon. New York: Pantheon Books. 1980.

——. *Discipline and Punish: The Birth of the Prison*. Trans. Alan Sheridan. New York: Vintage, 1979.

——. *The History of Sexuality*, vol. 1. Trans. Robert Hurley. New York: Pantheon Books, 1978.

——. *Birth of the Clinic*. New York: Pantheon Books, 1973.

——. *The Archaeology of Knowledge*. Trans. Alan Sheridan Smith. London: Routledge, 1972.

Fox, Ann. "Development of a Bisexual Identity: Understanding the Process." In L. Hutchins and L. Kaahumanu, eds., *Bi Any Other Name: Bisexual People Speak Out*. Boston: Alyson Press, 1991, pp. 29–36.

Fox, Ronald. "Bisexual Identities." In A. R. D'Augelli and C. J. Paterson, eds., *Lesbian, Gay, and Bisexual Identities Across the Lifespan*. New York: Oxford University Press, 1995.

Frank, Arthur W. "For a Sociology of the Body: An Analytical Review." In Mike Featherstone, Mike Hepworth, and Bryan S. Turner, eds., *The Body: Social Process and Cultural Theory*. Newbury Park, Calif.: Sage Publications, 1991, pp. 37–102.

——. "Bringing Bodies Back In: A Decade Review." *Theory, Culture, and Society* 7, no. 1 (1990): 131–162.

Franklin, C. W. *The Changing Definition of Masculinity*. New York: Plenum, 1984.

Freedman, Diane. "Writing in the Borderlands: The Poetic Prose of Gloria Anzaldúa and Susan Griffin." In Linda Perry, Lynne Turner, and Helen Sterk, eds., *Constructing and Reconstructing Gender: The Links Among Communication, Language, and Gender*. Albany: State University of New York Press, 1992, pp. 211–217.

Freedman, Eric. "Confidentiality Clause in Johnson HIV Suit Not Unusual, Lawyers Say." *Detroit News*, December 13, 1993, p. B5.

Freudenheim, Milt. "Merck and Lilly Post Strong Earnings and Sales." *New York Times*, October19, 1994, p. D3.

——. "The Drug Makers Are Listening to Prozac." *New York Times*, January 9, 1994, p. F7.

Freund, K. W. "Diagnosing Homo- or Heterosexuality and Erotic Age-Preference by Means of a Psychophysiological Test." *Behavior Research and Therapy* 5 (1967): 209–228.

Frintner, Mary Pat and Laurna Rubinson. "Acquaintance Rape: The Influence of Alcohol, Fraternity Membership, and Sports Team Membership." *Journal of Sex Education & Therapy* 19, no. 4 (Winter 1993): 272–284.

Frye, Marilyn. "The Necessity of Differences: Constructing a Positive Category of Women." *Signs: A Journal of Women in Culture and Society* 21, no. 4 (1996): 991–1010.

——. *Willful Virgin: Essays in Feminism, 1976–1992*. Freedom, Calif.: Crossing Press, 1992.

——. "Some Reflections on Separatism and Power," *The Politics of Reality: Essays on Feminist Theory*. Freedom, Calif.: Crossing Press, 1983, pp. 95–109.

Fuss, Diana. "Monique Wittig's Anti-Essentialist Materialism." *Essentially Speaking: Feminism, Nature, and Difference*. New York: Routledge, 1989.

Futuyma, Douglas and Stephen Risch. "Sexual Orientation, Sociobiology, and Evolution." *Journal of Homosexuality* 9, nos. 2/3 (1983/1984).

Futuyma, Douglas and Stephen Risch. "Sexual Orientation, Sociobiology, and Evolution." In Jon DeCecco and Michael Shively, eds., *Bisexual and Homosexual Identities: Critical Theoretical Issues*. New York: Hawthorn, 1984, pp. 157–168.

Gallagher, John. "Johnson Disclosure brings AIDS Issues to Middle America." *Advocate* (December 17, 1991): 14–16.

Gallop, Jane. *Thinking Through the Body*. New York: Columbia University Press, 1988.

Gardiner, Judith Kegan. "Can Ms. Prozac Talk Back? Feminism, Drugs, and Social Constructionism." *Feminist Studies* 21, no. 3 (Fall 1995): 501–517.

Gates, D. "White Male Paranoia: Are They the Newest Victims or Just Bad Sports?" *Newsweek* (March 29, 1993): 48–-54.

George, Nelson. *Elevating the Game: Black Men in Basketball*. New York: Harper Collins Publishers, 1992.

Giddens, Anthony. *The Constitution of Society*. Berkeley: University of California Press, 1984.

Gilman, Sander and Jan Zita Grover. "Constituting Symptoms." In E. Carter and S. Watney, eds., *Taking Liberties*. London: Serpent's Tail, 1989, pp. 147–160.

Goffman, Erving. *Stigma: Notes on the Management of Spoiled Identity*. Englewood Cliffs, N.J.: Prentice Hall, 1963.

Goldenberg, Naomi. *Returning Words to Flesh: Feminism, Psychoanalysis, and the Resurrection of the Body*. Boston: Beacon Press, 1990.

Goldsby, Jackie. "Queens of Language: Paris Is Burning." In Martha Gever, Pratibha Parmar, and John Greyson, eds., *Queer Looks: Perspectives of Lesbian and Gay Film and Video*. New York: Routledge, 1993, pp. 108–115.

Goldstein, Arnold P. *Violence in America: Lessons on Understanding the Aggression in Our Lives*. Palo Alto, Calif: Davies-Black, 1996.

Goodman, Ellen. "Un-Magic Moment." *Boston Globe*, November 12, 1992, p. 19.

——. "Magic Embodies a New Era." *Minneapolis Star Tribune*, November 23, 1991, p. A16.

Gorman, C. "Are Gay Men Born That Way?" *Time* (September 9, 1991): 60–61.

Gram, Lars. "Drug Therapy: Fluoxetine." *New England Journal of Medicine* 331, no. 20 (November 1994): 1354–1361.

Gramsci, Antonio. *Selections from the Prison Notebooks*. Quintin Hoare and Geoffrey Nowell-Smith, eds. New York: International Publishers, 1971.

Gray, Herman. "Black Masculinity and Visual Culture." *Black Male: Representations of Masculinity in Contemporary Art*. New York: Whitney Museum of American Art, 1994, pp. 401–405.

Greenberg, Roger, Roberth Bornstein, Michael Zborowski, and Seymour Fisher. "A Meta- Analysis of Fluoxetine Outcome in the Treatment of Depression." *Journal of Nervous and Mental Disease* 182, no. 10 (October 1994): 547–551.

Griffin, Susan. *Woman and Nature: The Roaring Inside Her*. New York: Harper and Row, 1978.

Gross, Larry. "Is Tyson Case Helping the Stereotype?" *Chicago Defender*, February, 1, 1992, p. 48.

Grosz, Elizabeth. *Space, Time, and Perversion: Essays on the Politics of Bodies*. New York: Routledge, 1995.

———. *Volatile Bodies: Toward a Corporeal Feminism.* Bloomington: Indiana University Press, 1994.

———. "Intensities and Flows." In Grosz, *Volatile Bodies,* pp. 160–183.

Hale, Jacob. "Are Lesbians Women?" *Hypatia* 11, no. 2 (1996): 94–121.

———. "Blurring Boundaries, Marking Boundaries: Who Is Lesbian?" (A Claudia Card Symposium) *Journal of Homosexuality* 32, no. 1 (1996): 21–42.

Hall, Wiley A. "Some of Wilt's Bedroom Tales are Really Incredible." *Minneapolis Star Tribune,* November 16, 1991, p. E 9.

Halperin, David. *One Hundred Years of Homosexuality and European Greek Love.* New York: Routledge, 1990.

Hamer, Dean and Peter Copeland. *The Science of Desire: The Search for the Gay Gene and the Biology of Behavior.* New York: Simon and Schuster, 1994.

Hammonds, Evelyn. "Missing Persons: African American Women, AIDS and the History of Disease." *Radical America* 24, no. 2 (1992): 7–24.

Hanke, Robert. "Hegemonic Masculinity in thirtysomething." *Critical Studies in Mass Communication* 7 (1990): 231–248.

Hansen, C. "Bisexuality Reconsidered: An Idea in Pursuit of a Definition." *Journal of Homosexuality* 11, nos. 1/2 (1985): 1–6.

Haraway, Donna. "A Cyborg Manifesto." *Simians, Cyborgs, and Women: The Reinvention of Nature.* New York: Routledge, 1991, pp. 149–181.

———. "The Biopolitics of Postmodern Bodies: Determinations of Self in Immune System Discourse." *differences* 1 (1) (1989): 3–43.

———. *Simians, Cyborgs and Women: The Reinvention of Nature.* New York: Routledge, 1991.

———. "The Biopolitics of Postmodern Bodies: Constitutions of Self in Immune System Discourse." *Simians, Cyborgs and Women: The Reinvention of Nature.* New York: Routledge, 1991, pp. 203–230.

———. "The Promises of Monsters: A Regenerative Politics of Inappropriate/d Others." In Lawrence Grossberg, Cary Nelson, and Paula Treichler, eds., *Cultural Studies.* New York: Routledge, 1992, pp. 295–337.

Harper, Suzanne. "Subordinating Masculinities/Racializing Masculinities: Writing White Supremist Discourse on Men's Bodies." *masculinities* 1, no. 4 (1994): 1–20.

Haug, Frigga, ed. *Female Sexualization : A Collective Work of Memory.* Trans. Erica Carter. London: Verso, 1987.

Heckman, Susan J. *Gender and Knowledge: Elements of a Postmodern Feminism.* Boston: Northeastern University Press, 1990.

Hennessey, A. C., K. Wallen, and D. A. Edwards. "Preoptic Lesions Increase Display of Lordosis by Male Rats." *Brain Research.* 370 (1986): 21–28.

Henry, W. "Born Gay?" *Time* (July 26, 1993): 36–38.

Herdt, G. "A Comment on Cultural Attributes and Fluidity of Bisexuality." *Journal of Homosexuality* 10, nos. 3/4 (1984): 53–62.

Herek, Gregory. "Stigma, Prejudice, and Violence Against Lesbians and Gay Men." In John C. Gonsioret and James D. Weinrich, eds., *Homosexuality: Research Implications for Public Policy*. Newbury Park, Calif: Sage Publications, 1991: 60–80

———. "Beyond 'Homophobia: A Social Psychological Perspective on Attitudes Toward Lesbians and Gay Men." *Journal of Homosexuality* 10, nos. 1/2 (1984): 1–21.

———. "Heterosexuals' Attitudes towards Lesbians and Gay Men: Correlates and Gender Difference." *Journal of Sex Research* 25, no. 4 (1988): 451–477.

———. "On Heterosexual Masculinity: Some Psychical Consequences of the Social Construction of Gender and Sexuality." *American Behavioral Scientist* 29, no. 5 (May/June 1986): 563–577.

Herek, Gregory and Kevin Berrill, eds. *Hate Crimes: Confronting Violence Against Lesbians and Gay Men*. Newbury Park, Calif: Sage Publications, 1992.

Hiestand, Michael. "Ad Agency People Agree on Disparity." *USA Today*. November 21, 1991, p. C2.

Higgins, Lynn. "Nouvelle Autobiography: Wittig's Le Corps Lesbian." *Sub-Stance* 14 (1976): 160–166.

HIV/AIDS Surveillance Report. Centers for Disease Control. Atlanta: United States Department of Health and Human Services, Public Health Service, Center for Infectious Diseases, Division of HIV/AIDS. Rockville, Md: National AIDS Information Clearinghouse (distributor), April 1992.

Hoagland, Sarah Lucia. *Lesbian Ethics: Toward New Value*. Palo Alto, Calif.: Institute of Lesbian Studies, 1988.

Hocquenghem, Guy. *Homosexual Desire*. London: Allison Busby, 1978.

hooks, bell. "Is Paris Burning?" *Black Looks: Race and Representation*. Boston: South End Press, 1992.

———. *Talking Back: Thinking Feminist, Thinking Black*. Boston: South End Press, 1989.

Hutchinson, G. E. "A Speculative Consideration of Certain Possible Forms of Sexual Selection in Man." *American Naturalist* 93 (1959): 81–91.

Irigaray, Luce. *The Sex Which Is Not One*. Trans. Catherine Porter with Carolyn Burke. Ithaca: Cornell University Press, 1985.

Jack, Dana Crowley. *Silencing the Self: Women and Depression*. Cambridge: Harvard University Press, 1991.

Jackson, Peter. "Black Males: Advertising and the Cultural Politics of Masculinity." *Gender, Place, and Culture* 1, no. 1 (1994): 49–60.

Janis, Ashby. "Festival Forum." *Lesbian Connection* 14, no. 4 (1992): 11–12.

Johnson, Earvin "Magic." *What You Can Do to Avoid AIDS*. New York: Times Books, 1992.

Johnson, Earvin "Magic" and Arsenio Hall. "Time Out." Video: Paramount, 1992.

Johnson, Earvin "Magic" with William Novak. *My Life*. New York: Random House, 1992.

Johnson, Earvin "Magic" with Roy S. Johnson. "I'll Deal With It." *Sports Illustrated* (November 18, 1991): 16–26.

Jones, Ann Rosalind. "Writing the Body: Toward an Understanding of *L'Ecriture feminine*." *Feminist Studies* 7, no. 2 (1981): 247–263.

Kadi, Joanna. *Thinking Class: Sketches from a Cultural Worker*. Boston: South End Press, 1996.

Kakutani, Michiko. "The Examined Life Isn't Worth Living Either." *New York Times*, September 20, 1994, p. B2.

Kane, Mary Jo. "Resistance/Transformation of the Oppositional Binary: Exposing Sport as a Continuum." *Journal of Sport and Social Issues* 19, no. 2 (1995): 191–218.

Kantrowitz, Barbara, Emily Yoffe, Patricia King, and Anthony Duignan-Cabrera. "From Hero to Crusader: Activists Debate What Magic Should Do Next." *Newsweek* (November 18, 1991): 69.

Kaplan, G. and L. Rogers. "Breaking Out of the Dominant Paradigm: A New Look at Sexual Attraction." *Journal Of Homosexuality* 10 (1984) 71–76.

Karp, David. "Taking Anti-Depressant Medications: Resistance, Trial Commitment, Conversion, Disenchantment." *Qualitative Sociology* 16, no. 4 (Winter. 1993): 337–359.

Katz, Jackson. "Reconstructing Masculinity in the Locker Room: The Mentors in Violence Prevention Project." *Harvard Educational Review* 65, no. 2 (1995): 163–174.

Keating, AnnLouise. *Women Reading Women Writing: Self-Invention in Paula Gunn Allen, Gloria Anzaldúa, and Audre Lorde*. Philadelphia: Temple University Press, 1995, pp. 241–259.

——. "Writing, Politics and *las Lesberadas: Platicando con Gloria Anzaldúa*." *Frontiers: A Journal of Women's Studies* 14, no. 1 (1993): 105–130.

Keller, Elizabeth Fox. *Reflections on Gender and Science*. New Haven: Yale University Press, 1985.

Kessler, Suzanne and Wendy McKenna. *Gender: An Ethnomethodological Approach*. Chicago: University of Chicago Press, 1978.

King, Samantha. "The Politics of the Body and the Body Politics: Magic Johnson and the Ideology of AIDS." *Sociology of Sports Journal* 10 (1993): 270–285.

Kinsey, A., W. Pomeroy, and C. Martin. *Sexual Behavior in the Human Male*. Philadelphia: W. B. Saunders, 1948.

Kinsey, A., W. Pomeroy, C. Martin, and P. Gebhard. *Sexual Behavior in the Human Female*. Philadelphia: W. B. Saunders, 1953.

Kitzinger, Celia. *The Social Construction of Lesbianism*. London: Sage Publications, 1987.

——. "Heteroapatriarchal Language." *Gossip: A Journal of Lesbian Feminist Ethics* 5 (1978): 15–20.

Klein, Fritz, B. Sepekoff, and T. Wolf. "Sexual Orientation: A Multi-Variable, Dynamic Process." *Journal of Homosexuality* 11, no. 1/2 (1985): 35–39.

Klobuchar, Jim. "Reactions of Magic Show How Much Our Attitudes Have Changed." *Minneapolis Star Tribune*, November 9, 1991, p. B3.

Kramer, Peter. *Listening to Prozac: A Pschychiatrist Explores Antidepressant Drugs and the Remaking of the Self*. New York: Viking Penguin, 1993.

Kristeva, Julia. *Powers of Horror: An Essay on Abjection*. Trans. Leon S. Roudiez. New York: Columbia University Press, 1982.

Kroker, Arthur and Marilouise Kroker. *Body Invaders: Panic Sex in America*. New York: St. Martin's Press, 1987.

——. *The Postmodern Scene: Excremental Culture and Hyper-Aesthetics*. New York: St. Martin's Press, 1986.

Kroll, Jack. "Smile Though Our Hearts Are Breaking." *Newsweek* (November 18, 1991): 70.

Laqueur, Thomas. *Making Sex: Body and Gender from the Greeks to Freud*. Cambridge: Harvard University Press, 1990.

——. "The Social Evil, the Solitary Vice and Pouring Tea." In Michel Feher and Nadia Tazi, eds., *Fragments for a History of the Human Body* (Part Three). New York: Zone, 1989, pp. 3–342.

Leershen, Charles, Donna Foote, Jeanne Gordon, Emily Yoffe, Frank Washington, Vern Smith, Debra Rosenberg, John McCormick, Regina Elam, and Elizabeth Leonard. "Magic's Message." *Newsweek* (November 18, 1991): pp. 58–62.

Lehne, Gregory K. "Homophobia among Men." In D. David and R. Brannon, eds., *The Forty- Nine Percent Majority: The Male Sex Role*. Reading, Mass.: Addison-Wesley, 1976, pp. 66–88.

Lerner, Gerda. *The Creation of Patriarchy*. New York: Oxford, 1986.

LeVay, Simon. *The Sexual Brain*. Cambridge: Massachusetts Institute of Technology Press, 1993.

——. "A Difference in Hypothalamic Structure between Heterosexual and Homosexual Men." *Science* 253 (1991): 1034–1037.

Lewontin, R. C., S. Rose, and L. J. Kamin. *Not in Our Genes*. New York: Pantheon, 1984.

Linstrum, Cathy. "*L'Asile des Femmes*: Subjectivity and Femininity in Breton's Nadia and Wittig's Le Corps Lesbien." *Nottingham French Studies* 27, no. 1 (1988): 35–45.

Lloyd, Genevieve. The Man of Reason: "Male" and "Female" in *Western Philosophy*. Minneapolis: University of Minnesota Press, 1984.

Longino, Helen. "Gender, Sexuality Research and the Flight from Complexity." *Metaphilosophy* 25, no. 4 (1994): 285–292.

Lopresti, Mike. "Magic Takes Last Chance to Hold Court." *USA Today*, January 31, 1996, p. C4.

Lorde, Audre. *Sister Outsider: Essays and Speeches*. Trumansburg, N.Y.: Crossing Press, 1984.

——. "Uses of the Erotic." *Sister/Outsider: Essays and Speeches*. Trumansburg, N.Y.: Crossings, 1982.

Lugones, Maria. "Purity, Impurity, and Separation." *Signs* 19, no. 2 (1994): 458–479.

———. " 'Playfulness,' 'World'-Traveling and Loving Perception." In Jeffner Allen, ed., *Lesbian Philosophies and Cultures*. New York: State University of New York Press, 1990.

MacDonald, A. P. "A Little Bit of Lavender Goes a Long Way: A Critique of Research on Sexual Orientation." *Journal of Sex Research* 19, no. 1 (1983): 94–100.

MacKinnon, Catharine. *Toward a Feminist Theory of the State*. Cambridge: Harvard University Press, 1989.

———. *Feminism Unmodified : Discourses on Life and Law*. Cambridge: Harvard University Press, 1987.

MacPherson, K. I. "Menopause as Disease: The Social Construction of a Metaphor." *Advances in Nursing Science* 3, no. 2 (1981): 95–113.

Maddox, J. "Is Homosexuality Hard-Wired?" *Nature* 353 (1991): 13.

"Magic: How He Got AIDS Virus—His Wild Sex Life With More Than 1000 Women." *National Enquirer* (November 26, 1991): 30–31, 33, 36–37.

Majors, Richard. "Cool Pose: Black Masculinity and Sports." In Michael A. Messner and Donald F. Sabo, eds., *Sport, Men, and the Gender Order: Critical Feminist Perspectives*. Champaign, Ill.: Human Kinetics Books, 1990, pp. 109–114.

Majors, Richard and Janet Mancini Billson. *Cool Pose: The Dilemmas of Black Manhood in America*. New York: Macmillan, 1992.

Mapplethorpe, Robert. "Untitled 1972." In Robert Mapplethorpe. Whitney Museum of Art. New York: Bullfinch Press, 1988, p. 22.

Marks, Elaine. "Lesbian Intertextuality." In George Stambolian and Elaine Marks, eds., *Homosexualities and French Literature: Cultural Contexts/Critical Texts*. Ithaca: Cornell University Press, 1979, p. 372.

Martin, Biddy and Chandra Talpade Mohanty. "Feminist Politics: What's Home Got to Do with It?" In Teresa de Lauretis, ed., *Feminist Studies/Critical Studies*. Bloomington: Indiana University Press, 1986, pp. 191–212.

Martin, Emily. "The End of the Body?" *American Ethnologist* 19, no. 1 (1992): 121–141.

———. *The Woman in the Body: A Cultural Analysis of Reproduction*. Boston: Beacon Press, 1988.

Martyniuk, Joy. *Adverse Effects of Fluoxetine (Prozac): January 1987 through June 1991*. Bethesda, Md.: U.S. Department of Health and Human Services, 1991.

Mauss, Marcel . "Body Techniques." *Sociology and Psychology (1936)*. Trans. Ben Brewster. London: Routledge and Kegan Paul, 1979.

McCallum, Jack. "Unforgettable: Magic Johnson, the Player Nonpareil, Was an Outsized Paragon of Style and Grace." *Sports Illustrated* (November 18, 1991): 29–37.

McCormack, Thelma. "Hollywood's Prizefight Films: Violence or 'Jock Appeal.' " *Journal of Sport and Social Issues* 8, no. 2 (1984): 19–29.

McGrath, Ellen, ed. *Women and Depression: Research, Risk Factors, and Treatment Issues: Final Report of the American Psychological Association Task Force on Women and Depression.* Washington, D.C.: American Psychological Association, 1990.

Meese, Elizabeth. *(Sem)Erotics: Theorizing Lesbian Writing.* New York: New York University Press, 1992.

Melnick, Merrill. "Male Athletes and Sexual Assault." *Journal of Physical Education, Recreation and Dance* (May/June 1992): 32–35.

Mercer, Kobena. "Just Looking for Trouble: Robert Mapplethorpe and the Fantasies of Race." In Lynne Segal and Mary McIntosh, eds., *Sex Exposed: Sexuality and the Pornography Debate.* New Brunswick, N.J.: Rutgers University Press, 1993, pp. 92–110.

——. "Imagining the Black Man's Sex." In Pat Holland, Jo Spences, and Simon Watney, eds., *Photography/Politics: Two.* London: Methuen, 1986.

Messner, Michael A. "When Bodies Are Weapons: Masculinity and Violence in Sport." *International Review of Sociology of Sport* 25, no. 3 (1990): 203–219.

——. "Sports and Male Domination: The Female Athlete as Contested Ideological Terrain." *Sociology of Sport Journal* 5 (1988): 197–211.

Messner, Michael and Donald Sabo, eds. *Sport, Men and the Gender Order.* Champaign, Ill.: Human Kinetics Books, 1990.

Meyer, Richard. "Rock Hudson's Body." In Dianna Fuss, ed. *Inside/Out: Lesbian Theories, Gay Theories.* New York: Routledge, 1991.

Modleski, Tania. "Cinema and the Dark Continent: Race and Gender in Popular Film." In *American Feminist Thought at Century's End: A Reader.* Edited by Linda Kauffmann. Cambridge: Blackwell, 1993, pp. 73–91.

Mohammed, Abdul Jan. "Sexuality on/of the Racial Border." In Domna C. Stanton., ed., *Discourses of Sexuality: From Aristotle to AIDS.* Ann Arbor: University of Michigan Press, 1992, pp. 94–116.

Mohr, Richard. "Knights, Young Men Boys': Masculine Worlds and Democratic Values." *Gay Ideas: Outing and Other Controversies.* New York: Beacon, 1992.

Montre, Lorrain Kee. "Magic Flap." *St. Louis Post-Dispatch*, October 24, 1992, p. C1.

Montville, Leigh. "Like One of the Family: When Magic Delivered His Shocking News, It was, for So Many People, the First Time the AIDS Epidemic Had Really Hit Home." *Sports Illustrated* (November 18, 1991): 44–45.

Moraga, Cherríe. *Loving in the War Years: Lo que nunca pasù por sus labios.* Boston: South End Press, c1983.

Mores, Margaret. "Sport on Television: Replay and Display." In E. Ann Kaplan, ed., *Regarding Television: Critical Approaches.* Los Angeles: University Publications in America, 1983, pp. 44–66.

Morgan, Kathryn. "Women and the Knife: Cosmetic Surgery and the Colonization of Women's Bodies." *Hypatia* 6, no. 3 (Fall 1991): 25–53.

Morrison, Toni. "Introduction: Friday on the Potomac." In Toni Morrison, ed., *Race-ing Justice, En-gendering Power: Essays on Anita Hill, Clarence Thomas, and the Construction of Social Reality*. New York: Pantheon Press, 1992, pp. vii–xxx.

———. *The Bluest Eye*. New York: Washington Square Press, 1972.

Mullen, Michael. *Africa in American: Slave Acculturation and Resistance in the American South and the British Caribbean: 1736–1831*. Urbana: University of Illinois Press, 1988.

Myles, Eileen. "Gender Play." *Outweek* 5 (December 1990): 48–49.

Nagell, Thomas. *A View from Nowhere*. New York: Oxford University Press, 1986.

Neisen, Joseph. "Heterosexism: Redefining Homophobia for the 1990s." *Journal of Gay and Lesbian Psychotherapy* 1, no. 3 (1990): 21–35.

Nestle, Joan. *A Restricted Country*. New York: Firebrand Books, 1987.

"New Bodies for Sale." *Newsweek* (May 27, 1985): 64–69.

"The New You." *Psychiatric Times* (March 1990): 45–46.

News Services. "The World Has Magic on Its Mind." *Minneapolis Star Tribune*, November 9, 1991, pp. A5, C5.

"No Magic Bullet." *Equal Time* (November 22, 1991).

Norden, Michael. *Beyond Prozac: Brain-Toxic Lifestyles, Natural Antidotes, and New Generation Antidepressants*. New York: Regan Books, 1995.

Oches, Robin. "A Letter to the Editor." *Out/look* (Summer 1990), p. 78.

Olalquiaga, Celeste. *Megalopolis: Contemporary Cultural Sensibilities*. Minneapolis: University of Minnesota Press, 1992.

Olano, Pamela J. "Throw Over Your Man, I Say, and Come: Reading Virginia Woolf as a Lesbian." Manuscript, 1992.

Omi, Michael and Howard Winant. *Racial Formation in the United States: From the 1960s to the 1980s*. New York: Routledge, 1986.

Oomura, Y., A. Aou, Y. Koyama, and H. Yoshimatsu. "Central Control of Sexual Behavior." *Brain Research Bulletin* 20 (1988): 863–870.

The Oprah Winfrey Show. "Everything You Wanted to Know About the Happy Pill" (Chicago: Harpo Productions, March 7. 1994), Burrelle's Information Services, Livingston, N.J.

"Ordinary Pleasures and Prozac for All." *Psychology Today* 27, no. 4 (July/August 1994): 44–49, 72, 80–81.

Orr, Jackie. "Theory on the Market: Panic, Incorporating." *Social Problems* 37, no. 4 (November 1990): 460–484.

Pascarelli, Peter. *The Courage of Magic Johnson* . New York: Bantam, 1992.

Pateman, Carole. *The Sexual Contract*. Stanford: Stanford University Press, 1988.

Patton, Cindy. *Inventing AIDS*. New York: Routledge, 1990.

———. "Heterosexual AIDS Panic: A Queer Paradigm." *Gay Community News* (February 9, 1985): 3,6.

———. *Sex and Germs: The Politics of AIDS*. Boston: South End Press, 1985.

Paul, Jay. "The Bisexual Identity: An Idea without Social Recognition." *Journal of Homosexuality* 9 (1983/1984): 45–63.

———. "Bisexuality: Reassessing our Paradigms of Sexuality." *Journal of Homosexuality* 11 (1985): 21–34.

Paul, Jay and M. Nichols. " 'Biphobia' and the Construction of a Bisexual Identity." In M. Shernoff and W. Scott, eds., *The Sourcebook On Lesbian/Gay Health Care*. Washington, D.C.: National Lesbian and Gay Health Foundation, 1988, pp. 259–264.

Penelope, Julia. "Heterosexual Semantics: 'Just Two Kinds of People in the World.' *Lesbian Ethics* (Fall 1986): 58–80.

———. "The Patriarchal Universe of Discourse." In J. Penelope, ed., *Speaking Freely: Unlearning The Lies of The Father Tongue*. New York: Pergamon, 1990.

Perez, Emma. "Irigaray's Female Symbolic in the Making of Chicana Lesbian Sitios y Lenguas (Sites and Discourses)." In Laura Doan, ed., *The Lesbian Postmodern*. New York: Columbia University Press, 1994, pp. 104–117.

Perry, Donna. "Gloria Anzaldúa." *Backtalk: Women Writers Speak Out*. New Brunswick: Rutgers University Press, 1993, pp. 19–42.

Pfeil, Fred. *White Guys: Studies in Postmodern Domination and Difference*. London: Verso, 1995.

Pfohl, Stephen. *Death at the Parasite Cafe: Social Science (Fictions) and the Postmodern*. New York: St. Martin's Press, 1992.

Pharr, Suzanne. *Homophobia, A Weapon of Sexism*. Inverness, Calif.: Chardon Press, 1988.

Phelan, Shane. *Getting Specific: Postmodern Lesbian Politics*. Minneapolis: University of Minnesota Press, 1994.

The Phil Donahue Show. "Prozac—Medication That Makes You Kill." Telecast. (February 27, 1991).

Piaget, Jean. *The Child's Conception of the World*. Totawa, N.J.: Littlefield, 1972.

Pleck, Joseph H. *The American Male*. Englewood Cliffs, N.J.: Prentice-Hall, 1980.

———. *The Myth of Masculinity*. Cambridge: MIT Press, 1981.

Plummer, K. "Homosexual Categories: Some Research Problems in the Labeling Perspective of Homosexuality." In K. Plummer, ed., *The Making of the Modern Homosexual*. Totowa, N.J.: Barnes and Noble Books, 1981, pp. 53–75.

Ponse, Barbara. *Identities in the Lesbian World*. Westport, Conn.: Greenwood, 1978.

Poovey, Mary. "Speaking of the Body: A Discursive Division of Labor in Mid-Victorian Britain." In Mary Jacobus, Evelyn Fox Keller, and Sally Shuttleworth, eds., *Body Politics: Women and the Discourses of Science*. New York: Routledge, 1990, pp. 29–46.

Pratt, Minnie Bruce. "Identity: Skin Blood Heart." In *Yours In Struggle: Three Feminist Perspectives on Anti-Semitism and Racism*. New York: Long Haul Press, 1984, pp. 11–63.

Pronger, Brian. *Arena of Masculinity*. New York: St. Martins Press, 1990.

Pugliesi, K. "Women and Mental Health: Two Traditions of Feminist Research." *Women and Health* 19, no. 2/3 (1992): 43–68.

Radicalesbians. "The Woman-Identified Woman." In Anne Koedt, Ellen Levine, and Anita Rapone, eds., *Radical Feminism*. New York: Quadrangle, 1973.

Ramazanoglu, Caroline, ed. *Up Against Foucault: Explorations of Some Tensions Between Foucault and Feminism*. New York: Routledge, 1993.

Rapkin, Bruce. "Do You Believe in Magic? The Public Health Consequences of Magic Johnson's Announcement for Inner City Women. 1992." Paper presented at the North American Society for Sociology of Sport, November 1993.

Rappaport, David. video "Rock Hudson Home Movies" 1991.

Raymond, Janice. "Putting the Politics Back into Lesbianism." *Women's Studies International Forum* 12, no. 2 (1989): 149–156.

——. *A Passion for Friends: Towards a Philosophy of Female Affection*. Boston: Beacon Press, 1986.

Rebolledo, Tey Diana. *Women Singing in the Snow: A Cultural Analysis of Chicana Literature*. Tucson: University of Arizona Press, 1995.

Reid-Pharr, Robert F. "The Spectacle of Blackness." *Radical America* [This issue subtitled: "Becoming a Spectacle: Lesbian and Gay Politics in the Nineties"] 24, no. 4 (1990): 57–65.

Reinisch, June M. and Ruth Beasley. *The Kinsey Institute New Report on Sex: What You Must Know to be Sexually Literate*. New York: St. Martin's Press, 1990.

Reinish, June Machover, Stephanie A. Sanders, and Mary Ziemba-Davis. "The Study of Sexual Behavior in Relation to the Transmission of Human Immunodeficiency Virus: Caveats and Recommendations." *American Psychologist* 43, no. 11 (November 1988): 921–927.

Remafedi, Gary. "Predictors of Unprotected Intercourse Among Gay and Bisexual Adolescents: Knowledge, Beliefs, and Behavior." *Pediatrics* 94, no. 2 (1994): 163–168.

Reuman, Ann S. "Wild Tongues Can't Be Tamed: Gloria Anzaldúa's (R)Evolution of Voice." In Deidre Lashgari, ed., *Violence, Silence, and Anger: Women's Writing as Transgression*. Charlottesville: University Press of Virginia, 1995, pp. 305–319.

Rich, Adrienne. "Notes Toward a Politics of Location." *Blood, Bread, and Poetry: Selected Prose 1979–1985*. New York: Norton, 1984, pp. 210–231.

——. "Compulsory Heterosexuality and Lesbian Existence." *Signs* 5, no. 4 (1980): 631–660.

——. *Of Woman Born*. New York: Bantam, 1977.

Richardson, Diane. "The Dilemma of Essentiality in Homosexual Theory." *Journal of Homosexuality* 9 (1983/4): 85.

Riska, Elianne and Elizabeth Ettorre. *Gendered Moods: Psychotropics and Society*. New York: Routledge, 1995.

Roberts, George. "Brother to Brother: African American Modes of Relating to Men." *Journal of Black Studies* 24, no. 4 (June 1994): 379–390.

Robson-Scott, Markie. "Who Is the Real Ms. Prozac?" *The Guardian* (September 21, 1993): 16.

Roediger, David. *The Wages of Whiteness*. London: Verso, 1991.

Roof, Judith. "Lesbians and Lyotard: Legitimation and the Politics of the Name." In Laura Doan, ed., *The Lesbian Postmodern*. New York: Columbia University Press, 1994, pp. 45–66.

Rosenfeld, Marthe. "The Linguistic Aspect of Sexual Conflict: Monique Wittig's Le Corps Lesbien." *Mosaic: A Journal of Interdisciplinary Study of Literature* 17, no. 2 (Spring 1984): 235–241.

Ross, M.. "Beyond The Biological Model: New Directions in Bisexual and Homosexual Research." *Journal of Homosexuality* 10 (1984): 63–70.

Rothman, David. "Shiny Happy People: The Problem with 'Cosmetic Psychopharmacology.' " *New Republic* (February 14, 1994): 34–38.

Rotundo, Anthony. "Romantic Friendship: Male Intimacy and Middle-Class Youth in Northern United States, 1800–1900." *Journal of Social History* 23 (Fall 1989): 1–25.

Rubin, Gayle. "Traffic in Women." In Rayna Reiter, ed., *Toward and Anthropology of Women*. New York: Monthly Review Press, 1975.

Rugg, Deborah. "Changes in Behavioral Intentions Among Adolescents Following HIV National Sports Celebrity Disclosure." A paper presented at the AIDS International Conference on AIDS, Amsterdam, July 19–24, 1992.

Ruse, Michael. "Are There Gay Genes? Sociobiology and Homosexuality." *Journal of Homosexuality* 6 (1981): 5–34.

Rust, Paula. "The Politics of Sexual Identity: Sexual Attraction and Behavior Among Lesbian and Bisexual Women." *Social Problems* 39 (1992): 366–386.

——. " 'Coming Out' In The Age of Social Constructionism: Sexual Identity Formation Among Lesbian and Bisexual Women." *Gender-Society* 7, no. 1 (1993): 50.

——. "Neutralizing the Political Threat of the Marginal Woman: Lesbians' Beliefs about Bisexual Women." *Journal of Sex Research* 30 (1993): 214–228.

Ryder, Robert W., Robert W. Ryder, Mibandumba Ndilu, Susan E. Hassig, Munkolenkole Kamenga, Denise Sequeira, Mwandagalirwa Kashamuka, Henry Francis, Frieda Behets, Robert L. Colebunders, Alain Dopagne, R. Kambale, and William L. Heyward. "Heterosexual Transmission of HIV-1 Among Employees and Their Spouses at Two Large Businesses in Zaire." *AIDS* 4, no. 8 (1990): 725–732.

Sagarin, E. "The Good Guys, the Bad Guys, and the Gay Guys." *Contemporary Sociology* 2, no. 1 (1973): 3–13.

Scarry, Elaine. *The Body in Pain: The Making and Unmaking of the World*. New York: Oxford University Press, 1985.

Scheman, Naomi. "Anger and the Politics of Naming." In Sally McConnell-Genet, Ruth Borker, and Nelly Furman, eds., *Women and Language in Literature and Society*. New York: Praeger, 1980, pp. 174–187. Reprinted in *Engenderings: Constructions of Knowledge, Authority, and Privilege*. New York: Routledge, 1993, pp. 22–35.

——. "The Body Politic / The Impolitic / Bodily Politics." *Engenderings: Constructions of Knowledge, Authority, and Privilege*. New York: Routledge, 1993: 185–192.

——. "Though This Be Method, Yet There is Madness in It: Paranoia and Liberal Epistemology." *Engenderings: Constructions of Knowledge, Authority, and Privilege*. New York: Routledge, 1993, pp. 75–105

Schulman, Sarah. "Laying the Blame: What Magic Johnson Really Means." *My American History: Lesbian and Gay Life During the Reagan/Bush Years*. New York: Routledge, 1994, pp.223–225.

Schulz, Alfred. *Reflections on the Problem of Relevance*. New Haven: Yale University Press, 1970.

Sedgwick, Eve Kosokofsy. *Tendencies*. Durham: Duke University Press, 1993.

——. *Between Men: English Literature and Male Homosocial Desire*. New York: Columbia University Press, 1995.

Segal, Lynne. *Slow Motion: Changing Masculinities, Changing Men*. New Brunswick: Rutgers University Press, 1990.

Shaktini, Namascar. "The Revolutionary Signifier: The Lesbian Body." In Karla Jay and Joanne Glasgow, eds., *Lesbian Texts and Contexts: Radical Revolutions*. New York: New York University Press, 1990.

——. "Displacing the Phallic Subject: Wittig's Lesbian Writings." *Signs: Journal of Women in Culture and Society* 8, no. 1 (Autumn 1982): 29–44.

Shilts, Randy. "Speak for All, Magic: In His Fight Against HIV, Magic Johnson Should Not Confine His Concerns to Heterosexual Victims." *Sports Illustrated* 1991: 130.

Shively, Michael and J. DeCecco. "Components of Sexual Identity." *Journal of Homosexuality* 3 (1977): 41–48.

Shuster, R. "Sexuality as a Continuum: The Bisexual Identity." In Boston Lesbian Psychologies Collective, eds., *Lesbian Psychologies: Explorations & Challenges*. Urbana: University of Illinois Press, 1987, pp. 56–71.

Silverman, Kaja. *Male Subjectivity on the Margins*. New York: Routledge, 1992.

Slimp, J. C., B. L. Hart, and R. W. Goy. "Heterosexual, Autosexual, and Social Behavior of Adult Male Rhesus Monkeys with Medical Preoptic-Anterior Hypothamic Lesions." *Brain Research* 142 (1978): 105–122.

Smith, Dorothy. *The Everyday World as Problematic: A Feminist Sociology*. Boston: Northeastern University Press, 1987.

Smith, K. T. "Homophobia: A Tentative Personality Profile." *Psychological Reports* 29 (1971): 1091–1094.

Smith, Sidonie. "The Autobiographical Manifesto: Identities, Temporalities, Polits." In Shirley Neuman, ed., *Autobiography and Questions of Gender*. London: Cass, 1992, pp. 186–212.

Span, Paula. "The Man Behind the Bitter Pill Debate: Lawyer Leonard Finz Presses the Case Against Eli Lilly and Prozac." *Washington Post*, August 14, 1991, pp. C1-C3.

Spelman, Elizabeth V. *Inessential Woman: Problems of Exclusion in Feminist Thought*. Boston: Beacon, 1988.

Spivak, Gayatri Chakrovorty. "Subaltern Studies: Deconstructing Historiography." In *Other Worlds: Essays in Cultural Politics*. New York: Methuen, 1987, pp. 197–221.

Starr, Mark. "Yakety-Yak: Do Talk Back." *Newsweek* (December 21, 1992): 60.

Sternback, Nancy Saporta. " 'A Deep Racial Memory of Love': The Chicana Feminism of Cherríe Moraga." In Asuncion Horno-Delgado et al., eds., *Breaking Boundaries: Latina Writing and Critical Readings*. Amherst: University of Massachusetts Press, 1989, pp. 48–61.

Stoltenberg, John. *Refusing to Be a Man: Essays on Sex and Justice*. Portland, Ore.: Breitenbush Books, 1989.

Storms, M. "Theories Of Sexual Orientation." *Journal of Personality and Social Psychology* 38, no. 5 (1980): 783–792.

Suleiman, Susan. "(Re)Writing The Body: The Politics of Female Eroticism." In S. Sulieman, ed., *The Female Body In Western Culture: Contemporary Perspectives*. Cambridge: Harvard University Press, 1986, 7–29.

Suppe, Fred. "In Defense of a Multidimensional Approach to Sexual Identity." *Journal of Homosexuality* 10 (1984): 7–14.

Swabb, D. F. and E. Fliers. "A Sexually Dimorphic Nucleus in the Human Brain." *Science* 228 (1985): 1112–1114.

Swift, E. M. "Dangerous Games: In the Age of AIDS Many Pro Athletes Are Sexually Promiscuous, Despite the Increasing Peril." *Sports Illustrated* (November 18, 1991): 40–43.

"Tale of Revenge Stirs AIDS Furor: Woman Claims She's Trying to Infect Men, Prompting a Surge of Concern." *New York Times*, October 1, 1991, p. A16.

Tanouye, Elyse. "Critics See Self-Interest in Lilly's Funding of Ads Telling the Depressed to Get Help." *Wall Street Journal*, April 15, 1993, pp. B1, B4.

Tatum, Jack. *Final Confessions of NFL Assassin Jack Tatum*. Coal Valley, Ill.: Quality Sports Publications, 1996.

Theweleit, Klaus. *Male Fantasies*. Trans. Stephan Conway in collaboration with Erica Carter and Chris Turner. Minneapolis: University of Minneapolis Press, 1987.

Torres, Eden. *Caras vemos, corazones no sabemos: Their Faces We See, Their Hearts We Don't Know*. PH.D. diss., University of Minnesota, 1997.

Trebilcot, Joyce. "Taking Responsibility for Sexuality." *Dyke Ideas: Process, Politics, Daily Life*. Albany: State University of New York Press, 1994, pp. 97–109.

Treichler, Paula A. "AIDS, Gender, and Biomedical Discourse: Current Currents for Meaning." In Elizabeth Fee and Daniel M. Fox, eds., *AIDS: The Burdens of History*. Berkeley: University of California Press, 1988, pp. 190–266.

Troiden, Richard R. "The Formation of Homosexual Identities." *Journal of Homosexuality* 17 (1989): 43–73.

Udis-Kessler, Amanda. "Bisexuality in an Essentialist World: Toward an Understanding of Biphobia." In T. Geller, ed., *Bisexuality: Reader and Sourcebook*. Ojai, Calif.: Times Change Press, 1990a, pp. 51–63.

——. "Present Tense: Biphobia As A Crisis Of Meaning." In Loraine Hutchins and Lani Kaahumanu, eds., *Bi Any Other Name: Bisexual People Speak Out*. Boston: Alyson, 1990b, p. 354.

Vaid, Urvashi. *Virtual Equality: The Mainstreaming of Gay and Lesbian Liberation*. New York: Anchor, 1995.

Vamplew, Wray. *A View from the Bench: Coaches and Sports Violence in Australia*. Canberra: Australian Sports Commission, 1991.

"Violence Goes Mainstream." *Newsweek* (April 1, 1991): 46–52.

Walker, Alice. *You Can't Keep a Good Woman Down*. New York: Harcourt Brace Jovanovich, 1981.

Watney, Simon. "AIDS, Language, and the Third World." In Erica Carter and Simon Watney, eds., *Taking Liberties*. London: Serpant's Tail, 1989, pp. 183–192.

Weinberg, George H. *Society and the Healthy Homosexual*. New York: St. Martin's Press, 1972.

Weiner, Jay. "Teams in State Discuss AIDS Testing, Awareness." *Minneapolis Star Tribune*, November 5, 1991, pp. C1, C5.

Weissman, Myrna and Mark Olfson. "Depression in Women: Implications for Health Care Research." *Science* 269 (August 11, 1995): 799–801.

Wenzel, Hélène. "The Text as Body/ Politics: An Appreciation of Monique Wittig's Writings in Context." *Feminist Studies* 7, no. 2 (Summer 1981): 264–287.

White, Garland F., Janet Katz, Kathryn E. Scarborough. "The Impact of Professional Football Games upon Violent Assaults on Women." *Violence and Victims* 7, no. 2 (Summer 1992): 157–171.

Whitford, Margaret. *Luce Irigaray: Philosophy of the Feminine*. New York: Routledge, 1991.

Williams, Patricia J. *The Alchemy of Race and Rights*. Cambridge: Harvard University Press, 1991.

Wilson, E. O. *On Human Nature*. Cambridge: Harvard University Press, 1978.

——. *Sociobiology: The New Synthesis*. Cambridge: Harvard University Press, 1975.

Wilson, Robert A. *Feminine Forever*. London: W. H. Allen. 1966.

Wilton, Tasmin. *Lesbian Studies: Setting the Agenda*. New York: Routledge, 1995.

Wings, Mary. "A Letter to the Editor." *Out/Look* (Summer 1990): 79.

Winterson, Jeanette. "The Cells, Tissues, Systems, and Cavities of the Body." *Granta* (Special Issue: The Body) 39 (Spring 1992): 125–136.

Wittig, Monique. "The Mark of Gender." *The Straight Mind and Other Essays.* Boston: Beacon, 1992, pp. 76–89.

——. "On the Social Contract" *The Straight Mind and Other Essays,* pp. 33–45.

——. "The Point of View: Universal or Particular?" In *The Straight Mind and Other Essays,* pp. 59–67.

——. *The Lesbian Body.* Trans. David LeVay. Boston: Beacon Press, 1986. French edition published in Paris by Editions de Minuit, 1973.

——. *Le Corps Lesbien.* Paris: Les Editions de Minuit, 1973.

——. *Les Guerilléres.* Trans. David Le Vay. London: Owen, 1971.

Wong, David, Frank Bymaster, and Eric Engleman. "Prozac (Fluoxetine, Lilly 110140), the first Selective Serotonin Uptake Inhibitor and an Antidepressant Drug: Twenty Years Since Its First Publication." Life Sciences 57, no. 5 (June 1995): 411–441.

Wrathall, John. *Take the Young Stranger by the Hand: Same Sex Relations in the YMCA.* Chicago: University of Chicago Press, 1998.

Wurtzel, Elizabeth. *Prozac Nation: Young and Depressed in America.* New York: Houghton Mifflin, 1994.

Young, Iris. "The Scaling of Bodies and the Politics of Infinity." *Justice and the Politics of Difference.* Princeton: Princeton University Press, 1990, pp. 122–155.

Zinik, G. "Identity Conflict of Adaptive Flexibility? Bisexuality Reconsidered." *Journal of Homosexuality* 11 (1985): 7–19.

Zita, Jacquelyn N. "Feminist Philosophers Rethinking Sexuality." In Allison Jaggar and Iris Young, eds., *A Companion to Feminist Philosophy.* (Oxford: Blackwell, forthcoming 1998.

——. Review Essay. *Signs: A Journal of Women in Culture and Society* 21, no. 3, 1996, pp. 786–795.

——. "The Feminist Philosopher's Revolutionary Toolbox and the Unavoidability of Queerness." Paper presented at the American Philosophical Association, Central Division, Kansas City, Mo., May 4–7, 1994.

——. "Lesbian and Gay Studies: Yet Another Unhappy Marriage." In Linda Garber, ed. *Tilting the Tower: Lesbians Teaching Queer Subjects.* New York: Routledge, 1994, pp. 258–276.

——. "Male Lesbians and the Postmodernist Body." *Hypatia* 7, no. 4 (1992): 106–127. Reprinted in Claudia Card, ed., *Adventures in Lesbian Philosophy.* Bloomington: Indiana University Press, 1994, pp. 112–132.

——. "Transsexual Origins: Reflections on Descartes's Meditations." *Genders* 5 (1989): 86–105.

Index

Abjection, 37

AIDS: and African-American men, 12; and African-American women, 20; and the AIDS body, 15, 23; as heterosexually acquired, 22–23, 213*n*37, 214*n*48; and immunological metaphors, 230*n*71; origin story of, 31,54, 219*n*81; phobia, 12; queerity of, 22, 30–32; and race, 216*n*57; and vectors of HIV transmission, 12, 19–20, 213*n*37

Alexandria, Minn., 2

Anzaldúa, Gloria, 143, 167–83; and blood, 177–80; on body hatred, 178; and bone, 176–77; and Coatlicue, 174–75, 263*n*20; and dualities of the North, 180; and face, 172–73; and *una herida abierta*, 168–71, 180; on historical trauma, 171, 262*n*14, 263*n*21; on language, 170–71; and morphogenisis, 180–82; and new meztiza, 178–79, 181–83, 262*n*15; and sixth sense 181, 261*n*11; and skin, 173–74; and the space of Cartesian negation, 183; and soul, 172–73, 180, 182; *see also* Body as Anzaldúan

Anzaldúan body, *see* Body as Anzaldúan

Athleticism: and disciplined black masculinity, 27–28; and male superiority, 28–29; and male violence, 18, 212*nn*26, 27, 217*n*66; and physical sublimity, 13, 18; and race, 13, 15

Atkinson, Ti-Grace, 115

Attribution theory, 94–96; and sex categories, 105

Augustine, 204

Bartky, Sandra Lee, 70

Basketball: and race, 27; and black aesthetics, 29, 217*n*71

Bisexualities: and biphobia, 125, 245*n*13; and multidimensional measures, 134, 246*n*27; and omission from research, 123, 124, 131, 135; and the omnisexual nomad, 4, 135; and stereotypes, 119

Black masculinity, *see* Athleticism, and disciplined black masculinity; Heteromasculinity, and race

Body: as activity, 168; as Anzaldúan, 143, 168–83; as articulation, 4–5, 7–9; as biology, 145; as Cartesian, 5, 160, 166–67; as corporate body, 14, 24; as disarticulation, 4–5, 81–83; as discursive, desiring production, 4, 9,

Between Men~Between Women
Lesbian and Gay Studies
LILLIAN FADERMAN *and* LARRY GROSS, *Editors*

Judith Roof, *A Lure of Knowledge: Lesbian Sexuality and Theory*

Claudia Schoppmann, *Days of Masquerade: Life Stories of Lesbians During the Third Reich*

Alan Sinfield, *The Wilde Century: Effeminacy, Oscar Wilde, and the Queer Moment*

Jane McIntosh Snyder, *Lesbian Desire in the Lyrics of Sappho*

Chris Straayer, *Deviant Eyes, Deviant Bodies: Sexual Re-Orientations in Film and Video*

Dwayne C. Turner, *Risky Sex: Gay Men and HIV Prevention*

Ruth Vanita, *Sappho and the Virgin Mary: Same-Sex Love and the English Literary Imagination*

Thomas Waugh, *Hard to Imagine: Gay Male Eroticism in Photography and Film from Their Beginnings to Stonewall*

Kath Weston, *Families We Choose: Lesbians, Gays, Kinship*

Kath Weston, *Render Me, Gender Me: Lesbians Talk Sex, Class, Color, Nation, Studmuffins . . .*

Carter Wilson, *Hidden in the Blood: A Personal Investigation of AIDS in the Yucatán*

Jacquelyn Zita, *Body Talk: Philosophical Reflections on Sex and Gender*